With Our Good Will

30 YEARS OF SHAKESPEARE IN IDAHO

Let the sky
rain potatoes.

~ Falstaff, *The Merry Wives of Windsor*, V, v.

With Our Good Will

30 YEARS OF SHAKESPEARE IN IDAHO

Doug Copsey

Caxton Press
Caldwell, Idaho
2006

I will never forget that blissful, innocent summer when the Idaho Shakespeare Festival was born. I suspect we all knew we were to be a part of the magic, but if we didn't know it then, I have no doubt we do now.

Library of Congress Cataloging-in-Publication Data

Copsey, Doug.
With our Good Will : 30 years of Shakespeare in Idaho / by Doug Copsey.
p. cm.

ISBN 0-87004-456-7
1. Idaho Shakespeare Festival (Boise, Idaho).
2. Shakespeare, William, 1564-1616—Stage history—Idaho—Boise.
3. Theater—Idaho—Boise—History. I. Title.

PR3105C67 2006
822.3'3—dc22 2006008311

Lithographed and bound for
CAXTON PRESS
Caldwell, Idaho
173762

Printed in Canada

Dedicated to the

communities of Boise and the Treasure Valley,

whose steadfast support remains the primary reason

the Idaho Shakespeare Festival

exists today.

The Team

David Bogie, Photography

Chris Latter, Art Direction

Cheri Workman, Appendix

Alan Virta, Indexing

The Publisher

CAXTON PRESS

Ordering Information:

Caxton Press

312 Main St., Caldwell, Idaho, 83605

www.caxton press.com

208-459-7421 ,

800-657-6465

This book was made possible in part by a grant from the Boise City Arts Commission and with technical assistance from the Idaho Shakespeare Festival.

BOISE

Arts COMMISSION

Table of Contents

Photographers

We are grateful to the many individuals whose photographs appear in this book.

David Blain Bogie, DBB

Debra Lynn Bogie, DLB

Stacey Ericson, SE

Mary Erdmanczyk, ME

Troy Maben, TM

Norman Nelson, NN

Gage Williams, GW

Unknown, UK

Can one desire too much of a good thing? (As You Like It, IV,i)

Introduction

Boise has always been home to a thriving performing arts community—one that has consistently outpaced its growth.

Founded in 1948, Boise Little Theater is one of the oldest working community theaters in the country, and continues to provide a high quality outlet for community theater performers and patrons on a volunteer basis.

Over the years a number of attempts were made to establish professional theater companies, but one by one they all failed to attract an audience large enough to make them profitable. Many ambitious, talented young artists who wished to make at least a portion of their living at their craft were forced to seek theater employment elsewhere.

Nine years gone from Helen Farrer's healthy, ambitious drama department at Boise High School, I returned to my hometown in 1973 with a degree in Theater Arts, a season of professional summer stock under my belt, and four years of training in film and video production courtesy of the U.S. military draft. I brought with me a driving desire to resist the traditional "real job" market in favor of being paid for what I had been trained to do.

My first Boise theater experience came as a guest artist in a BSU production of *One Flew Over The Cuckoo's Nest*. The energy and talent in that group of students inspired me. Here was the next generation of performers, directors and designers about to be graduated into the "real world," and there was not one successful local professional outlet for their talents. There had to be a way to keep this wonderful talent pool from leaving like so many before them – to create the right combination of circumstances that would grab the attention of the city's already supportive arts audience and keep coming back for more.

Several members of that cast, along with what other friends we could cajole into chasing a wild and crazy dream, became the core of that first experiment in Shakespeare at One Capital Center during the summer of 1977 – our midsummer night's dream come true. We must have done something right, because to this day, local talent plays an important role in making ISF the successful company it is, and I'm very happy to say the audience is still coming back for more.

Doug Copsey

The Bull Goose Loonies: top row, left to right: Pat Nance, Bruce Richardson, Dan Peterson, Stitch Marker, Marv Koch. Bottom row, left to right: Mike Hoffman, Sal Sanzo, Doug Copsey, Jim Dobson.

Michael Hoffman: *What's interesting to me is Cuckoo's Nest is a play about redefining your reality, and not giving in to a sort of prescribed reality. With all the good things about the Boise State theater department, I think there was a general feeling that most people coming from the area and getting involved in theater might look forward to a career as a high school theater teacher, but there wasn't much else, really, that we were encouraged to set our sights on. Doug showed up with a lot of energy and an ability to dream and think bigger than what we were used to, and I think it was really infectious. Partly because of Doug, and in large part because of the director, Larry West, that show, I think, redefined a lot of people's notions of what their future could be. So for me, the start wasn't really A Midsummer Night's Dream, the start was Cuckoo's Nest.*

Beginnings

The Downtown Years

1977-1980

Biondello, hie you home, And bid Bianca make her ready straight; And, if you will, tell what hath h
Lucentio's father is arrived in Padua, And how she's like to be Lucentio's wife. Happily we met; the happ

Seelye Smith (above), Titania, *A Midsummer Night's Dream*; Background for this and opposite page One Capital Center blueprint, architects John Graham and Company. UK

The Festival's grass roots beginnings were a combination of like-minded community-based

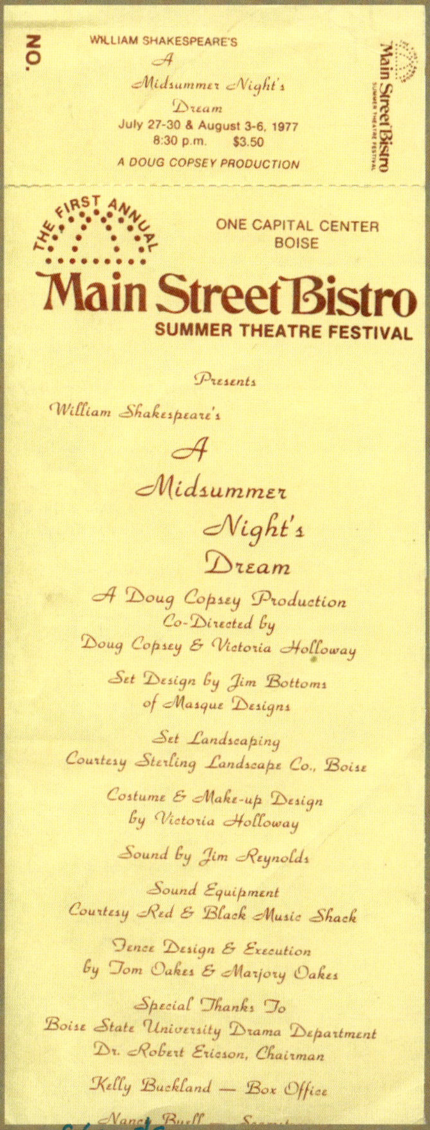

NO.

WILLIAM SHAKESPEARE'S
A
Midsummer Night's
Dream
July 27-30 & August 3-6, 1977
8:30 p.m. $3.50
A DOUG COPSEY PRODUCTION

Main Street Bistro
SUMMER THEATRE FESTIVAL

THE FIRST ANNUAL

ONE CAPITAL CENTER
BOISE

Main Street Bistro
SUMMER THEATRE FESTIVAL

Presents
William Shakespeare's
A
Midsummer
Night's
Dream
A Doug Copsey Production
Co-Directed by
Doug Copsey & Victoria Holloway

Set Design by Jim Bottoms
of Masque Designs

Set Landscaping
Courtesy Sterling Landscape Co., Boise

Costume & Make-up Design
by Victoria Holloway

Sound by Jim Reynolds

Sound Equipment
Courtesy Red & Black Music Shack

Fence Design & Execution
by Tom Oakes & Marjory Oakes

Special Thanks To
Boise State University Drama Department
Dr. Robert Ericson, Chairman

Kelly Buckland — Box Office

To try and say exactly how it all began, thirty years gone, is to discount a whole lot of water under many bridges, both real and proverbial, along the way.

Yet there remain occasional flashes of memory that bring forth visions of a sort. One such epiphany that continues to linger occurred in the spring of 1976 with my first view of the recently completed One Capital Center at Ninth and Main Streets. It wasn't so much the building itself, although its modern design was certainly unique to the city, as the sloping lawn that rolled from the sidewalk surrounding the northeastern third of the block down to a vast concrete patio one floor below street level, offering entrance to offices as well as a restaurant, as yet unopened, called the Main Street Bistro.

The patio was flanked by two wide staircases flowing down from street level like broad rivers emptying into a pristine lake. One ran straight down from the parking lot on the southeast corner of the block between the lawn and a descending series of large, freshly filled planter boxes, its series of cascading steps

The Play: ***A Midsummer Night's Dream***

Co-Directors: Doug Copsey and Victoria Holloway

Set Design : Jim Bottoms

Costume Design: Victoria Holloway

Lighting Design: Dan Andrews

Sound: Jim Reynolds

L-R, Patrick Delana, Demetrius, Linda Pommerening, Hermia, Michael Hoffman, Lysander, Barbara McKean, Helena, *Midsummer.* UK

Dramatis Personae
Theseus, Duke of Athens .... Doug Copsey
Egeus, Father to Hermia .... Dan Peterson
Lysander, in love with Hermia ..... Mike Hoffman
Demetrius, in love with Hermia .... Pat Delana
Hippolyta, Queen of the Amazons .... Seelye Smith
Betrothed to Theseus
Hermia, Daughter to Egeus...Linda M. Pommerening
In Love with Lysander
Helena, in love with Demetrius .. Barbara McKean
Quince, A Carpenter .... S. Galligan
Bottom, A Weaver .... Joel Far
Snug, Apprentice Joiner
Snout, A Tinker
Flute, Apprentice Tinker
Starveling, A Tailor
Liza, A Beauteous Wench
Oberon, King of the
Titania, Queen of
Puck or Rob

1977

The Main Street Bistro, One Capital Center. DBB

interrupted twice by small pools of landings before reaching patio level just behind a pair of tall flag poles set forward a few feet in a small notch of concrete. The other cut a broad arc down from Main Street bordered, like its counterpart, by the lawn toward Ninth Street while on the building side a sloping patch of top soil dotted with newly planted trees and shrubs stretched all the way from the patio's edge up to the sidewalk at street level – a small forest in the making. This stairway widened as it descended pausing at a pair of landings much broader than those on the opposite side. The lower one, just a few steps above the main patio, was at least fifteen feet across.

Downtown Boise's newest high-rise bustled with activity, but that empty expanse of lawn and concrete conjured up the feeling that here was an emptiness in need of filling. The blank, concrete whiteness cried out for the color of sets and costumes, the movement and action of actors, dancers and musicians. Likewise the lush, green lawn seemed wanting for crowds of people relaxing on picnic blankets, enjoying food and drink and friends as they laughed and cried and applauded the performers. Surely the designers must have had this in mind when they drew up their plans for this magnificent amphitheater, for that is indeed what it was, in the most Greek sense of the word.

I had known Skip since high school, so I went to see him in his office on the eighth floor, which just happened to overlook the patio and lawn. Ushering him to the window I asked him to look down and "think Greek." I was surprised to learn he had no such plans in mind, no sense at all, in fact, of the opportunity that had been created at the foot of their eleven story edifice. We consulted his father, Arthur, who was likewise oblivious to the concept. Then Skip suggested we speak to his brother, Doug, and no sooner had I explained it to him than destiny reared up on its haunches and roared approval.

Cast meeting, *Midsummer.* UK

Skip Oppenheimer: *In the original plans there was no amphitheater, no lower level plaza, just a flat grid with a jewel box bank, or something similar, on the corner. Right before construction started we were doing some conceptual planning with our partners, which were Simplot and Howard S. Wright, and we began thinking Boise could use a really good downtown restaurant and we could create sort of interesting urban space. That's where the whole thing came about, and they changed it very much last minute.*

DBB

"... look down and "think Greek."

Doug Oppenheimer: *I remember it was the perfect time, because it was a natural amphitheater and, frankly, we needed a hook to get people to come to the Main Street Bistro.*

Skip Oppenheimer: *The three people running that were Bob Barney, Shane Williams was the bar manager, and Riley McDevitt was the maitre'd. I remember getting together with them and they were all positive about it. They thought it would be very cool.*

Undaunted by a failed attempt to raise the money in time to mount a production of *Hair* before the Bistro opened in the late summer of 1976, discussions among our small group of artists that fall and winter turned to what we might do the following summer.

Michael Hoffman: *What comes to mind is a lot of conversation at Doug's old house on 12th Street. A lot of dreaming, a lot of hoping that there might be the possibility of creating professional theater in Idaho. Eventually it just reached a point where there was a certain kind of synergy that happened, and the house, the group of people, and Doug's positivity and talent became, in a way, a kind of funnel for that energy. He believed that it could happen.*

Shakespeare had always been a good draw for audiences, especially the comedies, and his plays were public domain, which meant no performance royalties. We also reasoned that a period piece, with a big cast, colorful costumes and an opportunity for unusual set designs, would work well outdoors. Add to that the fact that Shakespeare had only been performed in Boise once in a blue moon, and we decided we had the perfect recipe to fill the space and entertain crowds of unsuspecting Boiseans invited to picnic downtown at Ninth and Main.

The budget for such an undertaking, however, was a different story. Without non-profit status we could not ask for donations, and loan meetings with local bankers were met with rejections ranging from the impatient to the highly amused. I agreed to expand my one-man film production company, Doug Copsey Productions, to include theater productions, but with only about $1,000 in my bank account and a collective goose egg available from the rest of the group, we were far short of the funds needed to pull off even a meager production.

Barbara McKean: *In the spring of 1977, I sat in the back yard of Doug Copsey's house listening to his idea for a Shakespeare festival downtown at the base of the only skyscraper in Boise. I remember shaking my head and thinking he was absolutely crazy, but there was no way I'd ever turn down an opportunity to play Helena. So I threw my hat into the ring and off we went.*

Doug Oppenheimer: *If I recall, I asked about the budget, and Doug said it was tiny – he needed another $3,500 to pull this off. I thought it was a great idea to do Shakespeare and, frankly, we needed a hook to get people to come to the Main Street Bistro. It was kind of a win-win situation. So I wrote a check. It was one of those spur-of-the-moment decisions that I probably freaked out about later that day, but in hindsight it turned out to be a pretty good investment.*

Nonetheless, I approached the Oppenheimer family again the following spring with the idea of producing Shakespeare's *A Midsummer Night's Dream* that summer. They welcomed this new idea with open arms and a more than generous offer to grant us free use of the amphitheater – as long as we left it in the same condition we found it. But the set needed lumber, nails and paint, all of which were hard costs that no one was willing to foot for a group of young people with the wild idea of producing Shakespeare outdoors downtown. No one, that is, except Doug Oppenheimer.

With our total budget now at $4,500, we went to work. In order to give the new company some structure, it was decided that I would be Producing Director with Victoria Holloway taking the title of Artistic Director. She also took on the job of designing costumes. Her first move was to convince her former BSU theater professor, Steve Buss – with permission from Dr. Robert Ericson, Chairman of the Theater Arts Department – to give her free access to their costume storage. Then she and Seelye Smith set about scrounging the city for whatever other bits and pieces of fabric they could find. Meanwhile I concentrated on creating "a forest near Athens" fit for the antics of confused lovers and mythical "faeries" that could also double as a court for Duke Theseus and his soon-to-be bride, Hippolyta.

My one requirement from the outset was to fill the space. We could not afford to let our show get overpowered by the vastness of the concrete sea or the imposing eleven-story edifice rising above it. Jim Bottoms took my words to heart and designed a series of platforms that sprawled up from ground level some thirty feet to a broad ledge that extended out from the first

Lighting Rental
Illuminat lighting #3124
light hook-up
Set
Jim Bottoms

June 2, 1977

The First Annual Main Street Bistro
Summer Theatre Festival

Revised Budget: "A Midsummer Night's Dream"

1. Set Construction	$125.00
2. Light Rental	350.00
3. Costumes & Make-up	250.00
4. Props & Miscellaneous	100.00
5. Security	160.00
6. Publicity	500.00*

Total Main Street Bistro Expenses = $1485.00

Profit from fence advertising.................$875.00
To be used as follows: Light Rental.......225.00
Publicity..............

TOTAL BUDGET

...he check for the order ...
... on June 21, 1977. The order was as foll...

2 pair Green Ears #9 @ $2.95 each	= 5.90
2 pair Elf Ears #10 @ $2.95 each	= 5.90
1 Large Nose #17 @ $1.19 each	= 1.19
1 Large Clown Nose#21@ $1.49 each	= 1.49
1 Stein's Liquid Make-up, Green	= 2.25
	$19.68

... the t... ...ted over th... ...hone. ...

Set construction, One Capital Center. UK

Tom Wolfe and Barbara McKean. UK

Mike Hoffman, above, and right, with Seelye Smith. UK

floor windows. Chicken wire covered in a painted cloth mache would be used to shape them into a large mountainside seemingly growing out of the side of the building. In the dark of a summer's night it would seem as though the whole building were a giant mountain. This would allow for entrances from high above as well as down both staircases, and through a couple of hidden caves built into our "mountain," giving Oberon and his impish attendant, Puck, plenty of room to race about and confuse the four lovers lost in the woods. There was even a waterfall that tumbled into a pool at center stage where Titania and her sprites liked to lounge.

With design duties already occupying a considerable amount of time, Victoria and I decided to split directing duties as well. I was to play Oberon, so I took on the lovers and court scenes while she handled the Fairies and Rustics. Auditions were held in the late spring of 1977, with rehearsals to begin in early July.

Directors, actors, designers and crew were all one in the same. Everyone participated in literally every phase of the production – usually after working at regular jobs. This was going to be a professional theater, but before we could pay anyone we first had to create a company, and that meant producing a successful play. Contracts were simple: after the Oppenheimer loan and any other expenses were paid, everyone got an equal share of the profits – if there were any.

The first obstacle was finding a rehearsal space. There were vacant buildings in town that had been loaned to theater groups in the past, but since we would be performing outdoors, we wanted to rehearse outdoors, if for no other reason than to get our voices in shape so that we would be heard all the way to the back of the lawn. There was only one given – it had to be free.

Jeannie Peterson: *Dan and I were renting an apartment on Highland Street and there was a horse pasture out back with only one horse in it. I asked our landlord, Marty Priest, if we could use it for rehearsals, he said yes. Of course our cocker spaniel, Sunny, was right there in the thick of it.*

With Sunny dutifully keeping the horse at bay, rehearsals proceeded apace. But there was the business side of the company to run as well. Our use of the patio space at One Capital Center would close off the main entrance to the Bistro for two prime weeks in July. Guests could still get to the basement-level restaurant by entering the building at street level and taking the elevator down one floor, but we were definitely an interruption in their summer dining traffic.

In order to make up for any lost business due to this inconvenience we offered to let them sell drinks and food to our audience. They heartily agreed and made plans to set up a couple of grills and a bar on the lawn. However, the city ordinance for selling or consuming alcohol outdoors required an enclosed area, which meant a fence would need to be constructed completely around the lawn. It was an unplanned expense, and not in our already tight budget, but we also needed a way to control access for our ticket holders. Projecting voices from the patio all the way to the back of the lawn was no easy task, and using amplification was out of the question from a budget standpoint, but a fence might help with that obstacle as well. The only question was how to pay for it.

We had long since given up on the idea of a souvenir program. Printing costs were just too high. Instead we opted for a simple play bill that listed cast, crew and anyone else who had helped in any way. But the fence suddenly presented us with a huge blank canvas perfect for advertising. It could pay for itself. Downtown businesses were already in support of our festival because of the potential customers we would theoretically provide them each evening, so I had little problem selling mini-billboard space at Ninth and Main for two weeks in July. We easily made enough money to pay for the fence materials, and there was enough left over to provide a small stipend for an artist to paint the ads on four by eight foot sheets of particle board.

Left to right: Tom Wolfe, Starveling; Martha Peavey, Wench, G. Robert Fields, Flute, Joel Farmer, Bottom, Sue Galligan, Peter Quince. Midsummer. UK

By this time, Jim Bottoms had bolted together several of the set platforms for us to use at the rehearsal site and with a little imagination we could begin to see our mountainside take shape. The sweeping staircases and their large landings worked beautifully for the court scenes, but the landscaping around the building was only a year old, and had not even begun to fill in yet. After a couple of experiments with the cloth mache, using everything from old t-shirts and jeans to bedspreads, sheets and whatever rags we could dig up, we began to see that it would take more than a skillful paint job resembling rocks, earth, moss and lichens to create the illusion of a forest in the vast sea of concrete at One Capital Center

Enter Eric Olson, a long-time friend and a partner in Sterling Landscape. He took one look at the design and the space and agreed. We needed trees, lots of them, and we were running out of time. He and his partners, John and Lynn Sterling and

Sue Galligan: *I missed the first auditions because of illness. No tragedy that, though, since I was much too old to play a lover in Midsummer and lacked the natural "oomph" necessary for either Titania or Hippolyta. Then Victoria suggested Peter Quince. So there I was with a gray beard, a deep hood and a limp, trying to keep track of a pack of zanies as they ran completely out of control. I know of no greater thrill in my theater life than getting to stand on the concrete before 500 people sitting on the lawn at One Capital Center and starting the prologue to Pyramus and Thisbe. Miraculous and marvelous!*

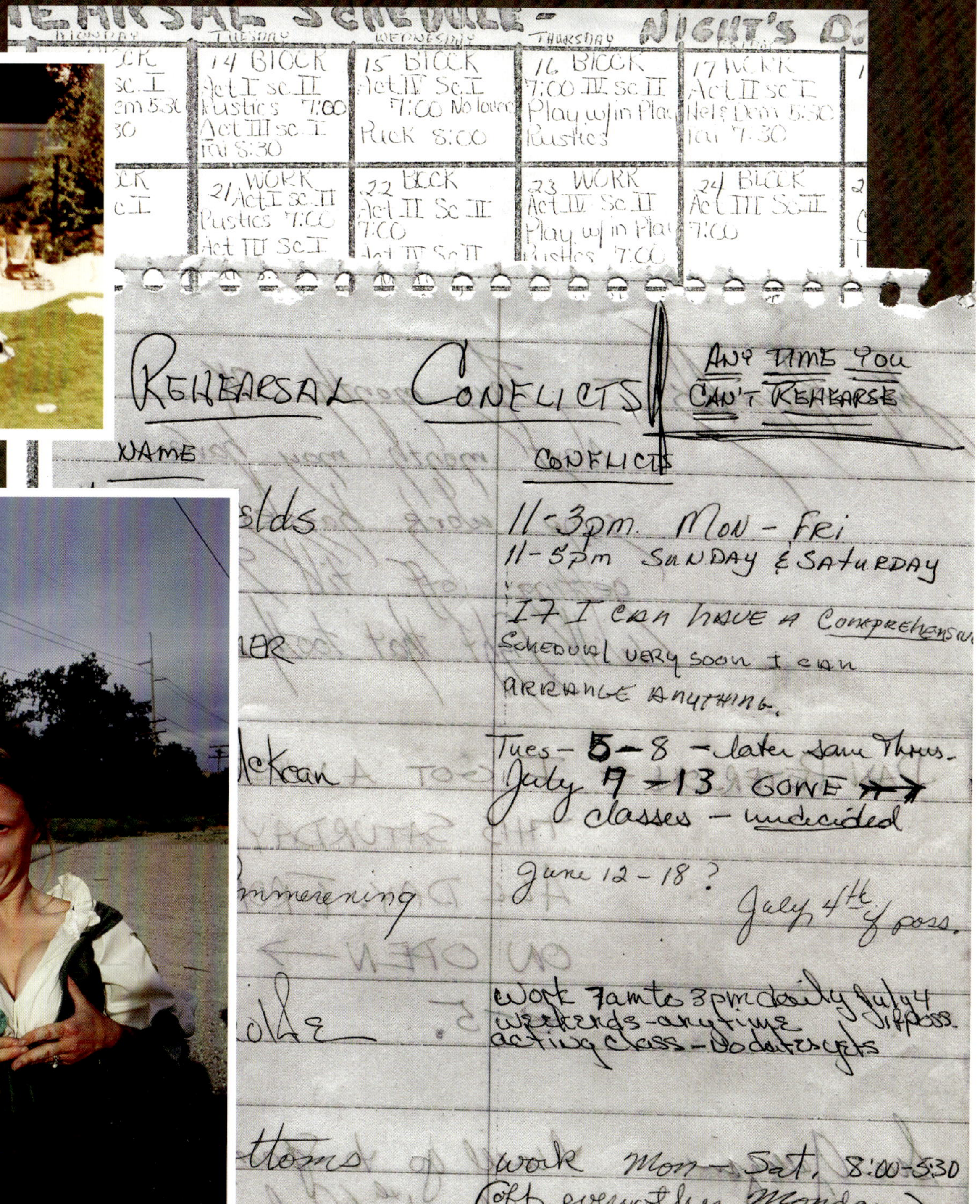

REHEARSAL SCHEDULE - NIGHT'S D

MONDAY	TUESDAY	WEDNESDAY	THURSDAY	FRIDAY
...CK sc. I ...em 5:30 ...30	14 BLOCK Act I sc. II Rustics 7:00 Act III sc. I Titi 8:30	15 BLOCK Act IV Sc. I 7:00 No lovers Puck 8:00	16 BLOCK 7:00 III sc. II Play w/in Play Rustics	17 WORK Act II sc. I Hel & Dem 5:30 Titi 7:30
...CK ...c. I	21 WORK Act I sc. II Rustics 7:00 Act III Sc. I	22 BLOCK Act II Sc. II 7:00 Act IV Sc. II	23 WORK Act IV Sc. II Play w/in Play Rustics 7:00	24 BLOCK Act III Sc. II 7:00

REHEARSAL CONFLICTS — ANY TIME YOU CAN'T REHEARSE

NAME	CONFLICTS
...olds	11-3pm. Mon - Fri 11-5pm Sunday & Saturday
...ER	If I can have a comprehensive schedual very soon I can arrange anything.
...cKean	Tues - 5-8 - later same Thurs. July 7-13 GONE → classes - undecided
...mmerening	June 12 - 18 ? July 4th if poss.
...olle	work 7am to 3pm daily July 4 if poss. weekends - anytime acting class - ...
...ttoms	work Mon - Sat. 8:00-5:30 (off ... Monday)

Victoria Holloway: *The Festival's grass roots beginnings were a combination of like-minded community-based theater artists, families and friends. Everybody took pride in their work. We were all exhilarated by the great literature we performed, the location, and the sense of belonging to a company.*

Ginger Scott
DLB

Joel Farmer, Bottom; Seelye Smith, Titania, *Midsummer*. UK

A calendar, a calendar! Look in the almanack; find out moonshine. Midsummer Night's Dream, III, i.

Tom Martin, had already agreed to let us use their trucks to transport our giant set pieces from the horse pasture downtown. Their nursery on Fairview Avenue was a small forest in itself, and they readily agreed to let us take as many trees and shrubs as we wanted, with the understanding that we would pay for any that didn't survive.

The peat pots in which most of them were kept held up the illusion of a forest floor well enough, and the only upkeep was making sure they were watered every night, a crew chore that became rather coveted over the five years that Sterling provided us with massive amounts of nursery stock, not to mention flowers, bird baths, fountains, and anything else that came to mind from their extensive inventory. Those trees completed the forest near Athens better than any set designer could have built with ten times the budget. We could never have done it without them, but as Eric simply put it, what are friends for?

Tom Oakes and his sister Marjory were also running out of time. They had drawn several ad logos on the fence panels and were starting to realize the enormous task that still lay before them. There was no way they could finish drawing all the ads and paint them as well. With no money to hire painters, our cast and crew all pitched in, trooping over to my back yard after rehearsals to spend another few hours painting. Talk about dedication.

We had long since given up on the idea of a souvenir program.

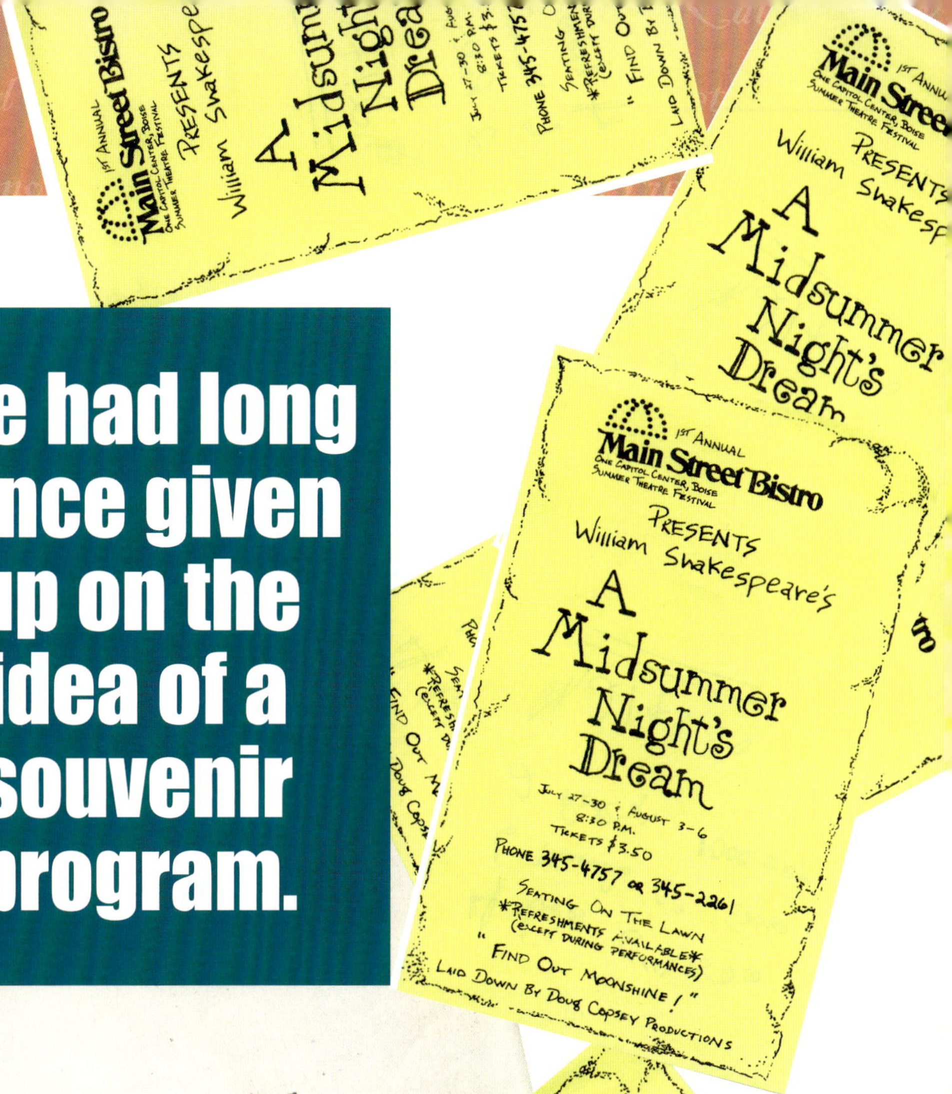

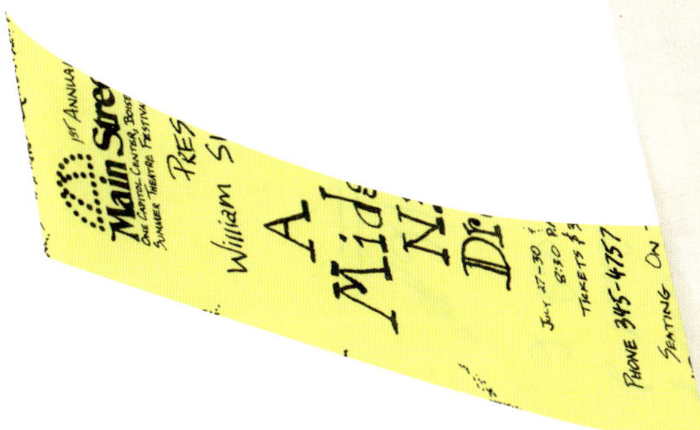

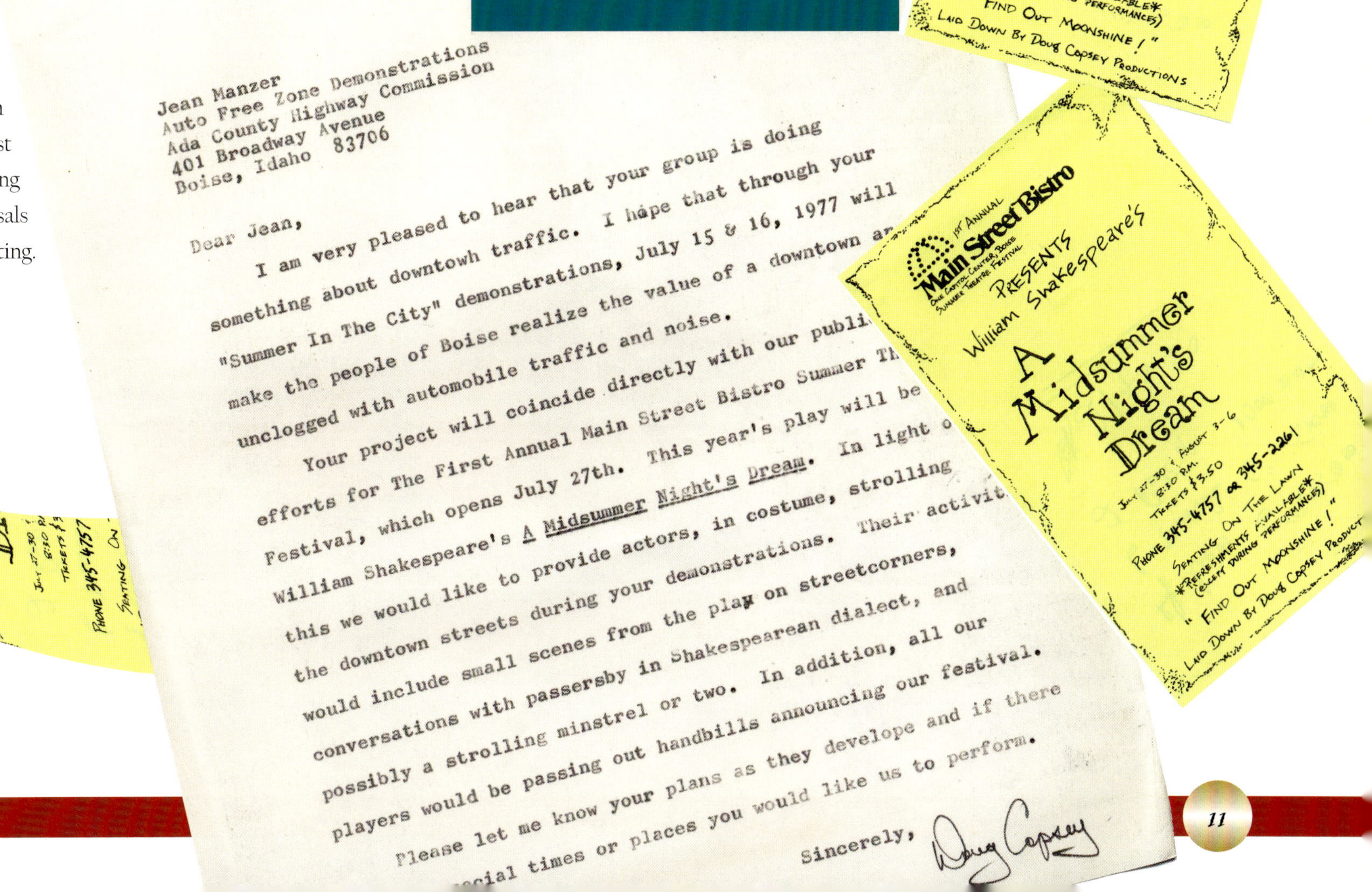

Jean Manzer
Auto Free Zone Demonstrations
Ada County Highway Commission
401 Broadway Avenue
Boise, Idaho 83706

Dear Jean,

I am very pleased to hear that your group is doing something about downtown traffic. I hope that through your "Summer In The City" demonstrations, July 15 & 16, 1977 will make the people of Boise realize the value of a downtown ar[ea] unclogged with automobile traffic and noise.

Your project will coincide directly with our publi[city] efforts for The First Annual Main Street Bistro Summer Th[eatre] Festival, which opens July 27th. This year's play will be William Shakespeare's A Midsummer Night's Dream. In light o[f] this we would like to provide actors, in costume, strolling the downtown streets during your demonstrations. Their activit[ies] would include small scenes from the play on streetcorners, conversations with passersby in Shakespearean dialect, and possibly a strolling minstrel or two. In addition, all our players would be passing out handbills announcing our festival.

Please let me know your plans as they develope and if there [are spe]cial times or places you would like us to perform.

Sincerely,

Doug Copsey

Seelye Smith: *We were down to such a deadline that we were all painting in the dark. One night someone unplugged the freezer on the back porch in order to plug in floodlights and forgot to plug it back in. After a few days in that summer heat there was this ungodly stench, and no one could figure out where it was coming from. Finally, someone opened that freezer and the smell sent everyone scattering.*

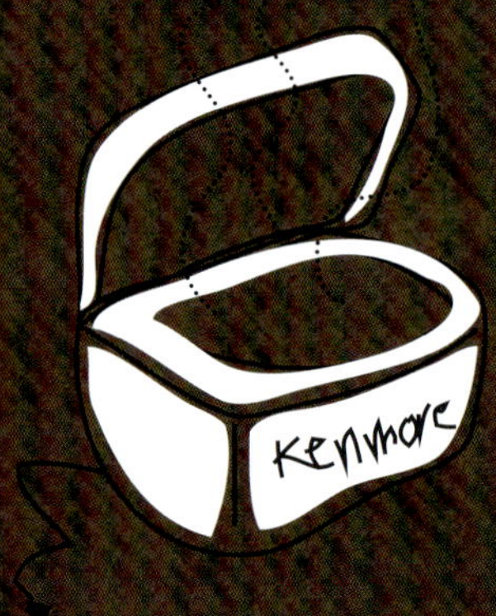

Doug Copsey, Oberon and Jim Bottoms, Puck, *Midsummer*. UK

Tom Oakes, G. Robert Fields, Victoria Holloway, Marjory Oakes, Pat Delana.UK

Victoria had completely taken over the apartment with her costume shop. She and seamstress Nancy Buell were sewing all hours of the day and night. If that wasn't enough, the posters we thought we had carefully proofread came back with the wrong phone number for tickets. With no money for re-printing, Kelly Buckland, who had been coerced into running the box office out of my apartment, graciously accepted the tedious task of cutting up printed sheets of the correct phone number and pasting them over the old ones one some 300 posters, in addition to answering the phone and taking reservations. Needless to say, anyone who happened to drop by during those frenzied weeks was quickly roped into working on something for as long as we could keep them there. It was truly a labor of love on the part of everyone involved, and all for a small share of profits that might or might not materialize.

About two weeks before we were scheduled to open, Mike Silva, a long-time Boise Little Theater director and actor who also happened to be an Ada County Highway Commissioner at the time, approached me with the idea that the traffic noise on Ninth and Main streets could be a problem. My planning process hadn't gone beyond the confines of the lawn, but it was easy to see – and hear – that, even with the fence, he was right. He helped us draw up a plan, get ourselves on the next ACHD meeting agenda, and with an impassioned speech about the value of the arts in our community to his fellow commissioners, led the vote to approve it.

Thanks to Mike, the usual bureaucratic red tape fell away like so much Christmas ribbon, and we found ourselves in possession of a dozen ACHD barricades and permission to block traffic at Tenth and Main, as well as Ninth and Idaho streets from 7:30 until 11:00 PM on the nights of our performances. Things really seemed to be going our way. But we had forgotten about one of Boise's favorite teenage summer pastimes.

Every Friday and Saturday night during the warm months any teenager who can get his or her hands on a car, or find a seat in one, seems driven to take part in the ancient ritual known as cruising. From Sixteenth and Main, they form an almost bumper to bumper, three lane rectangle down to Seventh, over to Idaho Street and back up to Sixteenth again. We were definitely outnumbered, and the barricades did not prove much of a barrier at first.

> **Tom Willmorth:** *In the early days, actors were part of the stage crew. We all helped raise the plywood fence around the theater and helped build and strike the set. I was part of the tree crew, and I helped set up wooden sawhorses to detour traffic – unbelievably allowed by ACHD to close down Ninth and Main. Because this was done as close to curtain time as possible we were already in costume. As you might imagine, a road crew in tights and tunics got a lot of honks and catcalls.*

During our final rehearsals we were regularly greeted with honking cars and shouting teens streaming down Main Street just outside our fence. The guards we posed at both intersections were powerless to do more than keep replacing the barriers each time someone knocked them down. With Mike Silva's help once again, we turned to the Boise Police Department and found they were only too glad to come to our aid. It seems many of the City's finest secretly relished the chance to interrupt the cruiser routine, which had been a sore spot to local law enforcement for quite some time, and were more than happy to put in a few extra hours on duty at the barricades. To everyone's delight, the Bard's lyrical iambic pentameter was no longer punctuated with car horns.

On Sunday morning, July 24, 1977, One Capital Center began its transformation. Piece by piece the giant set was hauled in on Sterling Landscape trucks, carried down the steps and bolted into place. More cloth mache was applied and painted to mask any gaps between platforms. The eleven stories of concrete rising above it gave our set a whole new

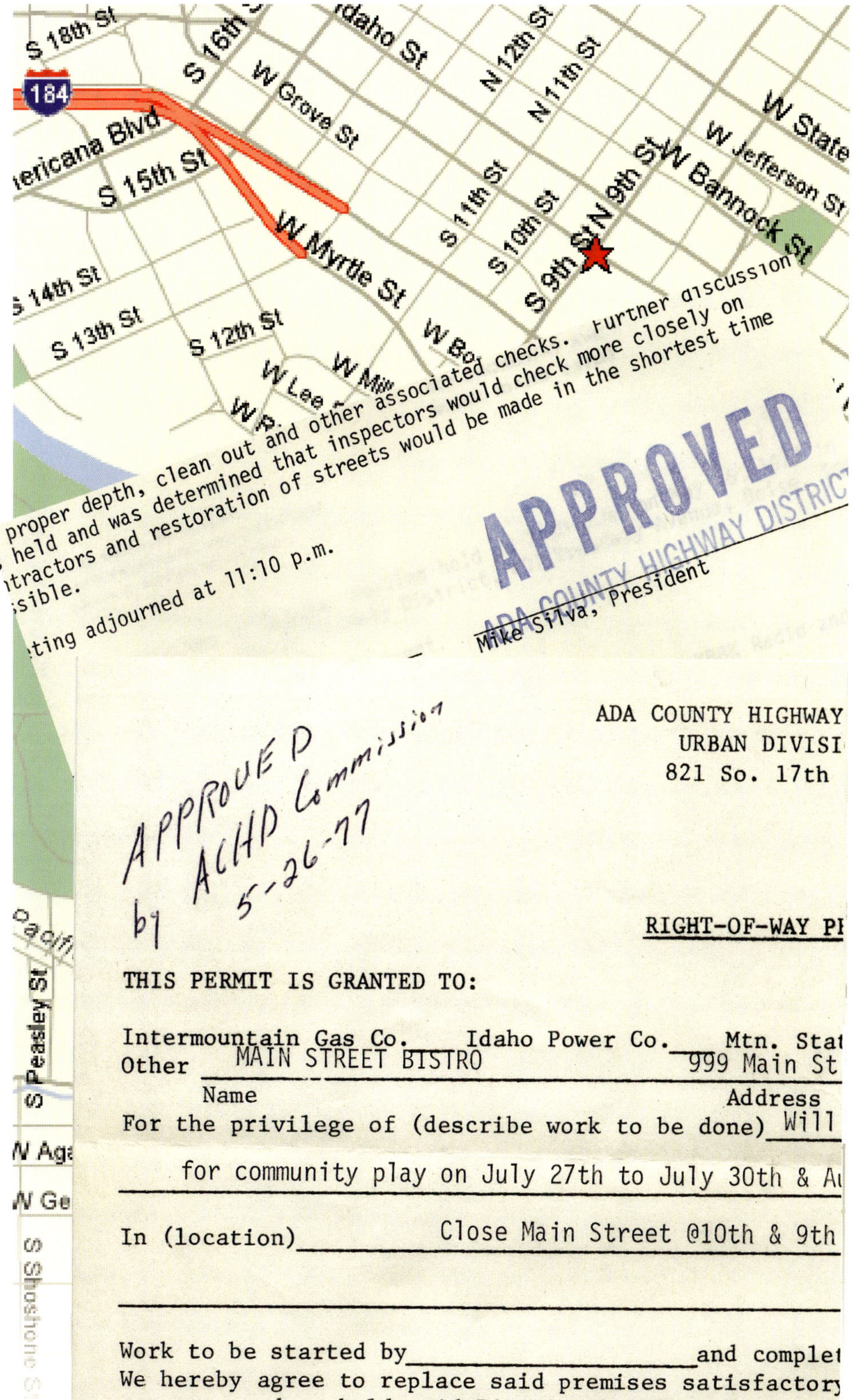

"This wild and crazy scheme was actu

Jim Bottoms, Puck, *Midsummer*. UK

dimension of size, creating an enormity we hadn't expected, and actors couldn't resist trying out entrances from the upper level.

At the same time, another crew began driving fence posts and stapling the four by eight foot painted panels into place along the sidewalk. Wielding the infamous post-pounders – heavy metal tubes with handles welded on each side – soon became a challenge, and everyone had to take a turn. Who could pound the most posts, who could last the longest without a break? It was a nasty, exhausting job made fun by a little impromptu competition, and those who excelled did so in part because the rest of the company cheered them on all day long. A new kind of energy took over as everyone realized that all their hard work was finally paying off and this wild and crazy scheme was actually going to happen.

We worked at a feverish pace. By afternoon truckloads of Sterling trees began arriving at the parking lot. One by one the heavy peat pots were wrestled down the steps and placed around the mountainside that was now firmly attached to the side of the building. Passersby stared in wonder at this ragtag group who appeared to be audaciously defacing Boise's newest downtown office building, no doubt wondering whether they ought to call the police. The fence, with its painted advertising helped allay their fears. If all those businesses were lending their names to whatever was going on it must at least be legal. And we had reserved one panel on each side to announce *The First Annual Main Street Bistro Summer Theater Festival* with performance dates and the box office number.

Michael Hoffman: *Just bringing trees into the space, that little bit of forest, created something really magical in terms of the design.*

Late that evening everything looked to be in place. We all sprawled on the lawn to admire our handiwork inside the protective enclosure of the fence. The

ng to happen."

barren patio had taken on a completely different look, and as exhausted as we were we couldn't resist running a few scenes and testing our voices to see just how much projection was really needed to reach the back of the lawn. As we had hoped, the fence actually helped in that regard, reflecting the sound back on the audience furthest away from the stage and improving their ability to hear. However, one thing immediately became very clear – we were going to need a lot more trees.

UK

The next morning I dragged myself out of bed early and went down to One Capital Center. I wanted to make sure the set and fence and trees hadn't mysteriously disappeared overnight – that I hadn't just dreamed the whole thing. But mostly I wanted to watch people's reactions as the city came to life on a Monday morning with a decidedly new look downtown at Ninth and Main.

UK

With just two days until opening night on Wednesday there was still much to do. Beginning first thing Monday morning, more truckloads of trees were hauled in to fill out the forest, and as tech rehearsal progressed, adjustments in their placement were made to allow for easier entrances and exits for the actors. Dan Andrews, a local one-man stage lighting company called Illuminauts, arrived to set up and we quickly learned that his two hydraulic towers, each holding a dozen or so lights would require a special $175 plug to be installed in order to prevent blowing out the Bistro fuse box. Once he got over the shock of seeing what we had done to his building, and most likely in a state of total disbelief, Doug Oppenheimer offered to take on that task himself, and by the next evening's dress rehearsal we had lights.

But our troubles were not over. The day before we opened I received a call from Skip Oppenheimer.

Skip Oppenheimer: *Some building code guy came into my office saying we had some signs that were in violation. And I said, "What signs? We don't have any signs."*

Doug Oppenheimer and I went to the City Attorney, who explained that the ads on the fence constituted billboards, and billboards were expressly forbidden in downtown Boise. We frantically tried to explain what were doing and begged for an exception to be made, but our pleas fell on deaf ears. Unwilling to give in, we went right to the top, appealing to Mayor Dick Eardley himself. He listened graciously, and promised to let us know within the next 24 hours.

Our final dress rehearsal that night was a bit strained. Had we come this far

only to be stopped by a zoning ordinance? Without the fence, the Bistro could not sell food and drinks, nor could our patrons enjoy their own picnic dinners. Without the fence, anyone sitting more than halfway up the lawn would not be able to hear the actors. Without the fence, we were doomed.

By noon the next day we still had not heard from the Mayor's office. I informed the cast that we would go on as planned, and get in at least one performance before they shut us down. Then, late that afternoon the call came in. Mayor Eardley had decided that no exceptions could be made, the fence must come down. I was stunned silent. After a moment, the caller asked how many performances we had planned. I told him the play would run Wednesday through Saturday for the next two weeks. There was a pause while he consulted with someone away from the phone, then he came back on line and informed me we had exactly two weeks to remove that illegal fence.

Victoria Holloway's costumes were extraordinary. In addition to the BSU costume pieces on loan she and her crew had done absolute wonders with an odd assortment of donated roll ends, discarded draperies, lace fragments and anything she could charm and cajole out of fabric stores, friends, even strangers. The nobility were regal, the Rustics were appropriately shabby, and both were a colorful contrast to the green and brown forest that now filled the patio almost to overflowing. The fairies and sprites were simple yet bizarre in green tights and leotards with an assortment of grasses, hair and rope hanging off them, and wild, green and gold makeup.

Ginger Scott: *My father died just a short time before we opened A Midsummer Night's Dream and I used to sit on the plaza and speak to him as I waited to go on as Snug the joiner. I told him how I wished he had been able to see what a group of eager young people had accomplished with almost no money, but a big dream.*

Three of the sprites, Cobweb, Moth and Mustardseed, were actually non-existent, but you could never convince an audience of that. Sound Designer Jim Reynolds created intriguing synthesized noises for each of them, and their musical "lines" in answer to Titania's commands made them as real as any actor on stage.

The box office was run by Jeannie Rice (soon to become Peterson), who set up a pair of folding tables, one at each entrance, and was responsible for the two small cash boxes I handed her each night. Ticket takers did double duty as ushers, although seating was first-come-first-served. Patrick Delana's

Jeannie (Rice) Peterson and Doug Copsey.

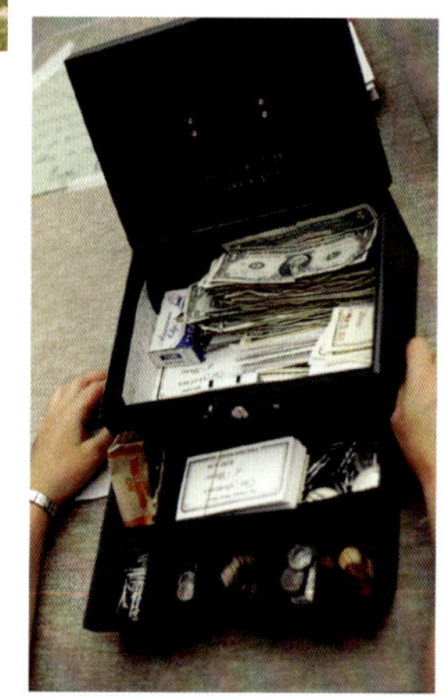

DBB

mother, Joyce, Edith Simmerman and my mom, Dee Dee, were among those who volunteered for that duty.

Others, like Dale Aspelund, patrolled the fence line to try and prevent eager patrons from sneaking under and seeing the show for free. Every dollar was important to our cause, a fact not overlooked by my father, Bob, who took it upon himself to stop on his way home from work each night to make sure the cash boxes were not left unattended, and to issue firm instructions to Jeannie each and every night that we get it to the bank as soon as possible and not leave it laying around somewhere so it could get stolen.

Joyce Delana: *Would anyone come was the major question in everyone's mind as the first curtain time approached. Did the people of the Boise Valley think we were all crazy to assume that they would* *enjoy Shakespeare sitting on a grassy hill? Would they appreciate the borrowed bushes, hand-painted sets and contrived costumes? No, they didn't think it was crazy, and they loved the play, with many coming for a second or third time. We ticket takers greeted friends as we helped them find places to sit and tried to fend off an occasional drunk who wanted to wander through the set on his way to the bar. There was an electricity in the air as each performance was greeted by a wildly appreciative audience.*

That first opening night we were astonished when over 300 people attended. Our only publicity had been the posters and flyers we spread liberally about town and that old, reliable standby, word of mouth – which from actors can be quite a lot. By all accounts we were already a success, but when the next night's attendance rose to 400, and the weekend saw 500-600 people each night, we knew we had created something special for our city.

Patrick Delana: *After rehearsing in a horse pasture for weeks, scavenging for costumes, painting advertising on the fence in a dark backyard, building the set, installing the fence, distributing handbills and flyers, and carrying in tree after tree to make the forest, it was opening night. Victoria came backstage and, in an amazed undertone and with a look of total disbelief, announced that there were actually 300 people in the audience. Just before the show began, the cast and available crew assembled in a circle to engage in a typical theater-type exercise of holding hands. I could feel the energy. About two hours later, from off stage right, we could watch Jim Bottoms doing Puck's epilogue – "If we shadows have offended..." Judging by the applause that followed, we hadn't.*

Even though the sun was still well up when the play started each evening at 8:00 PM, by the second half of the show, the east facing patio was in shade and lights were needed. Dan Andrews' hydraulic light towers worked beautifully, except when the wind blew and caused them to sway precariously back and forth. We staked guy wires to the ground and assigned two people to stand by each tower during the show just in case, but it was not the wind that caused our one lighting shutdown of the run.

L-R, G. Robert Fields, Flute; Ginger Scott, Snug; Dan Peterson, Snout; Martha Peavey, Wench; Tom Wolfe, Starveling, *Midsummer*. UK

For the past month, in a pasture in South Boise, a cast
15 actors and actresses have been preparing a unique event

About halfway through one performance it began to sprinkle lightly. It was nothing like real rain, and none of the audience was leaving, but rather than risk a short circuit the lights were cut off. There was still enough natural light to see the actors and, as we have come to expect of Boise audiences, no one seemed to mind. But we knew that towards the end of the show it would begin to get pretty dark. Backstage we were frantic. Should we risk turning on the lights? What if we got a bunch of flashlights and handed them out to the audience?

Before we could come up with any workable solution, Doug Oppenheimer, who happened to be in the audience that night, raced inside and instructed his building maintenance people to turn on the lights in all the offices on that side of the building. It was enough to light the stage through the end of the show and the cast, along with the audience showed their appreciation with quite possibly the only curtain call for a building in the history of theater.

Michael Hoffman: *I remember being initially suspect of starting the shows in the daylight and thinking, "Isn't that going to rob this Midsummer of the kind of magic it can have in a theater?" And then realizing that somehow it was just the opposite – that as the light changed, and as night fell, the magic sort of enveloped the audience, which is something I still love about the rhythm of the performances at the Festival.*

Doug Copsey, Oberon. Opposite: Joel Farmer, Bottom. *Midsummer.* UK

The only other near tragedy occurred on the final night of the first week's run. Sue Galligan, our Peter Quince, arrived about two hours before curtain to inform us that her nephew, Pat Delana, who was playing Demetrius, was in the emergency room receiving stitches to his face from a dog bite and would not be able to perform that night. After about ten minutes of frantic discussion on how to shuffle the cast around to fill the huge void left by the absence of one of the four lovers, it was decided that we would be better off leaving everyone in their own role and finding a replacement for Demetrius elsewhere. We would give him a script and announce the situation to the audience ahead of time, and hope they would play along with it.

Jim Owen, a good friend of Barbara McKean (Helena), had been rehearsing her lines with her for the past few weeks and was familiar with the role of Demetrius. He was also about the same size as Pat, so the costume would most likely fit. Barbara made the call, and a short time later Jim walked into the dressing room looking very dazed and confused.

I can only imagine what it must have been like in the audience that night as actors tugged, nudged and bumped Jim around the stage, covering for missed lines each time he lost his place in the script. I know it was an equal mix of pure joy and complete panic to watch from backstage.

Jim Owen: *There was this one scene where everybody is supposed to be asleep, and I'm sitting there not asleep, and Seelye Smith (Titania) leans in and goes, "You're asleep! Wait until somebody kicks you." Really, I was bruised and battered from people shoving me around. I'd be standing there with the book in my hand, trying to make it look like it was a prop, and all of a sudden I'd get these knuckles in my backbone and someone would whisper, "no, no, go to the left, go over and talk to Hermia."*

Not only did the audience play along, they embraced Demetrius' stand-in and cheered him along throughout the show. Fittingly, he received a standing ovation at curtain call. To this day it ranks as one of my all-time favorite

atre happening. Make your reservations by calling 345-4757.
The Main Street Bistro at 345-2261.

Press Release, 1977.

From an entry in the journal of Jim Owen, July 31, 1977:

Doug Copsey and Victoria Holloway came at me with script in hand. It had some yellow areas marked on it. "Read them," they said. And then they are telling me to speak "louder, louder!" And then, "Come over here, someone will do your makeup." Somebody else begins applying an instant curl machine to my hair. "Close your eyes, please." The smell of grease paint and then, "That's good, thanks." Lipstick, pancake, and more powder puff. "Oh, Jim" Victoria is at my side. She reads cues and reviews my entrances and exits. "Once again," she intones. "Oh, once again. Now once again." A hand blinds my left eye as hair spray goes on. The right eye catches Sue Galligan, who is playing Peter Quince, sending a glance my way that reflects the hope and doubt of the entire crew. Nobody here knows me and I don't know but Barbara.

And then there's Linda Pommerening (Hermia) shouting "Over here, come over here." She leads me to a corner where Helena and Lysander pace. Victoria provides a script. She and Doug stand off about twelve feet. Hermia, Helena and Lysander begin the rehearsal. The play begins in about twenty minutes. Soon there will be about 400 people on the lawn. God, I hope they get their money's worth.

performances in theater, anywhere, any time, and I'm pretty sure anyone who was there that night feels the same way. Fortunately, Pat was recovered enough to perform by the time the second week's run began the following Wednesday.

Jim Owen: *What really made that thing happen was the troupe. Because I remember when the play was over and we were all lined up, Doug stood up in front of the audience and made the announcement. I remember going up and taking bow and going, "Wow." And then I remember turning around and bowing to the troupe. And it was more like supplication, like, "You guys made it happen."*

To our amazement some 3,500 people attended our eight shows that first season, at $3.25 each. The reviews and the reaction of our audiences confirmed that our dream of a successful professional theater company in Boise was now a reality. Doug Oppenheimer's loan was repaid in full, all the bills were paid, and each company member was rewarded with a check for $225 for their eight weeks of hard work. It may not sound like much, but we were all ecstatic.

Michael Hoffman: *I remember so clearly Victoria saying to me, "I'm not going to act for free any more. I'm not going to pretend that people who cast me in things are doing me a favor." That was a big deal. It was a statement like, "As an actor, I really have something valuable to contribute and I'm going to acknowledge that value even if nobody else does." I always thought that through the Shakespeare Festival that whole idea was kind of injected into the community.*

The Oppenheimers and the Bistro staff were just as happy, so much so that after the closing performance they closed the restaurant and threw us a huge cast party to celebrate. After a brief period of recuperation, plans were begun for a second season.

Doug Oppenheimer: *We had no customers anyway, so it was an easy thing to do. I remember saying that it was the first time the restaurant had ever been full.*

Our dream of a successful professio

there were actually 300 people in the audience.

I always thought that through the Shakespeare Festival that

whole idea was kind of injected into the community.

The Idaho Free Press, Saturday, July 23, 1977 — 6

'Midsummer Night's Dream' opens in outdoor setting

Victoria Holloway, co-director of "A Midsummer Night's Dream," discusses details with director-producer Doug Copsey during a rehearsal for the Shakespearean production. The comedy opens Wednesday, July 27, at 8:30 p.m. and runs through Saturday, and then again Wednesday to Saturday, Aug. 3-6. On Aug. 3, half of the performance's proceeds will be donated to the Idaho Mental Health Association. Reservations for the outdoor performances at the Main Street Bistro may be made by calling 345-4757 or 345-2261 in Boise.

(Press-Tribune Photos)

By Marie Galyean
Idaho Free Press
Lifestyle Editor

BOISE—Chicken wire, a child's wading pool, wooden platforms and live rustling trees.

These are such "stuff as dreams are made on,"—and a veritable fairyland is being created—right in downtown Boise.

Producer Doug Copsey and his co-director, Victoria Holloway, are readying one of Shakespeare's most delightful and lighthearted plays, "A Midsummer Night's Dream," which will open Wednesday, July 27, outdoors in front of the Main Street Bistro, at One Capital Center on the corner of Ninth and Main Street.

According to Copsey, the cast of 15 actors and actresses have been rehearsing in a pasture in South Boise, so they could "get used to working outdoors, projecting their voices, and coping with the usual outdoor noises," and now the finishing touches are being worked on for the Wednesday opening.

Billed as the First Annual Main Street Bistro Summer Theatre Festival, the comedy will be presented at the restaurant entrance, and the audience, who may bring blankets and pillows, will sit on the grass in the gently sloping bowl-like grounds around the stage area.

Refreshments will be available from the Bistro before and after the show, as well as during intermission, and Bistro Assistant Manager Reilly McDevitt reported that a special late-night supper would be served, probably about 10:30, when the play ends for any theatre-goers who like to dine late. McDevitt was very enthusiastic about the idea of the play.

"I think it's very exciting," he commented, "and should be a good stimulus to bring people into downtown Boise in the evening."

Victoria Holloway, who says she is enjoying her directing chores, is more familiar to area audiences as an actress and she has been seen in productions at Theatre in a Trunk, Boise State University Theatre and on TV Channel 4. This is her first full-scale-production directing job and she is also in charge of costumes and make-up.

"A Midsummer Night's Dream" is a lively combination of lovers, fairies, royalty, and some very earthy peasants, all of whom combine to transport the audience to a land and time that never was.

Show dates are July 27-30 and Aug. 3-6, with curtain time at 8:30 p.m.

Tickets are $3.50 for adults and $1 for children under 12. Reservations may be made by calling 345-4757 or the Main Street Bistro at 345-2261.

Titania, queen of the fairies, embraces her love, under the effects of a magic spell, during a rehearsal of Shakespeare's lighthearted comedy. In the roles are Seelye Smith and Joel Farmer (who is not looking himself, these days).

ater company in Boise was now a reality.

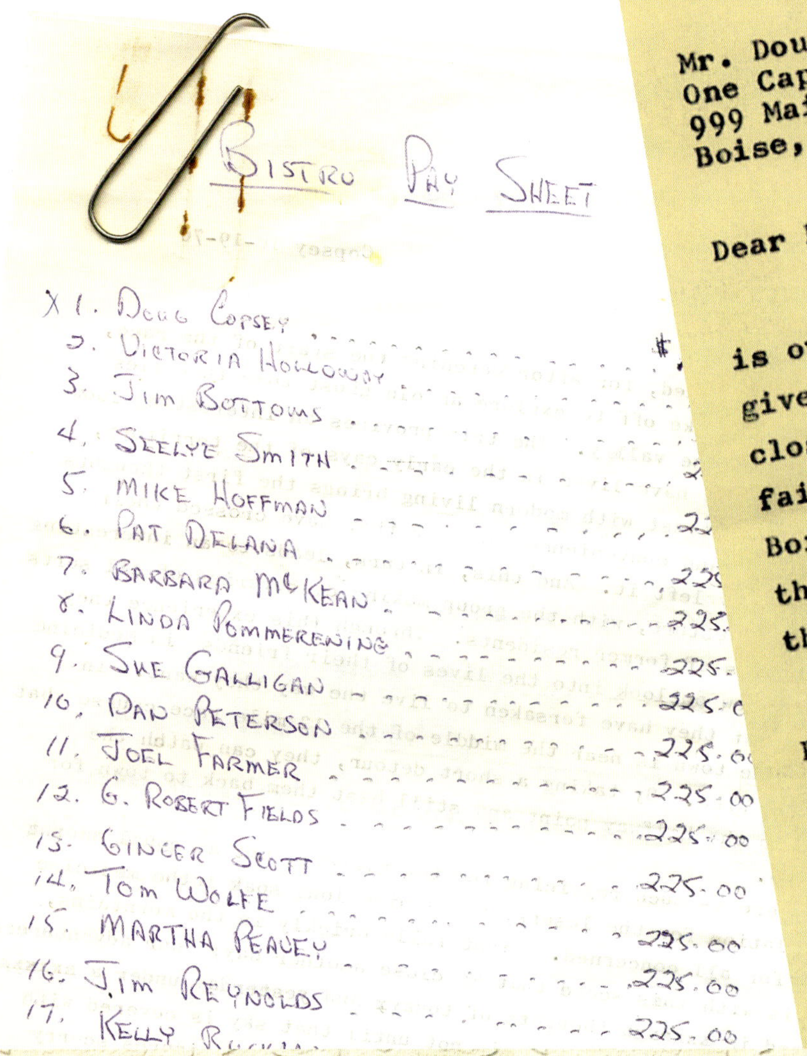

Bistro Pay Sheet

1. Doug Copsey . . . . #
2. Victoria Holloway
3. Jim Bottoms
4. Seelye Smith
5. Mike Hoffman 22
6. Pat Delana
7. Barbara McKean 225
8. Linda Pommerening . . . . 225.
9. Sue Galligan . . . . 225.
10. Dan Peterson 225.0
11. Joel Farmer 225.00
12. G. Robert Fields 225.00
13. Ginger Scott 225.00
14. Tom Wolfe 225.00
15. Martha Peacey 225.00
16. Jim Reynolds 225.00
17. Kelly R 225.00

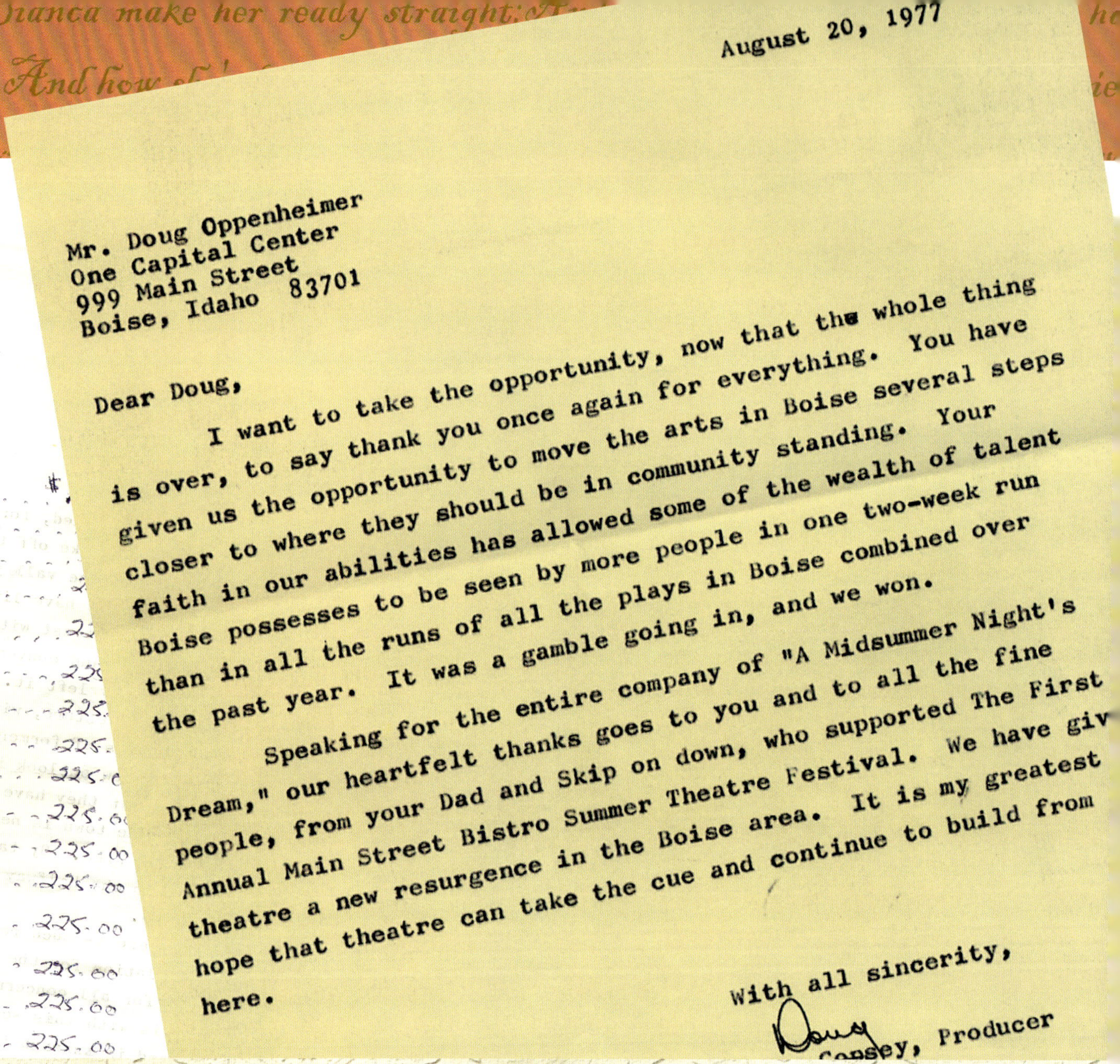

August 20, 1977

Mr. Doug Oppenheimer
One Capital Center
999 Main Street
Boise, Idaho 83701

Dear Doug,

I want to take the opportunity, now that the whole thing is over, to say thank you once again for everything. You have given us the opportunity to move the arts in Boise several steps closer to where they should be in community standing. Your faith in our abilities has allowed some of the wealth of talent Boise possesses to be seen by more people in one two-week run than in all the runs of all the plays in Boise combined over the past year. It was a gamble going in, and we won.

Speaking for the entire company of "A Midsummer Night's Dream," our heartfelt thanks goes to you and to all the fine people, from your Dad and Skip on down, who supported The First Annual Main Street Bistro Summer Theatre Festival. We have giv theatre a new resurgence in the Boise area. It is my greatest hope that theatre can take the cue and continue to build from here.

With all sincerity,

Doug Copsey, Producer

Barbara McKean: *Boise is one of those wonderful communities where the impossible become possible though the sheer force of energy and desire of the artists who have a vision for something. There seemed no time to question the outcome once we got started. We were like a train gathering steam with each day of rehearsal, with each panel of the fence in place, and once the play opened, we were off! I will never forget that blissful, innocent summer when the Idaho Shakespeare Festival was born. I suspect we all knew how lucky we were to be a part of the magic, but if we didn't know it then, I have no doubt we do now.*

Lord, what fools these mortals be! Midsummer Night's Dream, III, iii

Dennis Chase, cover art.

We were on a roll and didn't want to quit, so at the urging of Victoria and Seelye we decided to produce two small-cast shows that winter with the idea of raising money to help us get started with next summer's Shakespeare production.

The Play: ***The Two Gentlemen of Verona***
Director: Doug Copsey
Set Design: Jon Ostrove
Costume Design: Victoria Holloway
Lighting Design: Dan Andrews
Sound: Jim Reynolds

All the profits from our first summer had been distributed, so we were once again starting with an empty bank account, but there was a new confidence that made the decision somehow easier.

The first issue was an indoor performance space, an age-old problem for Boise arts groups. Boise State University had just built a brand new barn of an auditorium called the Special Events Center. It was booked through Christmas, but Victoria grabbed a two week slot for a show in January, then discovered the ballroom in the Student Union was available and booked it for a production of Robert Patrick's haunting work, *Kennedy's Children.*

Victoria directed, taking on one of the four monologue roles herself and casting Seelye, myself, Stitch Marker and Pat Patterson in the others. Bill Murphy, who managed the Royal Restaurant at the time, generously provided the bar supplies for Dan Peterson, who was the consummate silent bartender. Audiences were sparse at first, but excellent reviews brought larger numbers as the run continued. We didn't break any

L-R, Michael Hoffman, Speed, and Stitch Marker, Valentine, *Two Gentlemen of Verona*. DBB

1978

Dan Peterson, bartender, *Kennedy's Children.* DBB

records, but all the bills were paid and each member of the company once again got an equal share of what was left in the kitty.

We jumped into our second show right after the holidays. Victoria was proving to be an excellent director and enjoying it more than acting. She chose *That Championship Season*, and called on our favorite Ada County Highway Commissioner, Mike Silva, to play the Coach. Mike Hoffman, who played Lysander the previous summer signed on, with Dale Aspelund, Jon Ostrove and me rounding the group of aging high school basketballers reliving their dream season. After ten performances attendance had not topped 200, and we closed with our first red ink on the books. I managed to pay off all the bills on my own, but the actors were left wanting – a situation I did not want to repeat.

Seelye Smith, Carla; Doug Copsey, Mark, *Kennedy's Children.* DBB

In the spring, thoughts quickly turned to Shakespeare again, rousing us from the doldrums of our recent fallback. The Oppenheimers were happy to offer us free use of their amphitheater again, but financially we were on our own. The fence, or most of it, had survived the winter in my tumbledown garage on 12th Street, along with as much lumber as we could salvage from our previous productions. Likewise, costumes had been stored in my basement and were ready to be remade into a new look for a new show.

Auditions were held for *The Two Gentlemen of Verona* in May. Victoria wanted to get back on stage again, so I would direct. She took on the role of Julia along with her costume designing duties. Stitch Marker and Bruce Richardson, two of the original *Cuckoo's Nest* cast joined us for the first time playing Valentine and Proteus, respectively, with Mike Hoffman and Dan Peterson as their servants, Speed and Launce. Barbara McKean was back as Lucetta and Seelye Smith created a devastating Sylvia. She even wrote a song which she sang from her balcony each night.

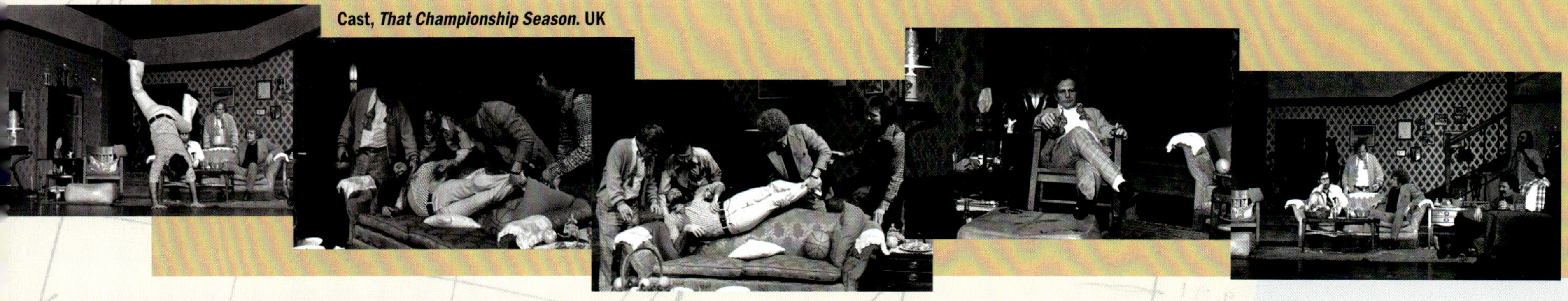

Cast, *That Championship Season.* UK

Seelye Smith: *I decided I would write a song about Julia and her attributes because my character, Sylvia, was so inflamed that Proteus was such a two-timer. I also just wanted to sing! It came very closely after Ed Simmerman sang his "Ode to Sylvia" in Act IV, sc.1 and went like this:*

If you look through the window and see what I see
You'd see the face of Julia, who's true love you should be.

Taking up Julia's cause in an earnest, heartfelt way, true to Shakespeare's character, Seelye's poetry was in the right vein – if not the right pentameter.

She's lovely, she's gentle, and so full of heed,
God bless this poor young maiden if she bears this man's bed and seed.
Oh Julia, fie Julia, you know not our lover man,
Or you'd not keep such foul company with this disloyal piece of spam.

The audience howled, and the company stumbled onto the kind of freedom Shakespeare allows, especially in his fondness for actors whose enthusiasm exceeds what may be found in the actual lines and punctuation of the text. Naturally, she kept going.

He's false, he's mean and oh so full of needs,
The only thing he's fit for is riding out of town on his smelly steed.
If you look through the window and see what I see,
In your heart you will know what should be will be, will be, will be...

Seelye's unexpected diversion from the script may have caught a few ardent Shakespeare students by surprise, but it proved to be one of the highlights of the show. In hindsight, it was perhaps a pivotal moment in the beginning of our reputation as a company that has never been afraid to take a few liberties with the Bard. While we always took our work seriously, we never shied away from wherever our good will led us.

We set up rehearsals in the horse pasture behind Dan and Jeannie Peterson's apartment once again. There was also plenty of room for Dave Bogie, Jim Campbell and crew to construct Jon Ostrove's set design on-site. However, the landlord didn't take too kindly to all the hammering and sawing going on in the quiet, south Boise neighborhood, and told us we had to leave. Fortunately, the kind folks at Boise Cascade offered us free use of an empty lumber yard on Third Street, just off Main. The large cement slab in the middle of an otherwise gravel lot was a hot and dusty place to work, but the price was right and both the size and the substance approximated our performance space at One Capital Center, minus the stairs.

Michael Hoffman: *At one point during rehearsals, Doug asked one of the actors, I don't remember who, to make a cross, and I don't know if they were arguing with him or what but they asked, "What's my motivation?" Bruce Richardson (Proteus) was up on a platform in the background with a saw working on the set and I can hear his voice saying, "$35 a week."*

Jim Campbell: *We actually built a bunch of stuff in the basement of the Patterson apartments over at 12th and Washington. We ripped all the siding there that Jon spackled and painted to look just like the concrete at One Capital Center. We were running all that chipboard through a table saw and the whole place was just covered with chipboard dust, which we found out later is full of formaldehyde. No dust masks. Oh man, that was ugly. Well, we had it all cut, and it took all day,*

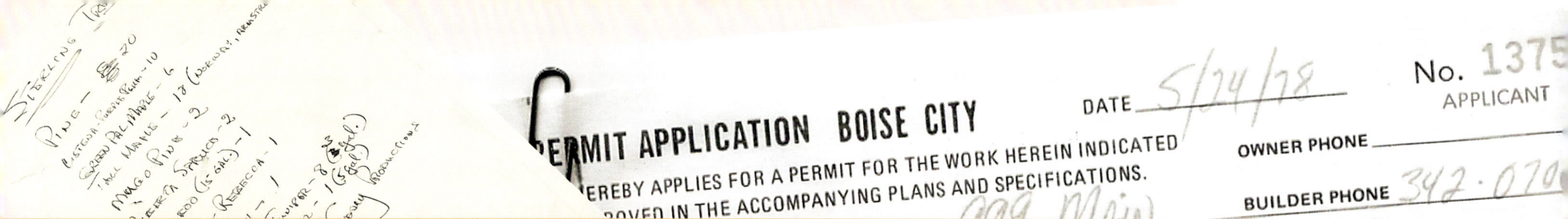

right? Jon comes back and says the dimensions are wrong, we need to recut every piece.

Once tempers subsided, Jon ended up re-cutting it all himself, and as each piece of the mock palace was finished, he applied his masterful painting skills to bring it to life. It looked so good a lot of people thought it was concrete. They would actually come up and touch it and be surprised it was wood.

Though the majority of the play takes place in two cities, there are several scenes in a forest as the characters travel between Verona and Milan. So once again the Sterling Landscape trees were hauled down the steps, pot by pot. Jon gave the outlaws inhabiting the forest their own secret entrance through a large rock with a hidden door. Here again his painting skills stood us in good stead, and each night the audience was surprised as the huge boulder opened up and several actors crawled out of hiding. This motley crew was led by two women, Debra Groves and Ginger Scott, who played Snug the Joiner in *Midsummer* the year before.

Set construction, *Two Gents.*

Ginger Scott: *Learning to fence in a field and getting to wear thigh-high green, suede boots and a full red wig while sword fighting fulfilled any fantasy I might ever have.*

The fence panels were brought out from the garage and once again encircled my back yard. Tom Oakes was not available that year, but his sister Marjory stepped up to offer her services once again to design and paint them. Although we could no longer sell ad space the city ordinance did allow us to promote our own event, so the fence became one giant ad for *The Second Annual Summer Theater Festival at One Capital Center*, complete with show dates, times and the box office phone number. It also proved, inadvertently, to be spectacular advertising for the new restaurant that now occupied the basement level of the building. The Main Street Bistro was no more. A seafood restaurant out of Seattle called Ray's Oasis had leased the space over the winter, and its managers were, to put it mildly, a bit stunned when we approached them with plans for our summer season.

Skip Oppenheimer: *I remember getting the word that we had a new restaurant coming in and thinking, "Oh god, oh god...*

Doug Oppenheimer: *Because when we first talked to Russ Wallers, the owner, there was some concern.*

Skip: *We really thought that he wouldn't want to continue for some reason.*

Doug: *Because he had this very successful restaurant in Seattle and he had a format he was very comfortable with. But he was very supportive of it.*

Skip: *The Ray's guys just blended right in.*

Doug: *Yeah, it was a very seamless transition.*

Once that little hurdle was cleared, the Ray's staff could not help getting caught up in the spirit of the event, and pitched in with all the support they could muster. However, we were left without the cash flow provided by the fence ads the year before. The only way to recoup that was to sell ads in an actual program, so once again I took to the streets, this time with help from Victoria Holloway and Pat Delana, seeking support from community businesses. Perhaps spurred in part by the first season's success, the community responded in spectacular fashion. Ad space was snapped up in record time.

Local graphic artist Dennis Chase created beautiful cover art that made us wish the season posters had not already been printed. A full-fledged program meant

David Bogie: Back then I just carried my camera everywhere anyway, so I just started shooting. I knew almost everybody so it was easy to point a camera at them. There was always something to shoot, the move, the construction, the rehearsals.

L-R, Stitch Marker; Valentine, Deb (Groves) Bogie, Outlaw Queen; Michael Hoffman, Speed, *Two Gents.* DBB

there was also room for a scene-by-scene synopsis of the play, and we even added pictures and brief biographies of the entire company courtesy of photographer Dave Bogie. Dave had approached me earlier in the spring with the idea of creating a photo documentary of the entire summer. We had all been disappointed at the lack of photos from our first season and the fact that I had no budget didn't seem to deter him, so I readily agreed. We had no idea what we were in for.

Just when we thought things were smoothly on track, crisis struck again. Ten days before opening, the Duke of Milan disappeared. Calls went out to friends and relatives alike but the actor was nowhere to be found, so John Elliott was hired to

L-R, Set Designer Jon Ostrove works on set construction with Jim Campbell, *Two Gents.* DBB

The fence goes up. DBB

Alas, how love can trifle with itself! Two Gents, IV, iv

take his place. It was a very short period of time to plug in a major character such as the Duke, but John's comic improvisation skills proved more than up to the task. Catching up to the pace the rest of the show had attained by that time, however, was a bit of a problem at first. I wanted the show to move quickly, to keep the comedic bits coming one right after another, and the Duke's role called for quick entrances and exits with lots of action in between. Learning the lines in short order was one thing, but learning the movements designed into the show was quite another.

L-R, Dan Peterson, Launce; Victoria Holloway, Julia; Stitch Marker, Valentine, *Two Gents.* DBB

John Elliott: *In late June, 1978, Doug Copsey walked into my living room with a tale of woe every director fears. I agreed to step into the role of the Duke with only eight short days left before the premiere, and in that time I went through costume fittings, rehearsed scenes and did my best to bond with the other company members, many of whom I had never met. It was fast, furious and fun. We opened, and there I was with a gorgeous costume made up of a 40 pound false torso piece under a heavy velvet and brocade tunic, and a velvet robe, and outside temperatures were over 100 degrees.*

During auditions, a pair of Capitol High theater students had expressed a desire to get involved in any way we wanted to use them. We could always use another body or two for the myriad of chores involved with putting together the show, but like any aspiring actor they wanted their moment on stage as well. Martha Peavey's success as the Rustics' wench in *Midsummer* the year before inspired

L-R, Bruce Abas, page; John Elliott, Duke; David Painter, page. *Two Gents.* DBB

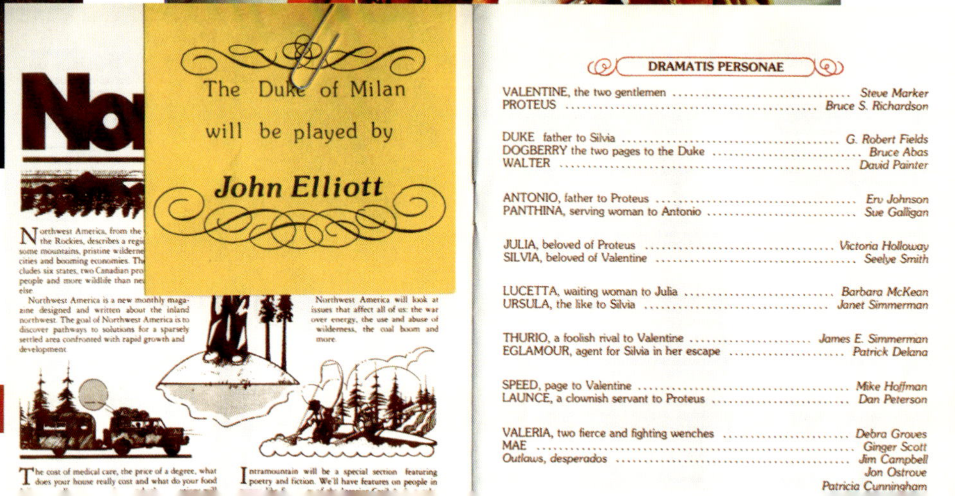

L-R, Bruce Abas, David Painter, pages, *Two Gents.*

Above, L-R, Stitch Marker, Valentine; Seelye Smith, Sylvia, *Two Gents.* DBB

the thought to once again cast outside the script, so David Painter and Bruce Abas became Pages to the Duke.

David Lee Painter: *It was a life changer. I remember One Capital Center – riding around in the elevators, hanging out in the bowels of the building watching all these real actors do what they do. Seventeen years old. I also ran the box office that summer, which was in the windowless pantry of Ray's Oasis. It was at least 8 x 8, with capers. I'd never seen a bottle of capers in my life. And I sat there and I would answer the phone – D.C. Productions. And I dreamt great dreams.*

We had been working on how to best utilize them in those created roles when the dilemma of the missing Duke arose. In rehearsal with John, I asked them to help make sure he got wherever he needed to be however they could. There was only one requirement – they had to do it in character. The boys took my instructions to heart and pushed, pulled, cajoled, tricked and otherwise manipulated John all over the stage, all very apologetically of course, as was appropriate for any Page in dealing with his Duke. The bits became so hilarious, and John's response to them so delightful that it was almost as though the Pages were in charge and a woefully beleaguered Duke was merely following their lead. By the time we opened, the Duke's scenes had become one of the hits of the show.

David Lee Painter: *John was instantly the Duke. He ordered Bruce and me around from the first moment. Being kids in that whole process was really great, because nobody was getting any money, everybody was doing it because they loved it. And the idea that a person could have an idea like that and make it happen, I think, set the tone for my whole life, really.*

Michael Hoffman: *In one scene I was on stage with Bruce Richardson, and John had a turkey leg to chew on and no matter what else was going no one could take their eyes off that turkey leg. I never, ever knew what he would do with it or where it was going to go. One night that whole scene became about him having a piece of turkey stuck in his teeth. It was like there was nothing else*

L-R, Victoria Holloway, Julia; Bruce Richardson, Proteus; Stitch Marker, Valentine; Seelye Smith, Sylvia, *Two Gents.* DBB

L-R, Michael Hoffman, Speed; Dan Peterson, Launce, *Two Gents.* DBB

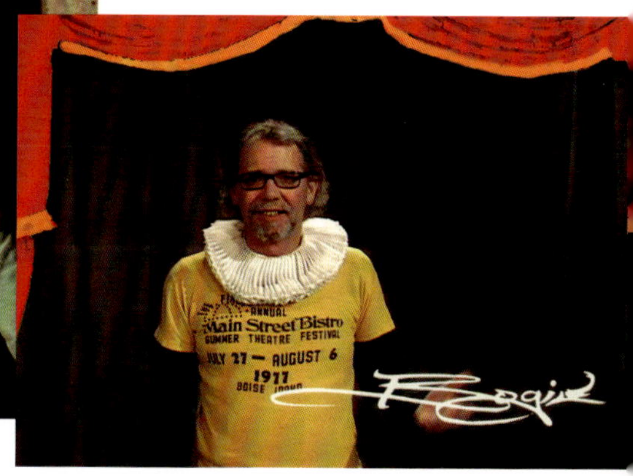

going on. If anyone else had a moment, it was gone.

David Lee Painter: *He would smack anyone with it, costume or not. I remember one night Victoria lit into him because he smacked somebody with that turkey leg and it left a grease stain on the shoulder. That was a hot moment.*

Ed Simmerman, Barbara McKean, Dan Peterson. DBB

The Pages weren't the only casting that was done outside the script. Jim Reynolds was back to create another of his unique sound score for the show and in the process, he created a role for himself. Jim fancied himself a wizard of sorts. He even had his own costume, complete with a pair of rubber pointed ears. Using his own, pre-recorded score, we opened the show with him sitting alone on the steps reading from a huge volume of Shakespeare. Timing his movements perfectly with the music he actually appeared to conjure up the show, populating the streets of Verona and bringing Proteus and Valentine together for the opening scene. As it began, he pulled his own disappearing act, returning again at the end of intermission each night to start things up again in equally magical fashion.

He fancied himself as a wizard of sorts.

Jim Reynolds, Sound Wizard. DBB

The offices we used for dressing rooms on the first floor of One Capital Center the summer before had been leased, and the only other available space was on the eighth floor, which made everyone a little nervous. One stuck elevator might turn a late entrance into no entrance at all. Strict orders were issued that once the show started no one was to go back up there unless was an extreme emergency. The basement level hallway between Ray's Oasis and Mountain Bell's audio visual room became a sort of Green Hall, as opposed to a Green Room.

Ray's had really gotten into the spirit of things, allowing us to use the restaurant's phone number for reservations in addition to our own box office, as well as providing free soft drinks and water for the cast and crew during the show each night. It was no small gesture. We extended our season to three weeks that summer, adding a fifth night each week for a total of 15 performances. The Ada County Highway District, no doubt bolstered by the covert joy of the Boise Police Department at the possibility of disrupting the cruisers once again, granted our permit to barricade Main and Ninth Streets during the shows as we had before.

We didn't have to wait long for the audience to return. Word had gotten out early that the Bard was back in downtown Boise and box office phones were ringing off the hook. Each night around six o'clock blankets and picnic baskets began appearing on the lawn and Ray's fired up the grills and began selling burgers and chicken. Soon, wine corks and beer cans would pop, ice would clink in glasses amid

the sound of people having a good time. And each evening, watching that lawn fill up with people anxiously awaiting the start of the show, I couldn't help but feel like the luckiest person on the planet.

Jim Owen: *What can I liken it to? It was kind of like a beehive, where it appears to be mass pandemonium but in reality all the bees are doing exactly what they should and performing their function. Then, all of a sudden, they fly away from the hive and they come out in perfect formation, and it's beautiful.*

Set design, Jon Ostrove, *Two Gents*. UK

But our three week run was not without moments of panic and terror as well. Dan Andrews' infamous hydraulic towers were once again providing the lighting for our stage, and while rain was not a problem that year, the wind paid us more than one blustery visit. On those occasions when the towers had to be dropped for safety reasons, the audiences, perhaps used to it by now, took it in stride, even coming to our aid when necessary, and never let it interrupt their enjoyment of the show.

Patrick Cunningham: *Who could ever forget being upstaged by the occasional disoriented customer from Ray's blundering his or her way out onto the stage during a performance? What must have gone through those poor people's minds at being thrust into some Elizabethan twilight zone?*

The fence, however, was another story. The four-by-eight-foot particleboard panels were stapled to three-inch-diameter poles, a sturdy enough arrangement for a calm summer's eve. But evening wind storms were a predictable event in the high desert, and were more than capable of wreaking havoc on four-by-eight-foot particleboard panels stapled to three-inch wooden poles. Gusts reaching forty or fifty miles-per-hour could easily rip them apart and send them flying into the street. The first time someone noticed a panel had come loose we simply put it back in place and stationed someone to hold it there until the winds subsided. One night, though, about midway through the run, we arrived to begin preparations for the show only to find whole sections of the fence in shambles.

Several panels had been blown into the street, some were broken in pieces. Only a supreme effort by the entire cast and crew got them all back in place in time for the show, and even then there were two or three gaps in the fence where panels were too demolished to be usable. The next day, new panels were purchased, repainted and put back in place, and thereafter, the slightest hint of wind caused a cadre of crew and other volunteers, often including audience members, to rush up and hold it in place. A few times, even that was not enough and an unattended panel or two was sent sailing.

But through it all, we were blessed with another hit. Audiences laughed and cheered almost every scene. Mike Hoffman's nearly non-stop performances as Speed brought consistent applause. Little did they know that in order to allow him to do all that running and tumbling all over our concrete stage each night Victoria and her costume crew had lined his costume with foam rug padding.

It may have helped him avoid some injuries, but it was also unbearably hot in the

I think one of the things I loved about when it started is that it was kind of a work in progress. People were kind of defining themselves and the roles. Not just the theatrica I remember the first season,

. . . backbone, because it created this wonderful kind of camaraderie that was just inspiring.

ninety-plus degree heat. Dan Peterson played Launce, and his hand-crafted wooden dog, Crab, complete with four wheels and floppy leather ears nearly stole the show each night, and Crab became the official company mascot that summer.

At the end of the run, attendance had topped 4,500. It was more than any of us had hoped for, and for the second year in a row, each company member received a share of the profits. Our success attracted attention from the media as well, and Channel 7 sent a brand new, young reporter named Dee Sarton to interview me the day after we closed. It's always easy to talk about success, but she managed to throw me for a loop when she asked what we were doing next year. Fresh off a mind-numbing summer of production and all that entailed, I think I was as surprised as she was when I realized I hadn't had time to give next week a thought, much less the next summer.

Dee Sarton: *When I first moved here and watched the Shakespeare Festival begin to develop I thought, wow, that really says a lot about your community, that it supports this great work.*

We had recruited more than 1,000 new festival supporters, among them the owners and managers of Ray's Oasis, who, with a healthy profit from food and drink sales, were already talking about next summer. On closing night they showed their appreciation for our hard work by closing down the restaurant and throwing a whale of a cast party for the cast and crew. But the real highlight was Dave Bogie's slide show.

David Bogie: *The idea to do the slide show was really kind of out of the blue. There were a lot of folks that didn't know what was going on. There were a couple of people who had seen my work from Theater In A Trunk and they were expecting some decent photography. But they weren't expecting the documentation from building the set and really early on. That was six or eight weeks ago and they had gotten all wrapped up in the show and had forgotten what had gone into it. That was a trip.*

What we expected out of his generous offer to document our second season gratis is anyone's guess. The energy and camaraderie reflected in those images, all set to a soundtrack, enhanced the summer's hard work, sweat and sacrifice beyond measure. When it was finished there was not a dry eye in the house, and I daresay the very thought of it would bring a moistness to any of our eyes today. Thankfully, it was not to be the last.

L-R, Michael Hoffman, Speed; Deb Groves, Outlaw Queen; Stitch Marker, Valentine; Jim Campbell, Jon Ostrove, Outlaws; Ginger Scott, Outlaw Queen; Patrick Cunningham, Outlaw, *Two Gents.* DBB

Victoria Holloway, Julia, *Two Gents.* DBB

different roles they played rehearsing, painting the fence, where do we change costumes – just figuring out how to put the shows on in that space I think it became a cultural . . .

ing rehearsals and stuff – the energy, the passion, the unbridled enthusiasm – that was great to witness for me. It was wonderful to be a part of it.

Dan Peterson: *Crab is the only "real" named animal that appears in all of Shakespeare. As we tried to figure out how to cast this part, many ideas flew around. "Use a real dog!" "Mime it!" "Puppet!" My idea was to build a little dog from an orange crate and put him on wheels with a pull string. As I began to build this dog I realized that he looked very like a horse. There wasn't time to rebuild, so I cooked up this little story that Launce, as a little boy, had somehow received a little hobbyhorse on wheels which he named Crab. As he grew up, he noticed that Crab stayed the same size, and one day he discovered that Crab the steed, had transformed into Crab the dog, which he has remained to this day. As audience members walked by and saw Crab and me waiting to enter each night, they would always speak to Crab, never to me. Crab was the best scene partner I ever had. He's gone where the good dogs go, and I think about him all the time.*

DBB

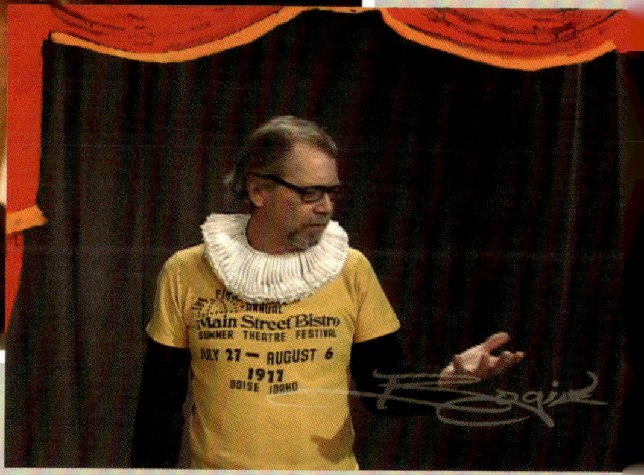

Lucentio's father is arrived in Padua, And how she's like to be Lucentio's wife. Happily we met; the happi

n. And now by law, as well as reverend age, I may entitle thee my loving father: The sister to my

Dennis Chase, cover art.

The Festival began to take on the feel of an annual event. Certainly the comments we received from our audiences and supporters, as well as the press, seemed to expect that another summer meant another season of Shakespeare at One Capital Center.

The Play: ***Romeo and Juliet***
Director: **Victoria Holloway**
Set Design: **Seelye Smith**
Costume Design: **Victoria Holloway**
Lighting Design: **Dan Andrews**
Sound: **Jim Reynolds**

The Play: ***The Merry Wives of Windsor***
Director: **Pam Abas**
Set Design: **David Bogie**
Costume Design: **Bitsy Bidwell**
Lighting Design: **Dan Andrews**
Sound: **Jim Reynolds**

Who were we to argue? We were doing what we loved and making it pay, although it didn't pay much and it was, at best, seasonal employment – at least for the actors and designers. As for me, managing this growing new business was becoming a year-round job.

Selling ad space for the fence that first summer, my pitch to potential buyers was that we were not just another fly-by-night arts organization seeking a handout, we were a business, just like theirs, and we planned to be around for a long time to come. I remember thinking at the time that I needed to keep reminding myself of that as well, and as our third season bore down upon us that mantra rang a

Joel Farmer, Master Page; Nancy Suiter, Mistress Page; Tom Willmorth, Slender; Jon Ostrove, Justice Shallow; Pat Cunningham, Dr. Caius; David Painter, Rugby, *Merry Wives of Windsor.* DBB

1979

Why, sir, for my part I say the gentleman had drunk himself out of his five senses. The Merry Wives of Wind

good deal louder than it ever had before. As the clock rolled over into 1979, discussions on the upcoming summer centered around two areas – how to expand our season without over-extending our budget capabilities, and developing a fundraising program to help make the first a reality.

We all agreed the Festival needed to grow in some tangible way. From a production standpoint, the natural progression was to offer two shows instead of one. Ray's and the Oppenheimers agreed to adding a fourth week to our run in their amphitheater, which would give us two weeks for each show. But while we could create two casts out of pretty much the same group of actors, we would also have to build two sets, construct twice as many costumes, collect twice the props – in short, increase our expenses considerably. The business of creating art had definitely taken on a focus of its own, and I was beginning to wear my producer hat a lot more than my acting and directing hat.

But I was learning that there is an art to business as well. Erv Johnson, who played Antonio in *Two Gents* the previous summer, ran his own marketing company. I approached him about helping us organize a fundraising effort and he jumped in with both feet, organizing an advertising campaign that would promote the summer season in print, on radio, and television. Joyce Delana, who had helped out as a ticket taker the first two seasons in order to watch her son, Pat, in the acting company, created our first Patron Program, outlining various levels of giving for potential sponsors of the Festival. She and her Patron Steering Committee, which consisted of Louann Blome of Nampa, Alice Radcliffe Green, Carmelyn Johnson, Carolyn Johnson, Dianne Robertson and Peggy Stoddard, all of Boise, gathered about 30 volunteers with the goal of raising $15,000 for the summer productions.

> **Joyce Delana:** *That first year (1977) I asked if there was anything Icould do and they said come on down and take tickets. And I'll never get over wondering that first night, will people pay to come down and sit on this lawn and watch Shakespeare? Edith Simmerman and I were handing out programs and they came, and they sat, and they loved. And they came back. It was the most exciting thing I've ever seen. And then we thought, well, why don't we get a group of volunteers together and do some more.*

The centerpiece of the fundraising campaign was to be "An Evening with Shakespeare," April 27-28 in the Hoff Building's Crystal Ballroom. There would be no admission charge. Invited guests would be treated to drinks, hors d'oeurvres, and a show, after which they would be expected to write a check to support the Shakespeare Festival.

The room had no stage, it was just, well, a ballroom, complete with chandeliers

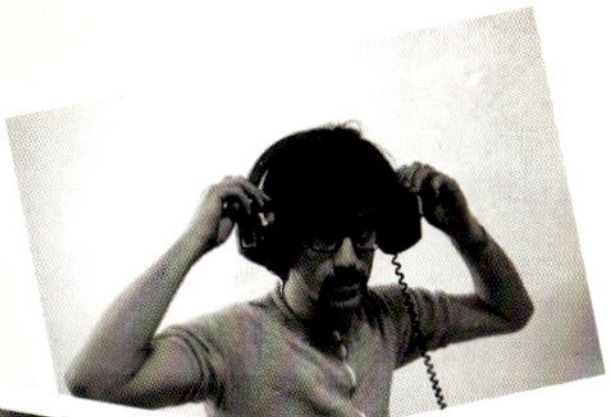

Top to bottom: Jim Reynolds; Barbara McKean and Dan Peterson; Michael Hoffman, *An Evening With Shakespeare.* UK

Pam Abas, Director, *Merry Wives.* DBB

Rebekah Oakes, Juliet; Stefan Wisniewski, Romeo. DBB

L-R, Stitch Marker, Simple; Tom Willmorth, Slender, *Merry Wives.* DBB

Tom Willmorth: *Pam needed a young dweeb who couldn't grow a beard to play Slender. I fit that pretty well, and she knew I had the British dialect, so that was my first Shakespeare contract.*

and a low ceiling, so our show had to be presented in a very minimalist fashion. Thinking it would be interesting and fun if a troupe of actors sort of magically appeared at the party, put on a show, and then magically disappeared, we put together a series of scenes from Shakespeare's most memorable plays that ran just over an hour and cast it with actors who were already becoming familiar to Boise theater-goers.

The set was a series of small, bare platforms flanked by black curtains. On the top platform, approximately four feet off the ground, sat an old, battered trunk, from which the actors emerged, one by one, like circus clowns from a tiny car. As the show progressed, any costume pieces and props were also gotten from the magical trunk, and when the show was over, everything disappeared back into the trunk. This naturally required having someone under the stage passing costume pieces and props up through the trunk. That job fell to Ed and Janet Simmerman, both of whom had joined the company as cast members in the previous summer's *Two Gents*. Ed played Thurio and surprised everyone with his marvelous singing voice, performing "Who is Sylvia," while Janet took on another of our "created" roles as the maid, Ursula.

Both evenings were well attended, and our efforts were rewarded not only by applause, but with a stack of checks that totaled around $5,000. It was short of the Patron Committee's goal, but by any measure, our first fundraising event was a success.

We also used the occasion to announce that the third season of Boise's Summer Shakespeare Festival would present *Romeo and Juliet*, opening July 10, followed by *The Merry Wives of Windsor*. Victoria was back in the director's chair for *R & J*, and Pam Abas, who had directed numerous productions in the Boise area would bring her extensive experience and rapier British wit to *Merry Wives*.

Above, Doug Copsey and Seelye Smith compare fat suits.

Below, L-R, Kassie Reckamp, Anne Page; Bitsy Bidwell, costume designer, *Merry Wives.* UK

Elledge, Anne Page, *Merry Wives.* DBB

Trace Hollenbeck, Mercutio, *R&J* DBB

L-R, Patrick Delana, Balthasar; Tom Pfenninger, Gregory, *R&J.* DBB

By this time, word of our success had spread to friends outside Boise, and many of them wanted to audition for the company. It had been a year of "firsts" so far, with a professional marketing campaign, an active Patron Committee and a successful fundraising event, and now we were bringing in our first "guest artists." We also continued to utilize young local talent from area high schools. Tom Willmorth had been an active participant in Caldwell's Snake Basin Drama Guild, which was run by Anna Marie Boles and Pam Abas.

Rebekah Oakes, recent graduate of San Francisco's American Conservatory Theater and sister of fence artists Tom and Marjory, returned to Boise to play Juliet opposite Stefan Wisniewski's Romeo. The two met while pursuing acting careers in New York City and fell in love. What better background for their summer in Boise playing Shakespeare's most famous couple? Trace Hollenbeck grew up in Nampa and attended BSU with several of the original company members before setting his sights on San Francisco. We lured him back with the role of Mercutio. Victoria met Ellen Maraneck when she was performing in Sun Valley with the Yale Repertory Company of New Haven and was so impressed she hired her on the spot.

Pam agreed to cast Ellen as Mistress Ford in *Merry Wives* sight unseen, but Victoria couldn't stand not to use her talent as well, so she cast outside the script once again, creating the role of Percy, serving woman to the Capulets, which turned out to be a hilarious tour de force. All three arrived with the understanding that the financial arrangements would be the same as with everyone else – work your butt off all summer long at whatever tasks needed doing for an unspecified share of any

L-R, Ellen Maraneck, Mistress Ford; Dan Peterson, Master Ford; Doug Copsey, Falstaff; Nancy Suiter, Mistress Page, *Merry Wives.* DBB

Pam Abas: *All I can remember about Merry Wives is that heavenly opening when the cast poured onto the stage to the Handel music I can hear in my head now, Bogie's heart-stopping cherry tree that turned instantly into Herne's Oak, Pat Nance and his live rabbit, Danny Peterson's brilliant Mr. Ford, an Ed Simmerman saying, "There's cheese and pippens to come." As for limited rehearsal space, costume difficulties, budget restrictions, I remember nothing. I always fell in love with my productions after they opened and forgot all the rest.*

profits that may or may not accrue. They rolled up their sleeves and dove in with the rest of us, hauling trees, building sets and costumes, and hefting the now notorious post-pounders to put up the fence, which bore artist Steve Merrill's design that year. Dennis Chase convinced me that by designing both the poster and the program cover he could bring more consistency to our marketing efforts, and produced his usual stunning work, as he would for the next several years with the Festival.

Rehearsals began May 14 on the most ideal site we had yet found. There was an old, empty house with a huge yard just off the freeway at Curtis Road. The owners were not planning to develop the property until after the summer and we were given free run of the place. The biggest drawback was that there was no water, but on the up side the only bill we had to pay was for electricity. The generosity and support of the community was once again proving to be the backbone of our success. With plenty of giant shade trees surrounding the lot, working there was like having our own little slice of theater heaven right here in Boise.

Victoria and crew immediately set up the costume shop in the house. She was designing for *R & J* but her directing duties for that show left no time for anything else. Tapping into the rich pool of local talent once again, Bitsy Bidwell became the first costume designer other than Victoria to design a show, taking on *Merry Wives*.

Janet Simmerman: *I remember sewing my own costume, and because Bitsy insisted on doing everything authentic we wore those corsets with metal staves, and because of the heat we all got sweaty and they just rusted right on your body. I had rust marks for weeks.*

The set designers laid out their plans in the yard, which was easily able to accommodate both sets back-to-back so we could hold simultaneous rehearsals for the two shows. Seelye Smith, who was playing Juliet's Nurse, came up with a massively elegant design for *R & J* which Jim Campbell, a high school math teacher turned commercial builder, agreed to construct as he had the year before, as always with help from the cast and crew.

Dave Bogie, our company photo-archivist presented a design for *Merry Wives* that was the proverbial offer we couldn't refuse. Consisting entirely of three giant flats painted on both sides so they could be rotated to depict a scene change, it was not only elegantly simple and easy to build, but wonderfully inexpensive. Jon Ostrove's masterful painting skills brought the scenic backdrops to life, and Bogie being Bogie, it had its own unique touch as well.

David Bogie: *We had $250 to build the set. I think Seelye had $300 because she needed a platform, so she got another $50 for the lumber. But we had to build on the cheap. It had to look good, it had to withstand the weather, and we had to move it across town. Pam said she wanted something British and soft, like water colors, so I spent a day at the library looking up famous English water-colorists from around the 1820's and found some wonderful images. Jon Ostrove rendered the ones we chose on double-sided flats so they could be flipped for scene changes. But at the end of the play, when everything changes to the forest at Herne's Oak, we wanted to do something magical. I finally came up with the idea that, well, it's an oak, so it should have a big knothole in the trunk, and the drop could be pulled through the hole. Then we added a*

o life is a shuttle. I am in haste; go along with me: I'll tell you all, Master Brook. Since I plucked geese, played truant and top, I knew not what 'twas to be beaten till lately. Follow me: I'll tell you strange things of this knave Ford, on whom to-night venged, and I will deliver his wife into your hand. Follow. Strange things in hand, Master Brook! Follow.

DBB

flickering light that would give it a kind of strobe effect, and once the drop was yanked through a little door was closed and the light became two little eyes inside the hole looking out.

The first test of the effect was a huge success, and the "yank crew," as they were affectionately known, quickly became proficient at making the action smooth and fast. So much so, in fact, that they began experimenting with giving the drop a twist as it was pulled through the hole, causing the trailing end to spin one direction or the other, and pulling it up or down to cause a sweeping effect in the opposite direction. It was a wonderful surprise near the end of the show each night, and audiences loved it.

Pam Abas: *All I can remember about Merry Wives is that heavenly opening when the cast poured onto the stage to the Handel music I can hear in my head now, Bogie's heart-stopping cherry tree that turned instantly into Herne's Oak, Pat Nance and his live rabbit, Danny Peterson's brilliant Mr. Ford, an Ed Simmerman saying, "There's cheese and pippens to come." As for limited rehearsal space, costume difficulties, budget restrictions, I remember nothing. I always fell in love with my productions after they opened and forgot all the rest.*

Another exciting first for this season was the addition of sword fights in *R&J*. I ordered several rapiers and epees from a theatrical supplier in San Francisco and Dr. Max Callao, a BSU professor and amateur tournament fencer, signed on as our fencing coach and fight choreographer. Most of the actors had never held a rapier, much less tried to fight with one. Rehearsals were long and strenuous but the young men of the Montague and Capulet families took to their new weapons quickly, and by opening night, the fights were fast, furious and some of the most spectacular we have ever had.

David Lee Painter: *I came home from college that summer and got to play Peter to Seelye's Nurse in R&J, and I got to have a moment that was really transformational for me. In the fight between Tibalt and Romeo one night, Romeo's sword got knocked clear out into the audience, and I gave him my sword and I felt like John Wayne at the Alamo. But I always wondered where that sword went.*

The week before opening we began our annual invasion of the outdoor amphitheater at One Capital Center. It was always an exciting time, not just because the shows were about to open, but because the whole community seemed to come alive as they watched the sets take shape, the trees hauled in and final rehearsals underway. There always seemed to be a small crowd of onlookers peeking over or around the fence trying to catch a glimpse of what the new season's show would be like. And we always had a booth set up at the entrance ready to accommodate any spur-of-the-moment ticket buyers. This year we even had our volunteers in costume.

L-R, Rebekah Oakes, Juliet; Stefan Wisniewski, Romeo. DBB

Romeo and Juliet was as big a hit as we'd ever had. It played to packed houses Tuesday through Saturday for two weeks, and reviews were glowing. The cast was excellent and the costumes were the most colorful and elegant we'd ever had. The only incident that took away from one of the greatest romances ever written happened when a very inebriated gentleman somehow got past our security volunteers one night and wandered onstage looking for the entrance to Ray's, right in the middle of the famous balcony scene. The scene continued as he was quickly steered inside to the bar. It was one of those moments that was tense at the time, but remembered only with laughter. As always, the audience took it completely in stride. A few even asked if it was a part of the show.

The highlight of the show for me was making two of my entrances as Escalus, Prince of Verona, with a live, Red-Tailed Hawk on my fist, courtesy of Morley Nelson, Boise's famous raptor expert. It was our first use of live animals and I was almost always completely upstaged by the hawk, but talk about coming on stage with authority. In the opening scene, the Prince enters on a platform above during a massive sword fight in the town square. Each night the hawk, frightened by all the clamor, would flap his wings and try to fly off my arm. It was never planned, but it certainly got everyone's attention in a hurry.

L-R, Jon Ostrove, Sampson; Doug Copsey, Prince Escalus; Tundra, red-tailed hawk. R&J. DBB

Patrick Cunningham: *I'll never forget the night Pat Nance, as Lord Capulet, was carrying Juliet down the steps and his costume tripped him up. Down they came – a fall of ten or twelve feet! There was a collective gasp, followed by hushed silence in the audience. Some quick thinking backstage brought an entrance that signaled an end to the scene, and the injured actors were rushed off stage. Both Pat and Rebekah were badly bruised, especially Pat, who had landed, cradling Juliet in his arms, on his forearms on the concrete patio, but they both finished the performance, as well as the rest of the run.*

When *R&J* closed on the second Saturday night there was no cast party, no celebration. The entire cast and crew quickly changed into work clothes and began dismantling the set. On Sunday we cleared out the last remnants of Padua and shift-

Left, L-R Jeannie (Rice) Peterson and Dan Peterson, take a break at load in. Above, L-R, Connie (Cremeens) Merrill and Jeannie (Rice) Peterson, run the box office. Right, the infamous post-pounders. DBB

ed over to the confines of Windsor, then had a tech run-through to set light cues and look for any problems we hadn't anticipated. Thankfully there were none worth mentioning. Monday was spent rehearsing individual scenes, with a full dress rehearsal that night, and we opened *The Merry Wives of Windsor* on Tuesday for an identical two week run.

> **Tom Willmorth:** *That was my first real introduction to professional theater, because Stitch was playing my servant, Simple and he was also playing Paris in R&J. So all during our rehearsals he was as dashing as could be, a perfectly well-groomed, moustachioed Paris, and then that play closes and we only have a couple of days to get the other show up. I show up at rehearsal the next day and Stitch has shaved off his moustache, cut his hair into a bowl, and removed his two false front teeth. He completely transformed himself into this hideously hilarious caricature. It was a real lesson for me.*

Dan Peterson played Master Ford in that production, and part of his disguise as Master Brook included a hook in place of his left hand. At the end of Act III, when Falstaff brags about his newest rendezvous with Mistress Ford, Brook (Ford in disguise) stands frozen in amazement, his hands out in front of him, believing he is a cuckold. Dan and I worked out a bit where, as I exited as Falstaff I would fling my hat back over my shoulder in a gesture of superiority, thinking that if it landed on the hook it would be a great laugh. Because I never looked back I never saw where it landed, but out of the eight performances it hit Dan or the hook three or four times, actually landing on his head once. It wasn't until one of the final nights that the audience reaction left no doubt our no-look pass had finally worked.

Our luck held, and so did the audiences, and we closed our third season with over 8,500 attendees, more than double the previous season. And once again we had all learned valuable lessons, not the least of which was that our humble Shakespeare Festival had really come into its own as a professional quality theater company with the support of an entire community. There was no longer any question about whether we would be back the next year, or for many years to come. It was simply expected.

Stitch Marker, Simple, *Merry Wives*. DBB

L-R, Ed Simmerman, Montague; Jenny Sternling, Lady Montague; Steve Wisniewski, Romeo; Rebekah Oakes, Juliet; Doug Copsey, Prince Escalus; Deb Groves, Lady Capulet; Patrick Nance, Capulet, *R&J*. DBB

But this time, as the actors, designers, crew and volunteers dispersed at the end of summer as they always did, one of the pillars of our company and our first Artistic Director, went with them. Victoria Holloway was off to try her luck at a theater career in New York with some of our new-found friends. She had been instrumental in the founding of our company, and someone we all relied on heavily for everything from advice and support to her considerable talents as an actor, director and designer. She planned to return the following summer, and in the meantime would continue to expand our family of actors on the east coast through auditions there, but for the first time since the company began I felt its weight settle squarely onto my shoulders alone.

Above, L-R, Stitch Marker, Paris; Stefan Wisniewski, Romeo, *R&J*. SE

Left, L-R, Ellen Maraneck, Mistress Ford; Doug Copsey, Falstaff, *Merry Wives*. DBB

Below, L-R, David Bogie, set designer; Jon Ostrove, scenic artist; Kathy Ostrove, scenic painter, *Merry Wives*. DBB

There was no longer any q

L-R, Patrick Nance, Capulet; Deb Groves, Lady Capulet; Rebekah Oakes, Juliet; Seelye Smith, Nurse, R&J. SE

...ether we would be back the next year, or for many years to come. It was simply expected.

It was a new decade, and we were feeling good about the Festival's accomplishments in its short, three-year existence.

Dennis Chase, cover art.

L-R, Curt Baker, Lucentio; Patrick Nance, Gremio; Seelye Smith, Kate, *Taming of the Shrew* DBB

One Capital Center had no complaints about our use of the site, Ray's loved the business we brought them each summer, and the Boise community had embraced us with open arms. But if we expected to keep growing, we had to get organized on a larger scale.

The Patron Committee had also provided crucial support for our efforts, and played a key role in our financial success that summer. However, it was now clear that we must begin to look seriously at becoming a non-profit organization so that future donors could be enticed with more than just professional quality theater. It was a basic reality – donations to arts organizations were expected to be tax deductible. There was much to be discussed, and many plans to be made, and I had learned that it was never too soon to start. I was also about to learn first hand the truth of the old adage, timing is everything.

Alan Minskoff lived just across the alley from my 12th Street apartment at the time. He was the editor of *Idaho Heritage Magazine*, a non-profit entity, so I enticed him over one afternoon with a cold beer to discuss the ins and outs of the not-for-profit world. He pondered our dilemma for about thirty seconds before proposing a solution.

Victoria Holloway, Portia; Curt Baker, Bassanio, *Merchant of Venice*. DBB

1980

The Play: ***The Taming of the Shrew***	**The Play:** ***The Merchant of Venice***	**The Play:** ***The Comedy of Errors***
Director: Larry West	**Director:** Larry West	**Director:** Barry Press
Set Design : Jerry Osborne	**Set Design :** Jerry Osborne	**Set Design :** Jerry Osborne
Costume Design: Victoria Holloway	**Costume Design:** Martha Shafer	**Costume Design:** Martha Shafer
Lighting Design: Lane Thomas	**Lighting Design:** Lane Thomas	**Lighting Design:** Lane Thomas
Sound: Jim Reynolds	**Sound:** Jim Reynolds	**Sound:** Jim Reynolds

Seelye Smith, Kate and Doug Copsey, Petruchio, *The Taming of the Shrew*. DBB

There's small choice in rotten apples. The Taming of the Shrew, I, i

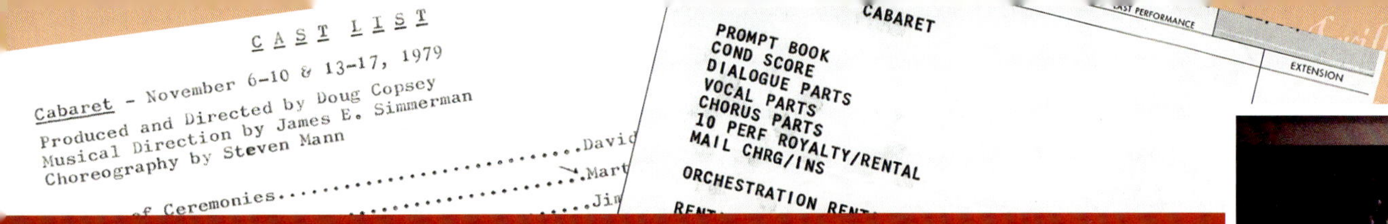

CAST LIST

Cabaret - November 6-10 & 13-17, 1979
Produced and Directed by Doug Copsey
Musical Direction by James E. Simmerman
Choreography by Steven Mann

CABARET

PROMPT BOOK
COND SCORE
DIALOGUE PARTS
VOCAL PARTS
CHORUS PARTS
10 PERF ROYALTY/RENTAL
MAIL CHRG/INS

ORCHESTRATION RENT

Alan Minskoff: *We had just finished this huge grant to study small towns in Idaho. We had people looking into agricultural issues, social issues, all kinds of stuff, and the work was so intense that all I was doing was managing all these people, doing the magazine had sort of become second or third position. We started saying, "Why can't we just do a magazine?" So we started Northwest America as a for-profit company and now we're sitting on Idaho Heritage, which we no longer need. So when Doug began talking to me about the Shakespeare Festival's growing pains I thought, "Well, maybe we can meet a couple of needs here."*

Coincidentally, Jim Owen, our famous one-night-stand-in during our first season, happened to be working with Idaho Heritage at the time, so we brought him into the mix and at the next meeting of their board, everyone unanimously approved a motion to appoint me as President, Victoria Holloway and Louann Blome as Vice-Presidents, and Ed Simmerman as Secretary. Then the original members were voluntarily voted off the board, with the exception of Jim, who remained so that the move would not be construed as a wholesale giveaway of the company. In a comparative blink of an eye, we became, officially, Idaho Heritage, Inc., dba The Idaho Shakespeare Festival.

Alan Minskoff: *It was a very simple transfer. Our original charter was to do anything published, produced, presented – we did a variety of programs prior to Shakespeare so it all just made sense. The fit was perfect. I always felt like we were there for a millisecond at the creation of the Festival.*

Things began to move quickly after that. Steve Brown, of Ellis, Brown & Shiels, was an old high school friend, and readily agreed to serve as legal counsel in the preparation of by-laws and articles of incorporation. Jim Owen took the position of General Manager and Sue Galligan signed on to handle office duties and research grant possibilities. We immediately applied to the Whittenberger Foundation and the Union Pacific Foundation for funding to cover directors' salaries for the upcoming season, and plans were made for a fall production of *Cabaret*.

With Victoria gone, the duties of Artistic Director fell to me in addition to my producing duties, and I had

Martha Peavey, Sally Bowles, *Cabaret*; Jim Owen, Clifford Bradshaw, *Cabaret*. DBB

Willkommen, bienvenue, welcome

David Six, Emcee, *Cabaret*. UK

at she rail; why then I'll tell her plain She sings as sweetly as a nightingale: Say that she frown, I'll say she looks as clear As morning roses
commend her volubility, And say she uttereth piercing eloquence: If she do bid me pack, I'll give her thanks, As though she bid me stay by
and when be married. But here she comes; and now, Petruchio, speak.

Victoria Holloway, *Comedy of Errors.* DBB

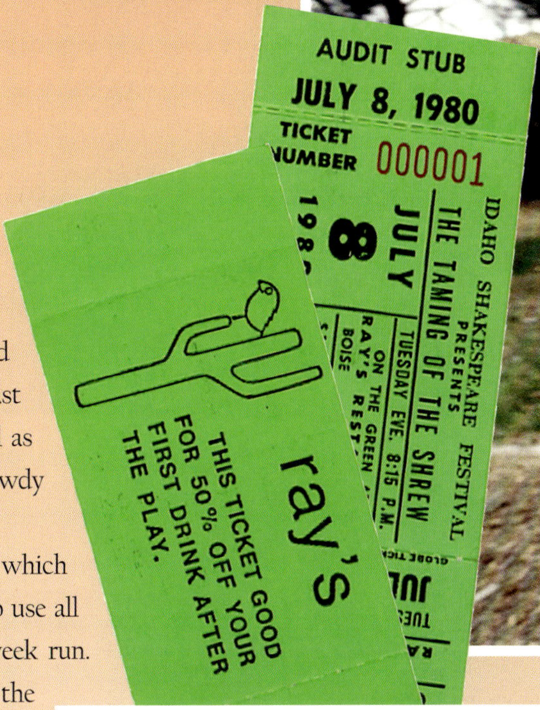

always wanted to direct a musical. We found an excellent choreographer named Steven Mann working with the Dance Spectrum company in Boise and Ed Simmerman agreed to be our Musical Director. The cast was full of familiar faces from past summers, as well as several new ones, mostly among the wonderfully bawdy girls of the infamous Kit Kat Club.

We struck a deal with Old World Catering, which occupied a building at Federal Way and Overland, to use all three of their adjoining banquet rooms for a two-week run. Attendance was sketchy the first few nights, but when the review hit the Idaho Statesman on Friday, word spread fast that this was a show not to be missed. We packed the house for the rest of the run and even extended into the following week to accommodate everyone who wanted to buy tickets.

Flush with another success we immediately jumped into planning the fourth summer season, our first as a not-for-profit organization. Auditions for the next summer's acting company were scheduled the following spring in New York and San Francisco as well as Boise.

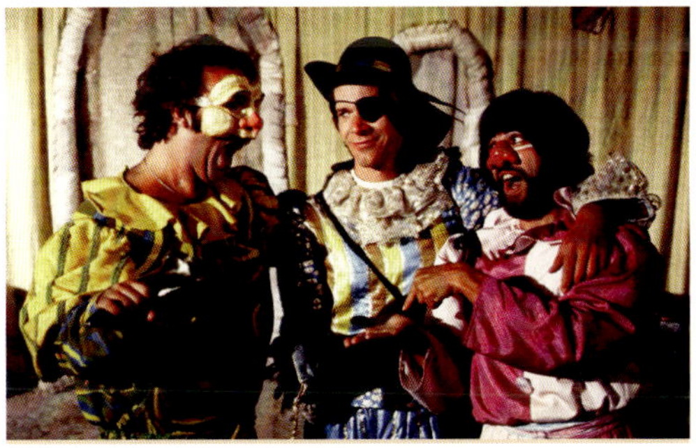

L-R, Patrick Nance, Town Crier; Curt Baker, Antipholous; Tony Cesare, Dromio, *Comedy of Errors.* DBB

With attendance growing by leaps and bounds each year, the new board agreed we should expand the season to three shows, and run in repertory. Larry West, who had directed that fateful production of *One Flew Over The Cuckoo's Nest* back in 1975, was excited about a return engagement in Boise, and signed on to direct *The Taming of the Shrew* and *The Merchant of Venice.* Victoria had met director Barry Press in New York, and when she learned he was moving to Seattle that summer, coerced him into a stopover in Boise to take on our third show, *The Comedy of Errors.*

Returning from New York, Victoria took on the task of Technical Director, overseeing set and costume design and construction as well as lighting and props, in addition to designing costumes for both *Shrew* and *Merchant.* She hired Martha Shafer, who had been working with Carroll's clothing store as their advertising and display director for several years, to design for *Comedy of Errors.* Carlos Salana, working with Bill McCombs, helped our budget crunch in a big way by coming up with a clever set design that could be used for all three shows. Their gigantic puzzle, built by Jim Campbell and crew, could be pulled apart and re-assembled with a minimum of effort to magically create the three different environs of Padua, Venice or Syracuse. And an old friend of Seelye's from New York, Jimmy Crowley, had heard about the new theatrical adventure out in Idaho and came to see what all the fuss was about. His organizational

It was just sort of serendipitous that this nucleus of peop

Louann Blome, Stage Manager. Below: Load-in, One Capital Center. DBB

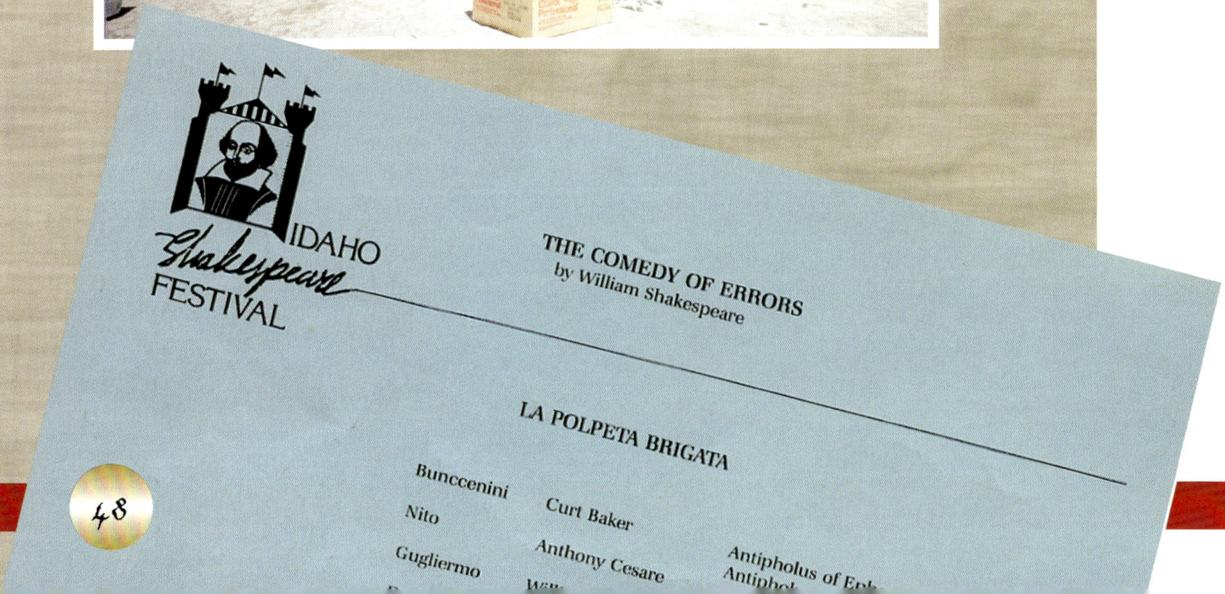

IDAHO Shakespeare FESTIVAL

THE COMEDY OF ERRORS
by William Shakespeare

LA POLPETA BRIGATA

Bunccenini Curt Baker
Nito Anthony Cesare
Gugliermo

skills, honed at the New York Theatre Studio, among others, made him the perfect choice for our new Company Manager.

Producing three shows not only required an increase in expenses for sets, costumes and the like, but a much larger company of actors as well. Studying the models of other successful theater companies around the country, two things became evident. First, we needed an apprentice program for young, aspiring local actors. They signed on for the summer without pay, just to gain experience in a craft they were interested in pursuing. In addition to helping out with literally whatever needed to be done, some were cast in smaller roles in the shows. Barbara McKean volunteered to head up the program and keep the apprentices busy, and Martha Peavey offered to instruct them in the various theater

Top, L-R, Jim Owen, Doug Oppenheimer, Festival opening night, *Taming of the Shrew.* Bottom, L-R, post pounders, Trace Hollenbeck, Stitch Marker, David Painter. SE

Opposite page, clockwise, Tony Cesare, Shylock; Trace Hollenbeck, Gratiano; Kevin Connell, Salerio; Tony Cesare, Shylock, *Merchant*; Larry West, Director, *Shrew* & *Merchant*. DBB

re all in this area at the same time to get some wild-ass theater going.

techniques she had learned in her first year of study at the American Conservatory Theater in San Francisco.

Second, we needed to restructure our contracts with company personnel. Even with our new non-profit fundraising capabilities in addition to ticket and ad sales we knew that our budget would be tighter than ever, and with the size of the company growing each year, the idea of simply splitting any profits equally among everyone as we had in the past would be unfair. We had become more specialized, meaning there was much less crossover between actors, designers and tech crews. So new contracts were drawn up, following the policies of other professional theater companies around the country, and people were hired at set rates for specific positions.

That is not to say, however, that time honored traditions such as moving from the rehearsal site to One Capital Center, putting up the fence, and hauling the groves of trees and shrubs still faithfully provided by Sterling Landscape off the trucks and down the steps to create our signature faux forest on the patio, then taking it all down at the end of the season, were forgotten. Those were the days when every last member of every summer company came to know what the making of theater was truly all about. And every summer, when the patio was literally scrubbed clean and restored to its original, pristine condition, we all sat on the lawn and marveled at what had been.

The shows themselves were the best we had produced to date. New York actors Tony Cesare and Curt Baker brought fresh faces and new talent to the company, but it was the directors who took our concept of outdoor Shakespeare to new levels of excellence for Boise audiences. Larry West tempered the intense drama of Tony Cesare's Shylock with a gentle, often humerous Portia, played by Victoria.

Nancy Lee Painter: *Martha Peavey and I were serving maids to Portia. Victoria named me Blythe. Our job was to help Bassanio choose the right casket, and as we sang this little song we would madly point to the right one.*

In *Shrew*, he gave my Petruchio fresh new insight into Seelye's Kate, and added an hilarious anachronism to the mix by giving the entire cast footwear – or in Kate's case, having her go barefoot – that was completely out of period and inconsistent with the costume design. Tom Willmorth's Biondello on out-of-control roller skates was a particular crowd favorite.

Larry West: *I knew I wanted to work with anachronisms, but I didn't know it would be shoes until I got there. I remember lining up a whole bunch of different shoes on the floor and asking each character to pick the ones they thought worked for their character. It ended up that the old men all wore dress shoes with garters, and the servants wore different kinds of sneakers. I can't remember who, but someone said right off, "Oh, I guess we're doing Taming of the Shoe."*

Barry Press's *Comedy of Errors* appeared to be presented not by the Idaho Shakespeare Festival company, but by a rag-tag group of itinerant actors called La Polpeta Brigata, loosely translated as The Meatball Brigade, who marched haphazardly down the steps of the amphitheater led by a pair of bleating trumpets and carrying a large wooden trunk from which many costumes and props for the show, among other things, were extracted at will.

He took the show yet another bizarre step away from reality with a fantastic set of *commedia dell'arte* masks, designed and created by Craig Brown of Seattle, which, judging by the howls of laughter from the audience each night, added a new level of hilarity to the show.

Nancy Lee Painter: *As a dresser for Comedy, I can remember those costumes being able to stand by themselves because they were just so full of sweat, and just the smell of different people's bodies from leaving the costume behind and walking out, and it would just stand there.*

David Lee-Painter: *During a pick-up rehearsal for Comedy later in the run, Victoria (Adriana) fell off someone's shoulders, splitting her forehead and requiring the assistance of a plastic surgeon. For two nights we all wore band-aids on our foreheads (and on our masks) commemorating her heroics.*

When it was over, attendance had topped 11,300 for the summer, a new record. It may have been expected because we were doing three shows, but considering we did them in the same four weeks as we had done two shows the summer before, increasing attendance by nearly 2,000 people is a real testament to what phenomenon the Festival had become in the Treasure Valley. All the bills were paid, contracts were met, and for the fourth year in a row we were in the black...but barely.

The summer ended with a huge cast party thrown by the owners of Ray's, the highlight of which was Dave Bogie's slide show, by now an annual ritual at cast parties chronicling each summer season.

David Bogie: *I had somebody come up to me after a show all excited about the thing. They'd really had a good time watching it and they told me about on particular image that really blew them away. But it wasn't there. I knew it wasn't there because I'd shot them all. I programmed the show. But there was no greater compliment. They were so into the show that they saw something that wasn't there.*

Stitch Marker: *I came to Boise to go to college, and at that point in time it was pretty much Boise Little Theater or college theater or nothing. So I think it was just sort of serendipitous that this nucleus of people were all in this area at the same time to get some wild-ass theater going. I mean, those first productions at One Capital Center were just maverick theater. They were just grab what you could and go. It was all about resourcefulness, there wasn't any money in it. But there was this goal.*

The Comedy of Errors. DBB

Load in complete. DBB

Above, Trace Hollenbeck, Angelo, Comedy. Below, Seelye Smith, Kate; Doug Copsey, Petruchio, Shrew. DBB

The Plantation Years

1981-1983

The Plantation site, Jim Owen and friend. DBB

Doug Copsey, Prospero, *Tempest*. DBB

Storm scene, *The Tempest*. DBB

Brian King, Ariel, *Tempest*. DBB

Dennis Chase, cover design.

It was early in March, 1981, when I got the phone call. Ray's Seafood Restaurant would no longer be occupying the basement of One Capital Center. A new restaurant called Angell's had leased the space, and they had plans to expand onto the patio with outdoor dining and live music, leaving no room for the Shakespeare Festival.

I remember distinctly the numbing sensation emanating from the pit of my stomach. Directors and designers had already signed contracts and were hard at work on our fifth season of Shakespeare. Acting company auditions

The Play: ***The Tempest***
Director: **Mark Cuddy**
Set Design: **Jerry Osborne**
Costume Design: **Michelle Thompson Black**
Lighting Design: **M. Lane Thomas**
Sound: **Homer Wise**

The Play: ***Much Ado About Nothing***
Director: **Eloise Bruce**
Set Design : **Jerry Osborne**
Costume Design: **Carrie Mather**
Lighting Design: **M. Lane Thomas**
Sound: **Jim Reynolds**

The Play: ***As You Like It***
Director: **Barry Press**
Set Design : **Jerry Osborne**
Costume Design: **Desiree McQueen**
Lighting Design: **M. Lane Thomas**
Sound: **Homer Wise**

1981

e is in Elysium. Perchance he is not drown'd: what think you, sailors? It is perchance that you yourself we
y poor brother! and so perchance may he be. Captain True, madam: and, to comfort you with chance, Assu
fter our ship did split, When you and those poor number saved with you Hung on our driving boat, I saw y

had been held in Seattle, New York and Boise and the walls of my office – my living room – were lined with head shots and resumes. We had just hired our first full-time Technical Director in the person of Jerry Osborne, the Patron Committee, now chaired by Dianne Robertson, was in full fund raising mode, and *Merry Wives* director, Pam Abas, in her new capacity as Public Relations Director, had developed a complete publicity campaign.

But all this seemed inconsequential at that moment. Oddly, I don't remember ever thinking that the Festival might be over, or even that there might not be a fifth season. The only question that leaped to mind was where can we go to put it on? After a few hasty phone calls, the board assembled on March 10th to discuss our options.

Organizationally the company was on a solid foundation. Plans for future growth had dominated winter board meetings. A local children's performing arts group, Idaho Public Theater, had approached us about taking over the management of their company. It seemed a natural extension of our community outreach and would give us a much broader base of support, not to mention avenues to additional grant funds under educational categories for which we did not previously qualify.

Coincidentally, the Alexander Building, just across the street from One Capital Center, was vacant at the time. Having used it for dressing rooms during the previous summer season I was convinced the historic, two story building would make a perfect headquarters for the Festival, with a 200-300 seat indoor theater utilizing the basement and first floors while offices and classrooms for a planned drama school occupied the upper floor. It could, we fantasized, make the intersection of Ninth and Main Streets a magnificent artistic gateway to downtown Boise, bringing new life to a downtown that had been in need of serious resuscitation for several years.

Now, however, all that had to take a back seat to the search for a new summer theater site. Needless to say, the board was not happy with the news. There was some panic, and talk of canceling the season before we got in over our heads financially, but we had come too far to turn back now. After much discussion, it was agreed that if we had not secured a new facility by April 1st, a one-season cancellation would be announced. Jim Owen and I were determined not to let that happen.

I knew that failure to produce a season in the upcoming summer would make it even harder to produce one the following year, and might become the death knell for the Festival. Jim and I began a frantic search for a suitable outdoor space, exploring parks, vacant lots, industrial areas, anywhere there was a large open space that could hold a stage, dressing rooms and a few hundred people, with room for parking. Our biggest problem was that we had no budget for building a new theater, and virtually all of the sites we looked at came with at least a small price tag attached.

Then we stumbled upon the old Penitentiary at the end of Warm Springs Avenue. In the undulating foothills just above the main compound, a broad gully opened onto a mostly flat area about 150 feet across. Initial conversations with the Idaho State Historical Society, which managed the site, were positive. Long range plans called for construction of a botanical garden complex in the area immediately adjacent, which seemed the perfect complement to an outdoor theater. We brought Eric Olson, our landscape guru, out to inspect the site and his assessment of the work required to transform the hillside with sod and grade the flat into an area suitable as a stage was equally positive. There were ready-made dressing rooms in the Penitentiary buildings and plenty of room to grow into the space over the coming years, once we were settled in with a season under our belts.

At its March 17th meeting the board approved a motion to present a formal proposal to the Historical Society, with the provision that they must reply before our April 1st deadline for cancellation. Meanwhile, all the work of preparing for a three-show summer season continued as though there was no doubt it would happen. Plans for a Patron Committee fund raising event on March 31st were well in hand, and Lane Thomas, our new Apprentice Director, had put together a wonderful program for high school students who wanted to intern for the summer.

At one end of it there was a pond adjacent to a lovely grove
drain. If we could accomplish that we could use the site f

Where, like Arion on the dolphin's back I saw him hold acquaintance with the waves So long as I could s

so, there's gold: Mine own escape unfoldeth to my hope, Whereto thy speech serves for authority, The like

Everything was looking rosy until our electrical and water needs entered the picture. Because the Penitentiary was a State-owned facility, we could not simply tap in to their existing lines, we would have to run our own, all the way from Warm Springs Avenue, several hundred yards down the road. It was highly cost-prohibitive, but Jim and I believed that with a concerted fund-raising effort, it could be done. The rest of the board was not so sure, but they gave us an extension until the April 17th meeting to come up with a plan.

At the same time, minor season preparation hiccups fueled the embers of failure smoldering in some minds. The turnout for apprentice auditions was disappointing, to say the least, but there were several good prospects, and Larry West, who was slated to direct *The Tempest* sent word that personal reasons would keep him from returning.

On April 14th I got another phone call, this time from Jim Owen, and our fortunes began to turn. The Plantation Golf Club was in the midst of constructing a housing development on some of their property. At one end of it there was a pond adjacent to a lovely grove of cottonwoods they needed to drain. If we could accomplish that we could use the site for our theater at no charge.

Clearing a space. UK

Jim Owen: *That's where a fortunate marriage of convenience came to pass. Three of the partners in the Plantation at the time were Alan Minskoff, Calvin Jensen and Ray Allen, all of whom I'd worked with at both Idaho Heritage Magazine and White Savage Associates. They had two things they needed to accomplish. One was to dredge that little lake, which was becoming a sewage problem, and secondly, they needed to bring attention to their development. In other words, they needed bodies out there. The interesting thing is that Calvin had actually approached me about moving the Festival there a year-and-a-half earlier. Naturally we declined because why would we ever want to leave downtown?*

ME

tonwoods they needed to theater at no charge.

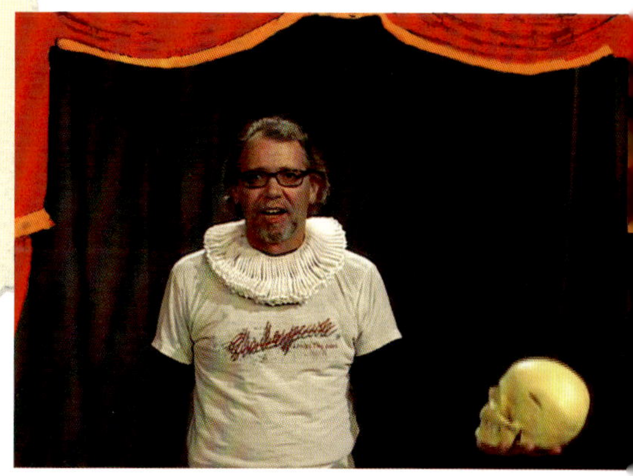

Alan Minskoff waxes eloquent, opening night, *Tempest.* UK

Barry Press, Director, *As You Like It.* UK

Top to bottom, Ursula Meyer, Rosalind; Beverly Hainault, Phebe, *As You Like It.* DBB

The next six weeks went fast and furiously. Soon after Larry West bowed out as director of *The Tempest*, Victoria accepted a terrific job offer in Florida and followed suit. Barry Press, who had been asked to follow up his *Comedy of Errors* the previous season with a production of *As You Like It*, had turned us down at first, then said he would like to do it but wasn't sure he could make his schedule work. The bottom line was, by early May, not one director contract was signed, and rehearsals were scheduled to start a month later.

Then I remembered that when we held auditions at the Denver Center earlier that spring, Mark Cuddy, one of their associate directors, expressed an interest in working with us. I called and asked him if he would like to direct *The Tempest*, and he quickly accepted.

Mark Cuddy: *There was someone at the Denver Center looking out for me who said, "there's a guy coming down from the Shakespeare Festival in Idaho to hold auditions. You should talk to him. You're a young director and he might be looking for young directors."*

Shortly thereafter, Barry Press did an about face and agreed to direct *As You Like it*. I then called on an old friend, Eloise Bruce, who was working with the Asolo Theater in Sarasota, Florida at the time. She was not keen on *Measure for Measure* or *All's Well*, but really wanted to take a stab at *Much Ado About Nothing*. It's a wonderful comedy, and we needed a director, so it was agreed. Besides, I had ulterior motives in bringing Eloise to Boise.

Plans for the Alexander Building and Idaho Public Theater had been shelved during our move from One Capital Center, but there was still a need for a professional children's theater in the Treasure Valley that could tour to schools and offer performances as well as workshops and classes to young people interested in the performing arts. Eloise was just the person to put it together. Even before the directing position came open I had tried to lure her to Boise with a seamstress position, just so she could see our operation and, hopefully, take a liking to the area. The chance to direct along with the possibility of starting her own company was too good to pass up, and we had our third director. Now the task was to convince everyone that they would have a theater by opening night.

That concept took a big step backwards when the three directors arrived to begin rehearsals three weeks before opening. Suffice it to say that when we proudly displayed their new work space – a duck pond in close proximity to the second tee of the Plantation golf course just behind a new shopping center – it was the only time I have seen any director, much less three at once, speechless.

Jim and I assured them that by July 6th there would be a gently sloping burm covered with sod, full of picnic blankets and happy patrons out to enjoy an evening of Shakespeare under the stars. To say they were skeptical would be a huge understatement, but with little hope of finding other summer employment at this late date, they dove into rehearsals – no pun intended – with all the energy of someone who actually had a stage to stand on. Since I was in rehearsal as well much of the time, Jim was left to manage the construction.

Being situated directly behind the Plantation Shopping Center, facing Glenwood Street, power was easily obtained, but running water was a luxury we would have to do without. We could not, however, do without bathrooms. The stores in the nearby strip mall were a long walk, and were all closed in the evening anyway, so that left us with only one option, porta-potties. Little did we know those little, green, plastic toilets would become an annual fixture at ISF over the next twenty years. Audiences and company members alike complained about them, but they all put up with them, and, thankfully, kept coming back.

We purchased a thirty-foot tent with wide, yellow and brown stripes to serve as dressing rooms, and Nancy Harms, our hair and make-up artist, went to work scrounging for costume racks, dressing tables, desks, chairs and mirrors to fill it. But with only one week to go before opening night, the theater was still not ready for audiences. The pond was drained and the berm had been shaped by our friends at Sterling Landscape, but it had yet to be covered with sod, and the stage itself remained the rough weed and rock surface it was when we first arrived. The good news was that sets, costumes and rehearsals were all on schedule, but even that was not accomplished without some extra effort.

David Painter, Jacques, *As You Like It.* DBB

Star Moxley: *I saw the first production in 1977 and thought this is something fun that I need to be involved with. I helped in the costume area with Two Gents the second year and just kept on helping out every year after that. I had been working on sculpture pieces and everything was tubes then for me, tube sculpture, tube stuff. So when we talked about headdresses for the fairies in Tempest I said, "Well, why don't we try something three-dimensional?" We did a prototype and Mark Cuddy liked it, so then we just went further and created that look, that world, for all the fairies, goddesses and sprites.*

Finally, just three days before opening, Jim Campbell and his crew laid the sod over the berm and its brand new sprinkler system. Everyone was told to stay off the grass

L-R, Nancy Lee (Painter), Celia; Ursula Meyer, Rosalind, *As You Like It.* ME

to allow it to take root, giving us nightmarish visions of the audience slowly sliding down the hill on sod strips that had not yet settled in.

> **Jim Crowley:** *I remember them laying the sod. It was literally down to the last minute, and we never thought the sod was going to take because only three nights later it was going to be full of people. That was my first season there and Jimmy Owen was a maverick. I attribute that whole move out to the Plantation and building that mound to him, which to me was sort of taking the Festival to its next stage. It was letting people know that it wasn't going away because we couldn't perform at Ray's. We were putting this festival on and it was a viable institution in town. Get used to it.*

> **Jim Owen:** *Sixty or so people worked on that production. The road that led us there had its ups and downs and bends, but when the sod began to go down on that hill, those sixty or so people began to talk to me in confident, conversational tones again.*

The last day before opening, the stage was graded flat and topped with a clay and sand road mix purchased from the Ada County Highway District. Wetted down thoroughly, it dried into a relatively hard, smooth surface that would work for all three plays. We could only pray that it would dry by the time we opened less than 24 hours later.

Fortunately, Mark Cuddy's *Tempest*, which takes place on a desert island, was the first show up.

> **Jim Owen:** *I remember Cuddy during the first Plantation season and he had this look on his face like, this isn't going to happen, this is just not going to happen, all through the rehearsal period. Then, all of a sudden, it was there, and I think he was genuinely impressed that we pulled it off.*

Of course the biggest question was whether or not the audience would show up. Ticket sales had not exactly been brisk, but we were hoping the wonderfully voluminous amount of press our move had received would work in our favor and bring people out to experience our new home. Ominous clouds began to fill the sky on that opening night, July 6th, 1981, darkening our hopes even further, but by showtime, much to our delight, the berm was full to overflowing. Excitement backstage was near fever pitch. The weather, which had continued to worsen, only caused the tension to increase.

Apprentices Johanna Winfield and Christina Gellert, were the sound and lighting crew for *Tempest*, and were firmly ensconced in a makeshift booth precariously attached to a large cotton-

> **Jim Owen:** *I was never more scared in my life than sitting there at the Plantation site and seeing a hill that wasn't done a week before we opened. I mean it's a week before we open and I'm sitting there just off the second tee box of the golf course going, "Oh my god, what are we going to do?"*

Statesman photos by Glenn Oakley

A cloudy sky enhances the set as *Tempest* audience watches opening shipwreck scene

By SUSAN SKOG
The Idaho Statesman

An enchanted island where invisible spirits ride with the wind and make mischief with their magic is the setting for *The Tempest*, the season opener for the 1981 Idaho Shakespeare Festival. The production, unveiled Monday, is a rare synthesis of fine acting, costuming, makeup and music.

The cast does a superb job in fabricating a dream-like

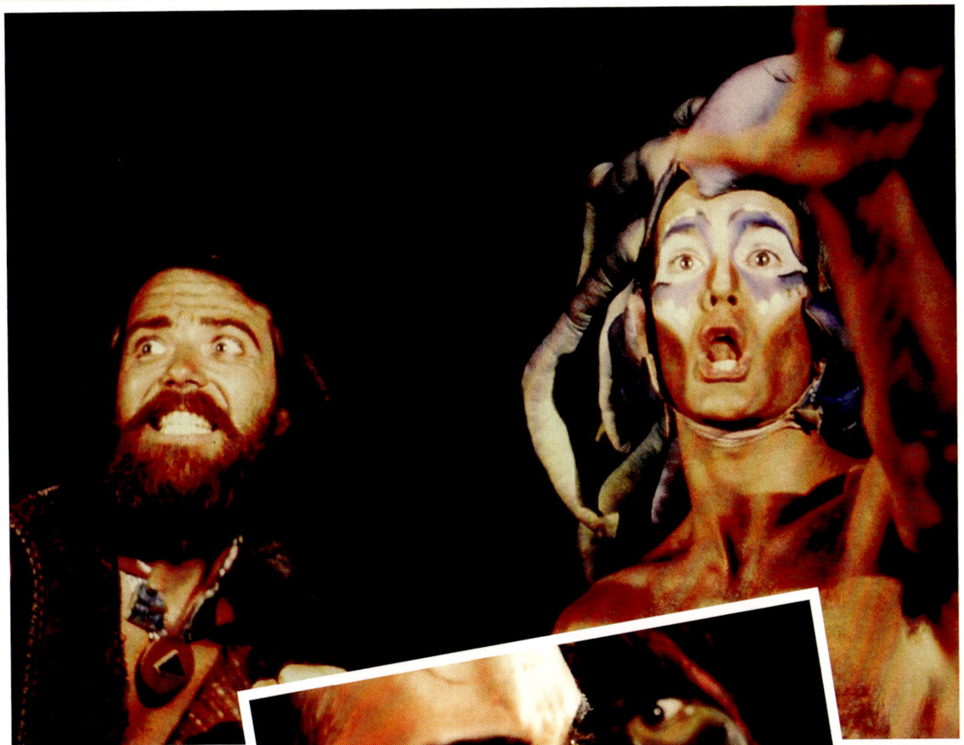

L-R, Doug Copsey, Prospero; Brian King, Ariel, *Tempest.* DBB

Dance of the Goddesses, *Tempest.* DBB

L-R, Matthew DeCaro, Stephano; John Cagan, Caliban, *Tempest.* DBB

Farewell to the Island, *Tempest.* DBB

wood tree to the right of the audience. Sound wizard Jim Reynolds had worked with the director and cast to create an exciting series of electronic sound cues to underscore the magical effects Prospero and Ariel produced throughout the show. Many hours of work had gone into timing those cues to the actors' movements so they happened at just the right moment.

But on opening night, Mother Nature took over, drowning out most of our created sound cues with some of her own. Speaking from the perspective of an actor playing Prospero I can tell you there is nothing quite like thrusting a wooden staff skyward to create a storm that will cause a shipwreck at sea and having the heavens respond with real thunder and lightning, or calling to the heavens for wind to conjure fairies and not being able to hear the taped wind noise over the sound of the real thing ruffling your hair.

David Lee Painter: *Opening night of Tempest I'll never forget in my whole life. That storm coming in and Doug on top of the platform and the wind coming down. I was up on the ship above the audience and he's down there conjuring this storm and the wind was really blowing. I thought we might stop the show, but I knew the Copsey weather factor would come into play. He ordered the wind to stop and it did.*

Brian King: *My unlikely casting as Ariel challenged my talents and produced solid notices, despite the fact that I sprained both my ankles during the second performance of the run leaping from rock to rock. The chemistry we shared on stage, the thunderous applause at curtain and the glorious headdress, costume and makeup designed by Star are very fond memories. If I had never worked again after opening night I could have retired happy as a performer.*

Perhaps because of all the people and the excitement of opening night, not to mention the weather, the ducks, no doubt unsure of their role in all this activity, stayed away completely. It was a luxury we were not to enjoy for long. Slowly over the next few nights, our displaced feathered friends apparently began to believe their pond was still there, somewhere, and as time went by their search for it became bolder and bolder until they were brazenly wandering among the pre-show picnickers and checking out the sets on stage. Attempts to shoo them away brought only temporary relief, in part because some of the patrons were feeding them.

Star Moxley: *One of my favorite things in The Tempest was watching Stephano (Matt DeCaro) from backstage. He wore that massive fat suit that was so hot, and when he gestured the sweat would come flinging out from his wrist across the audience. Then one night his pants were falling down in the back, and we had stitched butt cheeks into the fat suit, and he had no idea this was going on. People were riotous at that point, and he's just thinking, "Well I must be particularly good tonight," you know. Then he finally realizes his pants are down to his knees and he went with it. Then it was really big.*

Johanna Winfield, Sound Operator. DBB

Because all three shows took place in outdoor settings – *Tempest* on a desert island, *As You Like It* in a forest, and *Much Ado* in a garden – occasional entrances by our feathered friends could almost be justified, but as the ducks became bolder they also became more of a distraction. Apprentices were appointed to Duck Patrol and assigned to various points around the theater to keep them at bay, and pre-show announcements to each audience included a plea not to offer our feathered friends morsels from picnic baskets in the vain hope that they would lose interest and find

David Lee Painter: *We had ducks all summer. Every color duck you could imagine. I remember Jenny Brotherton out there catching ducks, running behind the set and putting them in this wire enclosure to keep them from going on stage. I noticed before the show there were some patrons out there throwing bread to them right on the stage.*

L-R, Rod Wolfe, Brian King, Doug Copsey and Matt DeCaro rehearse an entrance, *Much Ado*. ME

The soldiers' triumphant return, *Much Ado*. ME

another place to hang out. But alas, the ducks were not to be dissuaded.

Try though we might, the sneaky little devils managed to evade us more times than I care to remember. In the comedies, at least, it usually made for a humorous situation, including the night David Lee-Painter came on for Jacques famous soliloquoy in *As You Like It*. As a gaggle of ducks approached him no doubt looking for a handout, he shooed them off with his cane, ad-libbing, "Away, or the Duke will have you for dinner!"

The shows went on, with or without our additional cast members, and audiences were delighted with the innovations our new site allowed. Eloise Bruce's *Much Ado* was set just after World War I, and the Duke and his soldiers arrived home in an authentic Model A Ford that drove right across the stage, thankfully hardened by this time, to deposit the returning heroes. Because the back of our amphitheater was no longer a sidewalk on 9th street in downtown Boise, Mark Cuddy was able to stage the shipwreck scene that opens *The Tempest* at the top of the berm, and when the actors were forced to abandon the collapsing, storm-tossed vessel, they leaped into the unseen "boiling sea" that was in reality the soft dirt on the back slope of the berm.

Because he was able to build them on-site, Jerry Osborne's sets were massive. He used eight inch square beams for the structure of the *Much Ado* house, complete with functional second story balcony, and the platforms that supported the *Tempest* "rocks." It took about twenty people to lift and carry the set pieces

John Cagan, Don John, *Much Ado About Nothing*. DBB

Beverly Hainault, Beatrice, *Much Ado*. DBB

L-R, Brian King, Duke Frederick; Matt DeCaro, Benedick; Doug Copsey, Don Pedro, *Much Ado*. ME

L-R, Ursula Meyer, Hero; Sue Galligan, Ursula, *Much Ado*. ME

into place, looking much like some sort of multi-legged insect inching them into place and lowering them down at a specific cadence. It's a miracle no one was injured. Jerry told me afterwards that he was so concerned about making them look realistic, he hadn't thought about how much they weighed.

Nancy Lee Painter: *I had these huge peacock feathers in my headdress as Juneau in Tempest, and Beverly Hainault and Melanie Yellen carried me in on a bier. We had set the verse for the Goddesses in the text to some music we made up and we were quite proud of our little dance, but we got panned in the review. So we revamped that scene for everyone at the cast party and everyone got a good laugh.*

Attendance for our six week, 30 show season was just under 10,000, down a bit from the previous season downtown, but proof enough for us that we had weathered the frantic, last minute move to a new home. But the massive undertaking of building a new theater from scratch had taken a toll on our already strained budget and by season's end we found ourselves some $20,000 in debt. Company contracts were all paid, but we had acquired a long list of creditors. It was the first red ink in five years of summer Shakespeare, but there was still plenty of cause for celebration. Jim Owen summed it all up best in his letter for the program.

Welcome

"I'll tickle your catastrophe"
Falstaff, *Henry IV*, part 2

Sitting on this hill, a week before opening our fifth season, I am filled with wonder and amazement: wonder at whether we will be ready for opening; amazement at the amount of work that has been done by so many in order to bring the ISF here this year. There were moments (several) when I thought this would be the season that wasn't. Well — take a look around. This place is beautiful. Our catastrophe has been tickled. Not quite belly laughs — yet — but my smile is broader these days.

About a year and a half ago, White Savage Assoc., the developers of The Plantation, approached me with an invitation to more the Festival here. At that time our former location seemed to be the right place. We declined the offer. "But times do change and move continually," as Shakespeare's contemporary Edmund Spencer put it. And did they ever. That they moved and changed so quickly had us shifting gears often enough to burn out our collective clutch. The road that led us here has had its ups, downs and bends but when the sod began to go down on our hill, the sixty or so people working on this production began to talk to me in confident, conversational tones again.

All the people in the Festival production love this place; the cool green fairways, mature trees, the community of ducks in Lake Elmore. We are here due to the help and confidence of White Savage Assoc., Inc., Calvin Jensen, Alan Minskoff and Ray Allen, partners. This organization has been a supporter of art and culture in Boise for many years. They have donated office space to Idaho Heritage, Inc. since 1978 and have been Patrons of the ISF since the beginning. Their generosity and enlightened attitude toward local professional performing arts should be robustly applauded.

The Plantation Golf Club and staff, under the management of Bill Rundell, has been extraordinary in helping us get situated and settled here. Roy Johnson, Engineer and Wayne Wright Construction Co., Inc., worked double shifts to get our amphitheater built for you. Randy Sawyer drew the plans for the amphitheater and spent 12-14 hours a day overseeing it's construction. Eric Olsen and Sterling Landscape Co. worked their magic to make it beautiful and comfortable. Boise Cascade Corp., The Gannett Foundation and Ore-Ida Foods went beyond their normal limits to give us much needed financial assistance as did Idaho First National Bank thanks to the confidence of Mr. Chuck Hervey.

The Idaho Shakespeare Festival Patron Committee, chaired by Dianne Robertson, has given us aid and comfort and has produced and promoted events, the proceeds of which we could not do without. The members of that committee include Shari Ashbaugh, secretary, Joyce Delana, past chairwoman, Carmalyn Johnson, Helen Copple, Mike Coughlin, Emmet Herndon, Chuck Hervey, Bea Moe, Ann Murdoch, Kay Naeve, Chuck Newhouse, and Jaci Wilkins.

The merchants at The Plantation Shopping Center seem to be as excited about the ISF being here as the ISF is. Parking space is courtesy of these merchants, the Wright-Leasure Property Management Co., and Wells Fargo Mortgage and Trust Co. We appreciate their support and you can help the ISF by doing business with them. I would also like to thank the City of Garden City, Mayor Marge Mockwitz, Charlie Smith, Mrs. Pearl Hutchinson, The Idanha Hotel, the Belgravia Condominium Assoc., homeowners at The Plantation and members of The Plantation Golf Club who, upon arriving at the second tee have looked on with astonishment and shall I say guarded optimism as we prepared the site and our plays. . . . Thank you for bearing with us. Not to forget Watco, Inc., who has graciously allowed us to use land adjoining the Golf Course and amphitheater.

There are hundreds of people who have helped us through this difficult period of transition. Were it not for the press of deadlines, availability of space in this program and my own lapses of memory, every one would be listed here.

So sit back, relax and enjoy yourself; remember, as our friends at Burma Shave used to tell us . . .

"Don't loose your head
to save a minute
You need your head,
your brains are in it."

Jim Owen

We are pleased to announce that the Association for the Humanities in Idaho and Idaho Heritage, Inc., are presenting a lecture series on Shakespeare, his works and times to be held at the I.S.F. amphitheatre at The Plantation at 1:00 P.M. each Saturday afternoon. There is no charge for admission for this interesting and informative program. We urge you to attend with family and friends.

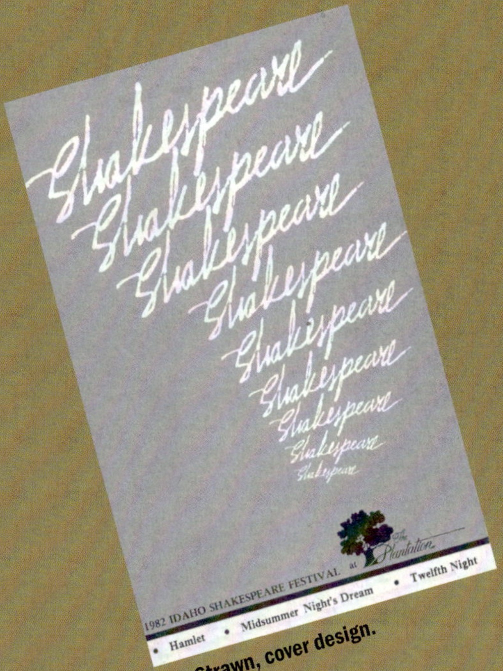

Ann Strawn, cover design.

In an attempt to rectify the red ink left over from the move to the Plantation, a bargain basement season was mounted in 1982.

In order to save the cost of hiring three directors, I opted out of the acting company and took on my greatest challenge ever as a director, *Hamlet*. Our first remake, *A Midsummer Night's Dream*, was directed by Eloise Bruce, who had not only developed a liking for Boise, but took my suggestion about children's theater to heart, launching Idaho Theater for Youth in September, 1981. Mike Hoffman, who had played Lysander and Speed in our first two seasons, was back from Oxford, England, where he was studying as a Rhodes Scholar and beginning a career as a feature film director and writer, to direct *Twelfth Night*.

In an effort to cut expenses, budgets were slashed at every level. We hired a smaller acting and technical company, expanding our apprentice program to help make up the difference. Lane Thomas, Apprentice Director the previous season, was given the position of Technical Director and actually lived on the site in a tiny trailer. Jenny Brotherton, one of Lane's former apprentices and an assistant director on *As You Like It*, returned to head up that program. Jerry Osborne, back for his third season as Set Designer, created a simple, unit set that could be used for all three shows with minor modi-

The Play: ***Hamlet***
Director: **Larry West**
Set Design: **Jerry Osborne**
Costume Design: **Martha Shafer**
Lighting Design: **Phil Brotherton**
Sound: **Sherilyn Paris**

The Play: ***A Midsummer Night's Dream***
Director: **Eloise Bruce**
Set Design : **Jerry Osborne**
Costume Design: **Star Moxley**
Lighting Design: **Phil Brotherton**
Sound: **Sherilyn Paris**

The Play: ***Twelfth Night***
Director: **Mike Hoffman**
Set Design : **Jerry Osborne**
Costume Design: **Odell England**
Lighting Design: **Rozanne Robertson**
Sound: **Sherilyn Paris**

1982

IDAHO Shakespeare FESTIVAL **Gazette**

Volume VI No. 1 Published by Idaho Heritage, Inc. Summer 1982

IDAHO HERITAGE, INC. PRESENTS THE 1982 SIXTH ANNUAL IDAHO SHAKESPEARE FESTIVAL JULY 6 - AUGUST 14, 1982

KING OF DENMARK ASSASSINATED HEIR SEEKS REVENGE

DENMARK (IH) Informed sources report that unusual circumstances have lead Hamlet, Prince of Denmark, to believe that his father the King died of causes

fications, and costume designers were told to keep it simple. Martha Shafer, who had designed the costumes for *The Comedy of Errors* in 1981, produced a splendidly elegant look for *Hamlet* using the simple theme of black and white with accents of red appearing at appropriately bloody moments.

Mike Hoffman's decision to set *Twelfth Night* in the 1930's helped our bottom line considerably by allowing Rozanne Robertson and Odell England to provide all the costumes from their vintage clothing shop, Cheep Chic. Star Moxley took on her first full design job for us with *Midsummer*, and took the three-dimensional soft sculpture she had used for the fairies in *Tempest* a step further, not only creating pieces for the fairies, but adding huge, fabric flowers and leaves throughout the forest, once again provided by our old friends at Sterling Landscape.

> **Star Moxley:** *It's really my favorite story of all, because I dyed every piece of fabric for that show in a toilet. It was the only source of clean, running water in that little space we shared with the scene shop over on Ninth Street behind 8th Street Marketplace. It no longer exists. All it had, literally, was a little hand basin and a toilet, and it's like, okay, how are you going to do this? I mean it sounds weird, but it's clean water, and it's flushable. I did all cold water dyes and dyed every piece that way. It was a $500 budget for the whole show.*

Over the winter, Jim Owen stepped out of his position as General Manager, although he remained on the board, and Jim Crowley was promoted in his place. Pam Abas had done such a marvelous job with publicity the past year everyone agreed we should sign her on for another season, and new board members Bea Black, Eloise Bruce and Alan Minskoff brought a fresh energy to the Festival that helped get us off and running once more. In a final attempt to help our bottom line, ticket prices were reluctantly raised from $6.00 to $7.00, with our first offering of a season ticket at $18.00 to try and soften that blow a bit. The season went off well, although attendance was down a bit, to just over 9,000 people.

In yet another attempt to attract patrons and new audience members, we presented a series of free seminars called, *Breaking the Shakespeare Barrier*. These weekly meetings, held in space donated by 8th Street Marketplace, included topics such as "Women & Shakespeare," "Shakespeare for the Modern Audience," and "Dream & Vision in Shakespeare's Plays," among others, all featuring guest scholars brought in from around the region.

It wasn't all work and no play for the company summer. Respite came in many forms, but one in particular was initiated that summer that struck a significant chord among a group of actors and theater technicians whose backgrounds, for the most part, did not include a great deal of mountain backcountry activities. Randy Andrews and Steve Herrick were a couple of river rats who spent at least as much time running their rafts down the rugged rivers of the northwest as they did tending to their budding real estate careers. But they had one other thing in common as well – they loved coming to the Shakespeare Festival.

They came to me that summer with an offer I couldn't refuse. In exchange for free tickets to the shows they would provide a day-long river trip for the actors and

Crew sets lights. DBB

June 8, 1982

PROPOSAL

Re: Idaho Shakespeare Festival move to 8th Street Marketplace

Idaho Heritage, Inc. (IH) proposed to the W. H. Moore, Inc., developers of the 8th Street Marketplace, that the Idaho Shakespeare Festival (ISF) be performed on the site of that development beginning in 1983 for a period of not less than ten (10) years.

The IH Board of Directors feel that returning ISF to downtown Boise would be a positive move, making Idaho's most highly attended cultural event even more popular while providing the 8th Street Marketplace merchants with

crew at no charge. Well, there was one small stipulation – we had to supply the beer. That trip down the south fork of the Payette did as much to relieve the stress of long hours and six-day work weeks as anything we did all summer long, and instantly became an annual event that ISF company members looked forward to and cherished almost as much as a full house on opening night. Nearly twenty-five years later, the trips continue to thrill those who partake, and Randy and Steve still attend almost every show, compliments of ISF. It's one of those rare perks that works both ways, and a wonderful addition to the community support that makes ISF a special place to work.

Despite total attendance dropping to around 9,000, the season went well, and by August we managed to pay off not only the company, but all of our creditors from the previous summer, some of whom generously offered to forego at least part of the debt in support of the Festival – yet another example of the ongoing community support that has always helped keep the Festival alive through good times and bad. However, we developed a new list of accounts payable from this season, some of which were repeaters. The Plantation site had served us well for two seasons, but we knew it was only a temporary home. And we had no idea how long it would be before the housing development overran us, forcing us into search mode once again. The board agreed that the Festival needed new fund raising ideas and new energy if it was to pull out of its financial slump.

One such idea came together in the form of a proposal to Winston Moore, Inc., developers of the 8th Street Marketplace, who had been generously providing us with free office space for the past year. We presented them with a plan to bring Idaho's most highly attended cultural event back downtown. Performances would be staged on the brick courtyard which served as the 8th Street entrance to the cinemas. ISF had acquired some 600 theater seats from the remodel of the old Ada Theater (now the Egyptian) which would be refurbished and mounted on specially built, moveable platforms to provide a variety of seating arrangements for various types of performances, from plays, to musical concerts. We even envisioned a series of summer, outdoor Philharmonic concerts.

The board felt that the increased business traffic during the summer months would be attractive to Marketplace merchants, and that the developing warehouse district surrounding it offered an ideal opportunity for long term growth that could provide a year-round program of professional theater and other entertainment. Idaho Theater for Youth, which had just completed its second successful season under Eloise Bruce, was a key component of the proposed program, providing not only children's entertainment, but classes, workshops, and a drama school for young people that would not only provide some basic theater training, but would contribute to the overall well being, self-assurance and general people skills of the participants.

Unfortunately the generosity of the Marketplace board did not extend quite that far, and our proposal was turned down. Still, as far as the general public was concerned the Festival was going strong, and indeed we were. Ticket sales indicated that our shows were very popular, and community support in general had never been better. But the hours and years had brought on a case of severe burn-out for me. It was time for a rest, but that was the one thing the Festival could not afford to do if it was to remain alive and growing.

ISF was becoming a large enterprise – larger than I felt capable of handling in addition to my other work. And as my businessman father reminded me, it was my "other work" that was

Jim Owen, Board of Director. ME

L-R, Louann Blome, Board Vice-President; Jim Crowley, General Manager. ME

Bless thee, Bottom!
Bless thee!
Thou are translated!

Midsummer Night's Dream, III, i.

ITY Season brochure.

ONE WOMAN PLAYS ENCHANT KIDS, ADULTS

Herald Tribune

The magic was in the quality of Lloyd's performance and in the amazing response she got from the children in the audience.

They answered her questions, sang, danced and helped with the fairy puppet show. Everyone (adults, too) participated in the play and contributed something unexpected.

You may be wondering how a group of small children can do all those things without getting completely out of hand. Doesn't someone spoil things?

No, no one does.

paying the bills. On top of that, I found myself becoming more of an administrator than an actor and director. So after much consideration and debate with family, friends, and myself, the word went out to friends and trade publications around the country that ISF was looking for a new Artistic Director. I would remain on the Board of Directors and help develop and guide that arm of the business, and remain available for acting and directing jobs, but the day to day activities of running the Festival would be put in the hands of someone we hoped would take what we had built so far to the next level.

Never was such a sudden schooling made. Henry V, I, i

ARTS RESIDENCIES AND WORKSHOPS

In addition to our Saturday morning performances, IDAHO THEATER FOR YOUTH now offers arts residencies and workshops in schools.

"Everyone, teachers, too, participated in the play and contributed something."
Louise Alexander
Principal
Middleton Elementary School

IDAHO PRESS TRIBUNE

"It has given the kids an experience they wouldn't usually get in a classroom. It has taught them discipline, respect for their director and increased cooperation with each other."
Cindy Bird
First Grade Teacher
Centennial School, Nampa

INVITE US!

All you have to do is lend us a 30' × 30' space, unlock the doors and bring on the kids! IDAHO THEATER FOR YOUTH travels with everything needed for professional performances of youth-oriented plays and musicals.

Performing and technical workshops can also be tailored to your group's needs.

Idaho Theater Youth

Idaho Heritage

IDAHO

1982 SEASON
APPRENTICESHIP POSITIONS
MAY 24 - AUGUST 15,

May 10, 1982

th THE GREAT ORIGINAL YARN OFF next Saturday.

0 in the bank and will break even or better

Glenn Oakley, cover photography.

The search for a new Artistic Director wasn't the only thing occupying the minds of the board. Financially, our four years at One Capital Center all ended in the black. The two subsequent years at the Plantation, however, produced a steady flow of red ink on the books, and some board members saw no end in sight.

During our first three years as a non-profit organization the board had been made up of a small group of people closely associated with the Festival. It was essential that we begin to expand our board into the community at large, not only to encourage fund raising growth, but to bring a more objective perspective on Festival operations. But before that could happen, we had to solidify the staff, as well as our own resolve to rectify financial difficulties and continue as a company.

The first test came when I proposed that Eloise Bruce serve a term as co-Artistic Director with me through the winter, and take over the position for the 1983 summer

The Play: ***The First Part of Henry IV***

Director: **Mark Cuddy**

Set Design: **Jeffery Hunt**

Costume Design: **Lowell Detweiller**

Lighting Design: **M. Lane Thomas**

Sound: **Catherine Mason**

The Play: ***Love's Labours Lost***

Director: **David Odie**

Set Design : **Jeffrey Hunt**

Costume Design: **Martha Shafer**

Lighting Design: **Katherine Mason**

The Play: ***The Merry Wives of Windsor***

Director: **Victoria Holloway**

Set Design : **Jeffrey Hunt**

Costume Design: **Rozanne Robertson**

Lighting Design: **Jonathon Perry**

1983

Shakespeare Festival names arts

By JUDY McCONNELL STEELE
The Idaho Statesman

An era ends. An era begins.

Mark Cuddy, former director for the Denver Centre Theatre Co., is replacing Doug Copsey as artistic director of the Idaho Shakespeare Festival.

Cuddy, who took over the position of artistic director March 4, grew up in Massachusetts and graduated from the University of Massachusetts at Amherst. Now 29, he was guest director of the Idaho Shakespeare Festival's 1981 production of *The Tempest*.

Mark Cuddy ...He'll hunt for festival site

Shakespeare Festival in 1975, will continue with the festival as a

His main function will be to find a permanent site for the festival, he said.

"We've been talking with several people, the City Parks Commission being one," he said. He also would not rule out the 8th Street Marketplace as a possible site, although he said the plays would not be in the cinema courtyard, as was earlier discussed.

The festival will stay for two more seasons at the Plantation golf course, Cuddy said. Festival productions have been there for the past two seasons.

This year's season will open on

directed by Cuddy. Other productions in the season are *The Merry Wives of Windsor*, opening July 9, and *Love's Labors Lost*, opening July 10.

The repertory company will include actors from Houston, Tucson, Los Angeles, Denver, Minneapolis and Nebraska, as well as Boise.

Merry Wives will be directed by Victoria Holloway, technical director of the Idaho festival for its first four years. During that period, she also directed *Romeo and Juliet* and portrayed Julia in *Two Gentlemen of Verona* and Portia in *Merchant of Venice* for the festival.

Governor John Evans opens a new season. DLB

David Odie, Director, *Love's Labours Lost.* DBB

season. The board actually approved this, then rescinded their vote a short time later. She was highly qualified, but she was also very busy running Idaho Theater for Youth, and the board felt the double responsibility would simply be too much for one person to assume. Then, in a surprise move while I was out of the room giving Eloise the bad news, a motion was passed to cease operations until all debt was paid off. It seemed I was not the only one suffering from burn-out.

Insisting the debate be re-opened, I argued that the only way we were going to pay off the debt was to produce another season of plays and work our tails off to make it successful. Where else was the money to come from? And who was going to donate anything to a company that was out of business? After considerable discussion, which concluded with my firm suggestion that the Festival would go on regardless of the vote, if necessary under another name and with a new board, another vote was held, and this time the majority was resolved to continue the Festival uninterrupted.

The festival gets a new stage. DBB

Nancy Harms works make-up magic on Suzanne Perreault. DBB

Eloise would continue to run ITY, and work to grow that organization to its full potential on its own, while the ISF board would work to expand its membership and fund raising efforts. But the first order of business for everyone was finding a new Artistic Director to lead us into the future. We didn't have to wait long. In January, 1983, Jim Owen was elected board President, and a short time later, he received a phone call from Mark Cuddy, who had directed *The Tempest* for us two years before.

Mark Cuddy: *I was freelancing out of the Denver Center when I heard Doug was leaving, and I just don't freelance well. I found out Jimmy (Owen) was President of the board, so I called him and said what's up, I hear Doug is leaving and I think I'd really like this job. That was before Eloise had been appointed for a short time and he said, "We have this big meeting and I can't go into details, but I'll keep you posted." Well, a few weeks later Jimmy called me and said they had another board meeting and it was done, I was in.*

Jim Owen: *Cuddy was a choice move. He was an ace move. I mean, he made stuff happen, stuff that Doug and I couldn't make happen. He knew exactly what he was doing. Doug and I were playing it by ear. It was jazz for us, but for him it was a symphony.*

Mark Cuddy: *I remember Doug's quote when they asked what he thought about me coming in as Artistic Director. Two years prior, when I directed Tempest, my hair was long and I dressed pretty wild – leather pants and things like that. His quote was, "He'll be great, you'll just have to buy him a suit."*

Governor John Evans makes it official. ME

Micheal Baltzell, Master Carpenter. DBB

Jim Crowley: *I remember him (Mark) coming in and he and I sat down. It was the first night he was there, and he pretty much laid out what he wanted to do – how he saw my role as General Manager and how it was going to function best. And I remember having a lot of confidence that this guy was*

coming here and knows what has to be done.

Aside from producing a season, Mark's goals for ISF were two-fold – get people out to the Plantation for now, but get to work on a long-term goal of finding a permanent home for the Festival right away. The board had decided to expand from six to eleven members in order to gain a broader outreach into the community we served, as well as valuable connections to that community from a fund raising standpoint. This was critical due to the red ink still flowing from the move to the Plantation. But most important, from a budget standpoint as well as the future of the Festival, was ticket sales, which had been the backbone of our community support since day one. That not only meant producing popular shows, but finding innovative ways of attracting people to attend.

Mark Cuddy: *One idea we had that first year was a critic's conference. I got a grant from the Idaho Humanities Commission and brought up Dan Sullivan from the Los Angeles Times, someone from the Seattle Times and another critic to hold a panel discussion on theatrical criticism. I had them see the shows, then taped the two hour criticism session where they talked about them. And I used all the good quotes in all our publicity and brochures for the next few years. It worked really well.*

For his debut season Mark picked *Henry IV, Part 1*, our first attempt at one of Shakespeare's histories, *The Merry Wives of Windsor*, a reprise from our third season that continued the story of Sir John Falstaff's adventures off the battlefield, and the romantic comedy, *Love's Labours Lost*. Naturally budget was a big consideration, and Mark was quick to pick up on a venerable ISF tradition – scrounging.

Mark Cuddy: *I got all the costumes and props for Henry from the Denver Center, from my mentor, Ed Call's production. I was his assistant at the time. He came and saw my production and said, "Hey, this is my show."*

Setting *Merry Wives* in the 1950's made it a natural for Rozanne Robertson to design the costumes from Cheep Chic, as she had for *Twelfth Night* the year before. And Martha Shafer, back for her third season as a designer, put her skills to work on a non-descript, futuristic *Love's Labours Lost*. Jenny Brotherton, making the move from Apprentice Director to Costume Shop Director, had her work cut out for her. Hair and Make-up Designer Nancy Harms also needed help, so she asked a long-time friend, local hairdresser Shirley Hurley, to help out.

New Stage Construction. UK

Lane Thomas inspects the progress. UK

Shirley Hurley: *I was always hanging around the Festival helping out when I could. I gave Tracy Hollenbeck a permanent when he played Mercutio in Romeo and Juliet when the Festival was still downtown, so by the time Nancy asked me to sign on* *full-time that third season at the Plantation, I was already hooked.*

Matty Shafer: *There was so much volunteer work. Everybody that stitched for me, none of them got paid, and we all worked long hours. It was that way across the company. No matter what part of the theater you worked in there were always a lot of volunteers.*

In addition to saving considerable money on the extensive costumes required for *Henry*, Mark directed the show as well. In an unusual move, he set the style for the other two shows before talking to the directors. Victoria Holloway, who was now Artistic Director at The American Stage Company in St. Petersburg, Florida, returned to handle those chores for *Merry Wives* while David Odie was brought in from Los Angeles to take on *Love's Labours Lost*.

Mark Cuddy: *For some reason I was saying, "ok, we have these three plays, they should be in different styles. So I asked each of them to direct in a very specific style, which was a mistake. The fifties sitcom version of Merry Wives worked, but the futuristic Love's Labours Lost was a bust.*

On the technical side, Mark brought in Jeffrey Hunt, a scenic designer from Seattle, and our first Production Stage Manager, Stephen Jimenez. Lane Thomas was back for a second season as the company's Technical Director and charged with the task of moving the scene shop to a new location before they could begin set construction. When he mentioned needing another pair of hands to help accomplish this not-so-small task to Jenny, she mentioned a friend who was between jobs.

Micheal Baltzell: *While I was helping Lane with the move, I mentioned that I had carpentry skills, and I could paint, and he hired me on for the summer right on the spot. It was just me and Lane and Jeffery. The only other tech staff they hired was designers. In the early years I actually think sometimes we did a better job when we had less to do it with. It was exciting because you had to come up with something clever because you didn't have any money to do anything else. So we found alternatives.*

The shows were all successful as far as the audience was concerned, and the Festival saw the best attendance since its move to the Plantation. General Manager Jim Crowley did a wonderful job of increasing the publicity on virtually no budget, but it was another Cuddy innovation that tipped the scales when it came to connecting with the audience and spreading the word that a night at the Shakespeare Festival was about much more than just going to see a play.

Michael Connor, Dumaine, *Love's Labours*. ME

The community's support weathered not only the move from downtown to a new site, but the parking, the porta-potties, the ducks and the occasional sprinkler system malfunctions that came with it. Mark took the reins of the Festival with both hands and mastered the running of it in such a short time that the company seemed to move forward almost seamlessly. So much so that he was already looking ahead to the next season.

Wendy Lawless, a member of the acting company that summer who came in from Minneapolis, was the daughter of the very well known and respected Guthrie Theater actor, James Lawless. When he came out to see his daughter perform in Idaho, Mark gave him a tour of the facility.

Mark Cuddy: *After the show he walked out on the stage and was looking at the giant trees that served as our natural backdrop and the little brook and said, "you know, you could do Robin Hood here." "That's a good idea," I said, "thank you very much."*

Mark Cuddy: *I so enjoyed the curtain speeches. It became a real opportunity to look at the audience in the daylight. Each night when I would deputize the duck patrol it seemed to galvanize the audience, to focus them on where they were and what they were there for. But as much as I loved that, I loved our sold out nights even more when about twenty or thirty minutes before curtain I would come out and say, "all right, we have a full house tonight, you've got to start scooching together." There would be 400 people in the bowl, all having dinner, and you'd think, I can't fit one more person. But all of a sudden coolers would go gack into their cars, blankets would fold up and boom, all this space would open up and we'd put another couple hundred people in there. The idea that everyone was working together to make that happen was extraordinary. You really felt that the audience was a partner.*

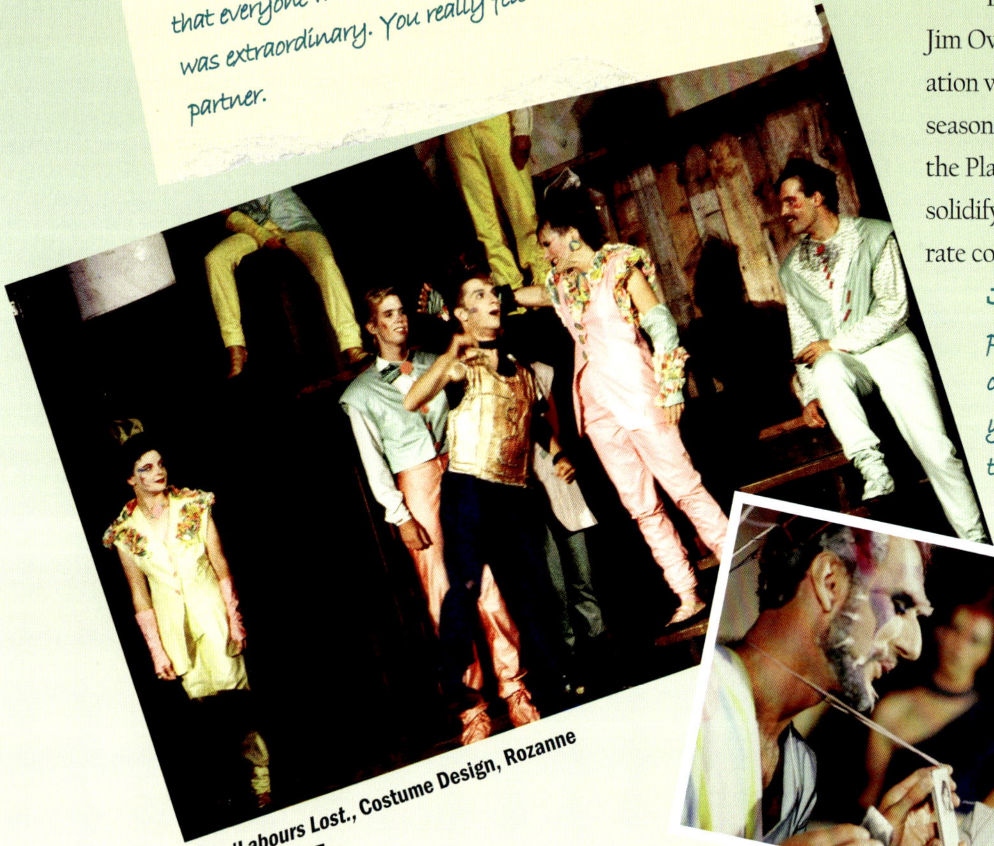

Love'Labours Lost., Costume Design, Rozanne Robertson. ME

Wayne Cote, Don Adriano; Ursula Meyer, Jaquenetta, *Love's Labours.* ME

When Mark was an undergraduate student at the University of Massachusetts – Amherst, he was cast in a play written by a graduate student named Don Nigro.

Mark Cuddy: *I didn't know that many playwrights, and I didn't know writers who had the breadth of writing an epic. Robin Hood was going to be a big story – an epic. I wanted it to be a comedy, and in his own quirky way, Don loves to skewer historical figures in their own historical time. It was the Festival's first commission. I think we sent him $500.*

The end of the 1983 season saw our new Artistic Director firmly ensconced as the head of ISF. The company, the board, and most importantly the community, had come to accept Mark as a leader who could get things done, and someone who could take the Festival into the future for a long time to come.

In November, Chuck Robertson was elected President of the Board, replacing Jim Owen, who was leaving to concentrate on the restaurant business. Jim's association with the Festival began as a last minute stand-in for an injured actor in our first season, and he played a key role in ushering us through the trauma of our move to the Plantation. His service as Company Manger and later as Board President helped solidify the company from within, and cement relationships throughout the corporate community that last to this day. He would be missed.

Jim Owen: *Who would have thought 30 years ago in Boise, Idaho, still pretty much an agricultural community, that a group of young actors could get together and put on a theater festival, and convince people that, yeah, this is going to be fun, and pull it off. It's kind of like, in some times, in some places, there is a coalescence of idea and ambition and motivation and goal, and on very lucky occasions, it just happens. And we just happened to be part of it.*

Mark Cuddy and Jim Crowley flank Governor Evans. ME

Ed & Janet Simmerman, Box Office Managers. DBB

That same month, the board voted to hire a Managing Director to work with Mark on the company budget and to direct sales efforts – two critical elements in gaining control of the company's debt. While a search was being conducted, the board, now expanded to twelve members and reorganized internally into committees, went to work on a fund raising program to increase membership and gain new corporate sponsorships. Dorothy Peavey, along with Chuck and Dianne Robertson, kicked things off by becoming our first two $1,000 donors, setting the bar for more to come.

Financially, things were beginning to look up, but there was still a long way to go before we would see black ink on the books again. To help pay off some of the debt immediately, a $25,000 loan was taken out. In addition to myself, Chuck Robertson, Bea Black, Chris Goode and Dorothy Peavey stepped up to sign as guarantors for the loan. It was an extraordinary precedent to set, and a heartwarming demonstration of loyalty by those whose connection to the Festival had, up to now, been as devoted fans and volunteer board members.

Brian King: *In those days, no one would loan the Festival any money unless there were personal guarantors. Serving as a guarantor certainly gave all of us who signed on a very personal interest in the success of the Festival.*

This Brian King was not the actor, but our board legal counsel from Boise Cascade. Among his many services during his tenure on the board was arranging for ISF to become a member of the Chamber of Commerce in order to heighten our public awareness and, hopefully, increase community participation in our membership and sponsorship programs. The success of our first membership meeting in December, 1983, prompted the scheduling of two more, in January and March of 1984 as a buildup to the season.

Mark's visits with potential corporate sponsors were likewise met with promising indications of support. Ore-Ida suggested a challenge to larger businesses to match the donations from small businesses, and Ed Simmerman, chair of the Business Membership Committee compiled a list of medium to small sized businesses for board members with the idea of appealing to them with personal letters. Lee Pulver followed up on that idea with a suggestion to ask the Chamber of Commerce to distribute a letter to its members asking for support. And the first issue of *Shake-Scene*, a new quarterly newsletter on Festival actitivies produced by BSU English professor Stu Evett went to press for a February release.

Mark was busy on the artistic front as well, and there was plenty of activity to report in that first issue of *Shake-Scene*. First Security Bank expressed a willingness to sponsor a North Idaho tour for one of our summer shows, and meetings with the Sun Valley Center resulted in a proposal to their board for ISF to do a week's residency there in August. He was also negotiating with Boise State University to become the first major tenant in the Morrison Center's new Stage II facility with a series of three contemporary plays.

In January, 1984, the board hired Ron Wachholtz as Managing Director. He arrived from Tennessee in February and hit the ground running with plans to develop five and ten year plans, restructure the subscription program, and expand the board yet again in order to achieve greater community outreach. He also proposed a gradual change that would drop Idaho Heritage from the Festival's name.

At the same time, the first draft of *Robin Hood* arrived. Everyone was anxious to read it but Mark insisted on having a live reading before too many people saw it. I was one of the select few that got to see the script before the reading and I was sadly disappointed. I told Mark I had some serious reservations. I could see how the fight scenes would be wonderful, but the plot was shallow and, bottom line, it just wasn't funny. Boy was I wrong.

A few nights later a group of the core acting company gathered in my living room to read the script aloud. From the first page to the last we were all howling with laughter, and by the time we finished, we knew we had a big hit on our hands. Once we had recovered, we discussed what few problems we could find and made some suggestions for changes and improvements.

Mark Cuddy: *Don and I had a great relationship. He would send me a draft and I would write comments all over it. And I would be brutal. "This is ridiculous." "What are you doing!?" "This is the cheap way out here." Then I would send it back. He, in Melbourne, Ohio, would yell and curse at me, we'd have this whole big fight, except of course I wasn't there. And then he'd calm down and ultimately take about three-fourths of my comments to heart, rewrite it and send me another draft. And that's how we worked together. We never really spoke about the script in person, or even on the phone. We would just do it via the mail.*

Michael Leopard, Falstaff, *Henry IV, Pt.1.* DBB

While Don Nigro was busily creating another draft of *Robin Hood*, Mark selected *The Taming of the Shrew* and *King Lear* to round out our eighth season. His appointment as Artistic Director had garnered the attention of some old friends in the Boston area, and the Idaho Shakespeare family was expanded to include Vincent Murphy and Tim McDonough, who would direct *Lear* and *Shrew*, respectively, and Kirsten Giroux, a marvelous addition to the acting company as Kate in *Shrew* and Goneril in *Lear*. Tim, also a great acting talent, was cast as Lear, and at six-foot-six made the ideal Little John in *Robin Hood*.

Mark Cuddy: *Tim was destined to play Little John.*

But though the ISF family was growing and expanding, the backbone of the company was still made up of local artists. I was thrilled when Mark asked me to play Robin Hood, and to be on stage with long-time ISF talents like Dan Peterson, Tom Willmorth, Carole Whiteleather, David Lee-Painter and Jay Sherlock.

Carole Whiteleather: *Cuddy always wanted that sense of company, you know, the feeling that everybody was on the same page, working together. So he would have auditions with the entire company. We would all be in one room and everybody from the interns to main company members would stand up and do an audition in front of the whole crowd. And what it did, immediately, was it made us all the same. Because we all knew what that nervousness was, and so everybody supported everybody, and there was that sense of family that was very, very strong.*

Behind the scenes David also served as Production Manager, Nancy Berger ran a tight ship in the costume shop working closely with designers like Bitsy Bidwell and Hair and Make-up Designer Nancy Harms, who was also an occasional actress, and Jim Campbell, who always seemed to be there, no matter what was needed. Nancy Lee-Painter, who was in the acting company for the 1980 and '81 seasons, and was slated to appear in *Crimes of the Heart* and *Sister Mary Ignatius Explains It All For You* in our spring series, was appointed to head up the Apprentice Program.

In Act I, Scene ii of *Julius Caesar*, A soothsayer admonishes Caesar to "beware the ides of March." Though the "ides" specifically refers to March 15, the soothsayer's warning had already proven prophetic to ISF in March of 1981 when we lost our original downtown site at One Capital Center. At the March 7, 1984 board meeting, President Chuck Robertson announced that we had lost our lease at the

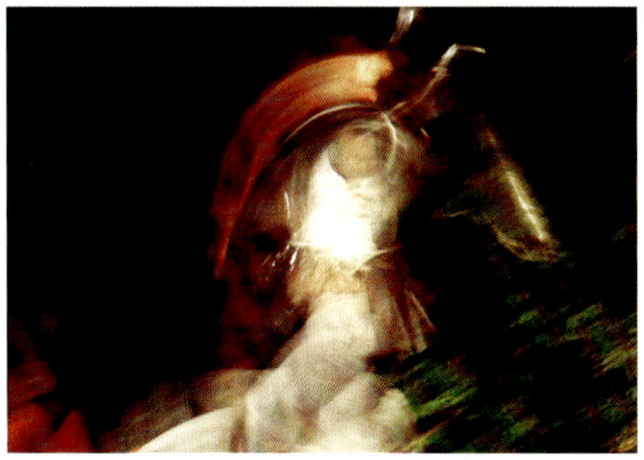

Sword play, *Henry IV, Pt. 1.* DBB

Michael Connor, Prince Hal; Sue Galligan, Mistriss Quickly, *Henry IV, Pt. 1.* DBB

Sword play, *Henry IV, Pt. 1.* DBB

Plantation site after only three seasons. It was not completely unexpected. The housing development had been moving closer and closer to us, and was now on the verge of engulfing the site itself. What was not expected was how bad the financial situation at the Festival had become.

> **Chuck Robertson:** *Mark called me one night and said he needed to talk, so Bea (Black) and I met with him and the story was incredibly bleak. I don't remember how many dollars we were in debt at that point, but Mark was the sole paid employee. He told us the Festival was out of money, he was out of money personally, the board was dissolved, and we had to decide right then if the Festival was go or no-go. I wrote him a check so he could live for a while and we could sort out some of these problems, and we agreed that Bea and I would be the board. The three of us were what we had. Mark went at it full time and we got a group of people together as a board, but the one thing we did that was really important was to decide that it couldn't go away.*

Once again the opportunity to buckle under was presented to the Festival, bolstered by the weight of additional debt. But this time there was no discussion of packing our bags and going home. The spring season at the Morrison Center's Stage II was set, as was the summer repertory, which included a world premier of our first commissioned play, *Robin Hood*, and Mark had traveled over 5,500 miles across the western states auditioning some 700 actors for the company. The word was out in arts communities across the country that the Idaho Shakespeare Festival was a dynamic new company that not only produced vibrant outdoor theater, but was an exciting and beautiful place to spend a summer.

At the time of the announcement, five potential sites for a new theater were already under discussion – Ann Morrison Park, the Western Idaho Fairgrounds, the Old Penitentiary, a ParkCenter site owned by Morrison Knudsen Construction, and, if only from a sentimental standpoint, a return to One Capital Center. Initial efforts were focused on the ParkCenter site, situated just south of the pond adjacent to Logger Creek. Although the Old Penitentiary and One Capital Center were not ruled out entirely, their consideration was put on a back burner for the time being.

Once again, time was of the essence. The spring season at the Morrison Center, under the bold heading, "The Great Potato Meets the Big Apple," was set to open on May 8 in the Recital Hall, with Dan Peterson starring in the one-man drama, *Billy Bishop Goes to War*. *Crimes of the Heart* would follow two weeks later in Stage II, with the third show, *Sister Mary Ignatius Explains It All for You*, running as a late night offering at 11:00 PM during the run of the other two. Contracts for these, as well as the summer repertory, had been sent out, but it was agreed they would not be signed until a new site was secured.

New board member Dick McChrystal, a Morrison Knudsen executive, put the wheels in motion by contacting the Morrison Foundation to obtain permission for the use of the site, while I contacted architects about preliminary sketches for a presentation. Meanwhile, the business of running the company continued apace. Brian Nye arranged for Ron Wachholtz to join the Chamber of Commerce's Goldbusters group, which would give the Festival listings in their newsletter, *Boise Business Today*. Ron also received a commitment from the Boise Board of Realtors to provide housing for 50 actors over the next three years. On the surface at least, it was business as usual.

But as we learned during our first move in 1981, in times of crisis help often comes from unexpected sources. Corporate support for the Festival had been growing slowly, in part because we had not only survived the move to the Plantation but prospered in doing so. At the same time our Board of Directors had begun to learn how to function as a fund raising arm of the company. One of those corporate supporters was Ore-Ida, a division of H.J. Heinz, whose headquarters was in ParkCenter. They had been generous with their contributions over the past few years, thanks in large part to Susan Gerhart, their Manager of Public Relations.

Susan Gerhart: *When they (ISF) first came to me I had never been to the Shakespeare Festival. I went out to the Plantation site and was impressed. It was my first experience with Shakespeare and it's been a series of wonderful experiences ever since. When they came to ask if Ore-Ida would contribute to the search, it came to me that we had this site next to one of our buildings. Normally when you give for bricks and mortar projects we had to go to Heinz, and it took a long time. I went to my boss, Don Masterson, General Manager of Human Resources, and he thought it would be a great use of the property. We took it to the Management Board, they approved it and that was that.*

Don Masterson: *As Sue's boss I was involved in the approval process, but it was her idea to let them use that vacant lot adjoining our property that we had purchased for future expansion. We had a year-to-year lease with the Shakespeare Festival for $1.00 a year. Ore-Ida's Management Board and Presidents Paul Corddry and Gerald Herrick were very supportive of the project, and our employees would enjoy watching behind-the-scenes rehearsals on lunch break strolls.*

Sue also offered the free use of Ore-Ida's two parking lots, which they only used during the day, to Festival-goers each evening. An agreement was signed in May, 1984, and once again we were pulled back from the brink by the support of the community. Even though the lease was only year-to-year, it was an offer we couldn't pass up. What's more, the empty land gave Mark a blank slate on which he could create a brand new theater.

Mark Cuddy: *So many decisions were made quickly, or the events happened so quickly. Boom, it was suddenly profit to non-profit. Boom, we're out of one site and we have to find another site. Boom, here's a new Artistic Director. Doug had his March, 1981 "you've gotta go" call to the Plantation and we had it in March of 1984. It's kind of extraordinary. It just feels like there was this path, there was sort of providence for the Festival. It was going to happen. But it's all part of the same thing – the energy of the early founders who were in that company. It didn't start as a group of artists doing their own little thing. It started smack in the middle of downtown as part of this business structure. It always had this sense that it came from the center up. It was part of the fabric of everything.*

The Festival hibernates. DBB

The Parkcenter Years
1984-1997

Amen. A man may, if he were of a fearful heart, stagger in this attempt; for here we h
orns are odious, they are necessary. It is said, 'many a man knows no end of his goods

DBB

King Lear. DBB

...le but the wood, no assembly but horn-beasts. But what though? Courage! As ...y a man has good horns, and knows no end of them. Well, that is the dowry of his

Mike Murie, cover design .

Dan Peterson, *Billy Bishop Goes to War.* UK

1984

In the midst of the organized chaos that resulted in a third home in only eight seasons of Shakespeare under the stars, our spring season at the Morrison Center started off smoothly.

Dan Peterson's *Billy Bishop* was a poignant journey back through the life of an aging World War I flying ace.

> **Dan Peterson:** *That was a huge thing for me, and I'll always appreciate that. I think it was kind of a big thing for Cuddy to go with me as Billy because I'm not a singer and I'd never really been a lead-type actor before. I was always – and still am – the character man.*

Audiences got an advance peek at Kirsten Giroux, the first of the Boston clan to arrive, in *Crimes of the Heart*, playwright Beth Henley's 1981 Pulitzer Prize-winning play about three eccentric southern sisters. Idaho Statesman

The Play: ***The Taming of the Shrew***
Director: Tim McDonough
Set Design: Jeffrey Hunt
Costume Design: Sarah Campbell
Lighting Design: Jonathan Langrell
Sound: David Miller

Vinnie Murphy, Director, *King Lear.* DLB

The Play: ***King Lear***
Director: Vincent Murphy
Set Design: Jeffrey Hunt
Costume Design: Sarah Campbell
Lighting Design: Jonathan Langrell
Sound: David Miller

The Play: ***Robin Hood***
Director: Mark Cuddy
Set Design: Jeffrey Hunt
Costume Design: Bitsy Bidwell
Lighting Design: Jonathan Langrell

The ParkCenter theater takes shape. DBB

reviewer Susan Lowman said Christopher Durang's *Sister Mary Ignatius Explains It All For You* was "simply superb theater," and Marie Devine Galyean of the Idaho Press Tribune called it "devilishly funny," bringing the younger, late-night audience Mark had been hoping for to see the sometimes controversial play in droves.

Amidst this trio of off-season successes, preparations for the summer season moved frantically along. At the May board meeting Mark announced that Production Manager David Lee Painter had hired Jim Campbell, our go-to guy for set construction since the second season of the Festival, as the Festival's new Technical Director. Along with that title came the daunting task of building a theater in the few short weeks remaining before our July 6 opening.

Jim Campbell: *George Stieger came in and built that hill for us. We had to get that landscaped, sprinkled, to get those light towers up and install the lights, build the stage, build the little kiosk on the outside, build the fence. I don't think we got the fence done that first year. I mean it was a real struggle.*

Mark Cuddy: *If it wasn't for Jim Campbell we never would have had a theater. He and his crew would show up after hours every evening with all this machinery and work late into the night. We kept asking the other contractors working around ParkCenter to dump the dirt from their projects there for the berm.. We basically built the theater out of nothing with no money. In the end, it was all about sod again – our lives were about sod. We went back to the well again with Eric Olson and the Sterling folks. I think we may have paid a little money this time, but we got a lot for a little.*

Jim Campbell: *I don't know who finally said it – it was theater by crisis. At one point we had to cut some holes to get power up those light trees, and the only way to do that was to get a torch up there. That meant getting oxygen up there, and we only had a short hose. So George Davis grabbed one tank and Chuck Raymond grabbed the other one and hauled them up the ladder and we hooked it all back together and they held those tanks on the ladder while I cut the holes, and I thought, wow, that's absolutely true. This is theater by crisis.*

DBB

Jim Campbell: *George Stieger came in and built that hill for us. We had to get that landscaped, sprinkled, to get those light towers up and install the lights, build the stage, build the little kiosk on the outside, build the fence. I don't think we got the fence done that first year. I mean it was a real struggle.*

Mark Cuddy: *And Jeff Hunt, our scenic designer, was just supposed to design scenery, but he ended up designing the whole theater! Because it's one thing to say, okay, let's build a hillside for the audience to sit on, but it's another thing to say, what's the stage going to look like? You have to build a back wall, you have to build wings, you have to create a sense of space. And Jeff did that. He was designing the whole environment.*

Jim Campbell: *When we were right down to the end, getting ready to open and everything, the City came down on me hard. We had no building permits or any of that, and here's the head building inspector out there just fuming, walking back and forth, and finally says, "You're in the flood plain and what we don't want is the river to flood and have this stage wash off here and get caught on the bridge." I said, "See these poles, they're buried six feet deep in concrete." Because the soil was just rocks and sand you couldn't dig it, couldn't backfill and compact it. so when we stuck the posts up for the theater we just poured a bunch of concrete in the bottom of every one of those things to anchor them, and then backfilled them. Once he found that out, he was good with it. And I'll remember this forever. Mark got up on stage opening night and he said, "There's three people I'd like to thank for this, the Bank of Idaho, Ore Ida, and Jim Campbell," and I thought, wow, I'm in good company.*

No one knew it at the time, but the environment they created was to become the Festival's home for the next thirteen years. But the Festival stayed on the move in other ways.

Mark Cuddy: *Everything moved a lot in those days. Storage was always moving, the offices were moving. It felt like we were constantly moving something. For years afterward, whenever I was asked for my definition of theater*

We basically built the theater out of nothing with no money. In the end, it was all about sod again – our lives were about sod.

A break in rehearsal. DBB

Ron Wachholtz, Managing Director. DBB

Mark Cuddy, Artistic Director. DBB

I said, "Well, theater is basically moving stuff around."

The 1984 season not only produced a new theater, but the biggest hit the Festival had ever seen. Don Nigro's *Robin Hood*, our first non-Shakespeare play, had audiences roaring with laughter and clamoring for tickets to see it again and again.

'Robin Hood' steals hearts with wit, acting

By SUSAN M. LOWMAN
The Idaho Statesman

Seeing *Robin Hood* again this year was like visiting favorite friends. The characters spun by playwright Don Nigro are visions out of glowing childhood memories, set off by the sophisticated flippancy that marks much of contemporary comedy.

This play, the biggest box office hit the Idaho Shakespeare Festival has ever had, is a smooth amalgamation of legend, comedy and satire. Don Nigro gives us politicians right out of *Doonesbury*. Their self-preoccupation ensures that our sympathies will stay solidly with Robin and the gang of outlaws, wholesome and conscientious beings that they are.

Doug Copsey stayed in the Idaho outdoors in this ParkCenter production, directed by Mark Cuddy and Paul Frellick, to star as Robin. His Robin is just such a nice guy there's nothing bad that could, in good conscience, be said about him. Copsey's wide-eyed repartee with Maid Marian marked him a real human male, susceptible to the charms of womanhood. Copsey's green thief led fearlessly when needed, and delivered a touching political treatise as the play drew to a close.

Maid Marian, described by Will Scarlet as one

Doug Copsey, Robin Hood. DBB

Bitsy Bidwell's costumes brought color and life to a nearly bare stage, and David Boushey's fight scenes were full of action and a sense of humor that belied the fierceness of wielding ten-pound broadswords and six-foot quarter-staffs in extremely close quarters on stage, not to mention mere feet from the front row of the audience. And then there was Grok, the court jester to end all court jesters.

Stitch Marker: *One of my favorite stories is the night a big gust of wind hit and that big plywood cut-out of Sherwood Forest just sort of popped off and floated down on top of the actors. Everyone just kind of crunched down and let it come down. In Nigro's script the Sheriff of Nottingham was always threatening to cut down Sherwood Forest to find Robin Hood. I'm standing way down right with Jeff Ware, who's playing Richard the Lionheart, and he turns to me and says, "Looks like they're cutting down the forest a little early tonight."*

Tom Willmorth: *He was like the ultimate showman from a culture that has not been discovered. He spoke no known language, although it was scripted. Nigro wrote the nonsense language and I learned it. I was spot on. He entered running, but in circles. The explanation that I had in my head was that he was from a rural mountain country, central Europe maybe, where they grew up as goat herders on mountain sides and the downhill leg was longer than the uphill leg so when Grok ran, he had to run in circles.*

Sarah Campbell, an old colleague of Mark's from the Denver Center, came in to design for both *Lear* and *Shrew*. She achieved a marvelous contrast between Vinnie Murphy's very Shakespearean *Lear* and Tim McDonough's dark, burlesque *Shrew*. Mark Cuddy made his on-stage debut for ISF as Petruchio, opposite Kirsten Giroux as Kate, in a production that challenged audiences with the notion that Petruchio, a first rank comic on the burlesque circuit is not looking for a wife, but rather a woman partner for his new marriage act. In the process of auditioning and rehearsing with Kate, he tames her by stifling any creative urges she may try to express and forcing her to submit to his will, leaving her truly lost in the end.

David Lee Painter, Yorick, *Robin Hood*. DBB

The equally dark *Lear*, with Tim McDonough in the lead role and Kirsten Giroux, Ursula Meyer and Laura Jones as his daughters, riveted audiences with Murphy's exploration of the nature of power, the control of destinies, and what that control can do to the powerful. By the end of the run, we were firmly entrenched in our new home, delighted that our loyal audience had followed us from the Plantation and that the community had once again sustained us through another crisis.

David Lee Painter: *1984 was a very stressful year for everyone. The production booth at the back of the theater was a plywood shack right at the back of the audience. There were six of us in there for King Lear each night. We had 120 light cues for the show on this little dimmer*

Tom Willmorth, Grock, *Robin Hood.* DBB

L-R, Mark Cuddy, Petruchio; Kirsten Giroux, Kate, *Shrew*. DBB

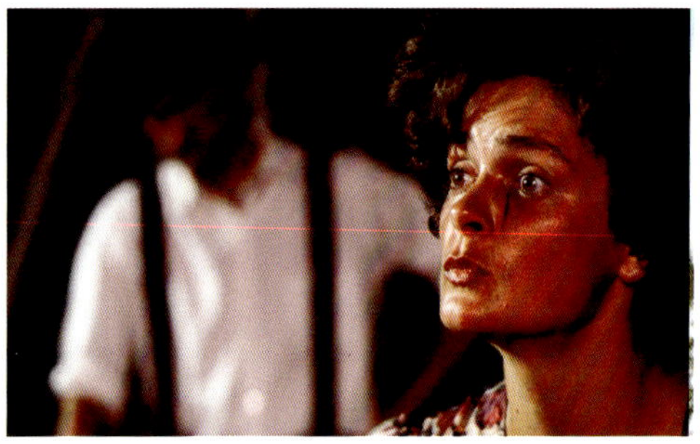

Top to bottom, Allan Batchelder, Biondelo; Tom Willmorth, Tronio; Doug Copsey, Pedant, *Shrew*. DBB

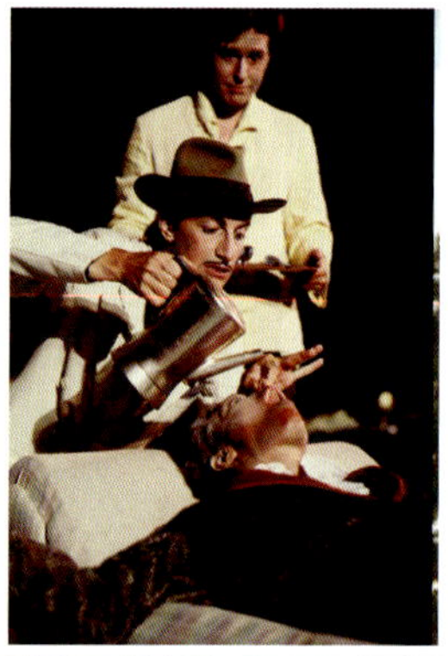

The Taming of the Shrew. DBB

board and 116 sound cues which were played on a boom box, so we're talking really primitive. And the six of us decided that on the last night of the production we would do naked-in-the-booth night. Shortly after intermission, at a prescribed, unspoken moment, we all disrobed and the rest of the night we were naked in the booth. It was like our own silent comment on the difficulty of that season.

Tim McDonough, *King Lear*. DBB

That fall, Chuck Robertson stepped down as Board President after shepherding the company through a tumultuous and trying year, agreeing to stay on as an advisor to the board. But an equally traumatic time lay ahead, and other board members were reluctant to follow in his rather large footsteps. When Mark asked if I would take on a fourth term as President, I agreed, but we all knew it would take the best efforts of each and every one of us to keep the Festival going. There was much to be done, not the least of which was addressing the "income gap" caused by the expense of having to move to a new theater twice in the space of three years. Unfortunately that gap was not going to be an easy one to close.

There were changes in the staff as well. After only one year, Ron Wachholtz moved on, and in his place Mark proposed that the board hire a full-time Development Director to organize and oversee fund raising efforts. By October, Vangie Osborn was hired for that position, Ore-Ida signed another lease for the following year, and Mark's title changed to Producing Director.

Mark Cuddy: *The move to ParkCenter almost felt as though we were starting over, or at least the beginning of some new era with all new challenges. Even though there was tremendous continuity with some of the actors and some of the people around the Festival, and certainly the audience, I remember a real sense at ParkCenter of beginning something. In a lot of ways it didn't feel like we were building off of Main Street Bistro or Ray's Oasis, and not even off of the Plantation, because it was such a new location. It was like plopping down in the middle of another country. Boom. My first year at the Plantation was building upon what had been built there. ParkCenter was a whole new ball game. It was a different part of town, it was really exposed, it wasn't hidden behind a shopping center. It felt like it was really higher stakes.*

L-R, Tony Carreiro, Edmund; Tom Willmorth, Oswald; Kirsten Giroux, Goneril, *King Lear*. DBB

Top to bottom, Wayne Cote, Edgar; Peter Giffen, Earl of Gloucester, *King Lear*. DBB

1985

Mike Murie, cover design.

The Costume Crew.

Vangie Osborn: *When I went to work there they had no staff. It was just Mark, and Pam Hawley had just started as the administrative assistant. Everyone else had left at the end of the season. And then a couple of weeks later, Mark left to do Taming of the Shrew back in Boston. So Pam and I are both new, the phone is ringing off the hook, people are yelling at us about owing them money. The files were a disaster. It was a mess. They didn't need a Development Director, they needed somebody to manage it, and that's what I really ended up doing. I mean, I was not a theater person so it was like, why am I doing this?*

She may not have been a "theater person," but in many ways, Vangie was exactly what the Festival needed at that time. Company members had all been paid, but community businesses were once again asked to carry the debt load created by our nomadic ways since departing One Capital Center. Becoming

The Play: ***The Two Gentlemen of Verona***
Director: Roberta Levitow
Scenic Design: Mike Baltzell
Costume Design: Deborah Trout
Lighting Design: Jim Henderson
Sound: David Miller

The Play: ***Richard III***
Director: Robert Clare
Scenic Design: Jeffrey Hunt
Costume Design: Deb Brunneaux
Lighting Design: Katherine Mason
Sound: David Miller

The Play: ***The Winter's Tale***
Director: Mark Cuddy
Set Design: Jim Campbell
Costume Design: Star Moxley
Lighting Design: Barb Feige
Sound: David Miller

The Play: ***Waiting for Godot***
Director: Vincent Murphy
Set Design: Jeffrey Hunt
Costume Design: Star Moxley
Lighting Design: Jeffrey Hunt

L-R, Pam Hawley, Office Manager; Vangie Osborn, Development Director. UK

R, Tedd McClellan, Gill Redcap; Dan Peterson, Constable Watt;
y Wilcox, Diccon Cruikshank, *Robin Hood.* DBB

a board member now came with the unofficial pre-requisite of agreeing to sign as a guarantor on bank loans for which there was no money to pay off. Some non-board members were even persuaded to sign on just to help keep the Festival going. Vangie's arrival shifted everyone's focus from the euphoria of a successful season in a new theater to the fact that the very life of the company was in jeopardy.

Vangie Osborn: *I mean, when you walk in and they have three desks and two of them are propped up with bricks... We borrowed a typewriter from Morrison Knudsen*

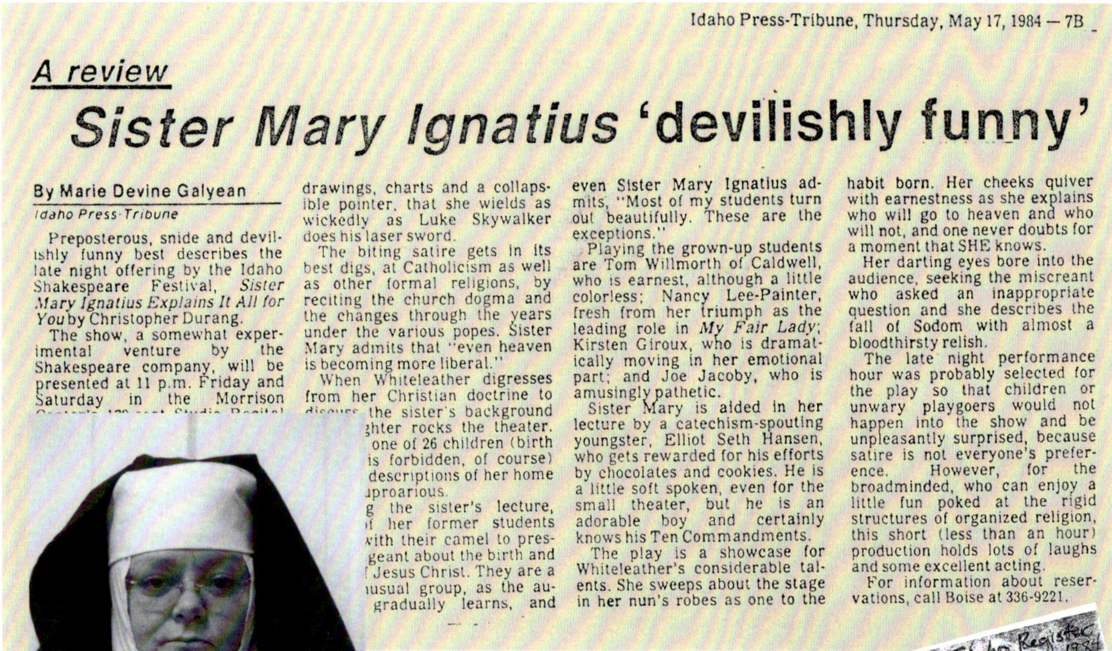

Idaho Press-Tribune, Thursday, May 17, 1984 — 7B

A review

Sister Mary Ignatius 'devilishly funny'

By Marie Devine Galyean
Idaho Press-Tribune

Preposterous, snide and devilishly funny best describes the late night offering by the Idaho Shakespeare Festival, *Sister Mary Ignatius Explains It All for You* by Christopher Durang.

The show, a somewhat experimental venture by the Shakespeare company, will be presented at 11 p.m. Friday and Saturday in the Morrison [illegible]

drawings, charts and a collapsible pointer, that she wields as wickedly as Luke Skywalker does his laser sword.

The biting satire gets in its best digs, at Catholicism as well as other formal religions, by reciting the church dogma and the changes through the years under the various popes. Sister Mary admits that "even heaven is becoming more liberal."

When Whiteleather digresses from her Christian doctrine to discuss the sister's background [...]ghter rocks the theater. [...] one of 26 children (birth [...] is forbidden, of course) [...] descriptions of her home [...]uproarious.

[...]g the sister's lecture, [...]f her former students [...]with their camel to pres[...]geant about the birth and [...] Jesus Christ. They are a [...]usual group, as the au[...] gradually learns, and

even Sister Mary Ignatius admits, "Most of my students turn out beautifully. These are the exceptions."

Playing the grown-up students are Tom Willmorth of Caldwell, who is earnest, although a little colorless; Nancy Lee-Painter, fresh from her triumph as the leading role in *My Fair Lady*; Kirsten Giroux, who is dramatically moving in her emotional part; and Joe Jacoby, who is amusingly pathetic.

Sister Mary is aided in her lecture by a catechism-spouting youngster, Elliot Seth Hansen, who gets rewarded for his efforts by chocolates and cookies. He is a little soft spoken, even for the small theater, but he is an adorable boy and certainly knows his Ten Commandments.

The play is a showcase for Whiteleather's considerable talents. She sweeps about the stage in her nun's robes as one to the habit born. Her cheeks quiver with earnestness as she explains who will go to heaven and who will not, and one never doubts for a moment that SHE knows.

Her darting eyes bore into the audience, seeking the miscreant who asked an inappropriate question and she describes the fall of Sodom with almost a bloodthirsty relish.

The late night performance hour was probably selected for the play so that children or unwary playgoers would not happen into the show and be unpleasantly surprised, because satire is not everyone's preference. However, for the broadminded, who can enjoy a little fun poked at the rigid structures of organized religion, this short (less than an hour) production holds lots of laughs and some excellent acting.

For information about reservations, call Boise at 336-9221.

Carole Whiteleather, Sister Mary. UK

Idaho Register June 1984

Mary Ignatius' called 'vicious tirade'

The Idaho [...] it was recommende[d ...] "religious renegades," I offered to see the production and review it for *The Idaho Register*. I wanted to find [...]

against it elsewhere.

But then, the play was being staged at the prestigious new Morrison Center on the Boise State University campus. Surely it would not permit a performance so rancorous as suggested by the League. What's more, the play is presented by the Idaho Shakespeare Festival, [...]

ship: Christ — then His Mother and Joseph. Frenzied and rabid, it leaves nothing undefiled. The play is an exercise of sheer, unrelenting hatred.

After some 40 minutes into this shameless little skit, I saw that my wife's eyes were brimming with tears, and we left. Having read the [...]

time of respect for social and religious pluralism?

Dark, sullen minds — clouded by a glazed hate — were once kept in check by a social consensus of decency and good-will. There used to be a lot of fretting about the "thin veneer of civilization". Well, by the intentions of this play, that decency, good-will and thin veneer is no more. It's back to bedsheets and torches.

While Americans have sometimes suffered discord over serious questions earnestly posed, they have always held tightly to the ethic encapsulated by the phrases "fair play" and "good sportsmanship." Americans have always prided themselves as good neighbors. In our town, these ideals are the final fallen victims of "Sister Mary Ignatius."

L-R, Russell Sommers, Sheriff of Nottingham; Doug Copsey, *Robin Hood*. UK

through Dick McChrystal and, well you know I exaggerate but I swear we only had one stapler and we all shared it.

The first step was to take out another loan, which board member Neal Hundt arranged. Then Vangie and Mark locked horns on the proposed budget for the 1985 season. Because of the move, the previous season had been shortened, and Mark felt that with a full season and the success of the new theater they could double the size of the audience. Vangie thought that was simply unrealistic. A compromise was reached, cuts were made, and they decided to re-mount *Robin Hood* for one week to kick off the season in the hopes that people would want to see the hit show again.

The re-mount idea sparked another fund raising possibility. Why not do the same thing with *Sister Mary Ignatius Explains It All For You*, the big hit from the successful spring trio of productions held at the Morrison Center the year before? The board agreed, so Carole Whiteleather and crew were brought back for another run, this time at The Flicks in downtown Boise.

Reviews were once again positive and supportive of the show, but this time they brought a stern rebuttal from a local State Representative. His suggestion in a letter to *The Statesman* that all federal and state funding for the Shakespeare Festival be withdrawn as punishment for producing such a "vicious tirade against the Catholic Church," sparked a storm of responses, pro and con, that played out in the media for some time after the show closed. Ironically the Festival was not receiving any taxpayer dollars whatsoever at the time other than individual donations from individual supporters, and we actually experienced a spike in contributions as a result of all the publicity. Ticket sales likewise soared, and though our first real controversy was not pleasant, the incident resulted in a small bright spot for our fund raising efforts.

Vangie Osborn: *It was pretty rocky that first year. There wasn't even money to meet payroll. We had several board members step up and help with some of the debt, and Pam Hawley and I became the masters of*

le but the wood, no assembly but horn-beasts. But what though? Courage! As
y a man has good horns, and knows no end of them. Well, that is the dowry of his

in-kind donations. Mark and the designers would give us lists of what they needed and we would just call people and ask them to donate stuff. Corporate contributions directors had pretty much written us off as dead, but we weren't.

Indeed, the wheel keeps on turning, and as sure as the swallows return to Capistrano, the family of ISF actors, designers and directors began to return to their summer home for another season of Shakespeare under the stars. There were faces which had been familiar to Boise audiences for many years, like Dan Peterson, Stitch Marker, Carole Whiteleather and Jay Sherlock, but with them came an assortment of new faces, as our Shakespeare family tree continued to sprout new branches.

One of those was the Stage Manager for Mark's reprise as Petruchio in the Boston re-mount of Tim McDonough's 1984 *The Taming of the Shrew*. During the course of that productions, one thing led to another and romance blossomed. Not long after Mark returned to Boise, the Festival had a new Associate Producer.

Christine Selian: *I'll never forget that he called me July 4th from a pay phone at a 7-11. I thought that was so romantic. I didn't know where Idaho was and here he was asking me to move out there. I came from Theater Works in Boston, which was very experimental, but Idaho was incredible. We were in a new theater, doing such new stuff, and one night I was managing the house when this lady walked out of the theater. I went up and asked her if there was a problem. "I've never been so offended," she says. I thought, this is Robin Hood, what could be so bad? Well that whole fart scene completely and totally offended her. I wanted to kiss her, because where I came from...farts? That's what you're so offended about? Ok, that's great.*

Recognizing the importance of box office to the company's bottom line, Mark decided to push the envelope and try another first – increasing our summer repertory to four shows. And he continued his experiments with non-Shakespeare plays as well. In addition to the re-mount of *Robin Hood*, he brought Vinnie Murphy back to direct Samuel Beckett's *Waiting for Godot*, which Murphy calls "a deliberately enigmatic play in which Beckett both wants and allows us to speculate on the nature of relationships."

Christine Selian, Associate Producer. DBB

"Breaking the Shakespeare Barrier"

July 6 "Will The Real Richard The Third Please Stand Up"
Robert Clare —
Royal Shakespeare Company.

July 13 "Beckett's Life of Silence and Murmurings"
Dr. Susan Brienza — UCLA

July 20 "Is Shakespeare Overrated?"
Dr. Ken Sanderson
Boise State University

July 27 "Spring Myth and Summer Magic in THE WINTER'S TALE"
Dr. Lawrence Eilenberg
San Francisco State Univ...

August 3 "How Nothing Happen...
WAITING FOR GODOT...
Dr. Cathering Burkman...
Ohio State University

All seminars are Saturdays at 3 p.m. and a... Restaurant in the Eighth Street Marketplace. C... informal, air-conditioned and free!

"Breaking the Shakespeare Barrier" is funded by... from the Association for the Humanities in Id...

Jeff Ware, Vladimir, Waiting for Godot. DBB

Jeff Ware, Vladimir, *Godot.* DBB

Another branch sprouted a grant from the Idaho Humanities Council for a series of Sunday afternoon lectures that brought in experts from around the country to discuss each of the summer shows at space generously provided by the Cedars Restaurant in the 8th Street Marketplace. Dr. Catherine Burkman from Ohio State University came in to discuss *Godot*, and since her talk didn't begin until 3:00 PM, Mark offered to show her a little of the countryside that morning. Along with Associate Producer Christine Selian and actor Al Oliver, two more new company faces, he began what he thought would be a nice, scenic drive up to Bogus Basin.

Mark Cuddy: *Someone had told me that a pretty way down was to go through the parking lot and take the road down the back side of the mountain, so we did that. But that eventually became a dirt road, and then it became a path, and we were clearly in the middle of nowhere. We had to back all the way up the path and finally got back to the Bogus parking lot about the time we were supposed to be at the Cedars for her talk. So I just drove like a madman down that hill. The poor woman was just white from the experience. We arrived about 45 minutes late and there were all these people, still waiting. They had all just started talking among themselves and agreed that this was just part of the talk – that Waiting for Godot was about waiting.*

Still, the season mostly belonged to the Bard. Mark picked *The Winter's Tale*, one of Shakespeare's more obscure "romance" plays, to direct. Roberta Levitow, whom Mark knew from his days at the Denver Center, and Robert Clare, a British actor who had toured the U.S. with the Royal

L-R, Dan Peterson, Estragon; Jeff Ware, Vladimir, *Godot.* DBB

Shakespeare Company but was doing his first work as a director in America, directed *The Two Gentlemen of Verona* and *The Tragedy of Richard III*, respectively. It was the second time around for *Two Gents*, which we produced in our second season, but *Richard* brought to the ISF stage, for the first time, one of the most notorious villains in all of theater.

The same was true backstage. Tim Ocel, took the Production Manager reins from ISF veteran David Painter, who had enchanted audiences as an actor since his first appearance as one of the Duke's Pages in our first production of *Two Gents* in 1978, when he was a high school intern. Likewise, three of the costume

Chasee Clayton, Mamillius; Allen Oliver, Leontes, *Winter's Tale*. DBB

***The Winter's Tale*. DBB**

designers were here for the first time. The fourth, Star Moxley, added to her growing list of ISF designs with *Winter's Tale*. But Star had been busy outside ISF as well.

Star Moxley: *When Eloise (Bruce) kicked off Idaho Theater for Youth I did the very first production and that started a long relationship. I did so many for ITY in those early years I can't even tell you what they were. Then about 1985 I thought it was time to figure out a different way of making a living. Even when I wasn't designing I always volunteered and sewed. I loved the freedom of that, to be able to actually stitch all summer and not be an employee. Having schlepped around all those clothes for so many years and seeing them get lost and damaged, I finally said, "Ok, there are a lot of costumes floating around everywhere in this town and no one has access to them and no one can take care of them. So I kind of cooked up the idea of The Costume Shop to make the best of both worlds.*

Her new business quickly became a clearing house for costumes of all kinds, and continues to be a primary repository and supplier for ISF costumes along with those of many other arts organizations in the area.

Meanwhile, the evolution of the company continued with Mark casting our first African American actors. Bob Devin Jones came up from Sacramento to take on the role of Pozzo in *Godot* and Polixenes, King of Bohemia in *Winter's Tale*, opposite Allen Oliver, another of Mark's acquaintances from Boston, who would play the lead role – Leontes, King of Sicilia. There was some trepidation with the casting choice because of a kiss between Leontes and his white Queen, played by Kate Levy.

Mark Cuddy: *I had this vision of the two kings being African friends, but hot-tempered warlords, and when Al kissed a white woman on stage, we had people walk out of the theater. Ironically, he had a white girlfriend in Idaho.*

Bob Jones also played Speed, in *Two Gents*, and when director Roberta Levitow wanted to use a live dog as Crab, they held dog

Allen Oliver, Launce; Micki, Crab, *Two Gents*. DBB

auditions. That particular item caught the attention of Entertainment Tonight, and ISF made national television that summer. Rehearsals went smoothly with the dog, but Bob was a little worried about his on-stage partner once the theater became filled with audience

Outlaw Gang, *Two Gents.* DBB

L-R, Stitch Marker, Edward IV; Bob Devin Jones, Lord Hastings, *Richard III.* DBB

members sitting just a few feet away. Little Micki proved to be a trooper, though, and performed her role like a true professional.

Micki wasn't the only animal in the company that summer. Roberta set her production in the Wild West of 1870 when the Civil War is over and Idaho Territory has just been annexed by the Union. Naturally that called for some fancy gunplay, good fights, and, of course, horses. Micheal Baltzell's first set design for ISF was true to form, as were Joseph McNally's fist fights, and every time the huge palomino galloped in from stage left, it brought the house down.

Micheal Baltzell: *I sort of designed something before, when we did The Curate Shakespeare As You Like It, but that wasn't really a full-blown design, it was more like gathering props. And I did some ITY building up to that. You know how it is, you're sitting around and they go, "Will you paint?" "Here, why don't you do this?" then, ten years later, you go, "How the hell did I get into this?"*

Mark Cuddy: *Before Two Gents, Mike was our Mister Gadget guy. He always came up with the oddest things. We'd need something South African or something and he'd go find it. He was very resourceful. He's also a talented artist, a painter, but he learned theater and set design easily. One person would dabble a bit and then go off and do something else, but he got hooked and stayed with it. That was the thing about ISF, we could take chances like that. The Festival gave so many opportunities to people for projects that in a larger, established theater they couldn't get the chance to do.*

Governor Dirk Kempthorne: *I'll always remember Two Gentlemen of Verona and that western theme. I remember the fight scene where one of the actors ended up in the horse trough, it was just tremendous. We always took our kids when they were small, but also the neighborhood kids. I just don't know how*

Top to bottom, Michael Connor, Proteus; Kevin Bahn, Thurio, *Two Gents.* DBB

many communities anywhere in the world where you have a situation that the neighborhood kids want to go with you to Shakespeare. That kind of creativity, where it's not always just the same period costumes, attracts an audience at a much earlier age. And then you've got them for life.

Richard was the one show that was true to Shakespeare's time, with a dark, brooding set design by Jeff Hunt, lots of chain mail in Deb Brunneaux's costumes, and exciting sword fights designed by director Robert Clare. Russell Sommers, who also re-created Tony Carriero's Sheriff of Nottingham in *Robin Hood* was witty and viscious as Richard, the consummate liar and manipulator. And like the infamous Sheriff, Richard is the man the audience loves to hate.

Russell Sommers, King Richard, *Richard III*. UK

Carole Whiteleather: *As the Duchess of York I had a great scene where I got to curse Richard. It was just the perfect kind of curse, and one night it happened just as a huge dust storm hit. It was blowing so bad we had to stop the show and everybody, audience included, went backstage to hold down the tent that was our dressing rooms. We all just stood there holding that tent until the storm passed, and then we went back out and finished the show. They audience loved it.*

It's a rainout. DBB

Despite the occasional calamity, the community had taken a liking to our new home and it was another successful season, enough so that a dent – albeit a small one – was put in the nagging debt hanging over the Festival's collective heads.

Vangie Osborn: *It started to turn around that first season at ParkCenter with Robin Hood. At least we didn't go further in debt. But the key was that we learned we could do it. It seems like so much happened in such a short period of time. Probably the first three or four years I was there I wasn't sure we were going to survive day to day. But the Shakespeare Festival always seems to pick itself up by its bootstraps and just move on, no matter what happens. It was always just like: it doesn't matter, we'll survive it. I don't believe it was anything significant that brought us back around, just year after year we got smarter. We did better at the box office, we became much more organized, the corporations really started kicking in. The Festival had enough support to keep it alive and some of the right people helping them at the time to keep it going.*

Mark Cuddy makes the announcement. DBB

Further testament to the community's loyalty came in the strange, but useful, form of garbage bags. Summer in Boise is pretty much a dry season, but there is always the occasional sprinkle or thunderstorm. Audiences, realizing, that these rarely last more than a few minutes, always stuck it out, and the show went on, but there were always those who were unprepared for inclement weather and left. On one such damp evening someone thought of passing out garbage bags to the audience and telling them to punch holes in them for their head and arms. It's a tradition that began back in the One Capital Center days, and exactly whose idea it was remains a mystery, but it has since become an official policy of the Festival.

Tom Willmorth: *And the other policy is that you can't go on stage in certain costumes when it's raining because they could be permanently damaged. So as you exit out of a scene in a light rain the costume people take your costumes and send you back out there in street clothes. You're acting to beat the band wearing a rain slicker, and the audience, in their garbage bag tunics, goes right along with it.*

Ten years are spent since first we undertook this cause. Titus Andonicus, I, i.

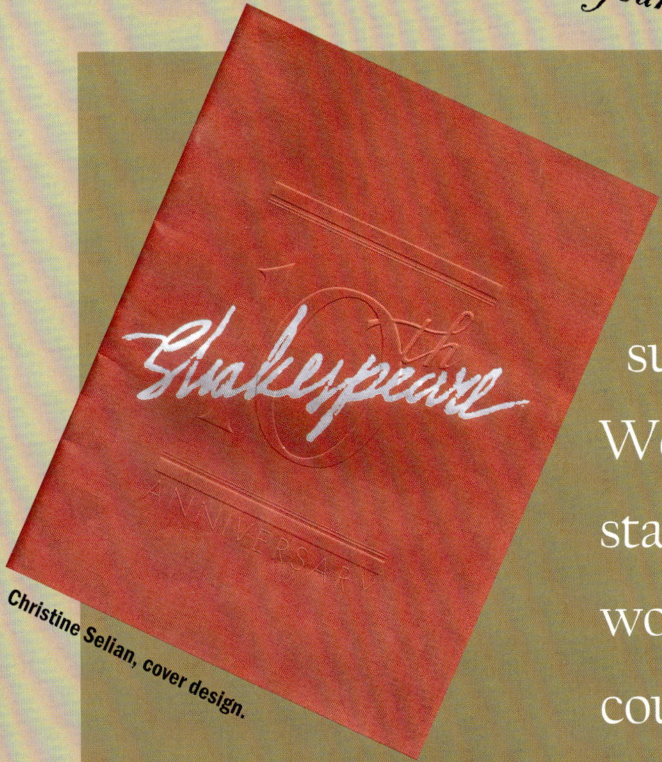

Christine Selian, cover design.

DBB

1986 was a year of surprises. For starters, virtually everyone was surprised that it was the tenth season. We had all just assumed that since we started in 1977 our 10th Anniversary would be 1987, so nobody bothered to count them up until plans for the season were being made. Indeed, there were those who were surprised we had made it that far.

Bitsy Bidwell: *Ten years ago I was one of those people who said, "This Shakespeare thing is really great, it's a shame it will never last." It's a pleasure to be able to celebrate the tenth season by designing costumes for A Midsummer Night's Dream.*

That quote from her program bio summed up the feelings of many people, both in the company and in the community. But we had survived, and with this milestone

The Play: ***A Midsummer Night's Dream***
Director: Mark Cuddy
Costume Design: Bitsy Bidwell
Lighting Design: Jeffrey Hunt
Sound: Tom Coatey
Music Composed by Joseph Weisnewski

The Play: ***Pendragon***
Director: Andrew Traister
Scenic Design: Michael Baltzell
Costume Design: Frances Kenny
Lighting Design: Tom Coatey

The Play: ***Othello***
Director: Vincent Murphy
Scenic Design: Philip W. Atlakson
Costume Design: Matty Shafer
Lighting Design: Tom Coatey
Sound: Joseph Weisnewski

The Play: ***All's Well That Ends Well***
Director: Paul Frellick
Scenic Design: Scott Beseman
Costume Design: Ted Bernard
Lighting Design: Shaun Sites
Sound: Joseph Weisnewski

1986

Early morning warm-ups start the day for ISF members.

Steve Matt as Othello rehearses fight with John Rice's Iago.

Othello and floating the river brought Vinnie Murphy back

Dan Peterson: *I'm playing Bottom, and we're rehearsing the Pyramus and Thisbe thing in the play-within-a-play. One of the great things about Cuddy was that you felt free, you felt allowed to do these kinds of things, and when we got to that scene I started singing and it turned into this big opera. It was one of those things that doesn't happen very often, where the actor and the director have notions that instantly bond, and you say, that's it!*

Dan Peterson, Bottom, *Midsummer.* DBB

marking our third season at the ParkCenter site, things were finally beginning to look up again.

Mark thought that giving the Festival a winter presence of some sort would help add to the coffers as well, and when Vangie mentioned an idea for a Christmas show suggested by Roberta Levitow, he approached Carole Whiteleather about producing something for the holiday season. She took some old Christmas stories she found, added a few Chrismtas carols, and offered a series of short shows that were perfect for company or private Christmas parties, or gatherings of any kind.

That idea worked so well, he decided to try something in the spring as well. The Idaho Humanities Council declined to fund his "Breaking the Shakespeare Barrier" series that year, suggesting instead that we try a tour. Taking a cue from the success of Idaho Theater for Youth he began bringing an abbreviated Shakespeare play to high schools around the area, with the help of the Idaho Humanities Council. He called the tour *Shakespearience*, and included question and answer sessions after each performance. It was a hit with students and teachers alike, and plans were immediately begun to continue the tradition the following year.

To mark the end of ISF's first decade, Mark led off the summer season with *A Midsummer Night's Dream*, the very first play we produced that inaugural season at One Capital Center. Victoria Holloway and I co-directed that original production, and her return to ISF for the first time since directing *Merry Wives* in 1983 was as a member of the acting company – playing Helena. This time Mark directed, and he was kind enough to cast me as Oberon, the same role I played ten years earlier and one of my favorites, with Carole Whiteleather playing a delightful Titania, and company mainstay Tom Willmorth as Puck.

The set consisted of two stairways descending to the stage from a platform above. Midway down each of them was small landing where the stairs changed angles, and each night as Puck and I approached a sleeping Titania I would jump from the top platform to the landing, then continue down the stairs. One night, the upper set of stairs was jarred loose from the landing and swung free. I continued with the scene, thinking the stage crew would just put it back in place.

L-R, Tom Willmorth, Puck; Doug Copsey, Oberon, *Midsummer.* DBB

Carole Whiteleather: *One of my favorite memories from that show is having my youngest son, Benjamin, play the Changeling Boy that Oberon was trying to get from Titania. At one point Mark wanted him to jump from the top platform into the arms of the fairies about ten feet below, and I was just like, "No Mark, that's not going to happen."*

Benjamin Whiteleather, Changeling Boy, *Midsummer.*

Tom Willmorth: *An entire bridge was broken. Nobody could travel up and down those stairs and we had too much staging built around those step units. Tim Ocel, the stage manager, who looked more like an alien than we did with his radio headset, strolled between us to inform the audience that we were going to stop the show, repair the steps and then continue. What were we supposed to do, drop character? He walked away and I turned to the audience and said, "Just sit back and drink your tea, we shall at Red Robin be." That's my story and I'm sticking to it.*

Victoria Holloway, Helena, *Midsummer.* DBB

Sprites, *Midsummer.* DBB

Dan Peterson: *End of the show one night, just a few lines left, I think Theseus is speaking. I wish I could remember what he's saying, but it's nice. We were all sitting down along the apron of the stage and we were all supposed to look out over the audience as he was speaking. I was just kind of leaning back on my elbows and looking up. The moon was full. It was just like it was meant to be. I remember telling myself, remember this. Remember this. Always remember this moment. To be there in that place and remember.*

The rest of the season was filled out with two Shakespeare plays we had never produced at ISF – *Othello* and *All's Well That Ends Well*, and a fourth show that had never been produced anywhere. The incredible success of *Robin Hood* inspired Mark to commission another script from playwright Don Nigro which came to be called *Pendragon*.

Mark Cuddy: *Just like the company before I came, we were always trying new productions and new concepts. It became a conceptual festival for a while. There was a feeling that you could try a lot of things. There was this whole Basque community in Boise so I had this idea for some kind of Basque romance. I asked Don to do some research, but his particular take on things was not to do something historical, and it didn't go down too well.*

L-R, Rick Robertson, Snout; Tedd McClellan, Flute; Lucas McClure, Starveling; Paul Frediani, Snug; Jay Sherlock, Peter Quince, *Midsummer.* DBB

Despite turning out to be somewhat less than the Basque romance it was billed, *Pendragon's* historical Boise references made it popular with audiences. *Midsummer* was the big hit of the season, no doubt for sentimental reasons. *All's Well*, under Paul Frellick's direction, saw Mark take the stage again as Parolles, but *Othello*, directed by Vinnie Murphy, proved to be one of the most successful tragedies we had produced to date, thanks in no small part to Steve Matt's powerful Othello, Victoria's wonderful Desdemona, and John Rice's stellar performance as Iago, all of which were aided by yet another of Matty Shafer's stunning costume designs.

Steve Matt and Victoria Holloway, *Othello.* DBB

Matty Shafer: *I loved designing Othello because I got to do it in a kind of contemporary mode, and when it was over, everybody wanted to buy their costumes. I was really honored by that.*

All's well with Shakespeare's dark comedy

Play review

By JEANETTE ROSS
Special to The Idaho Statesman

Shakespeare may have planted a toad or two in his garden of proverbs when he named this play, but I didn't see any warts — all's well on stage for the Idaho Shakespeare Festival's fourth show this summer.

A strong-willed director and the pick of the summer's acting crop have combined to reap a rich bounty in this production of *All's Well That Ends Well.*

C. Whiteleather
. . . a born countess

A collaborating artistic staff has ably supported Director Paul Frellick in turning one of the Bard's darker plays into a coherent comedy. Frellick imagines this play to be a conflict

off to Court! and then to War! to win fame and fortune. Meanwhile, the girl Helena (Judi Dickerson) must find a way to win his hand and his love. This fairy tale opening is emphasized with banners and music that change from bright innocent to a much darker hue when Bertram and Helena meet the real worlds of war and love.

Just as the background setting is engineered by designer Scott Beseman, the sound is much more than music in the hands of Joseph Weisnewski. So the audience is carried easily through complexities of plot and language.

As is too often the case, the young lovers aren't as interesting as they could be; Helena appears to have only Bertram on her mind, and Bertram, despite some sweetening up, is still rather crass.

Because of Frellick's choice of emphasis, the adults are much more than minor players. And given the quality of the actors, that's fine with me. Carole Whiteleather looks like

Clothes, music help set the stage

How do you present a play about two mismatched lovers for whom none of the verities work? In this play, even the title is ironic, and even though all seems well for a few moments, we are out of fairyland into the real world and the end can only be another beginning.

When costume designer Ted Bernard learned what director Paul Frellick had in mind for *All's Well That Ends Well*, he had to repack his bags and leave the lace and other pretty notions behind. In most Shakespeare comedies, the complications, confusion and misunderstandings seem closer to the author's own vision than the happy endings, which seem to be slapped on to suit prevailing taste.

In this play, cynicism is a deep dye that seeps through many characters and much action. Paul Frellick and his artistic staff explained how they dealt with this problematic play in the fourth part of the "Breaking the Shakespeare Barrier" series for the Idaho Shakespeare Festival.

The play has two major problems, Frellick pointed out. We see little to convince us that young Bertram deserves Helena's devotion. And the play ironies tracing through the play threaten to sabotage the apparent comedy. "I could imagine the actors coming out and sticking out their tongues" rather than taking bows, Frellick said.

The easy way out would be the way the play has been most often performed before, shining a light on the prince of flash, Parolles, and on his comeuppance, which is full of boffo,

See STAGE, Back Page

trayed by Mark Cuddy) who doesn't know that he's a fool, too, until he trips over his own words once too often.

and Peter Greenberg as the interrogator who does the impossible — getting Parolles to tell the truth.

Highlights: As designer Ted Ber-

top to bottom, John Rice, Iago; Steve Matt, *Othello.* DBB

Vinnie Murphy: *ISF is a gloriously humane institution teeming with daring and care for an audience that knows how to listen. All other Festivals please take note.*

Opening night was filled with local dignitaries, a ribbon ceremony, even a surprise appearance by Idaho resident Carole King who, though she didn't sing for us, stayed for the show and was highly complimentary about the company. Another successful season put a bigger dent in the debt and finally had everyone, the board included, breathing easier. But the surprises weren't over yet.

Mark Cuddy: *I had been out west about seven years, which at that time in my life seemed like a long time. I just wanted to get back east. Christine and I got married at the end of '86, so I pretty much decided that 1987 would be my final season with ISF.*

Such is a life in the arts. The very nature of change is what sustains the creative source. Stability can be stagnating. We must keep moving, seeking new stimulation, or risk stifling the creative urge. On the other hand, the institutions which nurture and support the art we produce must achieve that very stability and continuity or there will be no place for art to be seen by the audiences which complete

L-R, Steve Matt, Othello. John Rice, Iago; Tedd McClellan, John Plummer, Soldiers, *Othello.* DBB

L-R, Dan Peterson, Roderigo; John Rice, Iago, *Othello.* DBB

Judi Dickerson, Emelia, *Othello.* DBB

the equation. This cycle had come full-circle once again for ISF, and like it or not, change was coming at a time when it seemed change was the last thing the company needed.

Vangie Osborn: *It was interesting, you know, because I wanted to leave, too. I had tried to leave like a year earlier, and I didn't. But we couldn't both leave, you know, if you care about the organization. So we both agreed that one of us would have to stay until we got other people in place.*

Michael McCarthy took over as President of the board at the close of the 1986 season with the primary goal of addressing the remaining debt. Now he and his fellow board members were faced with the daunting task of finding a new Artistic Director as well.

Carole Whiteleather, Countess, *All's Well.* DBB

Dan Peterson, Lavatch, *All's Well That Ends Well.* DBB

Costume shop stitchers — Lisa Leftowich Mary Catherine Gilson.

Development Director Vangie Osborn, Publicity Director Trish Elledge, Concessions Manager Jeff Holley and Associate Producer Christine Selian pose with ISF's mascot, Monroe.

1986 Technical Staff: Master Carpenter George Davis, Sound Technician Catherine Mason, Site Manager Shaun Sites and Carpenter Charles Olson.

Keep up your bright swords, for the dew will rust them. Othello I, ii

Doug Copsey, John Rhys, Pendragon. DBB

Dan Peterson, Mark Twain, *Pendragon.* DBB

Mark Cuddy, Parolles, *All's Well.* DBB

Pendragon set design, Michael Baltzell

John Elliott, Teddy Roosevelt, *Pendragon.* DBB

Dennis Chase, cover art.

Fortunately Mark had given plenty of notice – he would remain through the 1987 season. So while Mark put together the first season of a new decade for ISF, a national search was launched for his replacement.

But although ISF was becoming pretty well known throughout the northwest, it was still a relatively new company and did not have the reputation that would attract top tier Artistic Directors. The truth was, our debt situation would most likely dissuade many of the top tier from accepting a position with us in the first place.

Because of the stressful move to ParkCenter in 1984 and potential liability the debt represented, several board members had resigned, and this year the rebuilding process was still going on. Glenn Selander was elected president after only one year on the board, as was his vice-president, Jim Brandstetter. The treasurer that year, Bill Keller, had just joined.

Bill Keller: *I think Vangie knew my wife, Celeste, somehow and she needed a treasurer, so they got together and said,*

1987

Daniel Richards, Helicanus, *Pericles.*

The Play: ***Romeo and Juliet***
Director: Mark Cuddy
Scenic Design: Jenny Guthrie
Costume Design: Michael Chapman
Lighting Design: Tom Coatey
Composer/Sound Design: Joseph Weisnewski

The Play: ***The Comedy of Errors***
Director: Dennis Bigelow
Scenic Design: Jenny Guthrie
Costume Design: Guy A. Beuttler
Lighting Design: Tom Coatey
Composer/Sound Design: Joseph Weisnewski

The Play: ***Pericles***
Director: Paul Frellick
Scenic Design: Micheal Baltzell
Costume Design: Ted Bernard
Lighting Design: Tom Coatey
Composer/Sound Design: Joseph Weisnewski

The Play: ***The Adventures of Sherlock Holmes***
Director: Timothy J. Ocel
Scenic Design: Tom Coatey
Costume Design: Nancy Phillips Berger
Lighting Design: Shaun Sites
Composer/Sound Design: Joseph Weisnewski

"you're it." We were something like $75,000 in debt with no prospects for paying it off. The budget at that time was maybe $250,000 at the most, and to make a profit on that amount would have been enormous. So one of my first jobs was to go around town with Vangie and talk to creditors and tell them we couldn't pay. We compromised a ton of debt with offers of tickets. Some people were pretty supportive, but some of the bridges were burned.

"A little comedy, a little tragedy. A little mystery, a little romance. A little fantasy, a little reality. Hopes fulfilled and dreams shattered. A cycle ends and a new one begins." So read the opening paragraph of Mark's program comments for that summer's four-show season.

Star Moxley: *I loved the Cuddy years because he just took tons of risks. I think he really helped this community mature for that reason. He was flying by the seat of his pants, but he had a talented group of friends along with him and I think it was a real shot in the arm artistically for this town.*

Looking for a way to make the season a little longer, Mark asked Dan to try and find a way to expand on his very successful portrayal of Mark Twain in 1984's *Pendragon*. Working with Cindy Gaede, they developed a two act scenario in which a young Mark Twain and a few friends opened the show, then returned after intermission on Twain's 80th birthday. To keep things in the Shakespeare vein, the show also included a piece of Twain's own, rather bizarre take on *Hamlet*. Produced as a pre-season benefit, *Mark Twain Hisownself* provided a much needed boost to the box office.

Mark Twain Comes to Life on Festival Stage

by Trish Elledge

MARK TWAIN, HISOWNSELF, produced as a pre-season benefit, proved to be a dynamic success for the Idaho Shakespeare Festival, financially as well as artistically.

The production starred Festival veteran Dan Peterson and grew out of a segment of last year's world premiere production of PENDRAGON. The fascination the audience had for Peterson's portrayal of Twain, coupled with the fascination Peterson developed for the character resulted in a creative compilation of wit, anecdotes, asides and just plain old charming *Twainisms.*

Peterson and his director, Cynthia Gaede, said they spent endless hours weeding through what seemed to be endless amounts of material. "There is so much information," sighed Gaede at an early interview when the show had just gone into rehearsal. "In addition to all of the stories and novels that everyone knows about, there are all of his newspaper columns, essays, speeches and letters, plus all of the darker, satirical works and short burlesques.

Neither Gaede nor Peterson were Twain fanatics before initiating the project. However, researching for the production helped each of them develop a special fondness for the man.

"Mounting this show has been an extreme challenge," said Peterson. "It has been of enormous value to have Cindy and her talents working with me."

By using much of the material from Twain's earlier, more obscure work, Peterson and Gaede were able to lend a newer, fresher perspective to the man. They said they wanted their audience to see more of the two sides of Twain, especially since most everyone has read at least some of his stories.

Gaede explained that there was a public and a very private side to Twain (in his later years he became a very bitter man). He "wanted to be accepted

Ever the innovator, he continued to push the envelope even in his last season with ISF, commissioning playwright Mark Rosenwinkel to create *The Adventures of*

Pericles **set design, Michael Baltzell**

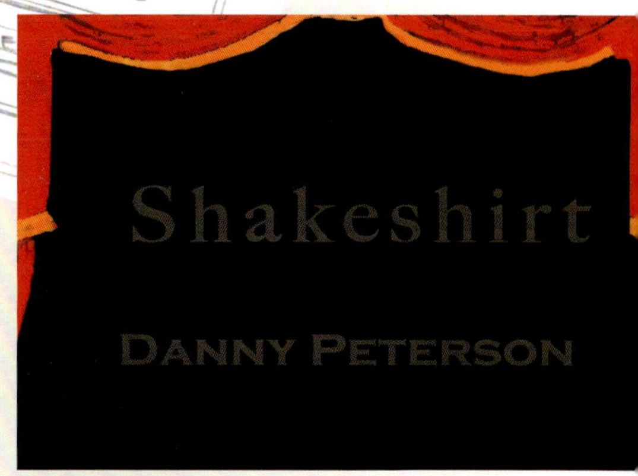

Stan Garner, *Sherlock* DBB

Arthur Glen Hughes, Mr. Nazim, *Sherlock Holmes.* DBB

John Rice, Dr. Moriarty, *Sherlock Holmes.* DBB

Sherlock Holmes. Audiences always love a good mystery, and such was the case with this show, which marked the centennial celebration of Holmes' and Watson's creation by Arthur Conan Doyle in 1887. It also marked the ISF directorial debut of Production Stage Manager Tim Ocel, who masterfully guided Stan Garner as Holmes, and Dan Peterson as Dr. Watson, through the labyrinth of a thrilling murder investigation.

Paul Frellick returned for his fourth season to direct *Pericles*, one of the Bard's later and more obscure plays, believed by many scholars to have been written only in part by Shakespeare, perhaps with the help of a young protégé. Ted Bernard's costumes launched us far into the future, where Tony Carriero's Pericles journeyed to distant planets in search of the answer to a riddle that would win him the hand of Antiochus' daughter.

Pericles costume designs, Ted Bernard.

Dan Peterson: *You could just watch that production run out of money as the evening went on. Act I, scene 1, man it was flashy, it was 25th Century stuff, and by the time you got to the end there were cardboard robots.*

Kevin Connell, Cleon, *Pericles.* DBB

Tony Carriero's return for a second season with ISF marked another first for the company – our first union involvement with Actors' Equity Association.

Mark Cuddy: *It was hard to pull off because the finances were so different than what we were used to paying, but I really thought we needed to take that next step. We were an established, non-Equity company that could bring in*

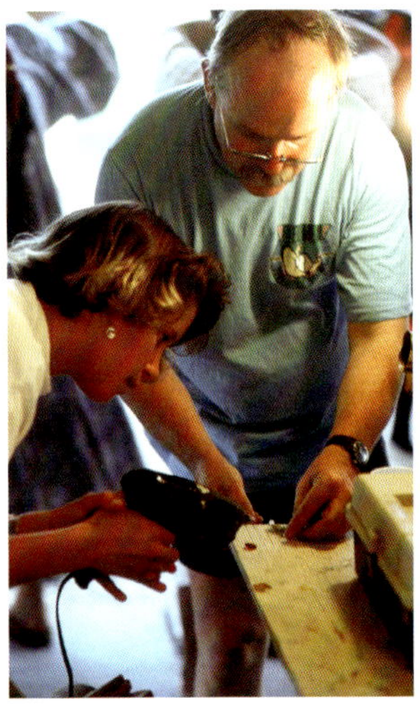

Ted Bernard, Costume Designer, *Pericles.* DBB

Carole Whiteleather, The Knower, *Pericles.* DBB

The role of Gower, which constituted the Chorus, was given another name for this fantastical production.

Carole Whiteleather: *We called it the Knower, but back stage it was known as the Know-it-all. I was a space creature with a large, bald head that was painted gold, and I had painted all these veins in green and aqua all over it. One night it started to rain and I literally started to melt. I had all these green and gold rivers running down across my face and it was really rather funny. But we just kept on going.*

L-R, James Newcomb, Romeo; Jennifer Langsam, Juliet. DBB

Arthur Glen Hughes, Tybalt, R&J. DBB

***Romeo and Juliet*. DBB**

two or three guest artists. Equity was very willing to work with us because they wanted to introduce Equity actors here. I knew those actors, and I knew they would be leaders in the company in a way that would pay off.

In addition to Tony, a second guest artist, Jamie Newcomb, was hired to play Romeo in Mark's production of *Romeo and Juliet*. He brought the audience further back onto familiar ground by bringing Dennis Bigelow up from the Sacramento Theater Company to direct a rousing *Comedy of Errors*. Nearly 20,000 people attended our 11th season, with season ticket sales reaching an all-time high and the list of donors growing yet again – a testament to Mark and Vangie's valiant efforts along with those of the board, to put the company back on an even keel. And through all this, Vangie spearheaded the search for his successor.

Cynthia Gaede, Assistant Director, R&J DBB

Tim Ocel, Director, *Sherlock Holmes* DBB

Vangie Osborn: *We narrowed it down to three people and brought each of them to town. I remember two of them were just not right for us, and then there was Rod Ceballos. No one was particularly enamored of him, but he had done quite a bit of Shakespeare and had some good qualities. And Mark was leaving.*

Glenn Selander's farewell letter for Mark appeared on the first page of that summer's program, and a few pages further in, right under Mark's own comments on his final season, was the announcement of Rod's hiring. Relieved to have that task over with, everyone went back to business as usual and enjoyed the summer season.

...from her handmaid do return this answer: The element itself, till seven years' heat, Shall not behold her face a...
But, like a cloistress, she will veiled walk And water once a day her chamber round With eye-offending bri...

Norman Armour, Dr. Pinch, *Comedy of Errors*. DBB

L-R, Arthur Glen Hughes, Dan Peterson, Dromios, *Comedy*. DBB

Mark Cuddy: My fondest time ever as an Artistic Director was getting hired by Idaho Shakes and coming to that little office in 8th Street Marketplace. It was all cubicles. Jimmy Crowley had an office for Idaho Theater for Youth and there was a desk for Idaho Shakespeare Festival. I arrived in March, 1983 and of course there were no other employees, it was just me. For two months I just worked virtually alone on putting together the whole summer. I remember putting pictures up on the wall and doing the booklets. It was a thrilling time because I really felt I was creating a company that I wanted to create. It wasn't from scratch because it was already there, but it was sort of given to me, I was given this gift. It was like, here you are, go for it. And to be able to just sit in my office for hours looking at resume photos up on the wall, picking a design, and it was great because I could do basically what I wanted. That spring of 1983 was my most thrilling time in the theater.

Guy Beuttler and Sue Trenery, both from Seattle, discuss fabric choices for COMEDY OF ERRORS.

Shakescene

Issue 5, 1987 — Idaho Shakespeare Festival — 211 N 8th St. — Boise, Idaho 83702

..."Thanks & Thanks & Ever Thanks"

By Glen Selander
(Reprinted from '87 Season Program)

Do you remember his burlesque role as Petruchio in TAMING OF THE SHREW? Or his yellow-clad fop in ALL'S WELL THAT ENDS WELL? How about his direction of A MIDSUMMER NIGHT'S DREAM? Or maybe your image is of his bringing the premieres of ROBIN HOOD, PENDRAGON and THE ADVENTURES OF SHERLOCK HOLMES to Boise?

Would you answer as a Festival trustee with a memory of the dynamic producer, always pushing us to believe we could overcome financial debt, produce a better summer season than before and become a major professional summer theater in the region? Mark fits all these visions, doesn't he?

Mark came as artistic director in ... producing di-

SHAKESPEARIENCE program. Audiences have increased from 8,500 in Mark's first year t... 18,000 during our 10th Anniversary a tribute to the high level of profe... sionalism Mark offers himself and the players, directors, and supporti... companies he brings year after ye... He also formalized the apprentice a... intern programs, providing a m... professional experience for th... young actors and actresses. Ma... made the Festival Idaho's only pro... sional theater company.

Behind the scenes, Mark is res... sible for an expanded Board of ... tees, presenting a deeper cross s... of the business and cultural co... nity. He's inspired the Bo... achieve the Festival's first brea... season financially-coincident the 10th Anniversary. Upon ... the Board is dedi...

ROD CEBALLOS

Artistic Director; Director-TITUS ANDRONICUS; Co-Director-AS YOU LIKE IT — **BOISE, ID**

Artistic Director: Shakespeare Festival of Chicago, Drake Theatre Repertory, Shakespeare Festival of Cincinnati; Artistic Coordinator: Lakeside One-Act Festival; Directed: ISF, Virginia Shakespeare Festival, Shakespeare Festival of Chicago, Body Politic Theatre, Williamstown Theatre Festival, Lakeside One-Act Festival, Shakespeare Festival of Cincinnati, Drake Repertory Theatre; MFA Ohio University, Actor Training Program; BA University of California, Santa Barbara, Dramatic Arts.

Lynn Bernisconi, cover art.

Rod Ceballos arrived in Boise toward the end of the season to begin the transition, and the only one who saw the storm clouds brewing on the horizon was Mark.

Vangie Osborn: *Mark and Rod were both here at the same time for a bit and Mark took a dislike to him. He even went to some board members and tried to get Rod ousted before he'd even started. He was obviously right, and I wish we'd all listened to him, but we decided not to and that was a mistake.*

Micheal Baltzell: *My first year was Mark's (Cuddy) first year. I started out as a scenic carpenter, helping out as a scenic artist, and then I turned into the scenic artist. I was sort of fed a design every once in a while, but not as a regular thing. Rod started giving me more and more of a chance, to the point where, actually, for a few years there, I was Tech Director and designing all four shows. That was also the time the shop started growing. He was hiring more people and we went through a string of really bad Tech Directors. We started complaining to Rod about it and he went, "Ok, I'm tired of listening to you guys. Here*

1988

The Play: ***Titus Andronicus***
Director: Rod Ceballos
Scenic Design: Micheal Baltzell
Costume Design: Ted Bernard
Lighting Design: Robert Parsley
Composer/Sound Design: Benjamin Masterton

The Play: ***As You Like It***
Director: William Glover and Rod Ceballos
Scenic Design: Michael Baltzell
Costume Design: Ted Bernard
Lighting Design: Robert Parsley
Composer/Sound Design: Benjamin Masterson

The Play: ***Quilters***
Director: Theresa Larkin
Scenic Design: Michael Baltzell
Costume Design: Guy Beuttler
Lighting Design: Robert Parsley
Music Director: Joseph Weisnewski

The Play: ***Measure for Measure***
Director: Peggy Shannon
Scenic Design: Michael Baltzell
Costume Design: Thom Heyer
Lighting Design: Robert Parsley
Composer/Sound Design: Benjamin Masterton

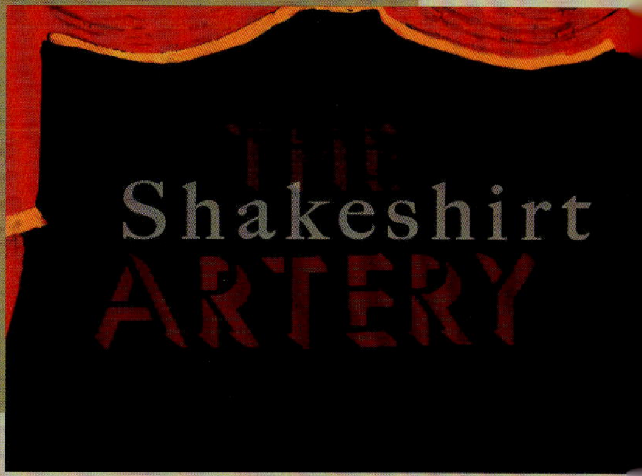

are the resumes, you hire the TD." With Mike Hartwell's help, and Bob Parsley, we had sort of a group thing. I was officially designated TD, but we always worked as a group, figuring things out together, everyone covering everyone else to make sure it's working.

The next three years marked a leveling off period for the Festival's rising star. While the shows maintained their high level of artistic quality, ticket sales dropped off. Rod's style was very different from that which Mark had developed in his five year tenure. Instead of becoming the public face of the Festival and embracing the community, a major part of any Artistic Director's job, Rod chose to immerse himself in directing shows.

Dan Peterson: *For him it seemed like the challenging part of it was the work. How it came out was how it came out. I don't mean to say that he didn't care about the production or anything, but it just seemed like working on the play was more important than the result.*

He began that fall by co-producing *Macbeth* with BSU, in the Morrison Center. It was the first full-length play to be staged in the main hall. David Bogie augmented his annual cast party slide show with a documentary film of the production which aired locally on KTVB, Channel 7 the following June. Then he kicked off the 1988 outdoor season with another Morrison Center production, *What the Butler Saw*, performed in Stage II that June. In addition, the spring tour of Shakespearience toured schools throughout the state for eleven weeks, playing to over 23,000 students and teachers, nearly doubling the audience of the 1987 tour.

Rod Ceballos (1988): *This has been a year of new ventures for the Festival. Audiences seem genuinely excited about the Festival and growth of the arts in Boise and Idaho. We are all responsible for this growth, both artist and audience alike. I look forward to participating in that growth and to being a part of the community in which the Idaho Shakespeare Festival was born and continues to be warmly embraced.*

The outdoor season that year included the Festival's first musical to be staged outdoors – Molly Newman and Barbara Damashek's *Quilters*, directed by Theresa Larkin. With Carole Whiteleather in the lead role, and Stitch Marker taking on the lone male part, this touching collection of stories, song and dances celebrating the spirit of pioneer women brought rave reviews from the audience and press alike.

Theresa Larkin, Director, *Quilters.* DBB

***Quilters.*DBB**

-le but the wood, no assembly but horn-bea... As
...y a man has good horns, and knows no en...

Carole Whiteleather: *I still have people come up to me and say, "Oh, I remember Quilters." I think because it was so western in its sensibilities, so much about what it was like to come across the West, that it hit people here very strongly. We still had the low fence around the back of the theater then, and the last night of that production the whole ISF company came and stood all around the back, leaning on the fence at the closing of the show. It was wonderful.*

Carole Whiteleather, Sarah Bonham, *Quilters.* DBB

Elizabeth Kelly, Phebe, *As You Like It.* DBB

Carol Whiteleather, Mistress Overdone, *Measure for Measure.* DBB

Susan Mundell, Celia, *As You Like It.* DBB

Tom Kelly, Orlando, *As You Like It.* DBB

L-R, Karen Fuller, Juliet; Mikel McDonald, Vincentio, *Measure.* DBB

rom her handmaid do return this answer: The element itself, till seven years' heat, Shall not behold her face a
But, like a cloistress, she will veiled walk And water once a day her chamber round With eye-offending bri

Peggy Shannon directed *Measure for Measure* while Rod co-directed *As You Like It* with William Glover, and took on the bloody drama, *Titus Andronicus*, by himself. However, when it came to making contact with the community and participating in fund raising activities, Rod chose to bow out.

Scott Olson, Chiron, *Titus.* DBB

L-R, David Painter, Demetrius; Scott Olson, Chiron; A. Bernard Cummings, Aaron; Sandra Lindberg, Tamora, *Titus.* DBB

Titus Andronicus. DBB

A. Bernard Cummings, Aaron, *Titus.* DBB

Tereasa Guy and Steve Welsh, cover art.

DBB

The business of the Festival continued apace. Personalities and job descriptions aside, the first year with a new Artistic Director had gone well. But a peek at the Administration section of the 1989 program revealed the storm clouds had not dissipated.

There, for the first time in the Festival's history, the General Manager took top billing over the Artistic Director. It was a subtle signal that the direction and mood of ISF was undergoing a change.

Vangie Osborn: *We all know the Artistic Director is way more than the plays and the company, it's the face of the community. And Rod just couldn't do it, and wouldn't do it. He didn't have the right personality.*

L-R, Jeana McClure, Office Manager; Maria Lewis, Concessions; Vangie Osborn, General Manager; Robin Smith, Publicity. DBB

The Play: ***Much Ado About Nothing***
Director: Douglas Jacobs
Scenic Design: Micheal Baltzell
Costume Design: Ted Bernard
Lighting Design: Robert Parsley
Musical Director: Susan Nelson Phillips
Sound: Benjamin Masterton

The Play: ***Waiting for the Parade***
Director: Penny Metropulos
Scenic Design: Micheal Baltzell
Costume Design: Guy Auguste Beuttler
Lighting Design: Robert Parsley
Sound: Benjamin Masterton

The Play: ***King Richard the Second***
Director: Kenneth Kelleher
Scenic Design: Micheal Baltzell
Costume Design: Pamela Davis
Lighting Design: Robert Parsley
Sound: Joseph Weisnewski

1989

The Play: ***Troilus and Cressida***
Director: Rod Ceballos
Scenic Design: Micheal Baltzell
Costume Design: Lisa Vollrath
Lighting Design: Robert Parsley
Sound: Joseph Weisnewski

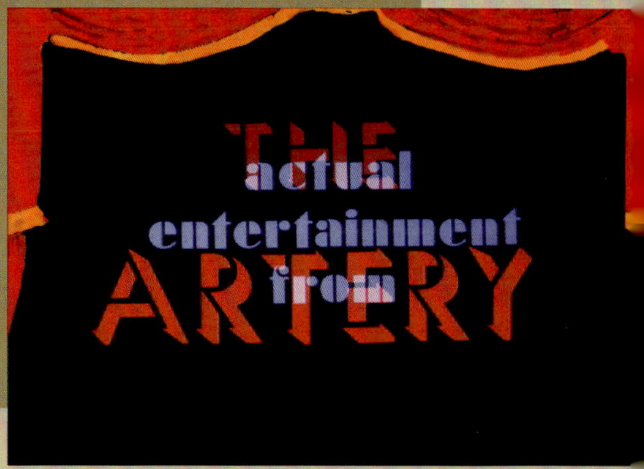

On the board, however, it seemed the more things changed the more they stayed the same. When Jim Brandstetter stepped down as board president, no one was exactly rushing to fill the vacancy, so in an unusual, though not unprecedented move, Glenn Selander volunteered to return for another year as president.

While Rod kept busy teaching at BSU, and producing fall and spring shows there for the Festival, Vangie and the board, with the help of the summer box office, whittled the debt to a more workable level. Rod's second summer season continued what had by now become the non-Shakespeare tradition with John Murrell's *Waiting for the Parade*, a series of stories told by five women waiting at home during World War II. Along with that were *Much Ado About Nothing*, *Richard II*, and *Troilus and Cressida*.

Stitch Marker: *We did some productions out there that he directed that I thought were really kind of groundbreaking in a way, like Troilus and Cressida, with the glamour boy Trojans and the biker Greeks going at it. He's got a kind of visceral approach to theater, you know, blood and guts.*

Dan Peterson: *One night with Troilus and Cressida somebody ran into a power pole somewhere nearby and we lost power at the theater. It's dark, it's late, what do we do? The tech guys scrambled for flashlights and brought them backstage, and the word was, "Whoever's talking, shine a light at them."*

Dave Bogie rushed to Idaho Power and brought portable lights and extension cords, which were run from the Ore-Ida building next door. Someone turned their car lights on backstage, and with the added illumination of a few lanterns, the show went on.

L-R, Robert G. Anderson, Pandarus; Stitch Marker, Thersites, ***Troilus and Cressida.*** DBB

L-R, Terri Dillion, Alexandra; Anne Marie Tremko, Cressida, ***Troilus.*** DBB

Sean O'Shea, Ajax, ***Troilus.*** DBB

Things won are done, joy's soul lies in the doing. Troilus and Cressida, I, ii.

Romeo and Juliet. DBB

Anne Marie Tremko, Ursula, *Much Ado About Nothing.* DBB

Sandra Lindberg, Margaret, *Parade.* DBB

Kevin Connell, Don Pedro, *Much Ado..* DBB

Kevin Connell, Richard II. DBB

William Salyers, Aumerle, *Richard II.* DBB

L-R, Mikel McDonald, Bolingbroke; William Salyers, Aumerle, *Richard II.* DBB

L-R, Sandra Lindberg, Margaret; Susan Mundell, Catherine; Karen Fuller, Eve; Tracey Komoski, Janet, *Waiting for the Parade.* DBB

Bethann Andersen, cover art.

DBB

The following year, 1990, was the State of Idaho's centennial year. By way of commemoration the Festival commissioned a play by R. N. Sandburg.

> **R.N.Sandburg (1990):** *The history and politics of Idaho have always fascinated me. Wealthy mines and a radical labor movement. Maverick politicians from the right and the left. One of the first states to grant women the vote and yet still a battleground on the abortion issue. Breathtaking quiet beauty and dangerous, rugged wilderness. So many provocative contradictions. A Shakespeare festival wanting to create a new play made perfect sense. Drama thrives on contradictions.*

Titled, *A Woman of Means*, the show gave audiences a glimpse into Idaho's formative years and the independent people who helped shape the new state. It was grouped with *Henry VIII*, which also helped to commemorate a royal occasion with its first production in 1613, *The Merry Wives of Windsor*, and *The Merchant of Venice*, both of which had been done during our downtown years at One Capital Center.

During Rod's three summer seasons Boise was growing, but Festival attendance remained stagnant. The artistic side of the company had grown

The Play: ***The Merry Wives of Windsor***
Director: Cynthia White
Scenic Design: Micheal Baltzell
Costume Design: Ted Bernard
Lighting Design: Robert Parsley
Sound Designer/Composer: Pete Weaver

The Play: ***A Woman of Means***
Director: Penny Metropulos
Scenic Design: Micheal Baltzell
Costume Design: Christina Rosendaul
Lighting Design: Robert Parsley
Sound Designer/Composer: Joseph Weisnewski
Lyricist: R. N. Sandberg

The Play: ***The Merchant of Venice***
Director: David Hay
Scenic Design: Micheal Baltzell
Costume Design: Paula Davis
Lighting Design: Robert Parsley
Sound Designer/Composer: Pete Weaver

The Play: ***Henry VIII***
Director: Rod Ceballos
Scenic Design: Micheal Baltzell
Costume Design: Lisa A. Vollrath
Lighting Design: Robert Parsley
Sound Designer/Composer: Joseph Weisnewski

1990

increasingly distant from the administrative side, and while the press remained upbeat there were increasing complaints from the audience. Rod continued to distance himself from the front office, leaving Vangie to handle not only her managerial duties, but all the fund raising as well. She had Jeana McClure managing the office and Trish Elledge as publicity director, but the financial responsibilities alone required more than she could handle, so she went to the board for help.

Glenn Selander had graciously accepted a third term as president. His reputation as a peacemaker stemmed from his stable leadership in that position two years earlier, and he knew it would take all that and more to keep the company on a solid track. He had considerable help from solid board members such as Mello Dee Thornton, Candice Allphin, Sandy Shook (Fery) and Brian King, but while they dealt with the larger picture, another board member was helping Vangie with some of the details.

Bill Keller: *I was sort of the unpaid staff, or one of them, during that time. Everyone was working around the clock, so I tried to take some of the burden off by dealing with some of the financial stuff that was going on. I even used to write checks because there just wasn't time to get someone else, especially during the season. So I really got involved, and I guess that's where my real affection for the organization started because it became sort of like my theater, too.*

Vangie Osborn: *He was like a rock to me. I talked with Bill almost every day, sometimes just to talk...nothing even to do with finances. So he became that board member that was so solid and knew everything, and everyone trusted him.*

Rod Ceballos, Shylock, *Merchant.* DBB

L-R, Julie Greenberg, Nerissa; Christina Lang, Portia, *Merchant.* DBB

J. Paul Boehmer, Bassanio, *Merchant.* DBB

Stitch Marker, Antonio, *Merchant of Venice.* DBB

By the end of the 1990 season the storm clouds were no longer threatening, they were ready to explode.

Vangie Osborn: *That first year we all gave him the benefit of the doubt, but after that I did start to say to board members that I didn't think this was going to work. Board members were slow to move, and it was just too hard to work under those conditions, with someone you just didn't believe was doing the right thing. I decided to leave, and that's when they made the decision to get rid of Rod and ask me to stay, because they did understand where the money came from and they had to have somebody who was responsible for that stuff. The search for his replacement was hard, but in the end it was right, because we didn't settle, like we had with Rod, and we ended up with Charlie.*

Financially, the Festival was nearly back on its feet again, but with another season fast approaching and no artistic management in place, Vangie was faced with adding those tasks to her already overflowing plate.

Tracy Young, Joe, *A Woman of Means.* DBB

Top to bottom, Scott Hayes, Harry; Susan Coromel, Lillian, *Woman of Means.* DBB

L-R, Julie Greenberg, Star; Susan Coromel, Lillian; Anne Marie Tremko, Katie, *Woman of Means.* DBB

L-R, Michael Picaro, Master Page; Dan Peterson, Master Ford, *Merry Wives.* DBB

Toni Rome, cover graphics.

One of the nicest things about ISF has been the close ties formed by members of the company over the years. Virtually everyone who has taken part, in any capacity, in the summer ritual that is the Idaho Shakespeare Festival considers themselves, and is considered by everyone else, to be family. And those family ties have come to the fore in times of crisis, as well as times of plenty, in many ways.

A growing number of actors, designers and technicians, not to mention board members, consider it their summer home, and even if they're not taking part in a given season, often show up just to watch a show or two and rekindle old friendships.

The Play: ***The Tempest***
Director: Doug Copsey
Scenic Design: Micheal Baltzell
Costume Design: Christina Rosendaul
Lighting Design: Robert Parsley
Musical Director: Joseph Weisnewski

The Play: ***Twelfth Night***
Director: Paul Frellick
Scenic Design: Micheal Hartwell
Costume Design: Ted Bernard
Lighting Design: Robert Parsley
Sound: Joseph Weisnewski

The Play: ***Spring Awakening***
Director: Dennis Bigelow
Scenic Design: Micheal Baltzell
Costume Design: Debra Bruneaux
Lighting Design: Deborah Penrod
Sound: Joseph Weisnewski

The Play: ***Macbeth***
Director: Kenneth Kelleher
Scenic Design: Micheal Baltzell
Costume Design: Ron Erickson
Lighting Design: Deborah Penrod
Sound: Joseph Weisnewski

1991

Shaun Sites, Master Electrician/Carpenter. DBB

Micheal Baltzell, Technical Director. DBB

Kate Shea, Apprentice. DBB

Bill Keller: *In those days we used to have a board night at the theater where we would be the ushers and run the concessions stand. It was always fun meeting the people and listening to them talk. And there were a lot of times when I would just go by the theater with nothing else to do and hang out for a while and watch part of the play.*

And then there are actors like Dan Peterson and Stitch Marker, who have rarely missed a summer since the Festival began in 1977. Apprentices and interns who have grown up with the Festival always leave to finish their education and find their way in the world, but every so often one will return to the fold in some capacity or other. Actors Tom Willmorth, David Lee-Painter, Karen Wennstrom are notable among them, as are costumers Nancy Berger and carpenter turned set designer Micheal Baltzell.

Many board members and community sponsors have taken on their own kind of ownership, finishing one term and taking a break, only to find themselves drawn back into service again. Alan Minskoff, who conveniently provided us with our non-profit status in 1980, was a crucial player in securing the Plantation site so that our fifth season could happen, and the following year, he joined our Board of Directors. Doug Oppenheimer was the key that opened the door to our first season at One Capital Center, and he has been a fan and supporter ever since. In 1988 he joined the Board of Trustees for a six year stint that revitalized his connection to the Festival.

I moved to Los Angeles after the tenth anniversary season in 1986, but always managed to make it home during the summer months to pay a visit to the Festival. Then, in April of 1991, I got a call from Vangie and my own repatriation began. She wanted to know what I had planned for the summer. It just so happened I was making a move to New York for a film project that started in the Fall. Even though I had been gone for four years I kept in touch, and was aware that Rod was no longer Artistic Director. When she asked if I would be interested in coming home to Boise to help see the Festival through a critical summer, I agreed on the spot.

ISF was perched, once again, on the edge of a precipice. It was not unfamiliar territory, but it was still scary, and somewhat demoralizing. Aside from that old itch to get back on the boards again that every actor and director can never seem to scratch enough, I could help fill out the staff for the Festival's fifteenth season and give the board the better part of a year to conduct a thorough search for a new Artistic Director. It was a chance for everyone involved to re-examine the past and the unique idealism that for fourteen years caused a diverse group of people from throughout the United States to hold on to one summer's experience as tightly as they hold on to family.

It was more than just the people themselves, it was the organization that brought them together, the community that embraced them, and the atmosphere that encouraged them to work long, hot hours for little reward other than the appreciation of an audience. Now it was time to stand up and be counted once more. It was an opportunity for each of us to discover the essence of our own involvement with ISF and work together to breathe new life into a festival that had grown tired. It wasn't a novel concept. In fact it was the very reason I stepped aside as Artistic Director in the fall of 1982.

The season Vangie and the board picked included *The Tempest*, *Twelfth Night*, *Macbeth*, and Frank Wedekind's dark, often controversial, *Spring Awakening*. Dennis Bigelow, who had directed for ISF in 1987 returned, bringing Rick Foster, who had done a translation and adaptation of the German script. Paul Frellick was back again to direct *Twelfth Night*, for which he chose the antebellum South as his setting, and

…le but the wood, no assembly but horn-beasts. But what though? Courage! As
…y a man has good horns, and knows no end of them. Well, that is the dowry of his

L-R, Erika Rolfsrud, Ariel; Rod Wolfe, Trinculo; Kevin Warren, Caliban; Stitch Marker, Stephano, *Tempest.* DBB

L-R, Debbie Funkhouser, Miranda; Erika Rolfsrud, Ariel, *Tempest.* DBB

Dan Peterson, Prospero, *Tempest.* DBB

Opening scene, *The Tempest.* DBB

Kenneth Kelleher, who came up from the San Jose Stage Company in 1989 to direct *Richard II* and just finished directing our spring Shakespearience tour, would handle directing chores for *Macbeth*. Tony Carriero put his burgeoning television and movie career in L.A. on hold to return to Boise in the lead role of a decidedly Latin production.

Part of my reason for returning was the chance to direct *The Tempest*. I had played Prospero under Mark Cuddy's direction in 1981, our first season at the Plantation, and memories of that electric opening night with Mother Nature providing her own special effects still burned strong in me. I was also excited that Dan Peterson agreed to play Prospero. After years of character parts it was past time for him to step into a strong leading role. And with Stitch Marker as Stephano and Rod Wolfe as Trinculo, I knew I had the makings of an excellent production.

Joseph Weisnewski created an incredible score of magical, stormy and ethereal sounds for the show and Micheal Baltzell outdid himself in the opening shipwreck scene with his creation of a billowing canvas sea that covered the stage and literally washed the disintegrating ship off the upper level, revealing Prospero in front of his cave below.

Keeping with tradition, a letter from Board President Mello Dee Thornton welcomed patrons to our 15th Anniversary Season, and offered, in part, some historical insight.

Mello Dee Thornton: *Our productions over the years have offered a wide variety of periods and styles, complete with healthy doses of drama, adventure, comedy and passion. It has been our vision to offer challenge and growth for our gifted artists, and to provide you, our audience, with*

Spring Awakening cast.
DBB

a wonderful presentation of intense emotion, energy, romance, sensitivity and (certainly!) silliness.

While all this was going on, Vangie and the board were embroiled in the search for a new Artistic Director. So much so, in fact, that no one noticed those pesky storm clouds brewing once again on the horizon. Dennis Bigelow had decided to add a little something extra to one of the scenes in *Spring Awakening* by having an actor appear nude on stage.

Vangie Osborn: *It was one of those situations where we had a director we knew, we liked him, and I don't think anybody really knew how far he intended to go with that scene. We never dreamed he would do something to hurt the organization.*

A couple of issues were at play here. First, public nudity is very clearly against the law in Idaho, especially where beer and wine are being served, and while the Festival certainly wasn't opposed to some tasteful, relevant show of skin on stage, in this instance a line was being crossed. Second, the organization itself was fragile – there was no Artistic Director, the company was being run by a General Manager who was exhausted from trying to do both jobs at once. It was also important to consider the possible reaction of the community and what that could mean for the future of the company. Finally, just days before the show was set to open, word of how that scene was going to be staged leaked back to Vangie. She immediately called Board Vice President Charlie Davis.

Charlie Davis: *When Vangie said to us that one of the performers told her there was a rehearsal that night and it would be a good idea if some board members went to see it, alarms went off. What I saw I thought was a brilliant performance, but a guy standing in a bathtub with his penis hanging out over the audience for about fifteen seconds wasn't going to fly. There were bound to be complaints and the Prosecuting Attorney's office would likely close us down. And though we may win the battle, by that time we'd be out of business.*

Naturally the scandal threw the company into an uproar. Dennis steadfastly refused to modify the scene and went so far as to threaten a walkout of the cast, virtually all of whom were in one or more of the other shows. It was dangerously close to opening night so the board decided to hold a private, preview performance for a small group of invited guests. On the basis of their reactions, the painful decision was made to cancel the show entirely.

Vangie Osborn: *We had lawyers on the board who were all saying we can't do this, we're at risk. We actually had a phone call from the police department. I know the actor was very uncomfortable with how far it went, I mean, the audience in that theater is just a couple of feet away from the stage. In most any community, in an outdoor theater, in broad daylight, it just went too far.*

A storm of media attention, both for and against the decision, followed throughout the summer. Nevertheless, the abbreviated season played to rave reviews, and the community turned out in fine fashion, confirming their continued loyalty by sitting through a rain storm on the opening night of *Twelfth Night*. By summer's end, the search for a new artistic director was in full swing. But true to Vangie's prediction, this time the search committee was determined to get it right.

Micheal Baltzell: *That committee almost had an anniversary. We worked for a whole year to try and find people.*

Initially the Search Committee received some 60-80 applications. Vangie and committee chairman Charlie Davis eliminated the obviously unqualified and then the rest of the committee, consisting of Vangie, Micheal Baltzell, Star Moxley and Steve

L-R, Kevin Fabian, Andrew Aguecheek, Ty Smith, Toby Belch, *Twelfth Night.* DBB

Stitch Marker, Malvolio, *Twelfth Night.* DBB

Buss, narrowed those remaining down to a batch of eight or ten, which they began calling.

Charlie Davis: *We didn't have a lot of money to offer. I think we were paying somewhere in the high $30,000 range at that time and $25,000 of that came from BSU along with the obligation that you had to teach the equivalent of two courses. That might have meant teaching a class, or directing a play, or however BSU defined it.*

After going through the first group of 10 with no viable winners, another batch of 10 was picked and the process was repeated. It was a time-consuming process, and by the time some eligible candidates were reached they had found employment elsewhere. The committee decided to re-open the application process, and that's when Vangie made a call to a potential candidate recommended by Rick Foster.

Kelly Dunn, Susan Murdoch, Martie Sanders, Witches, *Macbeth.* DBB

Oddly enough, Charlie Fee was already familiar with the Idaho Shakespeare Festival, and not in the best of ways. His acquaintance with Rick began at Sierra Rep, where he had done a few projects while Charlie was Artistic Director, but it blossomed when the playwright asked him to direct his new adaptation of *Spring Awakening* at a small Catholic college in the Bay Area in the spring of 1991. Needless to say, nudity was not included, and the play was very well received. Immediately after that production, Dennis Bigelow asked to use the same adaptation at ISF, with far less pleasing results.

Vangie's call just happened to come on the hectic weekend Charlie was opening his Sierra Rep production of *Hamlet*, the cast of which just happened to include a couple of actors from ISF's ill-fated *Spring Awakening*, and just after he had told Producing Director Dennis Jones that he felt he had done all he could there and would probably do one more season before looking for a new opportunity. Amidst the heady atmosphere of a successful opening night, the idea of moving to Boise seemed ridiculous, but the very next day, his fiance, Lidia, pressed him to at least go see Boise and meet the people. Reluctantly, he agreed.

Vangie Osborn: *When he and Lidia got off the plane and you saw them face to face, you've seen their information, you've heard the recommendations, and you're like, he's the guy. He could be the face that the Shakespeare Festival so desperately needs.*

L-R, Tony Carriero, MacBeth; Seth Jacobs, Macduff, *Macbeth.* DBB

John Farrage, Banquo, *Macbeth.* DBB

The attempt and not the deed confounds us. Macbeth II, ii.

Charlie Fee: *I got there and found a Board of Trustees that had gone through real hell that summer, but were not daunted by it. In some ways I think it really galvanized them. They were young and smart, and willing to really talk about the future of the company.*

For Charlie, that future would have to include a capital campaign to build a new theater, to which the board readily agreed. The Festival had never not been looking for a permanent home, and the board knew it would have to conduct a capital campaign to get one, so Charlie's sense of urgency about this issue was very appealing. But the real clincher came once again from Lidia, who was touring the city while Charlie was meeting with board members and learning about festival operations. She liked what she saw, especially when it came to home prices. Charlie had to agree, and that, coupled with the fact that he really felt ready to run a theater company focused on Shakespeare, tipped the scales in favor of Boise.

Susan Coromel, Lady Macbeth. DBB

Tony Carriero, Macbeth. DBB

Charlie Davis: *I was really nervous when he came in, feeling that we didn't want to be too anxious and see him through rose-colored glasses. We sat down and had a very long breakfast. He wanted to be assured that there was a reason this thing could grow, and I said that if he had already been an artistic director he should have certain characteristics: a sense of where we ought to go and a sense of practicality and staying on budget. He convinced me that he understood those things quite well, and had some ideas about how to deal with them, and I came away truly impressed.*

Macbeth curtain call. DBB

Tereasa Guy and Mark Lisk, cover art.

Charlie completed his contract at Sierra Rep and moved to Boise full-time in March to officially take over as the new head of the company, yet another critical "ides of March" event in the history of ISF. Charlie Davis was now President of the Board, but the search committee's work was not yet done.

Charles Fee

Vangie consented to stay through the summer, but that was it. A new Managing Director would have to be found by fall. Meanwhile, the new Artistic Director dove into preparations for his first season at ISF.

The good news was that he was starting with a relatively clean slate. Vangie, along with the staff and the board, had worked very hard to get the company back on track financially and they had succeeded. When Charlie arrived the Festival was once

The Play: ***Romeo and Juliet***
Director: Charles Fee
Scenic Design: Micheal Baltzell
Costume Design: Ron Erickson
Lighting Design: Shaun Sites
Musical Director: Peter Still

The Play: ***The Taming of the Shrew***
Director: Barry Edelstein
Scenic Design: Michael Baltzell
Costume Design: Ted Bernard
Lighting Design: Shaun Sites
Sound: Peter Still

The Play: ***Richard III***
Director: Bartlett Sher
Scenic Design: Deborah L. Jensen
Costume Design: Kim Krumm Sorenson
Lighting Design: Shaun Sites
Sound: Peter Still

The Play: ***Scapino!***
Director: Dale "AJ" Rose
Scenic Design: Deborah L. Jensen
Costume Design: Clare Henkel
Lighting Design: Deborah Penrod
Sound: Peter Still

1992

Ted Rooney, Buckingham, *Richard III*. DBB

again operating in the black. The only payments due were on the Shakespearience van, which were being made from grant funds, and on a copier they had purchased, for which the monthly payments were cheaper than the regular bills that had been piling up from various copy shops around town.

After familiarizing himself with local acting and designing talent and hiring a number of friends whose work he knew was good, among them Steve Tague, Janis Stevens, Ty Smith, Joe Golden, and sound designer Peter Still, he chose to title his season "The Good, the Bad and the Ugly." In an unusual move, he split the Festival's revolving repertory schedule in two, with The Good, *Romeo and Juliet*, and The Bad, *The Taming of the Shrew*, rotating in June and July, while The Ugly, *Richard III* was paired with Moliere's raucous comedy, *Scapino!* for August and the first two weeks in September.

L-R Marcel Shipman, Widow; Jeff Kramer, Petruchio, *Taming of the Shrew.* DBB

Steve Tague: *Charlie and I had been working together in California since '88 or '89. When he got the job at ISF he asked me what I would like to do his first year here. I didn't have any great ideas, I just said Richard III. I could have picked anything but that was the one that came up, and he said, "Great, that's what we'll do."*

Joe Golden: *It's Charlie Fee, he's to blame. I was fresh out of grad school and the head of my acting program, Dale Rose, who was going to direct Scapino! at ISF said, "You should look at that." Bart Sher, who had just directed my grad project, was also directing there, so it was this really weird kind of coincidence thing. After my audition Charlie comes out on a break and says, "Yeah, that Scapino! piece. I kind of liked that. He called me back in and the first thing he said to me, I'll never forget this, was, "You did Mercutio. I hated that. Let's look at that." He hated it and wanted me to do it again, to torture myself. So I re-did Mercutio and he says, "Yeah, that's just not you. You're not going to play Mercutio. You're like a Benvolio type. What else have you got?" We worked every piece I knew, then he said, "I think I've got a spot for you in my company." He didn't offer any specifics except Benvolio, which he'd probably promised to about 18 other guys, too.*

In an effort to improve audience sightlines, Charlie reconfigured the ParkCenter theater for the fifth time in its eight year history, adding wings to either side and giving the stage a rake to improve the dynamic relationship between the actors and the audience. Building on Mark Cuddy's initial "guest contract" relationship with Actors' Equity Association, which began in 1987, Charlie negotiated our first professional contract with the union to bring four Equity members into the acting company.

Joe Golden: *We were still dressing in that big tent from the Plantation, and when they brought in these Equity actors we had to hang bed sheets back there to separate out their dressing rooms. Sometimes we'd come back there and there'd be homeless people sleeping by the dressing tables, or we'd find them under the stage where somebody would have set up a little house. It was like, oh my god!*

Romeo and Juliet. DBB

Stitch Marker, Peter, *R&J.* DBB

For his ISF directing debut, Charlie picked the classic *Romeo and Juliet*, bringing in his old friend Bart Sher from the Guthrie Theater in Minneapolis to direct *Richard III*. Bart brought along a colleague from the Guthrie, to design costumes.

> **Kim Sorenson:** *It was hard that first year. The shop was rough. I'd never been out here. I didn't think it was beautiful. But then we went up into the mountains and it grew on me. We were led to believe that the local fabric stores would have everything we needed. That did not turn out to be the case, so we ended up dying everything. I would buy just any old fabric and shove it in this garbage can on top of an old, beat up stove down at the costume shop on Ninth Street, and we would be up there in 110 degree heat boiling fabric in this garbage can. It was very rugged.*

Barry Edelstein, a 1985 acting intern at ISF who had since begun to make a name for himself as a director in New York, returned to take on *Shrew*, reinforcing once again that strong family connection among the collective ISF company. Backstage, Micheal Baltzell remained on board as Technical Director, as well as designing sets for both *R&J* and *Shrew*, aided ably in the costume department by Ted Bernard, returning for his seventh season as a designer.

Aside from bringing in new faces, just as Rod Ceballos and Mark Cuddy had done before him, Charlie, too, felt the need to push for a bigger and better theater facility. Indeed, the secondary focus of the company ever since that first move from One Capital Center was forced upon us had always been finding a permanent home for the Festival. Charlie approached it with a new zeal and enthusiasm. He even knew the architects he wanted to work with.

> **Charlie Fee:** *Gene Angell and Brian Rawlinson had just designed the new California Shakespeare Festival. It was run by one of my grad school teachers, so I'd seen the space and loved what they'd done. I was convinced that we were going to open a new theater the next year, so I got Gene up here that first season to see the space.*

Mhari Sandoval, Lady Anne, *Richard III.* DBB

Charlie knew he couldn't do it alone, and Vangie made it very clear she was leaving. This presented him with the unique opportunity of re-structuring the top management tier of the company any way he wanted. But with the season in full production, he barely had time to think about what kind of partnership he wanted, much less who might fill that bill. Once gain, fate stepped in.

> **Mark Hofflund:** *I had taken some time off from my job at the Old Globe in San Diego and driven up to Ashland to see some friends with my fiancee, Lynn Allison. I knew Lynn wanted me to get away from the Globe because I had been married to it for about ten years, and she wanted me to marry her, which I thought was a really good idea, too. When we were ready to leave Ashland we decided to take a different route back home, and I mentioned that I had a friend in Idaho who had invited me to come by if I was ever in the area.*

The two went to grad school together, and Mark had done a directing stint for Charlie at Sierra Rep. The couple spent a leisurely couple of days in Boise, just missing the closing of Charlie's first season, and caught up on each other's careers. They

Almost immediately, Charlie and Mark began thinking about the next season. But though their initial focus was on building a new theater, they soon learned those thoughts were a bit premature.

Bethanne Andersen, cover art.

Capital campaigns take time to put together, and before they could even begin with that, both the staff and the board needed serious strengthening. Along with that, the attendance would have to grow as well in order to support such a massive effort. How better to start than by solidifying their newest partnership.

Mark Hofflund: *My view of politics and politicians, as an artist, especially in California, was that they were to be avoided. You just didn't associate with them. But here in Idaho it was a much different, and more pleasant, story. I couldn't believe it, "I can call the mayor on the phone!? And he'll talk to me?"*

Brent Coles: *I first met Mark at a social function and we became friends right away. We decided right on the spot that we needed to work together to find ISF a permanent home.*

The Play: ***Quilters***
Director: Theresa Larkin
Scenic Design: Micheal Baltzell
Costume Design: Star Moxley
Lighting Design: Shaun Sites
Musical Director: Michael Koerner

The Play: ***A Midsummer Night's Dream***
Director: Kirk Boyd
Scenic Design: Deborah L. Jensen
Costume Design: Peter Still
Lighting Design: Rick Martin
Sound: Joseph Weisnewski

The Play: ***Tartuffe***
Director: Charles Fee
Scenic Design: Deborah L. Jensen
Costume Design: Kim Krumm Sorenson
Lighting Design: Rick Martin
Sound: Peter Still

The Play: ***The Comedy of Errors***
Director: Barry Edelstein
Scenic Design: Narelle Sissons
Costume Design: Rafi Mercado
Lighting Design: Rick Martin
Sound: Peter Still

1993

Mark Hofflund
Managing Director

Mark is pleased to join the Festival following ten years at the Old Globe Theatre in San Diego, where he was a member of the artistic staff under Jack O'Brien, Tom Hall and Craig Noel. He has numerous acting, directing, dramaturgical, literary, and producing credits; and received degrees from the University of California (San Diego) and Princeton. Mark is recently married, and he and his wife Lynn are discovering the joys of their first home, their first garden, and their first year in Boise.

Romeo and Juliet. DBB

Stitch Marker, Peter, *R&J.* DBB

For his ISF directing debut, Charlie picked the classic *Romen and Juliet*, bringing in his old friend Bart Sher from the Guthrie Theater in Minneapolis to direct *Richard III*. Bart brought along a colleague from the Guthrie, to design costumes.

Kim Sorenson: *It was hard that first year. The shop was rough. I'd never been out here. I didn't think it was beautiful. But then we went up into the mountains and it grew on me. We were led to believe that the local fabric stores would have everything we needed. That did not turn out to be the case, so we ended up dying everything. I would buy just any old fabric and shove it in this garbage can on top of an old, beat up stove down at the costume shop on Ninth Street, and we would be up there in 110 degree heat boiling fabric in this garbage can. It was very rugged.*

Barry Edelstein, a 1985 acting intern at ISF who had since begun to make a name for himself as a director in New York, returned to take on *Shrew*, reinforcing once again that strong family connection among the collective ISF company. Backstage, Micheal Baltzell remained on board as Technical Director, as well as designing sets for both *R&J* and *Shrew*, aided ably in the costume department by Ted Bernard, returning for his seventh season as a designer.

Aside from bringing in new faces, just as Rod Ceballos and Mark Cuddy had done before him, Charlie, too, felt the need to push for a bigger and better theater facility. Indeed, the secondary focus of the company ever since that first move from One Capital Center was forced upon us had always been finding a permanent home for the Festival. Charlie approached it with a new zeal and enthusiasm. He even knew the architects he wanted to work with.

Charlie Fee: *Gene Angell and Brian Rawlinson had just designed the new California Shakespeare Festival. It was run by one of my grad school teachers, so I'd seen the space and loved what they'd done. I was convinced that we were going to open a new theater the next year, so I got Gene up here that first season to see the space.*

Mhari Sandoval, Lady Anne, *Richard III*. DBB

Charlie knew he couldn't do it alone, and Vangie made it very clear she was leaving. This presented him with the unique opportunity of re-structuring the top management tier of the company any way he wanted. But with the season in full production, he barely had time to think about what kind of partnership he wanted, much less who might fill that bill. Once gain, fate stepped in.

Mark Hofflund: *I had taken some time off from my job at the Old Globe in San Diego and driven up to Ashland to see some friends with my fiancee, Lynn Allison. I knew Lynn wanted me to get away from the Globe because I had been married to it for about ten years, and she wanted me to marry her, which I thought was a really good idea, too. When we were ready to leave Ashland we decided to take a different route back home, and I mentioned that I had a friend in Idaho who had invited me to come by if I was ever in the area.*

The two went to grad school together, and Mark had done a directing stint for Charlie at Sierra Rep. The couple spent a leisurely couple of days in Boise, just missing the closing of Charlie's first season, and caught up on each other's careers. They also had long discussions about what kind of partner might work best for Charlie and ISF.

Charlie Fee: *After they left, Lidia said to me, "That's your managing director." I thought she was crazy. Mark is totally entrenched in the Globe, he grew up there, he loves that company. Why would he leave that to come here? She just said, "Well, he's the right guy."*

Mark Hofflund: *As we were driving home through Nevada, Lynn asked if I had talked to Charlie about a job. I was surprised at the suggestion of imposing on his friendship and hospitality and Lynn was too sweet to pursue her idea. When we got back to San Diego there was message waiting to call Charlie. He shared his conversation with Lidia and my first response was, what a great idea! By the time I hung up I had agreed to talk with Lynn.*

Vangie Osborn: *I went down to San Diego and met with Mark, and it was the same as with Charlie. Immediately you're like, "This guy's perfect for it because he's smooth and kind and knowledgeable. He has the right personality for this community. He knows how to get down on your level and talk to you. He didn't really have the financial background, but that didn't matter because Charlie's the number cruncher. He likes the statistics. But Mark brings so much more into the mix, including his own artistic background, and he's such a great fundraiser.*

The board agreed with her assessment, encouraged by Charlie's enthusiasm, and Mark became the new Managing Director in the fall of 1992. He and Lynn were married in December and after a brief honeymoon they headed for Idaho in January. On the way he met Charlie in Cedar City, Utah for their first annual Shakespeare Theatre Association of America conference.

They both had some artistic experience with Shakespeare, but neither had run a Shakespeare company, so they were all ears. Scott Phillips and Fred Adams of the Utah Shakespearean Festival were hosting the conference and took the two new partners under their wing.

Charlie Fee: *They were just tremendous. It was the first thing Mark and I did together and that was a really fun way to start our partnership. In some ways, that really sealed the deal for Mark and me because it just felt immediately like our partnership running the company was going to be much stronger than either of us individually would have been able to pull off anywhere.*

Besides meeting a host of people who would become their colleagues during the coming years, an especially strong friendship was formed at that conference between the Utah festival and its much younger sister to the north. Charlie and Mark were now firmly entrenched in their new world and bursting with ideas and plans to make their festival bigger and better than ever.

Mark Hofflund: *The first thing was not what do Charlie and I need to do, it was what do I need to pick up and learn from Vangie. There was a month where we literally shared the desk. That was our mutual office. She was such an incredible caretaker of the Festival and she was so invested in everything she had done, but there was never a sense of turf or territory or anything. The first night I was here she took me to a party, and whenever there was a gathering we were off to meet people, always. "This is somebody you need to know," she would say, or, "This is something you need to know about." So there was just like a month of basics.*

The good news for the incoming regime was that the company was healthy. Essentially, the landlord kept them in the office space to keep the place from being vandalized or burning down. There were no real assets except a small collection of costumes managed by Star Moxley, with whom they shared the rustic building on Ninth and Broad Streets. The office was spacious, if

L-R, Thaddius Smith; Colin O'Conner, Brian McCarthy, Waiters, *Scapino!*. DBB

ancient and worn down, and the only other actual employee besides Charlie and Mark was Marketing Director Peter LeBlanc. There were, of course, perennial volunteers like Jay Sherlock, who for several years devoted many hours of his retirement to doing office work and playing "the old guy" in at least one of the shows each summer. Mark gradually displaced Vangie from the small office they shared, but before she took her leave, there was one last service she could perform.

The winds of politics had been been blowing in Boise, and in November, 1992, Mayor Dirk Kempthorne was elected to the U.S. Senate. When he departed for Washington, D.C., Brent Coles was appointed to fill out the remainder of his term. Vangie had known the new Mayor from his days on the City Council, when she was serving on the Boise city Arts Commission.

Brent Coles: *The first day I took office, the first appointment on my calendar was Vangie Osborn. She told me that if I was going to be a good mayor, I needed to support the arts, and that meant supporting Idaho's premier performing arts organization, the Idaho Shakespeare Festival. She also told me the Festival was changing hands. She said that with the new administration it was going to grow and become even more successful, and if I was smart I would get on board right away because we could help each other.*

Scapino! DBB

Vangie Osborn: *Whenever I tell people about the Shakespeare Festival, one of the things I'm always very happy about is the continuity of the organization, how Doug started it, and then Mark Cuddy, and then I was there, and now Charlie and Mark (Hofflund). So you have this group of people who have sort of passed the torch. And every time it goes a different direction it's allowed to get bigger and spread its wings even more. It's had very few people running it over the years, and very few issues with those people, and almost everyone's still around and available, which I think is very cool. You don't see other groups with that kind of history.*

Connecting the new City administration with the new ISF administration put new wheels in motion for the Festival. While City government had always been supportive, it was never really considered a partner in an arts organization, and ISF had, by this time, become one of Idaho's most important cultural institutions. For someone who was "not a theater person," Vangie became, quite literally, the glue that held the Festival together during some of its most difficult times. It was a fitting swan song.

Alan Minskoff: *Vangie had amazing, what my dad used to call, stick-to-it-iveness. She has a huge heart and a tremendous sense of what the arts needed.*

1993

Bethanne Andersen, cover art.

Almost immediately, Charlie and Mark began thinking about the next season. But though their initial focus was on building a new theater, they soon learned those thoughts were a bit premature.

Capital campaigns take time to put together, and before they could even begin with that, both the staff and the board needed serious strengthening. Along with that, the attendance would have to grow as well in order to support such a massive effort. How better to start than by solidifying their newest partnership.

Mark Hofflund: *My view of politics and politicians, as an artist, especially in California, was that they were to be avoided. You just didn't associate with them. But here in Idaho it was a much different, and more pleasant, story. I couldn't believe it, "I can call the mayor on the phone!? And he'll talk to me?"*

Brent Coles: *I first met Mark at a social function and we became friends right away. We decided right on the spot that we needed to work together to find ISF a permanent home.*

The Play: ***Quilters***
Director: Theresa Larkin
Scenic Design: Micheal Baltzell
Costume Design: Star Moxley
Lighting Design: Shaun Sites
Musical Director: Michael Koerner

The Play: ***A Midsummer Night's Dream***
Director: Kirk Boyd
Scenic Design: Deborah L. Jensen
Costume Design: Peter Still
Lighting Design: Rick Martin
Sound: Joseph Weisnewski

The Play: ***Tartuffe***
Director: Charles Fee
Scenic Design: Deborah L. Jensen
Costume Design: Kim Krumm Sorenson
Lighting Design: Rick Martin
Sound: Peter Still

The Play: ***The Comedy of Errors***
Director: Barry Edelstein
Scenic Design: Narelle Sissons
Costume Design: Rafi Mercado
Lighting Design: Rick Martin
Sound: Peter Still

Mark Hofflund
MANAGING DIRECTOR

Mark is pleased to join the Festival following ten years at the Old Globe Theatre in San Diego, where he was a member of the artistic staff under Jack O'Brien, Tom Hall and Craig Noel. He has numerous acting, directing, dramaturgical, literary, and producing credits; and received degrees from the University of California (San Diego) and Princeton. Mark is recently married, and he and his wife Lynn are discovering the joys of their first home, their first garden, and their first year in Boise.

The Barber Pool Conservation Area. TM

A permanent home. That phrase had become a mantra for the Festival since its earliest years, and was echoed by Charlie in his Artistic Director Notes for the season program where he introduced the community to his ambitious five- year plan stating, "Since neither myself nor my new partner can take credit for the incredible growth of this company, it falls on us to chart directions for the future."

Bill Keller: *One of Charlie's visions was that he and Mark were going to take us to the next level and build this new theater. We looked everywhere from Lucky Peak to Eagle Island for new sites. Charlie had done this before down at Sierra Rep, and his first analysis was that we could do it for $500,000, which we thought was a lot of money. Everywhere we looked we seemed to run into a wall of some kind or other, which turned out to be the best thing that happened to us.*

Enter developer Larry Leasure, of White-Leasure Development Company, and a board member of the Idaho Foundation for Parks and Lands. He had been working with local arts supporters to find a location for an indoor theater in downtown Boise when he got wind of the Shakespeare Festival's search and offered to show Charlie and Mark, along with their architects, a few possibilities.

Mark Hofflund: *As we were driving around with Larry, looking at old buildings, including the old Penitentiary, he said he had one other spot he wanted to show us. We kept going east on Warm Springs for some miles and all of a sudden he drove off the road. We weren't prepared for it because at that time there was no human habitat in evidence. He drove us down this barely visible two-track dirt path and pointed to a kind of depression just before you get to the river and said, "Do you think you could put a theater in there?"*

It was part of the Barber Pool Conservation Area, a 480 acre wildlife preserve donated by Boise Cascade in 1976 to the Idaho Foundation for Parks and Lands, of which Larry was a board member. This particular piece of it, however, had been a bone pile for the old Pullman Brick Company. Subsequently it had turned into a de facto dumping ground, and the sight of rusted vehicles, old logging cables and piles of brick deposited over the years did little to convince them that this might be the place for their Festival.

Charlie and Gene Angell politely explained that there was no telling what kinds of problems they might run into trying to build in a space like that, so close to the river. And frankly, it was just too far from civilization for comfort. Everyone promptly forgot about it and went back to the business of preparing for the upcoming season. The first thing was to get the Shakespearience tour of *Romeo and Juliet* out on the road.

Dan Peterson: *When Charlie came he wanted the Shakespearience tours to look like a bigger, more polished production. Now all of a sudden we're hauling scenery around in a trailer instead of everything fitting into the van, and at a stop sign in the middle of Shelley one day the*

To seek their fortunes further than at home, where small experience grows. The Taming of the Shrew, I, ii.

trailer just completely fell apart. There are set pieces and costumes all over the place. This guy comes out and says, "I'll give you $150 for the trailer frame there. I could probably weld that back together." I made an executive decision, took the money, and we rented a U-Haul.

Charlie brought Rick Foster back for his second season as the company dramaturg, and they put the final touches on a five year plan for ISF. Along with developing a company of artists, it included building a new theater and scene shop. The idea of a resident acting company on year-round contracts had become too expensive for most theaters around the country, and it required other revenue sources beyond the stage productions to support it. Still, he knew he wanted artists who would work together over several years, even though it was a seasonal company performing only in the summer.

With this in mind, he set about building on the small group of actors he added to the company his first season, bringing in Richard Klautsch and Susan Coromel, among others.

Richard Klautsch: *When Ann and I moved here to teach at BSU in 1992 we saw Richard III on what felt like a two-foot-square patch of grass in a packed theater, and that became one of the primary reasons I wanted to come and live here. Here was a place I could teach all winter and work on an Equity contract doing repertory during the summers. I auditioned for Charlie right away and he hired me.*

From the local talent pool, Karen Wennstrom, a former ISF apprentice, joined Dan Peterson, Stitch Marker and Carole Whiteleather, a long-time member of the Boise acting community who, because of her Equity status, had been unable to appear in her home town for many years. Carole was reprising her role as Sarah McKendree Bonham in *Quilters*, under the direction of Theresa Larkin, who had directed ISF's original production in 1988.

IDAHO *Shakespeare* FESTIVAL

ARTISTIC DIRECTOR NOTES: ". . .what's past is prologue . . ."

Thinking about the future is so seductive . . .

It is a time of change at the Festival. Exhilarating, challenging, possibly difficult, always alluring change. As we enter our seventeenth season, everyone in the company -- from the props assistant to the president of the board -- can feel the energy and excitement of a new beginning for the Idaho Shakespeare Festival.

Sound familiar? It should. Looking back through Festival archives (news releases, reviews, programs) two themes emerge as leitmotifs: optimistic plans for future growth and the quest for a permanent home. From founding directors Doug Copsey and Victoria Holloway, through Mark Cuddy and Rod Ceballos, nearly every season's greeting has sounded these twin refrains. The 1979 program announces, "This has been a growth year for us..., we look forward to continuing to build a professional theater company in Boise." Ten years later the 1989 program calls for the company to "continue developing a sense of worth and cultural place in the community. ...The continued growth that we at the Festival seek can only occur if both the Festival and the community make the commitment."

The quest for a permanent site is recorded almost every season in the press, with typical headlines reading "SHAKESPEARE FESTIVAL NEEDS NEW HOME" and articles quoting the joyful -- or worried -- artistic staff on the current state of the site. The Festival, like a perennial without its own flowerbed, is something of a miracle -- blooming again for the seventeenth time, taking root throughout the community, hoping to flourish and grow.

What makes me think this season is different? I recognize that in many ways our new beginning is really an old beginning, and that the sense of rejuvenation in the company is part of the legacy, part of the youthful energy and

Another full house.
DBB

Rounding out the 1993 season were *A Midsummer Night's Dream*, *Tartuffe*, and *The Comedy of Errors*, with former acting apprentice Barry Edelstein returning for his second season as a director.

Another ISF innovation began to percolate its way to the surface that summer. Greenshows, short presentations given before the play begins each night, have been common occurrences at theaters around the world since Shakespeare's time. They take many forms, from musicians offering pre-show music on the stage to wandering minstrels, clowns, jugglers and other entertaining characters who circulate among the crowd as they gather for the play.

Mark Hofflund: *It started as a way of introducing the idea of Tartuffe. Tom and Joe created a cleric and a royal. The cleric got onstage and said, "Go home. This is a blasphemous play." That was Tom. Then Joe, the royal came in and says, "Oh, don't believe him. I represent the king." And it was great, the audience loved it. Then the next year, they were doing Greenshows for all the plays. Pretty soon the political humor of the initial Moliere started going into the local characters.*

Joe Golden: *Tom and I met during auditions that summer. We were standing out in the hall, just kind of like laughing and joking around, and I was like, he's got the funny gene. I was kind of a clown growing up and could see it in him instantly. I was like, he and I are going to be friends.*

Tom Willmorth: *I saw Joe from the audience in '92 and I thought, "His Lucentio is just spot on. How entertaining is that? Then in '93 we get paired for the first time as Demetrius and Lysander.*

Joe Golden: *In Midsummer Tom and I get cast as the two least funniest guys in the whole show. The director actually asked us not to be funny, which was incredibly difficult. We snuck in little things where we could, but we were very unfunny.*

Tom Willmorth: *It was probably the fact that Joe and I were put into two roles like that, and disallowed any comic inventiveness at all, that made us the comic team we are.*

The architect team of Gene Angell and Brian Rawlinson, paid another visit to Boise that summer and continued working on plans for a new theater, but one pressing question remained – where were they going to put it? The Ore-Ida site at ParkCenter had served the Festival well for ten seasons, but it had always been on a year-to-year lease and there was no way to tell when the Heinz folks might decide to use it for something else. There were discussions of buying the property, but there were also plans for a connector bridge coming across the river at that point, which would severely impact the theater from a noise standpoint, and preclude any kind of real expansion. The search for an alternate site moved up a notch on the priority list.

Charlie Fee: *We're going through a fascinating process of evaluating places and we had some experiences we weren't prepared for, such as being told by neighborhood association after neighborhood association, "Don't you dare think of moving here." I'm not talking about one, I'm talking about every place we went. I didn't foresee them being so antagonistic to us.*

With the help of Mayor Coles and the Department of Parks and Recreation, Charlie and Mark, along with the board, had looked at several sites owned by the city, including a small site at the east end of Warm Springs Avenue, along the river just behind the Natatorium. Those meetings got particularly vocal, in an anti-Idaho Shakespeare Festival kind of way, and by the time the twentieth anniversary season was upon them, frustration was beginning to set in.

Charlie Fee: *We spent a lot of time on that one, only to get to the neighborhood association meeting and find a level of discussion I've never experienced in my life. All these people were standing up and literally screaming at us. And I'm thinking, "This is insane! It's not like we're proposing a nuclear reactor. This is the Shakespeare Festival!"*

Meanwhile the board continued to grow, and Charlie and Mark began to talk to them more seriously about the upcoming capital campaign. By this time the company was beginning to experience a growth curve. Attendance topped the 20,000 mark for the season, and financially they were in good enough shape to hire some help in the front office.

Mark Hofflund: *Helene Peterson is one of those indefatigable people who's not only tireless, but also tirelessly happy to be working. She was fresh out of a very good undergraduate program at the University of Colorado and after handling our concessions for the 1993 season, she became the person who was our front line, who picked up the phone every time it rang, and did all the many things that needed to be done.*

With two successful seasons under his belt, Charlie decided it was time to pursue an idea he had been nurturing since the previous fall, when he accepted an offer from the Actor's Theater of Phoenix to direct *A Christmas Carol*. The set designer for that production was Gage Williams, and the two became instant friends.

Charlie Fee: *They did it in this big proscenium house and it was really a great production. And I said, you know what, Gage, we should do this production in Boise. There's this theater there that would be unbelievable.*

Steve Tague, Scrooge.

Bethanne Anderson, cover art.

As soon as the summer season ended, he approached the Morrison Center board with his idea. His offer set a number of wheels in motion.

Charlie Fee: *For one thing, there was no Nutcracker that year, and the Morrison Center board was going through one of its meltdowns about the theater's relationship with the community. I went in and got to know Frank Heise, the executive director, and said, "Listen, let's make some money together." Well, all of a sudden I'm the poster boy for the theater – the one non-profit in town who doesn't seem to have any problem working in the Morrison Center. I was then asked to join their strategic planning committee, where I met Royanne Minskoff and John Parrish, and it became a really good intro for me to the world of leadership in town, which Mark and I knew was one of the key things that he and I had to work on for our capital campaign.*

The timing couldn't have been better. *A Christmas Carol* was a huge success, ISF's quest for a new home acquired some new players, and the mayor, City Council and several community leaders were ready to help the Festival move forward.

Opposite and this page, *A Christmas Carol*, The Morrison Center. DBB

L-R, Susan Coromel, Agnes; Debra England, Kate; JoAnn Johnson, Maggie; Lynn Allison, Chris; Ted Deasy, Gerry, *Dancing At Lughnasa.* TM

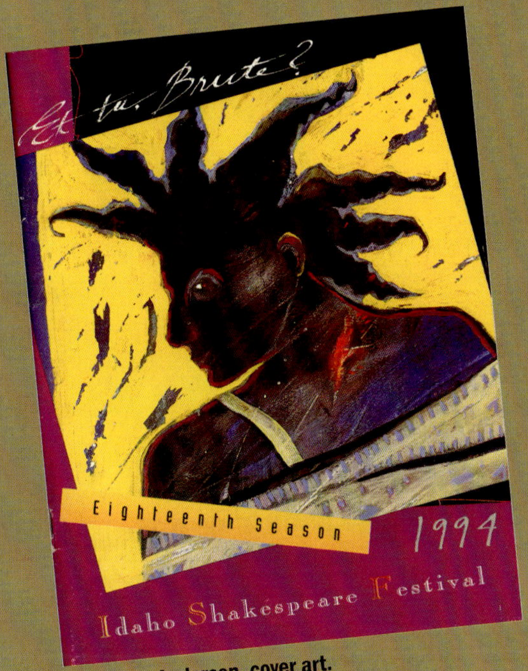

Bethanne Andersen, cover art.

L-R, Joe Conley Golden, Verges; Tom Wilmorth, Dogberry, *Much Ado About Nothing*. TM

Charlie sailed into 1994 on the news that ISF had been named one of the recipients for the 1996 FUNDSY charity auction. Besides being a large feather in the Festival's cap, it was a substantial bright spot to look forward to in the search for a new and permanent home.

Everyone knew that the contribution would be a large one, especially by ISF standards, and it provided new impetus to the idea of the capital campaign for which Charlie and Mark had been sewing the seeds among board members.

A lot of parallels can be drawn between the idea of reading a script, getting directors, designers, casting actors, rehearsing and then putting it on, and the idea of directing architects in the design of a theater, casting the builders and sub-contractors, doing the budget, getting all the permits and going ahead with construction. Both are very creative processes, and both require a tremendous amount of time and effort and help from a lot of people. And sometimes it isn't just how much you can do, it's also making the right connection at the right time.

The Play: ***Dancing at Lughnasa***
Director: Joan Robbins
Scenic Design: Micheal Baltzell
Costume Design: Ann Hoste
Lighting Design: Rick Martin
Musical Director: Peter John Still

The Play: ***Much Ado About Nothing***
Director: Charles Fee
Scenic Design: Gage Williams
Costume Design: Star Moxley
Lighting Design: Rick Martin
Sound: Peter John Still

The Play: ***Julius Caesar***
Director: Anne Justine D'Zmura
Scenic Design & Costume Design: Nephelie Andonyadis
Lighting Design: Rick Martin
Sound: Peter John Still

The Play: ***As You Like It***
Director: Bartlett Sher
Scenic Design: Jack Balance
Costume Design: Kim Krumm Sorenson
Lighting Design: Marcus Dilliard
Sound: Peter John Still

1994

Michael Hacker, Caesar; Dana Slamp, Cinna, *Julius Caesar*. TM

Mark Hofflund: *The first time we went out to the Arid Club it was with Odette Sutton, who had been a member of our board for a couple of years. She introduced us to Chuck Winder and said, "I want you to tell Charlie and Mark what you think is going to happen on that land. They're new in town and they need to know." And he said, "When I planned ParkCenter there was a bridge to go through your site, and I'd estimate you probably have a couple of years before it will actually start to happen."*

Shocking though the information was, it provided the catalyst Charlie and Mark needed to galvanize their board to action. It was no longer just their management team telling them time was running out, it was a major community figure. This created a new sense of urgency and motivated board members to parlay that deadline into some beneficial support from other community leaders and the political constituency.

By this time, Mayor Coles was working his way up the ladder of the National Council of Mayors, and in fact would be president in a couple of years. His constant talks about Idaho as a great place to live were peppered with references to the Greenbelt, the river and the climate, and he always managed to work in some positive support for the Shakespeare Festival, the Philharmonic and other arts organizations, touting Boise as a small town with big city arts opportunities. National publications like *Sunset*, *Forbes* and *Inc.* agreed, calling Boise one of the most desirable cities in the country in which to live. The city began to experience a growth surge unlike any it had seen before.

That summer brought more new additions to the company of actors, directors and designers. Local actor Glenn Hughes returned to the Festival as the lead

Idaho Shakespeare Festival Membership

The Idaho Shakespeare Festival counts on the support of our members – corporations and individuals who donate. Are you interested in joining our growing and distinguished membership?

Angels	$10,000+
Benefactors	$5,000+
Patrons	$1,000+
Donors	$500+
Sponsors	$250+
	$100+

A bird's eye view. TM

Joe Conley Golden and Tom Wilmorth, an early Green Show. TM

in Brian Friel's *Dancing At Lughnasa*, directed by Joan Robbins, who has also published work on the author. Her work on this Irish drama was complemented by the Idaho directorial debut of Ann D'Zmura, handling *Julius Caesar*, Charlie Fee's *Much Ado About Nothing*, and Bart Sher's return from last season's successful *Richard III* to direct *As You Like It*. Another new addition to the acting company came from Utah by way of New York and Colorado.

Mark Anthony Taylor: *I really wanted to do big time Shakespeare at a big time Shakespeare festival, so I came here because I thought it would be a stepping stone to Ashland. Lo and behold it was way cooler than Ashland. I just fell in love with the company. I fell in love with the people. Plus there's just so much of a family atmosphere. There always has been. When Charlie auditioned me he asked, "Why haven't you been working for me for three years already?" I was like, what do you mean? He goes, "You're an older actor with experience. You should be working for me now. You should have been working for me last year." I was like, you didn't know who the hell I was!*

Long-time ISF designer Micheal Baltzell created the quaint Irish homestead belonging to five, unmarried sisters, while Gage Williams, who designed the set for *A Christmas Carol* the previous winter, and for the spring Shakespearience tour of *A Midsummer Night's Dream*, was back to design *Much Ado*.

Star Moxley: *People always ask you what's your favorite play, or your favorite costume, and I've always told them that it's favorite moments on stage where it worked with what you designed. You're sitting in an audience and there's an audible gasp, or a hush, or there's applause or laughter at a point that's definitely related to costuming. One of those was at ParkCenter in Much Ado when all the cavaliers entered in the opening scene – sixteen men in full regalia with boots and spurs, wigs, capes, the lace, the cuffs, the gauntlets. We wrapped fabric around their faces to look like dust. You could hear their boots hitting the dirt on the path when they started coming, and the dust kicked up just a little bit like they had just come in on their horses. They came in a processional from both sides and all the women in the audience looked amazed. It was one of the most satisfying moments for me.*

In keeping with the tradition of the company as family, Steve Tague and his brand new wife, Kathleen, squared off as Beatrice and Benedick in *Much Ado*, which made the fireworks just a touch more personal, and the comedy a lot more fun. But probably no one in that cast had more fun than another pair of actors who suddenly found themselves free to become the clowns they always wanted to be.

Tom Willmorth: *Doing Dogberry was important to me. There was another actor that was being considered for it who couldn't come that summer and it fell to me. We would get called to rehearsal and two hours would go by while the rest of the cast went through staging and stuff, and we sat in the rehearsal hall figuring out bits and putting stuff*

Jazz Under The Stars '94

Hot nights and cool jazz - a perfect combination! The **"Jazz under the Stars"** concert series, presented by West One Bank, returns to the Idaho Shakespeare Festival Amphitheatre this summer, with three exciting performances featuring legendary masters of jazz, **Chuck Findley**, **Ernie Watts** and **Gary Burton**.

Chuck Findley
ith the Wind Machine Big Band **Monday, July 25th**
onsored by the US West Foundation)

ou've ever been to the movies, watched TV, or heard recorded music of any kind, chances are ve heard the unmistakable jazz solos of trumpeter **Chuck Findley**. With literally thousands of and movie credits to his name, Mr. Findley is one the world's most sought-after recording ians. Since moving to Los Angeles in 1969, he has performed with virtually every major ng artist, from Barbara Streisand and Frank Sinatra, to Steely Dan, Madonna, Michael Jackson rth, Wind & Fire. Chuck's movie credits include just about every major motion picture in the past twenty years, including *The Godfather*, *Rocky*, *Back to the Future*, *Kramer vs Arthur*, and *An Officer and a Gentleman*. In fact, Mr. Findley's recording career is such on, that he was the subject of a two page article in the Wall Street Journal! ck tours with several groups including Doc Severinsen's "Toni nd Barbara Streisand just to name a few. Chuck F

atts

L-R, Kathleen Tague, Beatrice; Steve Tague, Benedick, *Much Ado.* TM

L-R, Kathleen Tague, Beatrice; Steve Tague, Benedick, *Much Ado.* TM

Much Ado About Nothing. TM

together. It was Joe and me being left to our own devices. And Star created this amazing costume that was part English, part Spanish, part 16th Century, part 18th Century, just this magnificent stew of things. The pants were like four feet wide.

The results were predictably hilarious. Joe's Verges was the perfect foil for the bizarre Constable Dogberry, and a new comic team was born. Star Moxley's costume stew set them off even more, and provided the kernel of an idea for what has since become an ISF institution – The Fool Squad. That summer they did three Greenshows.

Joe Golden: *That was the first comedy team-up for us, and it started the whole thing off. NYPD Blue had just come out and we were kind of watching that show because we were playing cops in Much Ado. So we were like, "Let's be theater police."*

Tom Willmorth: *So we got the sound track and that's how we entered. That's where we got the accents.*

Joe Golden: *We decided we would talk in a kind of mishmash Chicago/New York kind of cop-guy thing.*

Tom Willmorth: *We didn't want to wear the Dogberry and Verges costumes for the Greenshows, so we went the opposite way. We wanted it to look as ridiculously cheap as possible, so we went down to Star's costume shop and found these lame plastic helmets spray painted gold, and just wore t-shirts and some kind of baggy pants.*

Joe Golden: *Those two guys allowed us to really break the wall and get out into the audience and make them a part of it, grabbing people's food and testing it, saying "It's drug test night" and drinking someone's wine. It's such a blast.*

Also that summer, the second season of Jazz Under the Stars, presented by West One Bank, brought such jazz luminaries as Gary Burton, Ernie Watts and Chuck Findley to perform with Idaho's own big band, The Wind Machine, led by trumpeter Lyle Manwaring. These popular performances filled the usually dark Monday night slots, and served the dual purpose of bringing new people to the theater and adding to the summer season's bottom line.

Now it was time to launch the capital campaign in earnest. To get the ball rolling they hired The Collins Group, a Seattle consulting firm, to do a feasibility study.

As You Like It costume designs, Kim Krumm Sorenson.

As the board went through that process they realized they needed to answer another huge question before they could go much further – who would take on the monumental task of chairing the campaign? Board President Ray Smith approached Alan and Royanne Minskoff with the idea of co-chairing along with another couple, but after talking with several people and getting no takers, Ray enlisted his Vice President, Bill Keller, and along with Charlie and Mark the quartet put a full court press on the Minskoffs to do it themselves.

L-R, Lynn Allison, Chris; Ted Deasy, Gerry, *Lughnasa.* TM

L-R, Louise Moore, Rose; JoAnn Johnson, Maggie, *Lughnasa.* TM

Royanne Minskoff: *Alan and I said there were a couple of things we'd want in order for us to take on this project. One was to hire new counsel. We had participated in The Collins Group feasibility study and didn't agree with the outcome of it. Basically they interviewed a number of prominent, philanthropic people in the community, as well as bank and corporate CEO's, and they came away saying that what Shakespeare needed to do was a $1.5 million campaign and that they had to find a major donor who would give a million dollars and get the other half-million from the community. We both knew that just wasn't going to happen. The other thing we told them was that the board had to really step up and make a significant gift, at least 10% of whatever the final campaign goal was, and that we had to build the board in conjunction with doing the campaign.*

Alan Minskoff: *I met Alice and Halsey North at a conference in New York and I said to Royanne, these people are great. They're extremely well organized, and they're working with theaters all over the United States. The Norths did several things that were fundamental to this campaign. First of all they said you guys are going to raise the money, not us. They taught us to fund raise.*

Bill Keller was the new president of the board, having just taken the reins of leadership from Ray Smith. After eight years as Treasurer he knew the job was not going to be a stroll through the park. Indeed, one of his first duties was to meet with the Collins Group and explain that their services were no longer needed. Once the North's were hired, it was a matter of learning how to fly.

Bill Keller: *The Norths were very instrumental in that first twelve months or so of the campaign when we really didn't know what we were doing. We thought we could do it, but we needed somebody to give us some help and encouragement, and point us in the right direction on some of these things.*

The first thing they had to determine was just how much money they needed to raise. The estimated cost of the project had already grown from Charlie's initial $500,000 to $1.5 million, and as the board and the campaign committee began to examine the potential costs in detail, everyone could see it was going to take considerably more than that.

Bill Keller: *I remember when we were going to Albertsons to ask for money. We were worried they would ask us how much we needed to raise, and we didn't know. We didn't have complete drawings yet, we just had kind of a vision, and none of us really understood the construction process. I think we were talking about $1.5 million at the time and I said, tell them $2 million. Then it kind of went up from there.*

The Norths were quick to point out that whenever a capital campaign gift was received, it was important that a percentage of it went into operating support. That way they wouldn't end up with a beautiful new facility and a bankrupt organization. Working with the Norths, Alan and Royanne put together a budget that compartmentalized the resources so donors knew they were getting credit for the total amount of the gift even though a percentage of it was going to operating support. It was a clever and effective way to build the level of the gift for a lot of people.

Bethanne Andersen, cover art.

The act of beginning the campaign in earnest seemed to generate a momentum of sorts for the Festival. Dee Fery was appointed Chair of the Idaho Commission on the Arts by Governor Phil Batt in 1995 and asked Mark to come on with her as an at-large member. This prestigious appointment added to ISF's already substantial cachet in the state-wide arts community and would lead, in only a few years, to national recognition.

The Play: ***The Two Gentlemen of Verona***
Director: **Anne Justine D'Zmura**
Scenic Design: **Jack Ballance**
Costume Design: **Elizabeth Hope Clancy**
Lighting Design: **Rick Martin**
Musical Director: **Peter John Still**

The Play: ***Love's Labours Lost***
Director: **Bartlett Sher**
Scenic Design: **Jack Ballance**
Costume Design: **Alec Hammond**
Lighting Design: **Rick Martin**
Sound: **Peter John Still**

The Play: ***The First Part of King Henry the Fourth***
Director: **Charles Fee with Rick Foster**
Scenic Design: **Gage Williams**
Costume Design: **Ann Hoste**
Lighting Design:Rick Martin
Sound: **Peter John Still**

The Play: ***The Second Part of King Henry the Fourth***
Director: **Rick Foster with Charles Fee**
Scenic Design: **Gage Williams**
Costume Design: **Ann Hoste**
Lighting Design: **Rick Martin**
Sound: **Peter John Still**

1995

Director of Marketing Peter LeBlanc, who had been a huge help in carrying ISF through several lean years, moved on, and in his place, Charlie hired Kristen Robertson (De Angeli), a young, energetic woman with a graduate degree in literature, who also happened to be the daughter of former board President Chuck Robertson (1984) and his wife, Dianne, a past president of the Patron Committee (1981). Chuck and Dianne have been staunch supporters of the Festival since the One Capital Center days, and instilled a love of the Bard in their children as well.

Kristen De Angeli: *When I was about 10 years old I got to hand out programs, and that got me backstage. I have a second season program that was signed by everyone. The third year I made my parents take me to Romeo and Juliet every night because I was convinced that if Romeo and Juliet could just get their timing right neither one of them would die.*

Helene Peterson

Helene Peterson continued to prove a valuable festival asset, utilizing her extensive dance background to choreograph the second production of *A Christmas Carol* that winter. It was a skill that would serve ISF on many productions well into the future. In the spring she was promoted to Educational Outreach Director, organizing and overseeing the Shakespearience tours each spring, while Shaun Sites, who began his long career as ISF's Site Manager in 1986, was named Technical Director. Also that spring the Festival received notice that the ParkCenter site had been leased to a commercial developer and would not be available after the summer season.

Charlie Fee (1995 program): *There is so much "new news at the old court" that it's difficult to know where to begin…so perhaps we should begin with an ending. This year we bid a fond farewell to our ParkCenter site. After twelve summers in a homey, functional, back-yard amphitheater the time has come for the Festival to move out of "the parents' house." Actually Ore-Ida has been more like favorite Aunts and Uncles than like parents – they let us invite a few hundred friends over for a party every night and stay up late playing Shakespeare! The Festival owes Ore-Ida a real debt of gratitude for their overwhelming generosity in providing a safe haven these many years.*

Momentum began to shift to a sense of urgency. Going through all the obstacles of finding another temporary site meant postponing the timing of the capital campaign, yet the search for a permanent site was still not complete. It had, however, been narrowed to a handful of realistic prospects, three of which were in Garden City. Mayor Ted Ellis and his Public Works director, Randy Dearden, convened a group of three or four regulatory agencies to give ISF an outline of what issues might come into play if the Festival chose to build on one of them. At the conclusion of that process, one of the Garden City sites still remained feasible.

But a second ParkCenter site, just a quarter-mile upriver, was still under consideration as well, and Yvonne Farrell, Director of the Idaho Department of Parks and Recreation, along with Larry Leasure and the rest of the Idaho Foundation for Parks and Lands board, continued to beat the drum about the brickyard dump site he had shown them two years earlier in the Barber Pool Conservation Area. As managers of the Barber Pool, the Parks Department had been trying to figure out a way to get the area cleaned up, and thought perhaps a partnership with the Festival might benefit both organizations. All this did little to assuage Charlie and Mark's initial reservations.

DBB

Charlie Fee: *It looked horrible. I mean it really did look awful. Except that the river's there, and the foothills are gorgeous there, and there's a lot of land there, not to*

L-R, Mark Fossen, Paul de Cordova, Outlaws; Doyne Mraz, Duke, *Two Gents.* DBB

L-R, Sally Anne Eames, Shana Wride, Karla Mason, Erin Neill, *Love's Labours Lost.* DBB

mention this amazing natural area. Suddenly there are all these movers and shakers from the foundation there, and it starts to get more and more interesting.

They began taking board members out to the site to get some more opinions. Most of them were not impressed. Despite being a beautiful location, the parcel of land itself was a mess, and besides, they argued, it was too far out of town. It was the same argument we heard in 1981 when the Plantation site was offered to us, but at least that side of town was where all the new construction was going on, even back then. The question remained, would people in burgeoning West Boise drive all the way over to the eastern edge of the city to see Shakespeare? To try and settle on one of the final three sites once and for all, Mark put together another meeting of the same regulatory agencies who had studied the Garden City sites.

Mark Hofflund: *It was like a contest between three suitors who wanted ISF's figurative hand. We convened about 20 agencies, showed the three sites and then debriefed them in the Parks Department's Summit Room. And that's where you saw that the Foundation for Parks and Lands and the Parks Department really wanted us to come out there. They wanted to win this contest. And it was also clear that the regulatory agencies gave IFPL the blue ribbon because it was going to be much easier for them to approve the project on that site than any of the others.*

Tom Willmorth, Launce, *Two Gents.* DBB

In the midst of all this, Charlie launched one of the most ambitious seasons ever undertaken. Dubbed "All Shakespeare, All Summer," it included two comedies – *The Two Gentlemen of Verona*, with Ann D'Zmura at the helm, and *Love's Labours Lost*, which brought Bart Sher back to direct again. Delving into the Bard's histories for the second time since his arrival at ISF, Charlie undertook the gargantuan task of directing *King Henry IV, Parts I and II*, bringing dramaturg Rick Foster in to co-direct.

Mark Anthony Taylor: *I had an entrance from a trap in the middle of the stage, which you had to crawl out to in the dark. They ran all the cable under the stage, too, so I'm crawling over cables and dodging spider webs and stuff. I'm sitting down there quietly waiting for my cue and I hear this rustling. I pan my little flashlight over and there's a skunk about six feet away. I've got nowhere to run, so I'm like, if I don't move, maybe he won't know I'm here. But he was cool.*

Ann Hoste came to BSU in 1990 as a costume designer for their theater department and immediately went to work on a co-production with ISF of *The Crucible*, directed by Rod Ceballos. When Charlie became Artistic Director he hired her to design *Dancing at Lughnasa* in 1994, and the following year he handed her the biggest assignment of her career – designing both *Henrys*.

There are several reasons why both parts of Henry IV are not usually done together in the same season, especially in repertory. Besides the large casts, almost all men, the time change from Part 1 to Part 2 makes it unrealistic to use the same costumes for both shows. Star Moxley's shop was still serving as the Festival's stichery, even though Star herself was busy designing shows for Idaho Theater for Youth that summer.

Ann Hoste: *For my money it was the best place to work. It was so miserably hot, but it was wide open. You had all this space and all this light. There was room to accommodate three or four designers without feeling cramped. Nancy Berger, the shop manager, would make homemade root beer and bring it in and we'd have a shop party. Those homemade root beer floats made it feel like a day at the lake or something. Nancy really had a way of making you feel like family when you were working there.*

Kristen De Angeli: *It is like a big family, a family of renaissance people. They're not just actors or designers or tech crew, they're people who have decided to make their lives doing something that is an art, and that they love. They travel, and they speak different languages, and they don't just have hobbies they truly have crafts that they do. They're very interesting as a group, and they're fascinating to work with. You feel like maybe some of it will rub off.*

Mark Anthony Taylor: *The worst person to be on stage with*

Peter John Still, Resident Sound Designer. *The Idaho Statesman*

Mark Anthony Taylor: *Peter Still, the resident sound designer, always wears black. Always. He'll say, "That's a great t-shirt, do they make it in black?" "No, I don't think so, Peter." "Darn, I can't get it then." Bart wanted him on stage playing the piano live during Love's Labour's, and because it was set in the forest and he had this little hunting scene, he told the costume designer to put Peter in hunter orange from head to toe. Somehow they even got fluorescent orange shoes. The first tech we had Peter came out with that costume on and he was like a newborn child. His steps were really tentative. He didn't know how to move in orange. It was hysterical. The sound guys loved it so much they kept pictures on the wall in the booth.*

Costume Design, Anne Hoste, Glendower, *Henry IV*.

Set Design, Gage Williams, *Henry IV, Pt.2*.

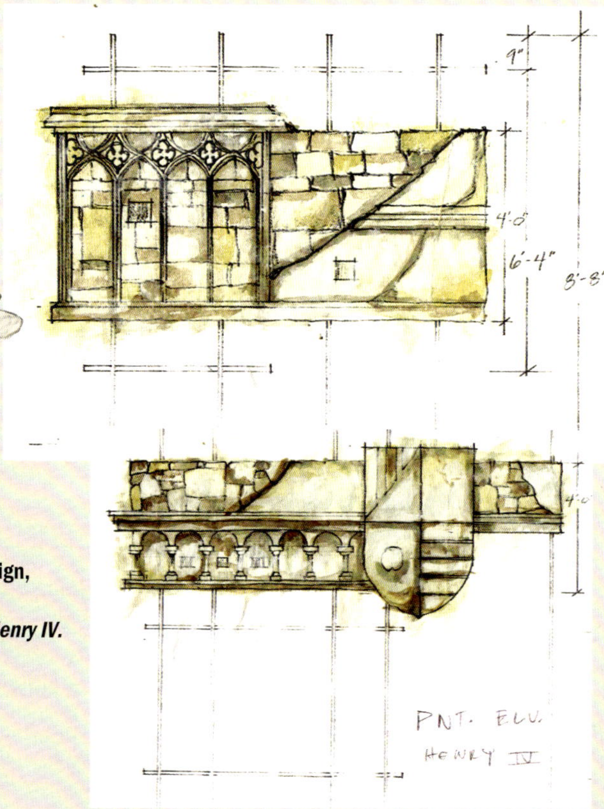

when odd things happen is Tom Willmorth. In Two Gents I played Speed and Tom was Launce. They didn't want to use a real dog for Crab, so they got a taxidermy dummy. Late in the run he says to me, "I've done all the dog bits except one, I never dragged my butt on the carpet." I couldn't really deprive him of that, so we worked out a time to do it, and as it got close I was already steeling myself because his bits were always hysterically funny to watch. So he says his line, gets down and drags his butt across the stage. I was ready for it, I thought, but when I started to say my next line I could not get my mouth around the words. That gave him just enough time to turn around and go back the other way, at which point the audience completely lost it. I just turned upstage and threw my hands up in the air in defeat.

While Charlie and company got the season up and running, Mark went to work creating a unique partnership that would, once and for all, put the Festival in a permanent home. A second round of site visits and brainstorming with regulatory agencies was held, this time with twenty of them, and the results yielded high marks for the Barber Pool site. Once that decision was made, the Festival still had to go through the lengthy, formal process of approval with each one of them. There were reports to be made, data to be collected, traffic studies to be done – but the big issue was access.

When Boise Cascade gave the 480 acres to the Foundation for Parks and Lands it had no formal access. It remained that way partly by design, since this was a park for wildlife, not for people. But if people were to appreciate this phenomenal resource that was a part of their city, they needed an appropriate way to get to it. So, Foundation president Don Weilmunster worked out a purchase agreement with George Pullman for his company's road side property that connected to the Pool. Welimunster then invited the IDPR to participate in a one-time administrative split, with the State Parks Department getting the majority of the brickyard property for their new administrative headquarters, and the Foundation getting an

Henry IV, Pt.2. DBB

I think Crab my dog be the sourest-natured dog that lives.

Two Gents, II, iii.

office inside the new Robert Smylie Headquarters Building. The next step was to give the area some identity and public usage, which would give the Foundation some visibility and name recognition. The Shakespeare Festival's capital campaign to build a theater was just the vehicle they needed to accomplish that.

Mark Hofflund: Another agreement, equivalent to the earlier split of the Pullman brickyard property, was reached whereby an administrative split of the Boise Cascade gift parcel carved out a 2.5 acre piece for ISF. Now the Festival would own the land for its buildings – so long as access could be arranged. At first we were going to share the entrance of the Parks Department parking lot, but the State Land Board could only give us a renewable ten year lease. The ISF board felt that if we were going to ask the community for millions of dollars to build a brand new theater, we needed more than a ten year commitment from the State. The County helped us in some ways as well, because it also wanted permanent access in order to approve the whole project. We all needed a new idea.

Working with Clive Strong in the Attorney General's office, an exception to the Land Board's ten year restriction was discovered for Parks Department property. When Governor Robert Smylie created the Idaho Department of Parks and Recreation in 1965, he gave the ultimate authority for park lands to the State Board of Examiners, not the Land Board. A special use permit was approved and purchase was announced at the Festival's annual fund raising gala. A document was prepared on a parchment scroll outlining all the terms of the partnership and what would need to be accomplished in order for the sale to go through. Foundation president Don Weilmunster took up a quill pen and signed, followed by ISF Board President Bill Keller, and the deal was sealed.

Mark Hofflund: *It was a great example of the State working together with the County to solve a problem that gave our Board and our donor base what it needed to raise the money to make improvements for our theater as well as enhancing the habitat in and around the Barber Pool Conservation Area.*

Henry IV, Pt.2. **DBB**

All that remained were a few political hurdles, and of course the small matter of raising the money to pay for it all. It was time for the capital campaign to go public and swing into full operation.

Royanne Minskoff: The first time it was announced to the Executive Committee that we were the Campaign Co-chairs everyone was thrilled. I said thank you, but now we've got some really thrilling news to share with you. We've set a campaign goal of $3.7 million. Everybody got really quiet. And then I said we've decided that the board has to contribute $350,000 to the campaign. And literally every head in the room just dropped. It can't be done, they said, it's impossible. Then we sat down and mapped how we were going to do it.

ISF wasn't the only arts organization in Boise to receive a jaw-dropping shock that spring. Across town at Idaho Theater for Youth, which had grown phenomenally under the capable direction of Eloise Bruce, another board meeting was taking place, one that would start it on a bumpy path leading back to where it began in 1981 – the Idaho Shakespeare Festival.

When I moved back to Boise in 1993 it didn't take long to realize that Charlie and Mark had things well in hand at ISF. The last thing they needed was an ex-artistic director and board president meddling in their plans. So when I was asked to join the ITY Board of Directors, I happily accepted. As one of two prospective new members attending our first meeting, and as yet unable to vote, I was perhaps more shocked than most when Managing Director Cynthia Gaede abruptly parted ways with the company. She had worked as an assistant director with ISF before joining Eloise Bruce at ITY to handle marketing and management duties, and had

Seated: Matt Ramsey, Sean Coleman, Matt Clark, Outlaws; standing: Dana Slamp, Julia; Jacque Drew, Lucetta, *Two Gents.* TM

become that company's driving force when Eloise left in 1988. Moments later David Lee Painter, another ISF alumni who had been ITY's Artistic Director for four very successful years announced he was leaving the following week to accept a teaching position at the University of Idaho. Those of us who were new to the organization began to wonder just what we had gotten ourselves into.

The next morning I received a phone call from David asking me to lunch with him and one or two of the board members. I eagerly accepted, dying to find out the reason behind the company's sudden loss of management. Since Eloise had taken on my challenge to create a theater company for young audiences fifteen years earlier, ITY had grown into the state's leading performing arts organization for young audiences, developing original plays which they toured twice a year to schools throughout Idaho and once a year to young audiences in seven western states. In addition, Terri Dillion had developed a very successful drama school program that offered a series of after-school workshop classes to kids each spring and fall.

Dan Peterson: *Eloise's original vision was to create this children's theater that would run during the school year and employ three actors pretty much full time. It was a hundred miles an hour for me and Terri Dillion and Linda Blome. We would do early morning shows on Saturday and Sunday for little kids at the BSU Reading Center. Then we would take shows for older students out to the schools each week. We also did one or two sort of major productions for the public each year.*

By the time Eloise left the company in 1988, the demand for ITY's unique brand of educational theater was employing a dozen actors and designers each year, and commissioning original works from playwrights acriss the country. Cindy, Dan and Terri decided to join forces to save it from ceasing operations. In 1991 they hired David Lee Painter as Artistic Director and the company began to gain a national prominence with productions such as an original adaptation of *Little Lulu* and Mark Rosenwinkel's captivating capsulization of *Moby Dick* . Since then they had twice been invited to participate in the Kennedy Center's Imagination Celebration and had just been selected to represent North America at the bi-annual International Children's Festival in Rostov-on-Don, Russia.

David Lee Painter: *I got there in January, 1992 and we were just about to go to the Kennedy Center with a production of Commedia de Lazzi which was just awful. I said this cannot go to the Kennedy Center. So we hired Tom Willmorth to do a re-write in a week and we re-cast the whole play and off we went.*

IDAHO THEATER FOR YOUTH PRESENTS
MOBY DICK

Clockwise from top, Dan Peterson, Ahab; Mhari Sandoval, Ishmael; Carole Whiteleather, Queequeg; Trini Sandoval, Starbuck, *Moby Dick,* adapted by Mark Rosenwinkel. UK

Instead of filling me in on all the juicy details behind the disconcerting events of the board meeting, however, David simply asked if I would accept the position of Interim Executive Director at ITY instead of going on the board, and oversee the hiring of new management. He was leaving for Moscow in just a few days, and rather than rely on the remaining staff to pick up the pieces, he felt a fresh perspective would be better when it came to sorting things out at ITY. I had not planned on diving back into the Boise arts scene head first, but after sleeping on the offer and seeing no other immediate short term option for the company, I agreed to a six month contract, at the end of which, with new management in place, I would re-join the board.

Meanwhile, the Shakespeare Festival's nineteenth season played to packed crowds all summer long as audiences flocked to pay their last respects to the ParkCenter site. The Monday night Jazz Under the Stars program grew even more popular. The capital campaign committee took to the streets making their pitch for the Festival's yet to be discovered new home, and Charlie's curtain speeches each night were peppered with pleas for contributions to the new amphitheater and inspiring stories of new donors who were beginning to toss their hats into the ring.

Alan Minskoff: *Halsey North went with me on a critical meeting with Key Bank where Halsey turned the key and I opened the door. When they told us, "we don't give money to bricks and mortar", Halsey said, "what about marketing?" And I said yes, you could be our marketing sponsor indefinitely. And they have been. That was one of the great meetings of the whole campaign.*

Dan Peterson: *In those early years we were doing three different shows in a school year, one in the fall, one in the winter and one in the spring. We'd go out and do 120 performances of each show over the course of a single school year. Four or five years of performing in front of people that often and I mean, good or bad, inspiring or uninspiring, that's where I learned the craft. That was my grad school.*

Audiences took it all to heart, and the community once again stepped up to help the theater company that had become such an integral part of Boise summers. Gifts from $5 to $5,000 began to fill the coffers, each one as crucial as the next. Royanne's advice to the board to work on "bite-sized pieces – one little step at a time," was working, but not nearly as fast as some had hoped. By the time the company said farewell at season's end it was clear that the road to Barber Pool was going to be a long one.

Another farewell was announced that summer in a small ad placed near the back of the program. David Bogie, who had chronicled the goings on of the Festival from rehearsals through closing night with his cameras since 1978, was taking his final bow. The infamous slide shows that graced each cast party, with equipment courtesy of his generous employer, Idaho Power, would no longer give the company a nostalgic look back at all they had accomplished that season. As a new era of growth was being ushered in with the capital campaign, another era was passing.

Micheal Baltzell: *Bogie's slide show was the event of the whole year for everybody. You know how it is, it's the end of the season and you're tired of looking at these people. You don't want to come into work any more. Then there's the closing night party and you're like, "Oh man, I don't want to go." But you do go, and then he shows that slide show with the music and all those pictures, and by the end of it everybody's all like, "I love you, man, I'm gonna miss you!" Somebody you weren't talking to an hour ago and now it's, "I'm never gonna forget you!" He was so good at encapsulating what we did, and now we could be proud of it in a different way. I miss that.*

L-R, Dan Peterson, Travis Swartz; Carole Whiteleather, Terri Dillion, *The "I" in Idaho.* UK

Bethanne Andersen, cover art.

Fall and winter came and went, and so did the commercial development planned for the Ore-Ida site. Another one-year lease was signed giving ISF a much-needed reprieve, and a home for its twentieth season.

The capital campaign was still a long ways from having enough cash in the bank to begin construction on the new theater, and Chuck Winder's Arid Club prediction was coming true as well. Connector construction was edging closer and closer to the east end of town, and the bridge connecting Myrtle Street with ParkCenter Boulevard was dangerously close to becoming a reality.

Just because a bullet had been dodged, this was no time to take a breather. Charlie and Mark knew they had to keep planning the theater as though the money was going to be there. In its first nineteen years 1,263 performances had drawn a total attendance of over 320,000. Ten years of the annual Shakespearience tour had provided 521 performances at high schools around the state, exposing the work of the Bard to more than 253,000 young people. The momentum was well

The Play: ***The Compleat Works of Shakespeare*** **(abridged)**
Director: **Charles Fee**
Scenic Design: **Gage Williams**
Costume Design: **Rebecca Hoffman**
Lighting: **RickMartin**
Musical Director: **Peter John Still**

The Play: ***The Merry Wives of Windsor***
Director:Sari Ketter
Scenic Design: **Jack Ballance**
Costume Design: **Kim Krumm Sorenson**
Lighting: **RickMartin**
Musical Director: **Peter John Still**

The Play: ***The Tempest***
Director: ***Bartlett Sher***
Scenic Design: **Alec Hammond**
Costume Design: **Kim Krumm Sorenson**
Lighting: **RickMartin**
Musical Director: **Peter John Still**

The Play: ***Twelfth Night***
Director: **Charles Fee**
Scenic Design: **Gage Williams**
Costume Design: **Star Moxley**
Lighting: **Rick Martin**
Musical Director: **Peter John Still**

1996

Danan Pere, Caliban, *The Tempest.* TM

established. The board and the capital campaign committee could not afford to let up.

Mark Hofflund: *Bill Keller ended up doing two years as board president just because we needed to keep him going to all those meetings. We needed to keep the continuum, and the guy was unbelievable. Always available, always there, always going to meetings. You wondered how he got his regular job done.*

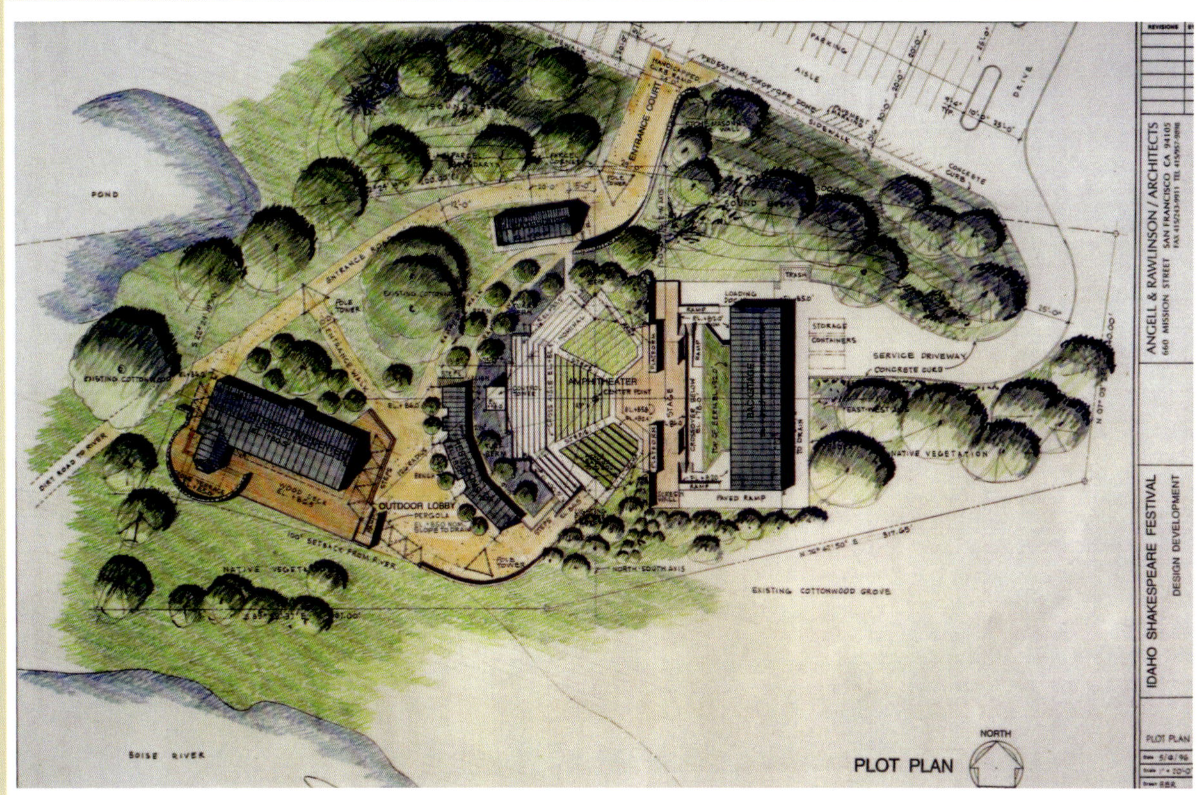

In order to bring some construction expertise to the board, Brent and Sandy Fery made a call to local architect Andy Erstad.

Andy Erstad: *I agreed to join the board not knowing that they wanted me to be on the Building Committee. My first committee meeting was in the old offices in Garden City and nobody showed up except Charlie and Mark. I said I think we have a problem, this isn't a committee, and they said that makes you the chairman.*

Andy realized that without a consensus group the construction would not be a true board effort, only the effort of Charlie, Mark and himself, so he set about establishing a committee. His first call was to his friend Brent Fery, a leader in the banking community. Campaign co-chair Royanne Minskoff was the next to join so she could keep as up to speed as possible on their progress. Joe La Marche, a dean among Boise architects who was on the verge of retirement, agreed to serve as the local ringleader for San Diego based theater architects Gene Angell and Brian Rawlinson, and proceeded to pull some phenomenal resources into the picture, including contractor Bill Mooney of Jordan-Wilcomb Construction.

Mark Hofflund: *In all fairness, board members and community volunteers had been working for years on a permanent theater. Vangie introduced Charlie and me to architect Brian Smith, who in turn got civil engineer Steve Sweet to work with Gene and Brian on concept drawings, donating all the local time and expertise we needed. Chris Beeson, the superb dirt lawyer did tons of work, along with surveyor Pat Tealey. The environmental and planning committees played huge roles with numerous field studies and site analyses. But ultimately the board needed one of its own involved in the same intimate details Charlie and I knew. That's where Andy became a lynchpin for the whole project.*

Meanwhile, the loyal Boise audience was beginning to ask questions. Last year's "farewell" season was supposed to be the last at the ParkCenter site. Now here they were back again. What happened? Where was this new theater the Festival had promised a year ago? Charlie's program notes declined to explain all the convoluted

Trinculo costume design, *Tempest*, Anne Hoste.

L-R, Danan Pere, Caliban; Tom Willmorth, Stephano; Rebecca Prescott, Ariel; Joe Conley Golden, Trinculo, *Tempest.* TM

The Tempest TM

L-R, Daniel Garton, Ferdinand; Sara Bruner, Miranda; Rebecca Prescott, Ariel, Steve Tague, Prospero., *Tempest.* TM

ins and outs of starting a capital campaign and searching for a new site. Instead, he kept his message simple.

> **Charlie Fee (1996 program):** *The good news is that our friends at Ore-Ida Foods have extended their invitation for another summer of Shakespeare – the bad news is that I'll be making the same curtain speeches as last year. So what does a theater company produce in its second good-bye season? Last year's "all Shakespeare, all summer" lineup was a rousing success…but this season – our 20th – we needed to go one better. The answer, "all OF Shakespeare, all summer."*

He chose to fill that outrageous bill by directing *The Compleat Works of Shakespeare (abridged)*, a raucous comedy in which three actors attempt to perform the entire canon, including all the sonnets, in a two hour show. Well okay, not really. To pull off this monumental task, he cast festival mainstay Dan Peterson along with Tom Willmorth and Joe Golden, whose Greenshow collaborations had been keeping audiences in stitches for several seasons now.

> **Joe Golden:** *Danny and I talked about it the year before, and he brought the script to Charlie. I asked what he thought and he said, "It's not very good. It's kind of cheesy. There are some lame jokes." I said, yeah, but we could mess with it, and he said, "Yeah, that's true."*

That turned out to be the understatement of the year. To round out the season, Charlie also directed *Twelfth Night*, and brought in Sari Ketter from the Guthrie Theater in Minneapolis to take charge of *The Merry Wives of Windsor*, while Bart Sher returned for his fourth season to direct *The Tempest*. In auditions at Boise State University that spring, several students vied for intern positions. One young Burley High School graduate was immediately impressive, and Charlie hired her on the spot. When the company came together to start rehearsals that summer, several of the younger actors were required to audition again for the other directors. They were likewise impressed with the young intern and she found herself playing Falstaff's young apprentice, Robin, in *Merry Wives* and Miranda, the lead female in *The Tempest*.

> **Sara Bruner:** *I had no idea how great it was because I was so excited. If I was to see an eighteen-year-old come here now and step in and do that I would probably be frightened for her. I put myself under such pressure because it was like, I'm on stage with Steve Tague now and I*

L-R, Dan Peterson, Bardolph (on floor); Drew Brhel, Falstaff; Mark Gladue, Host of the Garter, *Merry Wives.* TM

L-R, Sara Bruner, Robin; Ty Smith, Hugh Evans, *Merry Wives.* TM

L-R, Christina Lang, Mistress Page; Kathleen Tague, Mistress Ford, *Merry Wives.* TM

L-R, Stitch Marker, Justice Shallow; Danan Pere, Master Page; Danny Camiel, Slender, *Merry Wives.* TM

don't really know what that means, but I know I'd better do a really good job.

Kim Sorenson: *In The Tempest, Danan Pere, who was playing Caliban, was painted completely red, and at the end of the show each night there was no way for him to clean up because there was no running water. Nobody wanted the poor guy in their car. We tried to work a deal with the hotel across the street to let him use a shower there. It was a real struggle for him.*

Mark Anthony Taylor: *Sari read me for three things at auditions, but not for Doctor Caius, so when she asked me if there was anything else I'd like to read for I said yeah, I want to read for Caius. I read it once and she became hysterical. It became like my benchmark role here where I sort of rose to the occasion. One day Charlie pulls me aside and says, "My God, I didn't even know Caius was a good role."*

The opening pages of the program contained information about the new site and the planned theater complex, along with an architect's rendering of the design. Almost buried in the last paragraph about how the Festival staff was working with a host of people to finalize the design, obtain all the permits, develop construction cost estimates and launch a capital campaign to pay for it all, was the total proposed cost of the project, estimated at a cool $3.7 million.

The figure was shocking to some, impressive to others, but everyone was assured that the capital campaign was moving forward apace. And for those who wanted to see the Festival's new home for themselves, Ore-Ida sponsored "Hard Hat Site Tours." Each tour night, before the show, a bus departed from the ParkCenter theater to give people an up-close look at the new site, followed by a question and answer session. And each rider got a souvenir hard hat.

The project was known as the ISF Amphitheater and Reserve because it included a natural buffer of about ten acres surrounding the ISF parcel for the Festival to develop with parking, pathways, a large pond and native re-vegetation. It was by far the most ambitious undertaking the Festival had ever begun, and more than a few ISF patrons wondered privately if the staff and board could pull it off.

Kristen De Angeli: *This is a magical place to work in many ways. Despite the overwork and some frustrations, which you get in any job, you get to offset those by doing something your really believe in. There's nothing like going out to that theater and just feeling what's happening on stage and knowing you've been a part of that. There's a sense that you're doing something more important than just your daily* *job, that you've become a part of the fabric of this community and that you're creating, maybe, some new memories.*

At least one part of that question was answered on July 24, when Mark went before the Ada County Board of Commissioners for the final vote on the arduous process of re-zoning the Barber Pool property.

Mark Hofflund: *The day of the meeting I got a call from Morley Nelson, with whom I had talked a few times about what we were doing in terms of the wildlife in the reserve. He said, "I think I'd better come with you." We were way down on the agenda, and we were sitting there in the back of this very full room, when suddenly Vern Bisterfelt looks back at us and interrupts the entire proceedings. "Morley Nelson, is that you?" he booms out, waving a big arm. "Hello Vern," says Morley, waving back. "What are you doing here?" asks Vern. "Well, I'm here to help the Shakespeare Festival." And Vern says, "Well, they're coming up, but meanwhile, what do you think about this..." There was some issue about birds of prey that had been in the papers, had nothing whatsoever to do with the meeting. Morley gave his opinion, Vern thanked him, and they went back to the meeting.*

When the Festival did come up on the agenda, Mark's testimony was supported by comments from Joe La Marche, representing the theater architects, Chris Korte from the Idaho Park Foundation, Mike Wardle, project manager for the nearby Harris Ranch development. The lone opposition came from Oliver Gregerson, another property owner in Barber Pool and the Festival's closest neighbor, who was convinced that the noise, the lights and the people would all be detrimental to the area and the wildlife.

Then Morley stood up and said that he thought having the Festival in the Barber Pool was a good thing for the wildlife and everyone involved. He pointed out that ISF had given a lot of consideration to eagle habitat and the effect the Festival's presence will have on them, and that relocating the Festival there will give a lot of people the chance to see the eagles and learn more about them. The commissioners' approval was unanimous, and another hurdle was cleared on the way to a new amphitheater.

L-R, Matt Ramsey, Curio; Naomi Kingsbury, Dancer, *Twelfth Night*.. TM

Curio

Sailors

This page and opposite, *Twelfth Night* costume designs, Star Moxley.

Mark Hofflund: *Both Gary Glenn and Vern Bisterfelt had been subjects of humor in our Greenshows. At one point Tom and Joe actually made a spoof on them with two characters called Glenngass and Blisterbluster. So when I got up to testify, Vern looked at me very seriously, but with a twinkle in his eye, and said he had heard about some of the "goings on at our theater" regarding public officials. I of course disavowed any knowledge, and everybody started laughing. Then Roger Simmons piped up and said, "I think we might approve this so long as there's a guarantee that I'm never involved."*

It was probably a good thing that Ada County's elected treasurer, Barbara Bauer, who also happened to be an ISF board member and the capital campaign's first treasurer, was a close friend of all three very different men sitting on the Ada County Board of Commissioners at that time.

Meanwhile, the capital campaign was going full speed ahead. Since the beginning, Alan and Royanne had known that most of the big donations would come from corporations, so those were approached first. Then the focus shifted to the ISF board.

Royanne Minskoff: *The entire board campaign was set up two-fold. Every board member was being asked, and every board member was doing an ask. And doing an ask from a training standpoint, because they knew they were going to get a yes, but the experience would help prepare them for asking other people for contributions.*

Since 100% board participation was required for the campaign, early morning breakfast meetings included more training sessions provided on video by the National Center for Non-Profit Organizations. But there were other local people with plenty of experience in fund raising whose expertise could be called on as well.

Alan Minskoff: *I don't know how many meetings I went to with John and Dee Fery because they were critical to the success of this. John was like a godfather to us. He wanted to make sure that he knew what was going on, that he was happy with the process of the campaign and how the Reserve was going to be handled. He really helped a great deal.*

Toby Belch

L-R, Richard Klautsch, Toby Belch; Steve Tague, Malvolio, *Twelfth Night.* TM

L-R, Kathleen Tague, Viola (disguised); Steve Tague, Malvolio, *Twelfth Night.*

L-R, Kelly Kerslake, Olivia; Danan Pere, Orsino; Kathleen Tague Viola (disguised), *Twelfth Night.*

Royanne Minskoff: *Dee and John said they wanted us to be committed in the process of the campaign to making sure that the next generation was stepping up. They said it was time for that to happen and that this campaign had to be about more than getting a new amphitheater built, it had to bring in this whole new set of donors to the community.*

Set design, Gage Williams, *Twelfth Night.* GW

Bethanne Andersen, cover art.

In the spring of 1997 the capital campaign scored a direct hit that infused everyone's efforts with a new energy and excitement. Michael Hoffman, one of the original founding members of ISF, had achieved considerable success as a feature film director, working with some of the biggest names in acting along the way.

After a lunch with Alan and Royanne to discuss how he could best help the campaign, Mike made a call to his friend Kevin Kline, who graciously agreed to become the honorary chair and to attend a major fund raiser in Boise.

Mike Hoffman: *The Festival gave me a tremendous sense of possibilities for the life I could have in theater and film. The reason*

The Play: ***Private Lives***
Director: Charles Fee
Scenic Design: Gage William
Costume Design: Ann Hoste
Lighting Design: Tracy Odishaw
Musical Director: Peter John Still

The Play: ***The Merchant of Venice***
Director: Bartlett Sher
Scenic Design: Gage Williams
Costume Design: Kim Krumm Sorenson
Lighting Design: Tracy Odishaw
Sound: Peter John Still

The Play: ***The Taming of the Shrew***
Director: Sari Ketter
Scenic Design: Gage Williams
Costume Design: Kim Krumm Sorenson
Lighting Design: Tracy Odishaw
Sound: Peter John Still

The Play: ***The Tragedy of Macbeth***
Director: Charles Fee
Scenic Design: Gage Williams
Costume Design: Star Moxley
Lighting Design: Tracy Odishaw
Sound: Peter John Still

1997

Kevin Kline meets the press.

I came back is because I really wanted to be part of the community, and if anything meant community to me in Boise it was the Shakespeare Festival – that community of actors, all the hopes and dreams that we had as young people. And I was always amazed at the audience. The Festival created an audience of really intelligent Shakespeare viewers, which is extraordinary. I would listen to a play like Henry VIII with these odd little jokes obscured by four centuries of history, and there are people in Boise laughing at these really sophisticated literary turns of phrase that indicated to me that they had learned to listen to classical theater by sitting out on the lawn year after year. It's an amazing gift the Festival has given the city. So it was kind of a natural fit that I would come back and try to do what I could to push it forward.

The event was a huge success, raising $180,000 for the new theater in a single evening. In addition to the contributions of those attending, who also enjoyed wonderful readings from *Hamlet* and *Much Ado About Nothing* by Kevin Kline, there were a few additional announcements that brought applause. Not the least of which was a large donation from Alan Minskoff's mother, Marjorie Minskoff Schleifer, which caught the campaign co-chair completely unaware and, in a rare occurrence, rendered him momentarily speechless.

L-R, Kevin Kline, Honorary Campaign Chair; Charles Fee, Producing Artistic Director.

Artist's rendering Amphitheater, Sylvia Hofflund.

To give the summer season some extra fund raising incentive Charlie decided to call it the Festival's twentieth anniversary. It began in 1977, so in one way the math was correct, even though it was actually the twenty-first season of Shakespeare Under the Stars in Boise. By this time the list of capital campaign donors was a long one, and growing all the time, but there was still a long way to go if the goal of $3.7 million was to be reached.

In the summer program, board President Brad Andrews told patrons that "we are learning that many components of such an ambitious project may take more time to accomplish than originally expected. At times the process tests our collective patience, but your generosity and commitment continue to fuel our effort. The best is yet to come!"

Indeed, plans for the new theater were in the final stages, and though it had first been seen as little more than a dump site, further study revealed that the former logging mill pond is home to the largest remaining natural stand of black cottonwoods along the Boise River. The Barber Pool Conservation Area is also home to more than 200 species of wildlife throughout the year, including a large population of roosting Bald Eagles that winter here. All this within sight of a remnant of the Oregon Trail, which descends from the nearby bluffs above the river.

The program also featured letters from each of the Festival's former Artistic Directors, and a nod from Charlie to the "pioneers" of the Festival, "who carved out a path in the wilderness. The history of the Festival is filled with stories of perseverance and blind enthusiasm, of visionaries and dreamers, and of very practical people with the ability to solve problems – in short, a theater company."

The company that summer included many faces that were becoming familiar to audiences, and as usual there were new faces both on stage and behind the scenes. Charlie also ventured into new theatrical territory, directing Noel Coward's drawing room comedy, *Private Lives*.

Aerial shot, Barber Pool, pre-construction. TM

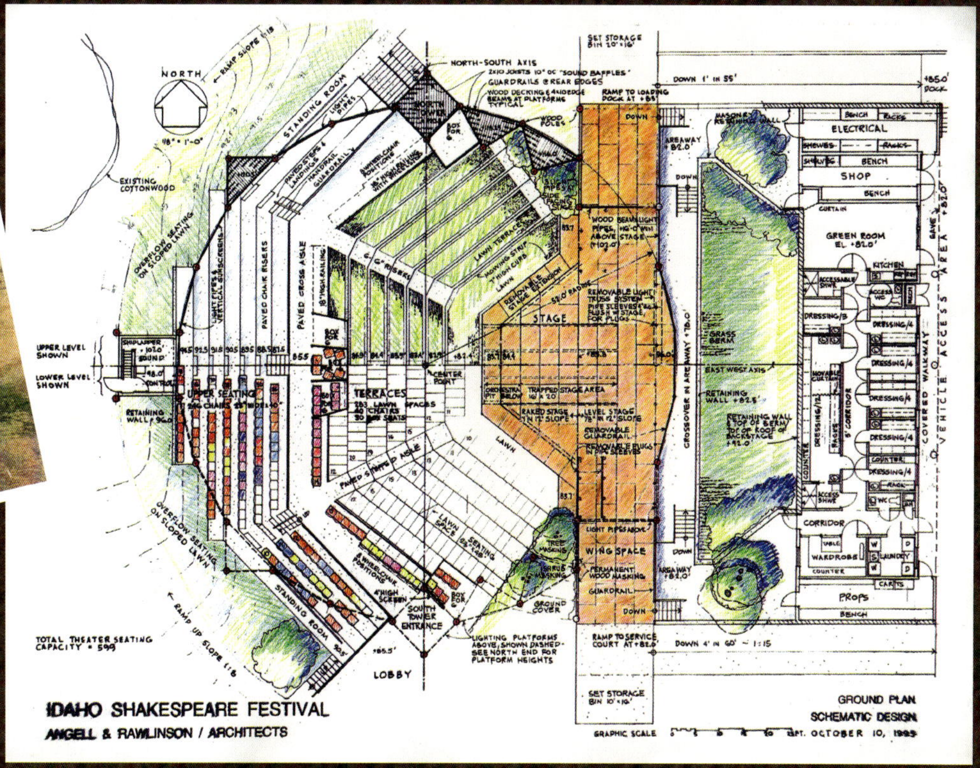

Gage Williams: *It was the first time Charlie and I had done a contemporary piece out there. The first scene takes place outside the hotel, and I came up with an idea for two big, curved walls with an awning that would open up and reveal this very modern, very elegant art deco interior. It looked great in the model, but when it got out there on stage we both took one look and said, "Oh no!" We had built a relationship with Davies-Reid, the antique dealer, and I remembered they had these carved columns in their basement from an Indian Buddhist temple. I went over there and got the columns and a bunch of rugs and some other things and redecorated the set the next day. It covered all the mistakes and just made perfect sense in the space. It must have been $60,000 worth of stuff they let us truck over and put on the set. They saved our lives.*

Richard Klautsch: *On opening night there was an absolute thunderstorm, and Boise audiences will stay out there no matter what. Charlie came back stage and asked us to go out and at least get through one act for the folks out there. All during the first act the rain increased in intensity, and every time you'd go off stage you'd take another costume piece off and put on a jacket or raincoat to try and keep from getting absolutely soaked, then go back out there and try to maintain the style and elegance of Noel Coward as you sat down in a puddle of water on those chairs. I'll never forget that night because it was just so damn much fun.*

As usual, there were three Shakespeare plays, *The Tragedy of Macbeth*, which Charlie took on himself, *The Taming of the Shrew*, directed by Sari Ketter, and *The Merchant of Venice*, which he put in the capable hands of Bart Sher, who gave it his own unique touch that actors and audiences had come to expect.

Mark Anthony Taylor: *I had a conversation with Bart one day and he said, "You know, I can't get away with this production anywhere else but here because there's a certain aesthetic that's been developed over the years that audiences are incredibly accepting and incredibly gracious and will go wherever you want."*

Gage Williams was now the Resident Scenic Designer, creating the backdrops for all the shows. Likewise, Peter John Still handled the Composing and Sound Design for the entire season. Kim Krumm Sorenson designed costumes for both *Merchant* and *Shrew*, with Ann Hoste creating the look for *Private Lives* and festival regular Star Moxley taking on *Macbeth*.

Richard Klautsch, Elyot Chase; Janis Stevens, Amanda Prynne, Private Lives by Noel Coward.TM

Gage Williams: *With the Scottish play we used devices associated with Japanese theater such as red silk for blood, live drummers and stylized costumes, hairpieces and physical movement. We were concerned with making a visual connection to the text that would somehow be recognizable by the words the actors were saying. The drums really supported that. I think it was a pivotal moment for us in terms of the Festival's design ideas. We were starting to let ourselves be a little more abstract*

Macbeth

Daiko drummer, *Macbeth*. TM

Steve Tague, Macbeth; Janis Stevens, Lady Macbeth. TM

Audiences loved the effect, especially Star's costuming of the witches and Charlie's use of their double-long arms, hidden in extended cloaks, to transform entire stage pictures.

Gage Williams: *Torches are always a dilemma in outdoor Shakespeare, both keeping them burning and not setting everything on fire. The prop person had this new thing where he rolled sawdust, bee's wax and kerosene into little balls that you could drop in your torch receptacle and flame up. Opening night one of them dropped onto the stage, and it had a nice little fire going. One of the actors went over and stomped on it but he had to make his exit, and even though it wasn't out he went ahead and left. So there's this fire still burning on the stage. Finally Charlie came down from the back of the house and walked up on stage and stamped it out. He looked at the audience and said, "Hey, live theater."*

Charlie's plan to solidify the company in all aspects was working. The Festival audience was really beginning to take notice of the improvements in artistic quality.

Mark Hofflund: *When Charlie did Macbeth the board actually said, "This is a great production, and it deserves a much better facility than this one. So the art was carrying us forward, as it always does and always needs to.*

The summer ended on a high note, with everyone confident that achieving a new home was closer than ever before.

Mark Hofflund: *We kept getting reprieves at ParkCenter. This was going to be our last year, no this was going to be our last year. The new bridge kept getting delayed. The sale of the land kept going on and then off. So we'd get another year out of it. And finally we got to the point where it was our last year, and we had torn the theater down in order for the current owner to go in. We called a scrap guy to come in and dismantle everything and haul it away, but it was so well constructed he was having a hard time of it. Finally, he was running out of time and it was costing him too much, so he said, "I'd just put up a sign saying free wood."*

Now there was no turning back. The capital campaign had raised around $1.7 million, less than half their goal, but fund raising efforts were ongoing. The board was nervous. How could they proceed when the funding was not yet in place? Building

The ParkCenter Theater comes down. UK

L-R, Brad Heberlee, Lucentio; Rebecca Prescott, Bianca; Mark Anthony Taylor, Hortensio, *Shrew.* TM

Committee chair, Andy Erstad, stepped in to echo Royanne Minskoff's entreaty at the beginning of the campaign – one step at a time.

Andy Erstad: *I still chuckle about the total disconnect between what it takes to build a building from a cost standpoint and what the board thought it was doing with the capital campaign. People thought we were just going to build it all at once. And I had to keep saying no, it's like anything else, you pay as you go. We're going to build what we can with the money available, but we're going to prioritize what our critical items are.*

L-R, Richard Klautsch, Petruchio; townspeople; Kathleen Tague, Kate; Joe Conley Golden, Grumio, *Shrew.* TM

When the contract to build the theater was awarded to Jordan-Wilcomb Construction, they agreed with Andy and Royanne that doing the project in phases was the most realistic approach to the job. And they were willing to treat it more as a civic partnership than a purely business arrangement. In November, 1997 everyone rolled up their sleeves and the work began. Debris was hauled away from the former dump site by a crew from the Ada County Juvenile Court Services, funded by the Private Industry Council, and once the palate was bare the artists began to create the Festival's new and, at last, permanent home.

L-R, Rebecca Prescott, Bianca; Kathleen Tague, Kate, *Shrew.*TM

Mark Hofflund: *Once laid out it was piece by piece, step by step, person by person, contractor by contractor, donation by donation. And then it's people like Stanley Wallace from Caldwall, who's been coming to your shows, and has a scraper, and he'll be happy to scrape the ground for you just as a first step. And I'd meet him out there on the hot August evenings after we'd had the bus tours that took people out to walk around the site. Nobody can quite see it yet, except the architects and Charlie.*

But while looking forward in time produced one vision, looking back produced another entirely. The broad valley that spreads north from the river and the cottonwoods was known to Native Americans as Peace Valley. It was here that the Shoshone, Bannock, Nez Perce and Paiyute tribes would gather each spring to replenish supplies depleted by the long winters. During these gatherings any hostilities among them were suspended so that they might come together and trade in the spirit of friendship. In light of this history, it seemed only fitting that representatives of these tribes offer a blessing for the success of the valley's newest members.

As the Festival's newest board member, Norena Gutierrez watched the new site take shape and wondered what she could give to the Festival. She knew from her Pueblo Indian ancestry that the eagles that roost there each winter made this a sacred site, and proposed to the board that they perform a Native American blessing. At sunrise on a brisk morning in early June, a group of staff, board members and friends stood around the nearly completed stage as Native American holy man Sam Puentes began the ceremony.

Richard Klautsch, Petruchio; Kathleen Tague, Kate, *Shrew.* TM

Andy Erstad: *They burned the sage and offered the smoke to the four directions and it was really moving. We were trying to be reflective of the past as well as the future.*

Norena Gutierrez: *The blessing is done to insure that there is a gift back to the land, so that when everybody comes to this place they know it is their home and their hearts would be filled with happiness and comfort. That's why I think when people get here they just breathe in the smell of the river and everything around it and just relax. And I think that people find themselves again in the stories Shakespeare tells, and truths of time are always acknowledged there.*

Gage Williams set design, *Shrew*. GW

The Taming of the Shrew. TM

When people get here they just breathe in the smell of the river and everything around it and just relax.

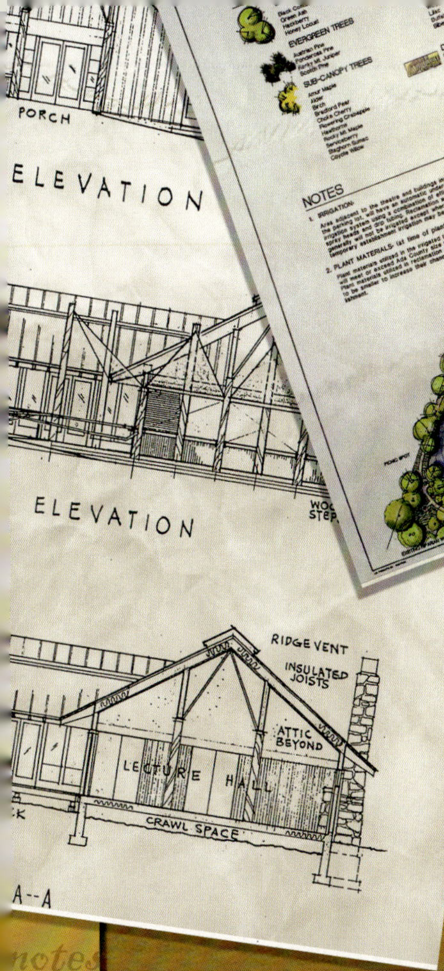

New Beginnings

1998 -

CENTER STAGE

'Amadeus' tells the tale with plenty of clowning

Photo by Katherine Jones / The Idaho Statesman

left, and Richard Klautsch

By Dana Oland
The Idaho Statesman

Quips and jokes fly when actors Richard Klautsch and Tom Willmorth are in the same room. The two take the leads in Peter Shaffer's "Amadeus" opening Saturday.

This play offers both actors a chance to stretch their range.

Klautsch, who heads Boise State's theatre department usually plays the king. This time he's Antonio Salieri, an Italian composer in the Austrian court who becomes confounded by a boorish, bratty musical genius named Wolfgang Amadeus Mozart, played by Willmorth.

"No one would know who Salieri was except for this play," Klautsch said. "He's a very twisted character. It's melodramatic and fun."

Willmorth, who runs the drama program at Capital High School, started with the festival as a teen-ager. He often plays the "clowny clown."

As Mozart, he uses his comic talents he picked up at Chicago's Second City com... too, but with a dramatic...

"Mozart ...

Amen. A man may, if he were of a fearful heart, stagger in this attempt; for here we h
orns are odious, they are necessary. It is said, 'many a man knows no end of his goods

L-R, Joe Conley Golden, Bottom; Dan Peterson, Flute; Sara Bruner, Snug; Tim Redmond, Starveling; Nathan Guisinger, Snout; Mark Anthony Taylor, Peter Quince, *Midsummer.* TM

Bethanne Andersen, cover art.

Shakespeare gets a home. TM

The theater's design appropriately pays homage to Shakespeare's Globe Theater in London. The ring of steel poles that encircle the theater proper is 100 feet in diameter, the same size as the original Globe.

The plans called for wooden poles, but structural engineers determined that steel towers placed in buried concrete footings that were all connected under the ground would be safer and longer-lasting. The increased cost had to be approved by the board, but that was pretty much a formality. They were in it all the way or not at all by this time. Besides, the Festival was on much better financial footing than it had been in several years, as noted by new board member Bob Wetherell.

Bob Wetherell: *I always like to tell people that I was the first member who came on the board in a long time who wasn't asked to sign as a guarantor on a loan.*

Indeed, those days were behind them now. The vote was unanimous, but when they began to excavate for the footings, another problem surfaced.

A private road leading to Barber Dam just off the greenbelt bike path is

The Play: ***A Midsummer Night's Dream***
Director: Charles Fee
Scenic Designer: Gage Williams
Costume Design: Star Moxley
Lighting Design: Rick Martin
Composer: Peter John Still

The Play: ***Cymbeline***
Director: Bartlett Sher
Scenic Designer: Gage Williams
Costume Design: Caitlin Ward
Lighting Design: Chris Akerlind
Composer: Peter John Still

The Play: ***Romeo and Juliet***
Director: Paul Barnes
Scenic Designer: Gage Williams
Costume Design: Janet L. Swenson
Lighting Design: Rick Martin
Composer: Peter John Still

1998

TM

all that remains of Silk Stocking Row, the first street in the town of Barberton. In 1906, the last milltown built in Idaho had 650 residents spread over eighteen square blocks with steam heated homes, a hotel, a community hall, its own municipal water system, school system, even a sewer system. It was also rumored to be the moonshine capitol of the valley. The Barber Lumber Company ran a two band sawmill and a wooden plank dam, and the area where the theater now stands was a part of the mill pond where logs were stored until they were ready to be milled.

Excavation hits a snag. TM

Andy Erstad: *We ran into a layer of logs that had been submerged and silted over. The Barber Pool was really a silt basin, so it was almost an archaeological dig to the degree of exposing all of the submerged logs and trying to figure out where we hit bearing soil. We had to sub-excavate and remove a lot of material and dirt that we hadn't planned on removing, and then fill it back in.*

The logs were scooped out, along with a thick layer of decaying vegetation at the water line. These were replaced with sand and cobble stones excavated from the shallow drainage pond just behind the theater. Landscape architect Don Belts and his partner, Eric Jensen, had been a part of the design team from the very beginning. In fact, Don was on the search committee that chose the Barber Pool site.

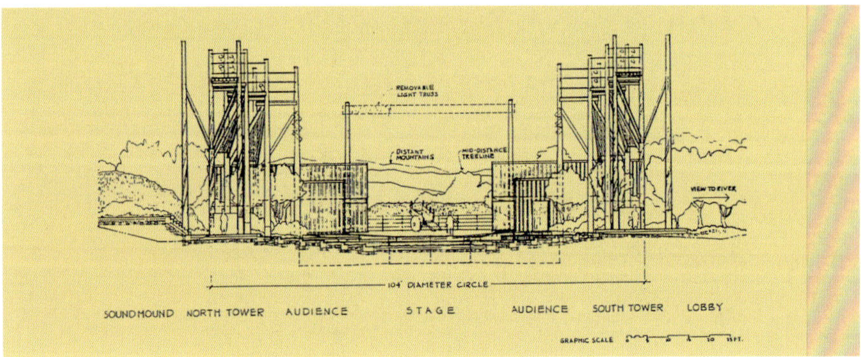

Angell & Rawlinson / Architects

Don Belts: *The rumor had always been that the swampy, narrow depression where the theater was supposed to be situated was an old barrow pit for work on Highway 21. It worked perfect for the extra fill material we needed, which ended up making a decent pond out of it, and an excellent water feature for the site.*

The big question was how to stabilize the area so the footings would be solid enough to support the ring of poles, not to mention the amphitheater itself. Mark took advantage of the Festival's partnership with the Parks Department and put in a call to the State Department of Transportation. They located an engineer who had built roads through Louisiana swamps who told them about a geotextile fabric that was used in just those types of situations. Rolled on top of the sand and cobble stone

That first season . . . we hadn't finished a whole lot of stuff . . . You could already feel how great it was going to be.

base and anchored with more stones, the fabric was then covered with a 60 foot mountain of dirt – more weight than the area would ever be required to support. After a month, the weight of all that dirt caused the site to settle more than an inch, and provided a platform for layers of fill dirt that were compacted by a roller, tested, and built up inch by inch to the desired elevation. Finally, construction could begin again on the new foundation.

By the time crews were able to begin pouring the footings the project was considerably behind schedule. Now it was winter, a time when the Barber Pool's most regal inhabitants come to roost in the trees along the river. Food sources are scarce for Bald Eagles during this time and it is critical that they conserve energy as much as possible in order to survive the coldest months of the year. The Parks Department was nervous that all the heavy equipment and construction would disturb the eagles and force them to be more active. But if the Festival had any hope of opening a season the following summer, construction had to continue. That's when the U.S. Fish & Wildlife Service, Idaho Fish & Game, the U.S. Geological Survey's biological unit, and Greg Kaltenecker of the Idaho Bird Observatory all got together and proposed the idea of doing an eagle study. Realizing at the end of the discussion that everyone was looking at him, Greg agreed to take it on.

Greg Kaltenecker: *I saw eagles come in and perch right there by the Shakespeare Festival during construction, while there were people walking around right underneath them. The thing is they don't really perch right at Shakespeare all that much. It's just not the right kind of*

Early construction. TM

The geo-textile fabric layer. TM

Buildling the mountain of dirt. TM

A curious neighbor. TM

The stage goes down. TM

The poles go up. TM

trees or something. It didn't seem like the construction affected them at all. There were still eagles in the pool, they still worked up and down the river and perched nearby.

As the work progressed, he watched to see if they changed their behavior patterns. The construction crews started early in the morning and ended late at night. There were protocols for what to do if an eagle perched in a nearby tree or on a piece of equipment. From December into February construction continued and the eagles barely noticed. In all that time only one eagle was flushed from a tree, and that was caused by an over-eager photographer.

In the midst of this turmoil, Charlie and Mark had to keep the company going. That spring, as acting company auditions were held and designers began work on sets and costumes for the inaugural season in their new home, a tremendous excitement set in. The theater may not be complete, but it would open, and the community that had seen ISF through good times and bad would be there to watch it take shape, piece by piece.

Charlie Fee: *We went in to that first season with an amphitheater and a stage. We hadn't finished a hell of a lot of stuff. No dressing rooms, no public bathrooms, no box office, no concessions, nothing. Just dirt around an amphitheater. We had spent most of what we had raised to get that far, but everything was going to be okay. All that had to happen was we had to get an audience in there and they had to dig it, which we really could tell that they would. I mean, you could already feel how great it was going to be.*

Construction delayed the opening of the season until July. As a result, for the first time since Mark Cuddy had grown the annual repertory season from three shows to four back in 1985, only three plays were produced. One of the delays was prompted by discussions about the raked stage, which was perceived by some as a potential liability. Charlie's argument that the rake was important in terms of voice projection, as well as for sightlines decided the issue and the Alaskan yellow cedar chosen for the stage surface was finally laid in.

Romeo and Juliet. TM

L-R, Nathan Guisinger, Romeo; Kenneth Merckx, Mercutio, R&J. TM

Gage Williams: *Charlie was about three things – trying to get the design and productions squared away, trying to get that new space built, and trying to get a core of actors that would return and continue to develop on that. As things became clearer for him working with designers, they also became clearer for him working with actors and how he wanted to produce a given text. So when we came to the new space with it's natural background instead of that old wall back there we were both like, wow, this space is really going to free us up. We don't always have to do a backdrop. We're going to be able to incorporate the foothills back there and play with that.*

To open the season Charlie returned to the roots of the Festival, directing the play that started it all, *A Midsummer Night's Dream*. He felt he couldn't go wrong pairing it with the classic *Romeo and Juliet*, and brought in Paul Barnes to direct. Paul called an actor he thought would be a good addition to the ISF family and asked him to audition with Charlie in San Francisco.

L-R, Richard Klautsch, Capulet; Rachel Sledd, Juliet, Marien Perry, Lady Capulet, Leslie Brott, Nurse, *R&J*. TM

Jeffrey Hawkins: *It just happened to be the same day that I was leaving San Francisco to go back home to Phoenix and do a show, so my car was packed with, basically, my life. I blew my first monologue and finally stopped about halfway through and said, you know, I'm going to start this again. I'm thinking I've blown the audition, but the piece went okay, and my second piece went well. Then Charlie says, "Well, great Jeffrey. I know Paul likes your work a lot, and I like your work from what I've seen so far, so come work for me." And he gave me seven months work right on the spot. It turned out to be the beginning of a very nice relationship.*

Bart Sher was becoming known to Boise audiences, and others as well, as a director who took chances. That strategy had paid off in the past, so Charlie told him to pick any show he wanted. Bart chose *Cymbeline*, one of the most obscure and least performed plays in the canon. He also chose the Festival's newest actor to play the lead.

Jeffrey Hawkins: *When the cast list went up I literally thought they messed up, because I was playing Posthumous, the romantic lead. I remember saying to a couple of people, he thinks I'm someone else.*

That summer Steve and Kathleen Tague were absent due to the birth of their son, Simon. That event opened the door for another new member of the ISF family. Charlie hadn't seen Aled Davies act

L-R, Jeffrey C. Hawkins, Abram; Kenneth Merckx, Mercutio; Richard Klautsch, Capulet, *R&J*. TM

since graduate school, eighteen years earlier, but he needed an older actor to fill Steve's spot in the company, so he took a chance on an old friend.

Aled Davies: *I hadn't been out of L.A. in about twelve years. I just thought, I've got to get out of town. I was no longer going to teach, I needed to act again. But I was always expecting to go back to L.A.*

Cast as Oberon and Theseus in *Midsummer*, Friar Lawrence in *R&J*, and one of the storytellers in *Cymbeline*, Aled quickly found himself immersed in both the company and the community.

Aled Davies: *I had a great, great summer. In '98 this still felt like a small, sleepy town to me, especially after L.A. It blew my mind that there were 25 mile-an-hour speed limits that people actually abided by. I owe my regional theater career to the Idaho Shakespeare Festival, and a great debt of gratitude to Charlie and Mark.*

Charlie knew he wanted to do something different for his show. It was the fifth time that play had been produced at ISF and the second time it inaugurated a new theater.

Gage Williams: *It was such an exciting time, but so frustrating. The theater wasn't finished. There were still backhoes out there, and carpenters. The sound system wasn't working yet, the lighting system wasn't cueing up yet, the set was behind, as usual. And when the idea came to us about the '60s – the clothes, the music – Charlie was nervous about it. Getting out of the puffy pants and tights and trying something more modern can be scary.*

Charlie Fee: *Midsummer has this big reveal at the beginning where you go from the court to the forest, and it had been hell to get the show opened. The last 36 hours were really tense because of the electrics. Basically we never did fully tech the show because it rained every night. We never did a run, we would just sort of tech a little bit, rain a little bit, tech a little bit, rain…I mean, it was a nightmare. So we're not even sure we could do this reveal where the wall opens up. We never got it right in tech.*

The weather finally broke for opening night. It was a beautiful evening. The audience began to arrive and make their way into the amphitheater, marveling at what had

L-R, Mark Anthony Taylor, Peter Quince; Dan Peterson, Flute; Nathan Guisinger, Snout; Joe Conely Golden, Bottom, *Midsummer.*

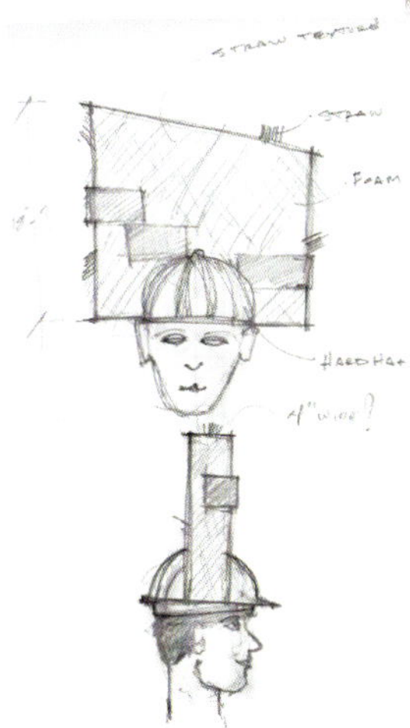

Wall headpiece design, Gage Williams, *Midsummer.* TM

Above, court scene, *Midsummer.* TM

L-R, Aled Davies, Oberon; Cheri Lynne Johnson, Titania; Tom Willmorth, Puck, *Midsummer.* TM

been built and trying to see the possibilities of what remained to be completed, but above all, thrilled to be sitting on new grass watching Shakespeare again. Charlie and Mark welcomed the first audience to the Festival's new home to loud and long applause, standing on the brand new Alaskan cedar stage named in honor of Chuck and Dianne Robertson. The efforts of everyone involved from the staff to the board, the campaign committee, the construction team and lots and lots of volunteers, were readily apparent.

Andy Erstad: *I look at some of the influential people that were involved when I was a part of it, and the expertise they brought, and just watching it all gel was a lot of fun. The other thing that was exciting was watching people come out to the site and seeing the light come on for the people who just didn't realize how big a project this really was.*

Taking their seats in the theater, opening night patrons were greeted by a large wall that filled the entire stage from one side wall to the other. It was impossible for the audience to see anything beyond the theater except sky.

Charlie Fee: *It hadn't truly dawned on me, even though I knew what I had covered up, but I knew that I had this moment in the play which would be cool. Well, we get to the moment and the wall opens up, and the audience is seeing the view from the theater for the first time, and it hit me just as it hit them. There was this gasp...a true gasp...and then the cheering starts. And frankly, that really was one of the most exciting moments in my career. We all knew it was back there, but we hadn't seen the frame created by the theater. It was so moving, I can't tell you, and so exciting. And then Tom came swinging in on that rope.*

Behind the wall, Gage arranged rows of dried grasses in different heights and in different colors to go along with the 60's motif and to provide a transition to the sun-burnished foothills beyond.

Kristen De Angeli: *When Aled Davies, as Oberon, came up through that trap door, I don't know that there was a moment as moving as that. He suddenly appeared and he was set against those foothills in that gorgeous sunset, and it was just spectacular.*

Tom Willmorth, Puck, *Midsummer*. GW

The show went on to become the biggest hit in ISF history, surpassing *Robin Hood*, which had held that record since 1984. The crowds continued to come, and even with the shortened season and only three plays, attendance topped 28,000, bettering the final season at ParkCenter by some 3,000. The big surprise of the summer, however, was Bart Sher's *Cymbeline*.

Jeffrey Hawkins: *I didn't really care for the show up until I was sitting out in the house watching him tech it. We had that big red floor and those crazy costumes and blue people. He walked up behind me and put his hand on my shoulder and said, "What do you think?" I said, "I think it looks really good." He said, "You sound surprised." And I said, "Well, to be honest with you I usually go for the more straightforward stuff, but the storytelling just comes alive, and the imagery really comes alive, and I really really like it." I think he liked that I liked it, and I really came to appreciate his work and his vision.*

Dan Peterson: *Originally he was thinking about mountain men, so I brought him that book on Buckskin Bill who lived up on the Salmon River. He looks at it and says, "I'm thinking more like cowboy. Can you do that?"*

Peter Still: *The first day of rehearsal Danny shows up and he's got on the red kerchief and the shirt, basically the whole thing, and he walked in to rehearsal and it was there.*

The only real downside to the theater's opening came in the form of some unwanted guests – hundreds of them. Several of the tall, steel poles that defined the circle of the amphitheater had metal pipes welded to them for various types of support, and the ends of these pipes were left open. No one thought of it at the time, but they were creating a perfect home for little mud wasps. The season was barely underway when patrons, actors and staff alike began swatting the air around them each evening to ward off the feisty little intruders. A welding crew was immediately dispatched to close off the pipes and the problem was alleviated. But wasps weren't the only distractions.

Aled Davies: *I never thought I'd do theater with mosquitoes. The first couple of years at the new sight, looking at the stage and seeing people act in a sea of insects in the lights. Geese flying over the stage in chevrons, honking. Charlie had that little hunting scene in Midsummer and Peter Still had dogs on the sound track, and after we played it, for fifty miles around, coyotes would howl into the night.*

The Cottonwood Dell. TM

The owner of the land right next to the site chose to paddock two llamas in there that summer. I don't know if they were same sex or opposite sex llamas, but for one performance of Romeo and Juliet, for 45 minutes, the most unnatural sounds you've ever heard in your life were roaring around the theater. Either they were having sex or a turf battle, or both.

One of the most satisfying, if little known, results of all the planning lay in the placement of the stage within the amphitheater. It was essential that they position the audience so that they were not looking into the setting sun each evening, a problem that had plagued the ParkCenter site. But this meant the actors on stage would have the sun in their eyes. Two fifty-foot cottonwood trees stood not far from the area set aside for the stage, and architects Gene Angell and Brian Rawlinson calculated the exact spot where their shadow fell at 8:00 PM during the summer months, and that's where they put the stage. When it came time to build the theater's back wall, however, they discovered that the natural repose of earth piled that high would necessitate removal of the trees.

Mark Hofflund: *There was all kinds of debate as to whether or not we wanted to keep the trees. Then we remembered the stone from the old Odd Fellows Lodge, which White-Leasure-Clark and Oppenheimer Companies had helped Pat McMurray and First Security Bank tear down a few years earlier and give to the Festival. The Boise Department of Public Works had stored the stone in a field out at the Joplin Water Treatment Plant, and once we got the approval for the donation they transported it all out to us and Gerhard Borbonus stacked it up to retain the wall and save those two cottonwood trees.*

Sure enough, at exactly 8:00 PM on the longest day of the summer, those trees cast their shadow precisely across the tongue of the stage from opening to opening, leaving both side walls

The light and sound booth goes up. TM

perfectly illuminated. In the process a small dell was created just behind the theater that became a beautiful spot for patrons to sit and enjoy the ambiance of the company's new home.

Gage Williams: *Theater is a big magic trick. That is, you want to make people believe they're seeing something, but if they get behind the magician they see it's completely false. With the Festival it's a double-edged sword. It opens in pure daylight, so you've got to design scenery that still looks pleasing with a bunch of harsh sunlight on it. You can't get away with traditional painting tricks, you've got to use a lot more texture and be much more dimensional. But once it turns night, it's just like being in a proscenium theater. We have that same kind of control with light where we can start to heighten and enlighten things.*

L-R, Tracy Sunderland, Helena; Jeffrey Hawkins, Lysander; Michael Shipley, Demetrius; Rachel Sledd, Hermia, *Midsummer*. TM

The success of opening night aside, there was still a long way to go to complete the theater complex. The campaign had raised about $2.9 million to that point, which left nearly a million dollars to go if they were to reach their goal of $3.7 million. But now the theater was open, and its full range of impact, though still in the future, could be addressed and appreciated.

Court scene, *A Midsummer Night's Dream*. TM

As Alan and Royanne Minskoff stated in their letter for the program that summer, "This is truly the prologue. This Amphitheater and Reserve benefits the arts and ensures the safekeeping of this historically significant and ecologically rich area as a park. In the months when the theater is dark this amphitheater and park will give our partners and neighbors at the Idaho Department of Parks and Recreation a unique place to observe and teach about bald eagles, great blue herons, osprey, and the more than two hundred species that share this riparian landscape. The amphitheater, the park that surrounds it, and the interpretive center that we plan to build, promise to educate, entertain and inspire thousands of Idahoans."

Lofty goals, and ones that would require continued support from the community that has nurtured this festival since its first days. Alan and Royanne, along with board President Sandy Fery, Governor Phil Batt and Mayor Brent Coles echoed that fact in letters for the season program.

Mark Hofflund: *You know the number of people who came together to build this was phenomenal, astonishing, unbelievable. I can't begin to get into all the trials and tribulations we all faced, but every time the summer rolled around they'd go out and see a play and they'd be newly inspired.*

One of those who was inspired was a young reporter who, after only two years on the Idaho Statesman staff, had landed the daunting task of reviewing the opening season.

Dana Oland: *My first year here I was a bit of a snob. I was used to Chicago Rep and ACT, Berkeley Rep and Cal Shakes. But the first season I went to the Shakespeare Festival I was blown away. Here was a top quality company here in this little place, and I couldn't quite get used to that. Since then I've written several times that the Idaho Shakespeare Festival is one of the most innovative, up-and-coming Shakespeare companies in the country.*

Brad Talbutt, cover photo.

1999

By this time, many of the leaders who had worked for years to bring the amphitheater to fruition were exhausted, but their new home was far from complete.

The next step was to create an entry into the theater and put up a box office. They also needed some way of controlling sound from the highway and all of the surroundings. Working with landscape architect Don Belts and the engineering teams from Quadrant and Atwood-Hinzman-Jones, a combination of concrete and earthen walls, or burms, was developed.

It was an efficient, effective design, but one that required a lot of dirt, and the pond had already been excavated. So Joe La Marche and Jordan-Wilcomb put out requests to everyone they knew for more dirt. In the end it came through another old-time Boise connection, and yet another example of the tremendous community support that has kept the Festival going through the years.

Andy Erstad: *One of the neatest things about the project was realizing how small Boise is and being able to call an old high school chum, Terry McEntee, at Central Paving and say, "We need dirt, what are you doing that you're having*

Entrance wall, artist's rendering, Sylvia Hofflund.

The Play: ***A Midsummer Night's Dream***
Director: Charles Fee
Scenic Designer: Gage Williams
Costume Design: Star Moxley
Lighting Design: Rick Martin
Composer: Peter John Still

The Play: ***Scapin***
Director: Christopher Bayes
Scenic Designer: Gage Williams
Costume Design: Caitlin Ward
Lighting Design: Tracy Odishaw
Composer: Peter John Still

The Play: ***The Winter's Tale***
Director: Charles Fee
Scenic Designer: Gage Williams
Costume Design: Star Moxley
Lighting Design: Trace Odishaw
Composer: Peter John Still

The Play: ***Titus Andronicus***
Director: Bartlett Sher
Scenic Designer: Deborah Jensen
Costume Design: Caitlin Ward
Lighting Design: Christopher Akerlind
Composer: Peter John Still

The Play: ***The Compleat Works of William Shakespeare (Abridged)***
Director: Charles Fee
Scenic Designer: Gage Williams
Costume Design: Rebecca Hoffman
Lighting Design: Christopher Akerlind
Composer: Peter John Still

A very gentle beast, and of a good conscience. A Midsummer Night's Dream, V, i

to lose dirt?" And having them bring in dirt that normally would have cost the Festival $20,000 or $30,000 and put it in place – just giving it to us. And having people like that, who really wouldn't have necessarily been involved in the Festival, all of a sudden having a very real tie to it.

Recent fires in the foothills north of Boise had city and county officials worried about the possibilities of flash floods. The end result was the digging of three large retention ponds at potential flood points along the Boise Front.

Mark Hofflund: *At some point the City Engineer said, you know, the city's going to be getting all this dirt. We don't have a place to put it, and maybe as part of the process we'll suggest the Shakespeare Festival as a location. McEntee was crucial on that because he bid it. Central Paving was one of four companies that offered to do our paving. We paid him anything for the dirt it was pennies on the dollar, and then he donated paving for the parking lot and the entry path on top of that.*

Truckloads of dirt began arriving at the Barber Pool site that fall, and continued through the winter. The following summer, people were entering the Festival between two massive berms. Bill Mooney, principal for Jordan-Wilcomb Construction, supervised the pouring of the long, curving concrete wall, designed by Joe La Marche, that supported a third, inner berm which formed the northern side of the amphitheater and completed the entryway. The box office and caretaker's cottage were scheduled to be housed behind it, as soon as the money could be raised.

Andy Erstad contributed his own design to the facility in the form of a staircase up the back wall of the theater. John and Dee Fery had already offered to create the park around the amphitheater, now they, too, stepped up again.

Mark Hofflund: *John Fery had become both chief skeptic and primary motivator in our displacing three portable shacks that were our box office, concession stand and souvenir/chair rental shed at the theater entrance. We all agreed that they looked awful, and John was worried they would be there a long time. So he was pleased to see them moved aside by Bill Mooney's signature entry wall. Then he offered to veneer it with sandstone through Gerhard and Hans Borbonus, and ultimately paid for the box office and caretaker's cottage as well, because we needed those to support the remainder of the wall. Together with funding for the park, John's was the largest single gift the campaign saw and moved the campaign firmly into phase two.*

Patrons arriving for the second season in the new amphitheater could now see the entire project taking shape. Passing through the broad new entryway and following the beautiful, curving, sandstone wall encasing the ticket windows, the amphitheater appears nestled in the midst of the larger park taking shape around it. Picnic areas, views of the river and frequent glimpses of the wildlife that call Barber Pool home made the short stroll around the Cottonwood Dell to the new south

Our first customers. UK

L-R, Samantha Quan, Hyacinte; Allen Gilmore, Argante; Jeffrey Hawkins, Leandre, *Scapin*. TM

L-R, Kathleen Tague, Hermione; Richard Klautsch, Leontes, *Winters Tale*. TM

L-R, Kathleen Tague, Tamora; Allen Gilmore, Aaron, *Titus*. TM

Tom Willmorth, *Scapin*. TM

Titus Andronicus. TM

Samantha Quan, Hermia; Jeffrey Hawkins, Lysander, *Midsummer*. TM

L-R, Richard Klautsch, Leontes; Tracy Sunderland, Paulina, *Winter's Tale*. TM

Aled Davies, Marcus Andronicus; Samantha Qua[n], Lavinia, *Titus*. TM

Ensemble, *Winter's Tale*. TM

entrance to the theater a truly pleasant one. In his program notes, Charlie proudly pointed out that "the policy of the Festival is to secure funding for each part of the project before we build. What you see is paid for. What's to come is up to all of us."

Perhaps the most evident need that remained in that yet to come category were the toilets. Rows of the infamous porta-potties that had been an unpleasant but necessary Festival fixture since our move to the Plantation in 1981, occupied most of the space that was slated to become the theater lobby.

Royanne Minskoff: *That was a strategic decision to phase the restrooms last because it was something audiences had always complained about at the other sites. So we could pitch them every year that if they really wanted flush toilets they were going to have to step up and build them. It was fun because it was not exactly a great naming opportunity for a donor. And of course the Fool Squad always managed to work that in to their Greenshows.*

Charlie also noted in the program that the second season in a new theater is notoriously dangerous. The common wisdom is to cut down on programming, pare back the overhead and begin to build an audience. Instead, he chose another plan – simple, but definitely dangerous. He wanted to do more plays, but he couldn't afford to do more plays, so his first proposal was to remount the hugely successful *A Midsummer Night's Dream*. Despite the fact that they could play off Michael Hoffman's film version of the play, which was opening around the country that summer, the idea was met with universal disapproval from staff and board alike.

Charlie Fee: *Everybody said it would never work, people won't come and see it again. The successful remount of Robin Hood was brought up, and that helped, but the problem is that nobody remounts plays. I argued that it wouldn't cost us much, and I can't possibly afford a fourth play any other way. Then I decided I wanted to go ape because it's our second season and this is our big opportunity, so let's do five plays. I'll bring back another successful play, Compleat Works, which only has three guys. Now the response was, "You're totally insane!*

But his reasoning proved sound. He was, in effect, producing five shows for the cost of three-and-a-half, and increasing the season enormously in terms of performances. *Dream* opened to even bigger crowds than it had the year before. Everyone who hadn't seen it wanted to, and everyone who had seen it wanted to see it again. Adding Moliere's zany French farce, *Scapin*, to the mix along with *The Winter's Tale* and the gory *Titus Andronicus* made for an ambitious and highly successful season.

Jeffrey Hawkins: *There was one particular night where all the elements came together. Steve Tague was playing Titus and I was playing his son, Lucius, and there's this one part where with his one remaining hand, he grabs me, his brother Marcus and his daughter, and there's that little oath of the Andronici where he kind of hovers over us and vows revenge. We're all kind of sweaty, and it's raining, too. So there's all this bloodiness all around and all this rain pouring down and I'm looking up at Steve as he gives me this big kiss to seal the deal and literally there's lightning flashing over his head. And we're like, wow, I don't know if anyone else caught that, but from here that was a pretty cool moment.*

The Compleat Works of Shakespeare, Abridged capped off one wild and crazy season. The show was first done at ISF in 1996, with Joe Golden, Dan Peterson and Tom Willmorth, but Tom was taking the summer off, so Jeffrey Hawkins was asked to step in. And by the time it came to student matinees in September, Joe had to leave as well, to teach at Albertson College of Idaho.

Clockwise from top left: Robert Anderson, Geronte; Allen Gillmore, Argante; Nick Garcia, Octave; Jeffrey Hawkins, Leandre, Scapin. TM

L-R, M.A. Taylor, Peter Quince; Joe Conley Golden, Bottom; Sara Bruner, Snug; Nick Garcia, Snout, Midsummer. TM

No profit grows where is no pleasure taken. In brief, sir, study what you most affect.

The Taming of the Shrew, I, i.

Mark Anthony Taylor: *I understudied it that summer, and when I was asked to step in for Joe I asked Danny what it was like to do the show. He said, "Oh, it's not as bad as it seems. You go out there and you do the beginning, then you do the football game, then you rest for about fifteen minutes, then you do the beginning of Hamlet and then you do the backwards Hamlet, then it's over." I was like, Danny, there's a hell of a lot of stuff that happens in between there, and he's like, "I have no idea."*

Jeffrey Hawkins: *It's true. The most painful part is starting. Once you push that boulder and it goes, it just goes.*

Mark Anthony Taylor: *It's so physically and emotionally exhausting to do that it really is a blur. You're going so fast and so furious that there's no time to take stock of what's going on. It's already past you and you have to think about it on the ride home or as you go to bed. Then you remember, oh, I didn't do that. Oh, kind of screwed that up. But it's really fun because you get to be rock stars.*

Jeffrey Hawkins: *The audiences were so great. That's what you miss. You don't miss the injuries and the sore muscles every morning. But the audiences, they absolutely carry you. In rehearsals we'd just be goofing off because there was no audience to play with, but the laughter and the people who come to this theater just carry you through the show.*

The huge season was a gamble, but it paid off. The people of Boise and the Treasure Valley were anxious to see what all their loyalty and support had wrought, and they turned out in a big way.

Charlie Fee: *All hell broke loose in terms of ticket sales. I mean it was staggering. We were completely overwhelmed. We still didn't have any decent box office systems running, we could not keep up with the phone at all, we had nothing but complaints all day from people who couldn't get tickets and we are selling like insane. We grew from 28,000 the year before to 41,000 total attendance for 1999. And we put $200,000 in the bank.*

L-R, ; Jeffrey Hawkins, Leandre; Tom Willmorth, Scapin; Nick Garcia, Octave, Scapin. TM

That fall, the Shakespeare Festival moved into new offices in downtown Boise, sharing the space with the newly formed Boise Contemporary Theater at Ninth and Fulton Streets. But the move brought much more than a change of location for ISF. In a merger that took place over the summer months, Idaho Theater for Youth returned to its roots, bringing the Shakespeare Festival a wealth of educational programming developed over nearly two decades of touring original plays for young audiences to schools throughout the state and region, and introducing young people in the Treasure Valley to the performing arts through its year-round Drama School.

Top: L-R, Kathleen Tague, Tamora; Richard Klautsch, Saturninus; Bottom: Allen Gilmore, Aaron, Titus. TM

When I accepted David Lee Painter's offer to step in as Interim Executive Director of ITY in the spring of 1995, my job was to oversee ITY's operations and work with the board to find new company management. With their touring and Drama School programs already well established and a seasoned staff in place to keep them that way, my main efforts went toward fund raising for those

This page and opposite, Idaho Theater for Youth school tours. UK

operations, as well as a trip to Rostov-on-Don, where the company had been selected to represent North America at the International Children's Theater Festival. When new Artistic and Managing Directors were hired the following winter I left the office and joined the board.

Over the following year the faltering economy began to cut into school budgets and tour bookings started to drop off. The Western States Tour was the first to go, and with it one of our staff, Diane Ragsdale. Not long after, Education Director, Terri Dillion, left for greener pastures. Both the Drama School and tour bookings remained strong, but by the spring of 1998, the company was mired in debt and it was clear that drastic measures had to be taken.

Theresa McLeod, ITY Board President: *During that time we had several board members resign, but what was left was a pretty awesome group of people who all recognized that the artistic integrity of the company and the Drama School were so strong that they warranted preserving in some form, permanently.*

After lengthy consultations, we agreed there was only one course of action that could be taken at that time. At a hastily called, early morning emergency meeting, the board voted to shut down everything except the school tour that was currently out on the road, and the Drama School. I went back into the office to oversee operations with the lone remaining staff member, Education Director John O'Hagan.

John O'Hagan: *I remember getting that phone call from Doug asking me to come to lunch with him and Theresa McLeod and Ron Eardley. I knew I was the newest hire and I knew we were in financial trouble, so I told my wife, Nikki, I think I'm going to lose my job today.*

But that was not the case. Although John had been on the ITY staff only a few months, his experience with the company dated back to his acting role in the 1996 touring production of *Opening Windows*. That, and the fact that he was willing to stay on and help see us through in the midst of a company meltdown, for a pittance of a salary, made him the hands down choice to fill the position of Interim Company Manager. Meanwhile, Ron Eardley approached Charlie and Mark with an idea that could turn ITY's troubles into a positive situation for both companies.

Mark Hofflund: *Our levels of operation were not that different. We had the land at Ore-Ida, but ITY was producing shows at BSU. The only thing we had that ITY didn't was the audience. We were beginning to cross over a little in touring because our Shakespearience high school tour had started doing some junior highs, which was ITY's main focus. But ITY had the seven-state tour, and we didn't have anything close to that. They also had international profile, and their own national profile which was way ahead of ours.*

Charlie had already been talking about expanding ISF's educational programming, and a merger with ITY would give the Festival an already existing means of doing that. So he and Mark brought a "merger committee" consisting of ISF Board President Cheryl Larabee, Bill Keller and Brent Fery to meet with Theresa, Ron and myself. Despite our argument that what we were offering was of some worth, which we valued at the amount of the debt, Brent was adamant that ISF was not in a financial position to take on any debt whatsoever.

Mark, fresh off ISF's successful first phase of the campaign, offered to help us launch our own campaign to eliminate the debt, and worked with us to develop the tools to go out and raise the money. By fall we not only cleared the debt, we arrived on the doorstep of the Shakespeare Festival with money in the bank. The only caveat ITY attached to the merger was that John O'Hagan, who had stuck with us through thick and thin, and championed the merger in many ways himself, had to keep his job as part of ISF.

John O'Hagan: *Once we knew the merger was going to take place I remember sitting with Charlie to go over the programming we were going to bring over. He knew about the tours, but we also talked about the drama school and the curriculum, the workshops were doing with some of* *the schools, and the artist-in-residence programs, and he said, "Wow, that's a lot, who does all that?" And I said I do. I don't think they were fully aware of how much we were doing.*

A number of people in the Boise arts community expressed to John the fear that this jewel of a children's theater would be lost in the vast corporate empire they believed the Shakespeare Festival had become.

John O'Hagan: *I told them it's either this and maintain the core of what ITY programming has been – bringing really quality programming to schools all over the state, or shutting the doors and it goes away completely. But there were also many who said simply, "It's about time ISF and ITY were back together. It just makes perfect sense."*

Along with John, ISF gained Theresa McLeod as a board member and Martha Ripple, who had helped guide the ITY board since its first reincarnation under David Lee Painter, as a Consulting Member of their board.

Theresa McLeod: *When you look at ITY today within ISF, the drama school is now seamless as far as ages. They start out in grade school and go all the way up through high school. And the great thing is that ISF actors are instructors, so at any given night out at the Festival the students can see their teachers up there performing. And they have maintained that ITY philosophy of developing new works for their school tours. We also brought this wonderful body of supporters into the Festival and they have either grown their support or continued it.*

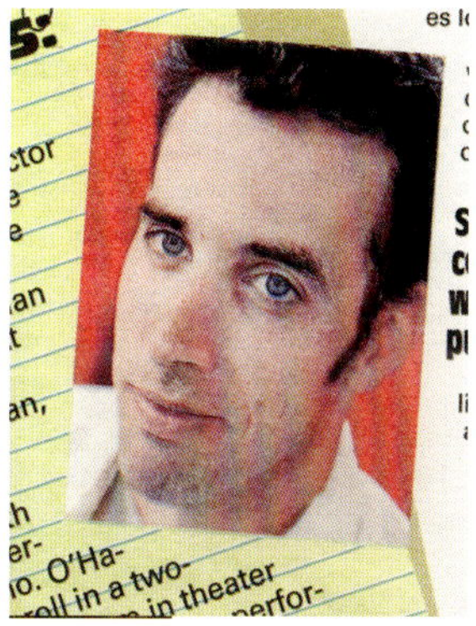

John O'Hagan
The Idaho Statesman

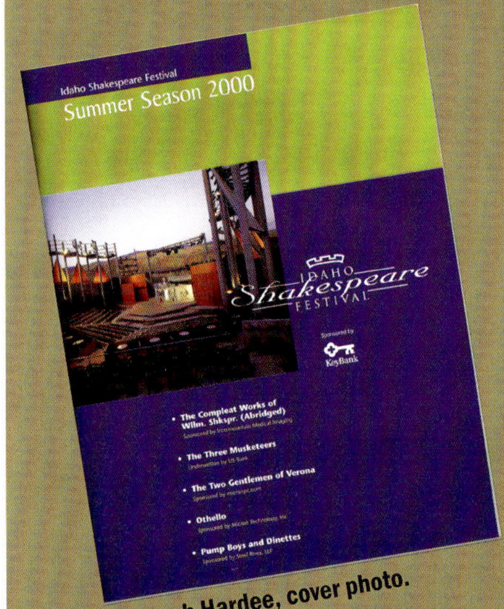

Deborah Hardee, cover photo.

Since Charlie and Mark attended their first Shakespeare Theatre Association of America conference in 1993 at the Utah Shakespearean Festival in Cedar City, Fred Adams and Scott Phillips had become two of their best friends in the Shakespeare community.

Shortly after making the pilgrimage to see the newest Shakespeare theater in the country open in 1998, they said that Idaho should host one. The upcoming 2000 conference was being held in the Bard's birthplace, Stratford-Upon-Avon, England, and they thought Charlie and Mark should toss their hats in the ring to host 2001.

Mark Hofflund: *We said you're crazy, and they said no, your community will support this. You have such a wonderful facility and we want you to inspire the STAA membership.*

Charlie Davis led the board discussion about whether or not they should pursue the idea. There was some initial resistance. Hosting the conference would require considerable resources. Some believed those resources would be better spent on their

2000

Enjoying the Reserve. UK

The Play: ***The Compleat Works of William Shakespeare (Abridged)***
Director: Charles Fee
Scenic Designer: Gage Williams
Costume Design: Rebecca Hoffman
Lighting Design: Rick Martin
Composer: Peter John Still

The Play: ***The Three Musketeers***
Director: Charles Fee
Scenic Designer: Gage Williams
Costume Design: Star Moxley
Lighting Design: Rick Martin
Composer: Peter John Still

The Play: ***The Two Gentlemen of Verona***
Director: Charles Fee
Scenic Designer: Gage Williams
Costume Design: Kim Krumm Sorenson
Lighting Design: Rick Martin
Composer: Peter John Still

The Play: ***Othello***
Director: Victor Papas
Scenic Designer: Gage Williams
Costume Design: Rose Pederson
Lighting Design: Tracy Odishaw
Composer: Peter John Still

The Play: ***Pump Boys***
Director: Dennis Jones
Scenic Designer: Dennis Jones
Costume Design: Kristin Cooper
Lighting Design: Mary Louise Geiger
Composer: Travis Jones

unfinished theater. But Scott Phillips came up from Utah to plead the case in favor of hosting the conference and ultimately the board was convinced. In January, Mark and Kristen De Angeli headed for England, accompanied by Mayor Coles and his wife, Julie, to attend the 2000 conference and lead one of the sessions. Mayor Coles also looked up his Stratford counterpart and invited her to the closing banquet, gaining some international appreciation from the Shakespeare Theatre Association for his thoughts on public commitment to the arts.

Back in Boise, John O'Hagan was busy setting up shop at ISF. But the wealth of ITY programming that already existed was not all he brought with him.

John O'Hagan: *There was this tremendous group of students who had all come into the Drama School at the same time under Terri Dillion. I started working with them in 1997. They were all friends, and they were constantly wanting to do more, but they had been doing the top level "Intensive" classes for so long as a group that they really weren't getting that much out of them any more. So I talked to Charlie about reviving the apprentice program with them and he said, go for it.*

John's goal was to create a daily program of tasks that would give them a balanced diet of everything the professional company was doing. There were morning warm-up and voice classes, walk-on roles in the shows that got them rehearsal time with the directors and acting company, and they also put in time at the set or costume shop every day.

John O'Hagan: *At the first company meeting that summer I told everyone that we were going to have a number of high school students around for the season. I asked everyone to welcome them as much as they could because we want them to feel like they're part of the company. I thought maybe I could get an actor or two to come in and talk to them once or twice, but the company embraced them. I had people lining up at my desk asking, "What can I do? I want to work with these kids."*

Interpretive Center, artist's rendering, Sylvia Hofflund.

Sandstone rubble. TM

2000 will forever be known as the "Year of the Bathrooms." Back at Barber Pool, the three-way partnership between ISF, the Idaho Department of Parks and Recreation and the Idaho Foundation for Parks & Lands was hard at work once again as construction began on S.J. Thoreson's design of the Interpretive Center. The concept behind this year-round educational and meeting facility was that it would serve the Shakespeare

Apprentice Showcase. TM

Finished Interpretive Center. TM

Mark Hofflund, Managing Director. TM

Charles Fee, Producing Artistic Director. TM

Festival during the summer months, and be utilized during the winter months for meetings and educational activities centered around the Barber Pool Conservation area, with a focus on the bald eagles who gathered there to roost.

The design incorporated the same sandstone motif which was now the dominant theme throughout the theater. Gerhard Borbonus' donation of the rubble – chunks left over from dressing the stones for the wall and the berms – was put to good use veneering the exterior of the Center, as well as the other major addition in 2000. The long-awaited restrooms remained a nightly part of Mark and Charlie's curtain speeches during the 1999 season, not to mention the infamous Greenshows, and one night Micron legal assistant Michelle Anderson and her husband, Mark, were in the audience to hear the plea. Mark Anderson just happened to be the head of the plumber's union training program and Michelle asked if he couldn't do something about this.

The Interpretive Center was being built as the result of a major donation, but there was no money specifically earmarked for the bathrooms. Needless to say, they were hardly a prime naming opportunity – unless perhaps you were a plumber. Mark Anderson agreed to coordinate what he could, and began contacting their suppliers, all of whom regularly took part in various community service programs. He convinced them that the Shakespeare Festival should be their program for that year, and in the four months from February to March, almost every member of the local plumber's union donated evenings and weekends to rough in, install, and ultimately finish off the much-anticipated facilities. The Board was willing to go into a little bit of debt to get the job done, and after a discount from the stone masons they managed to raise it all through future pledges and campaign donations. It was a huge contribution to the overall effort, and one that was perhaps more appreciated by the patrons than any other. Equally important, with real bathrooms in place and functioning, and no sign of the infamous porta-potties to be seen, the Festival had cast off of the last remnant of its humble beginnings.

Andy Erstad: *Basically everyone gave, whether it was money or sweat or blood or effort. And Jordan-Wilcomb was encouraging that all*

L-R, Joe Conely Golden, Dan Peterson, Tom Willmorth, *Compleat Works.* TM

along the way, helping Mark find leads, encouraging us, just carving it right out of their scope of work and letting other people deal with it. In many cases in a situation like that the contractor is reluctant to let someone not under their direct supervision work on a project because who do you go back to if something fails or goes wrong. With Jordan-Wilcomb that was never an issue.

That spring, working with Don Belts, Gerhard Borbonus and crew went to work landscaping the berms and some of the grounds.

Don Belts: *In terms of the overall planting concept, we really wanted to treat the immediate theater area a lot like A Midsummer Night's Dream. These wonderfully warm Boise evenings that we have just sort of go on forever, and the theater itself is magical. So we introduced a lot of fun plant material – purple leafed trees called Canada Red Cherries, butterfly bushes, the tulip tree that has a really odd flower that comes in the middle of summer – plants that were just a little different, a little unique, that might fit that forest in Midsummer.*

They hadn't gotten far before they realized they needed a groundskeeper to maintain everything they were planting. Eric Olson, a member of the original ISF family who, as a partner in Sterling Landscape, had provided all those trees that

I know bank where the wild thyme blows,
Where oxlips and the nodding iolet grows,
Quite overcanopied with luscious woodbine,
With sweet musk roses, and with eglantine.

A Midsummer Night's Dream, II, 1.

Dan Peterson, *Compleat Works.* TM

L-R, Sara Bruner, Kitty; Donald Sage Mackay, Count de Rochefort; Rebecca Prescott, Queen Anne, *Musketeers.* TM

L-R, Dan Hiatt, Roderigo; Steve Tague, Iago, *Othello.* TM

L-R, Jeffrey Hawkins, D'Artagnan; Carie Yonekawa, Mme. Bonancieux; Felton Page Kennedy, Jussac, *The Three Musketeers.* TM

L-R, Kathleen Tague, Countess de Winter; Steve Tague, Cardinal Richelieu, *Musketeers.* TM

L-R, Stitch Marker, Ensemble; Doug Miller, Duke of Venice; Lynn Berg, Ensemble; Dan Peterson, Gratiano, *Othello.* TM

L-R, Steve Tague, Cardinal Richelieu; Daniel Crane, Guard; Dan Peterson, M. Bonancieux, *Musketeers.* TM

L-R, Rebecca Prescott, Desdemona; Donald Sage Mackay, Cassio, *Othello.* TM

Allen Gilmore, Othello; Rebecca Prescott, Desdemona, *Othello.* TM

created the original *Midsummer Night's Dream* forest at One Capital Center back in 1977, and many other forests after that, stepped up to help once again. He had been talking with a friend who wanted to leave the corporate world and do what she always wanted to do, gardening. Eric recommended her to Don, and after an initial meeting and interview, she was hired.

Carol Cole: *When I came on in April the planters were already on site and the tulip trees were planted, then I begged and borrowed to get the plantings to put around them. The park had just been seeded with wild grasses and flowers that are native to the Great Basin.*

Don Belts: *The first year we did a wildflower mix out there, and quite often those mixes don't do all that well. But for whatever reason that first year there was an explosion of color and everybody marveled at that. Then all I could think of was how are we ever going to repeat that?*

The Shakespeare Park and Interpretive Center gave the theater a whole new feeling for crowds arriving for the Festival's 24th season, and they did indeed marvel at the colorful improvements, at least as much as they enjoyed the splendid productions. One of the most notable improvements was the Shakespeare Café, featuring John Berryhill's signature culinary creations along with an assortment of beverages. Picnic baskets were still encouraged, but now patrons had another alternative when it came to food and drink.

By now, remounting the previous summer's most successful show was a natural part of the summer season, and Charlie knew he could not go wrong by bringing back the zany three-man *Compleat Works of Shakespeare, Abridged*, with the original cast from 1996 – Tom Willmorth, Joe Golden and Dan Peterson. The antics of these three festival favorites kicked off the season with full houses each night.

Diving into new territory for the Festival, Charlie chose the swashbuckling Dumas classic, *The Three Musketeers*, adapted by Linda Alpers, Douglas Langworthy and Penny Metropulos. Ken Merckx was back for his third season with the Festival to choreograph the numerous sword fights, and Star Moxley was given the nod to design costumes.

Star Moxley: *You've got 30 different scenes with 55 characters, 70 to 90 some costumes and a budget that's like, "You've got to be kidding me!" And that's with foundation garments, period pieces, wigs, hats, swords, weaponry, boots…stocking…every accessory known to man, all in one show. That just about slayed me.*

Jeffrey Hawkins: *The first couple of weeks as D'Artagnan I had this awful wig that had a plastic dome that wouldn't allow any breathing. I was in the hospital from dehydration and finally the executive decision came down that we were going to cut the wig. I finally could see the people I was talking to. I had thirteen sword fights in that show and suddenly I could execute. I really had fun doing it. I wish I could do it again all the way through because I wanted to play that role since I was a kid.*

The tried and true *Two Gentlemen of Verona* and the Festival's second production of *Othello* completed the summer repertory. Still trying to save money wherever possible in order to continue construction, Charlie directed all but *Othello*, for which he brought in Victor Pappas, outgoing artistic director of the prestigious Intiman Theater in Seattle. Pappas' replacement at the Intiman was none other than seven-year ISF veteran Bart Sher. Bart chose to open his stint as artistic director with his highly successful ISF production of *Cymbeline*, taking Dan Peterson, Joe Golden and Aled Davies along for the ride to reprise their roles as Belarius, Cloten, and the invented Storyteller, respectively. The show received rave reviews there as well, and would go on to play in Stratford-Upon-Avon and New York, where Caitlin Ward received a Lucille Lortel award for her costume design.

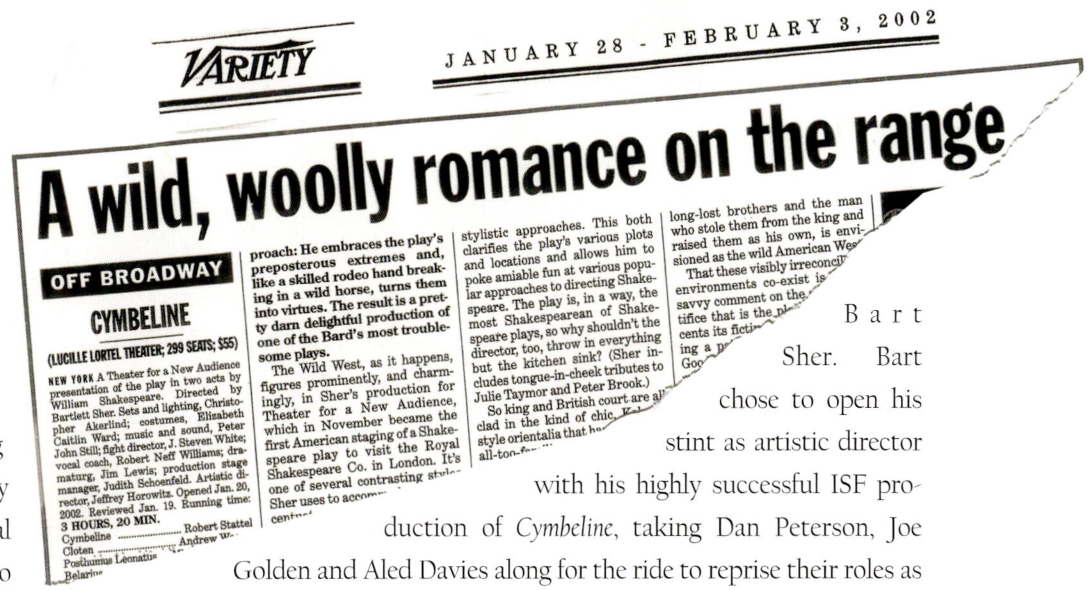
VARIETY JANUARY 28 - FEBRUARY 3, 2002

A wild, woolly romance on the range

OFF BROADWAY

CYMBELINE

(LUCILLE LORTEL THEATER; 299 SEATS; $55)

NEW YORK A Theater for a New Audience presentation of the play in two acts by William Shakespeare. Directed by Bartlett Sher. Sets and lighting, Christopher Akerlind; costumes, Elizabeth Caitlin Ward; music and sound, Peter John Still; fight director, J. Steven White; vocal coach, Robert Neff Williams; dramaturg, Jim Lewis; production stage manager, Judith Schoenfeld. Artistic director, Jeffrey Horowitz. Opened Jan. 20, 2002. Reviewed Jan. 19. Running time: 3 HOURS, 20 MIN.

Cymbeline .... Robert Stattel
Cloten .... Andrew W…
Posthumus Leonatus
Belarius

proach: He embraces the play's preposterous extremes and, like a skilled rodeo hand breaking in a wild horse, turns them into virtues. The result is a pretty darn delightful production of one of the Bard's most troublesome plays.

The Wild West, as it happens, figures prominently, and charmingly, in Sher's production for Theater for a New Audience, which in November became the first American staging of a Shakespeare play to visit the Royal Shakespeare Co. in London. It's one of several contrasting styl… Sher uses to accom… cent…

stylistic approaches. This both clarifies the play's various plots and locations and allows him to poke amiable fun at various popular approaches to directing Shakespeare. The play is, in a way, the most Shakespearean of Shakespeare plays, so why shouldn't the director, too, throw in everything but the kitchen sink? (Sher includes tongue-in-cheek tributes to Julie Taymor and Peter Brook.)

So king and British court are al… clad in the kind of chic, K… style orientalia that ha… all-too-f…

long-lost brothers and the man who stole them from the king and raised them as his own, is envisioned as the wild American Wes…

That these visibly irreconcil… environments co-exist is… savvy comment on the… tifice that is the pl… cents its ficti… ing a p… Goo…

L-R, Carie Yonekawa, Sylvia; Sara Bruner, Julia . *Two Gentlemen of Verona.* TM

L-R, Sara Bruner, Julia; Karen Wennstrom, Lucetta, *Two Gents.* TM

Clockwise from top, Jeffrey Hawkins, Proteus; Matt Ramsey, Valentine; Sara Bruner, Julia; Carie Yonekawa, Sylvia, *Two Gents.* TM

The success of 1999's extension into September and the addition of student matinees prompted a repeat, and for that Charlie invited Dennis Jones, his mentor from Sierra Rep, to bring his highly successful production of *Pump Boys and Dinettes* to the new theater. Part rock musical and part nightclub act, the show was another departure for ISF, this time into musicals. And it wouldn't be the last.

Aled Davies: *Charlie didn't have much of a season for me that year and I wanted a break. I drove down one day and walked into a rehearsal for Othello, and it was very instructive for me to feel the welcome and to greet people and to miss it. And to compare that with the model of theater whereby if you know the director at all it's by virtue of audition and call back, and you don't know anybody around the table. You make that attempt at an immediate intimacy for the six or seven weeks of the play, and then you say goodbye. It made me value the notion of company much more highly. I didn't realize that I had come to miss it and depend on it.*

The educational programming was also expanding, and when Helene Peterson left for graduate school that year, John O'Hagan was the logical choice to become the new Director of Education. By this time some of the initial group of students he brought with him had moved on to college, and the results of their training were being noticed.

John O'Hagan: *I meet teachers from schools where the kids have gone and they all say, "I don't know what you guys to with them, but they're amazing. Part of it is we spend a lot time telling them, "You're with professionals and we expect you to act like professionals and learn from them. This is not school, this is a unique opportunity for you. And 90% of them really take that to heart and learn a tremendous amount from the incredibly gifted artists we get here.*

The educational programming continued to grow that year with the addition of Splash Scenes, a series of student-prepared scenes performed on traditionally dark Monday nights, which gave apprentices the perfect opportunity to get on the stage in roles a bit meatier than walk-ons and crowd scenes. Once again the acting company rose to the occasion, giving up their night off to act with the apprentices. Their appearances brought out bigger audiences than might have come if it was just the students performing, and the rest of the acting company always seemed to show up just to watch these new, young members of the ISF family spread their wings.

Jack Sinclair, Julie James, Sandy Mulvihill, wow the crowd, *Pump Boys.* TM

Pump Boys and Dinettes. TM

Trula & Clayton Gorrie, landscape photo; Troy Maben, production photos.

2001 was a big year for the entire country. The economy was still riding the wave of the late '90's, business was good, the stock market was strong, and people were enjoying the good life in America.

In Boise, the year began with the arrival of the Shakespeare Theatre Association of America for their annual conference. The buzz created at the Stratford-Upon-Avon conference the year before carried over to the Treasure Valley as ISF and the community welcomed them with open arms, on the eve of the Festival's Silver Anniversary.

Mark Hofflund: *Scott (Phillips) said it just made sense for the STAA to go from the richest Shakespearean theater in the world to one that people haven't heard of yet, but that they could all aspire to become. And he was right. We featured some of the original company and the campaign leaders, we had education programs, corporate leaders, Shakespeare films in the Egyptian Theater – everybody contributed. A Bald Eagle even roosted outside the Interpretive Center during a midday lunch and tour we presented at the*

Costume design, Constanze, *Amadeus*, Ann Hoste

2001

The Play: ***The Two Gentlemen of Verona***
Director: Charles Fee
Scenic Designer: Gage Williams
Costume Design: Kim Krumm Sorenson
Lighting Design: Rick Martin
Composer: Peter John Still

The Play: ***Amadeus***
Director: Gordon Reinhart
Scenic Designer: Gage Williams
Costume Design: Ann Hoste
Lighting Design: M.L. Geiger
Composer: Peter John Still

The Play: ***Much Ado About Nothing***
Director: Drew Barr
Scenic Designer: Gage Williams
Costume Design: Kim Krumm Sorenson
Lighting Design: Rick Martin
Composer: Peter John Still

The Play: ***Hamlet***
Director: Charles Fee
Scenic Designer: Gage Williams
Costume Design: Star Moxley
Lighting Design: Rick Martin
Composer: Peter John Still

The Play: ***Forever Plaid***
Director: Jim Giancarlo
Scenic Designer: Gage Williams
Costume Design: Kerri Lee Robbins
Lighting Design: John Jay Espino
Composer: Peter John Still

site. And everyone was blown away by our new facility, even though it wasn't finished yet.

As winter rolled into spring, the Festival's impending 25th Anniversary gave added impetus to preparations for the upcoming season. Work was underway on the dressing rooms, the final piece of the five year, $6 million construction puzzle for the site. Although few patrons would ever see it, the acting company was more than ready to rid themselves of the temporary accommodations they had put up with while the rest of the theater park was being completed.

Dan Peterson: *Charlie brought in trailers, like the ones you see at constructions sites. There were usually 2 trailers, one for men and one for women. But in Shakespeare's plays, there are 50 men and 2 women and the trailers were the same size, so do the math.*

To make matters worse, there were no bathrooms or running water in them the first year. That situation was rectified for the next two years, but needless to say, the acting company was ecstatic when they arrived to find an actual building with a green room and dressing rooms with hot and cold running water, toilets, and air conditioning. The original building was a basic board-and-batton structure, but Gerhard Borbonus was still donating the sandstone rubble that had been used to finish the interpretive center and the rest rooms, and the plan was to do the same with the dressing rooms...when the money was available for the stone masons.

Don Belts' landscaping, begun in 2000, was starting to take hold, and that spring the grounds were ablaze with color. Then groundskeeper Carol Cole noticed a problem.

Carol Cole: *The berms were originally planted with creeping red fescue, but somehow a nasty little bug called a cranberry girdler came our way and the south facing slopes of the berms were just devastated before I figured out what was going on. Landscapers all over the valley were having the same problem, and they were using a mixture of different fescues to keep it from being a monoculture, so we raked everything out and over-seeded it with that blend, and it took care of the problem.*

One of the highlights leading up to the Silver Anniversary season was the announcement that ISF was the recipient of the Governor's Award for Excellence in the Arts. This prestigious honor served notice that the artistic mission of the Festival was stronger and more diverse than ever. This message was further defined by Board President Mike McIntyre's letter to patrons in the summer program.

Mike McIntyre (2002 program): *"Last year the Festival entertained almost 50,000 people, and expects to exceed that number this year. There are now two statewide school programs that reach 55,000 young people annually; a drama school where over 300 students learn public speaking, poise and confidence; school matinees that reach 6,000; a top-notch theater company; and a permanent, state-of-the-art performance space and nature preserve."*

Governor Dirk Kempthorne and Patricia Kempthorne present Excellence in the Arts Award to Artistic Director Charles Fee and Board President Brent Fery. TM

e **Williams:** *By this time Charlie and I began to talk in a d of short hand, and our process really changed. Before we ays spent hours pouring over research, that's why we had such itectural sets. But then Midsummer with just the grass and the ole arches, then moving on to Hamlet, which we sort of reduced n to a wall and a floor. Then I had this idea of having one portal, putting it up in the air so you had to climb up to get to it. Charlie , "What's behind it?" And I said there's nothing behind it, it's a al to nowhere. It's just like Hamlet's situation. It's the abyss.*

L-R, Stitch Marker, Osric; Chad Sheppner, Francisco; Aled Davies, Claudius; Kathleen Tague, Gertrude, *Hamlet.* TM

L-R, Douglas Frederick, Horatio; Steve Tague, Hamlet, *Hamlet.* TM

***Hamlet* set design, Gage Williams.**

Richard Klautsch, Banquo, *Hamlet.* TM

The 25th season of Shakespeare Under the Stars was reflective of the company's past, while looking toward the future at the same time. A remount of previous summer's *Two Gentlemen of Verona*, first produced for ISF's second season in 1978, led off the season, followed by *Much Ado About Nothing*, which helped inaugurate the Festival's Plantation site in 1981, directed in its fourth incarnation at ISF by festival newcomer, Drew Barr.

For only the second time in Festival history, *Hamlet* was on the playbill, the first production taking stage at the Plantation in 1982. One of the Bard's most famous works, arguably the most quoted, it has always been the subject of much discussion wherever it is produced. This time was no different as Charlie cast Steve Tague in the title role. Although he was firmly established by this time as the company's leading man, some thought him a bit too old for the part. The reviews, as well as the audience reaction, proved them wrong.

Steve Tague: *I liked the Hamlet for two reasons, the wholeness of the production and I thought it was some of my best work, even though I don't think I quite fit it perfectly.*

Stepping away from the Bard to explore new directions for the company, Charlie chose Peter Shaffer's award-winning *Amadeus*. Directing duties went to Gordon Reinhart, a recent Boise transplant from Detroit and Assistant Professor of Acting and Directing at Boise State University. Ann Hoste's costume design concept came right from the text.

Ann Hoste: *There's a line in the play where Salieri talks about everything turning golden. So I talked to Gordon about creating an entire world that was golden with the exception of Mozart and his wife. We would see them in contrast to that world, then how they gradually fit into the gold and then fell out of it again into darkness. Salieri was also a little bit out of the world of court and then moved*

L-R,; Jeffrey Hawkins, Proteus; Carie Yonekawa, Sylvia, *Two Gents.* TM

L-R, Chad Sheppner, Valentine; Tracy Sunderland, Speed, *Two Gents.* TM

into favor and into that beautiful gold suit.

Tom Willmorth: *Getting entrusted with the role of Mozart was really significant because any time I get to do a non-clown role, it's special. Playing on the surface to my type, which is the joker, but having to delve deep into this guy who's losing his confidence, losing prestige, just dying on stage...struggling and not understanding it. That was great.*

Richard Klautsch: *I probably felt more of a challenge doing Salieri than just about any other role I've played just because of the size and scope of it. And because Charlie looks to the senior members of the company as kind of the leaders, there was a sense that I needed to get out in front. So I always tried to be as prepared as possible and always made sure that whatever we were doing I was ready to give 110%. Every night it was a complete joy to do, and I think ultimately it took my own work to another level.*

Richard Klautsch, Saliere, *Amadeus.* TM

L-R, Tom Willmorth, Mozart; David Anthony Smith, Von Sweiten; Richard Klautsch, Salieri; Frederick Charles Canada, Von Strack, *Amadeus.* TM

Building on the success of *Pump Boys and Dinettes* the year before, with its small cast and big audience appeal, another musical closed out the season. This time it was *Forever Plaid*, directed by Jim Giancarlo, Artistic Director of the Oregon Cabaret Theater in Ashland.

L-R, Tom Willmorth, Mozart; Chad Sheppner, Major Domo; Kathryn Cherasaro, Constanze, *Amadeus.* TM

Left and above: Francis Kelly, Michael Jenkinson, Chad Sommervill, Jim Sorenson, Singers; John Jay Espino, piano, *Forever Plaid.* TM

It was the most successful season in festival history, with over 48,000 people attending the five shows. Further honors came to ISF that summer when Governor Dirk Kempthorne asked Mark to become the Chair of the Idaho Commission on the Arts. Since being appointed an at-large commissioner by 1995 Chair, Dee Fery, he had been asked to stay on in that capacity by two subsequent Chairs. He was sworn in on September 7, 2001. Four days later, on September 11th, the world changed in ways that still affect us all.

MYSTERIOUS AND COMPLICATED

HAMLET

Actor and director talk about the production, the role and meeting ghosts

By Dana Oland
The Idaho Statesman

For an actor, every role is a journey. It's a path from the self to a character in another reality, another self that exists in the world of a play. That journey is intensified for actor Steve Tague as he takes on Hamlet, Prince of Denmark, one of the most challenging roles, and one of the m... in the theatric...

From the director's chair

Charles Fee, directs "Hamlet." Hamlet's revenge for his father's murder destroys his mother, his lover, his kingdom, himself.

Q: Why do this play now?

Fee: One is always thinking about when one will do "Hamlet." I've been here 10 years. I have the actors. It's time.

Charles Fee

Q: What's the production's look?

Fee: Very, very minimal. We use Philip Glass' Tibetan inspired music for "Kundun."

The set is extremely severe, almost no furniture, very few props, only two pieces of gold silk that define the space. Hamlet is all in black against an all red court that is rich and opulent, almost garish. What really becomes apparent is Hamlet's loneliness and separation.

Q: How does this reflect in mood?

Fee: It will feel very classical. With the silk it will be a bit Asian but you'll feel a strong sense of the thriller in the play.

Q: How did you approach the text and the character?

Fee: I started out with the idea that Hamlet is the ultimate intellectual. But that's changed. When you get into rehearsals, you realize that characters are never just one thing. There's something different every moment.

— Dana Oland

Gerry Melendez / The Idaho Statesman
...the role of Hamlet, one of the most com... ...speare Festival's production of the pop... ...epertory through August. Tague has ...rking with the text and studying other

...me's Afoot
...nagram and enter a ...hakespeare Festi... ...r autographed by
NAME:
PHONE:

Two gents of the festival

Team charts Idaho Shakespeare's course

Charles Fee, 43, Idaho Shakespeare Festival's artistic director, works exuberantly with actor Jeffrey Hawkins during rehearsal of the 25th anniversary season opener, "The Two Gentlemen of Verona." Fee has spent the last 10 years at the festival's helm.

By Dana Oland
The Idaho Statesman

The first time Charles Fee and Mark Hofflund shared a stage 17 years ago, they barely knew each other. Fee played the bottom half of a nightmarish elk and Hofflund — in drag — was a decoy Ann Page with one word to say at San Diego's Old Globe Theatre's production of "The Merry Wives of Windsor."

Today, they share many a stage — and a friendship, a love of theater, an office and a working partnership that lies at the heart of the Idaho Shakespeare Festival's growth and success in recent years.

This marks Fee's 10th season as artistic director and Hofflund's ninth as managing director.

As this 25th anniversary season begins, the festival enjoys a growing national reputation; a talented company of creative artists who return to do theater in the Boise Foothills; and, finally, a completed amphitheater, though the campaign continues.

Fee and Hofflund have been instru... who was one of a band of actors who helped found the festival 25 years ago. "Mark and Charlie are a good match ...

AT CENTER STAGE: ACTOR JEFFREY HAWKINS

... coming to the Idaho Shakespeare Festival is like coming home.

Hawkins, 26, has made his way to Boise for the past four summers to act in roles such as Lysander in "A Midsummer Night's Dream," D'Artagnan in ...

Oliver Russell & Associates, cover design.

As America struggled to regain its balance after the devastating effects of 9/11, the 2002 Olympic Winter Games brought its message of peace and good will to nearby Salt Lake City, Utah in February. For ISF, things were finally starting to slow down after the hectic years of the capital campaign.

The significance of what they had all accomplished, enhanced by the milestone of the Festival's 25th anniversary began to settle in on board and staff members alike, and steadily growing attendance figures were a sure sign that the people of Boise and the Treasure Valley had embraced the new theater and all it had come to represent for their community.

The Play: ***Much Ado About Nothing***
Director: Drew Barr
Scenic Designer: Gage Williams
Costume Design: Kim Krumm Sorenson
Lighting Design: Rick Martin
Sound Designer: Peter John Still

The Play: ***Arms and the Man***
Director: Charles Fee
Scenic Designer: Gage Williams
Costume Design: Star Moxley
Lighting Design: Tracy Odishaw
Sound Designer: Peter John Still

The Play: ***Twelfth Night, or What You Will***
Director: Gordon Reinhart
Scenic Designer: Gage Williams
Costume Design: Clare Henkel
Lighting Design: Rick Martin
Sound Designer: Peter John Still

The Play: ***Macbeth***
Director: Charles Fee
Scenic Designer: Gage Williams
Costume Design: Star Moxley
Lighting Design: Rick Martin
Sound Designer: Peter John Still

The Play: ***You're A Good Man ,Charlie Brown***
Director: Drew Barr
Scenic Designer: Norelle Sissons
Costume Design: Jacqueline Firkins
Lighting Design: Rick Martin
Sound Designer: Peter John Still

2002

L-R, Douglas Frederick, Malvolio; Stitch Marker, Feste, *Twelfth Night.* TM

Aled Davies, Toby Belch; Kathryn Cherasaro, Maria, *Twelfth Night.* TM

L-R, Ira Amyx, Sailor; Sara Bruner, Viola; Aaron Preusse, Sea Captain; *Twelfth Night.* TM

[...]ely Golden, Andrew Aguecheek, *Twelfth Night.*

Richard Klautsch, Orsino, *Twelfth Night.* TM

Kristen De Angeli: *We've really become branded by this new theater, in a very nice way. We've changed from being a great family tradition to being a great family tradition in this absolutely world class setting. The idea that we are a professional theater, and that for everyone who works for us it is a chosen profession, effects how we fundraise, which, in effect, determines how we are able to spread the message of what we do. So that message then becomes filtered not just through our ticket holders, but through their kids, and through the work we do with state, city and private partnerships. We really have an impact throughout the state with school tours and residencies and apprenticeships and educator workshops. We do a whole year's worth of programming.*

As the company settled comfortably in to its new home, Charlie and Mark found they had also settled into their respective leadership positions, but not necessarily in the traditional way. Most artistic directors select the shows and hire the people to get them up and running, while the task of keeping track of expenses and growing the business of the company usually falls to managing directors.

Charlie Fee: *From day one we just kind of figured out, without ever talking about it, what we liked to do and what we're good at. So what Mark is doing is fund raising. He's creating all these relationships with individuals and corporations and the community that are obviously paying huge dividends. And while he's doing that I'm working on business models and budgets and all that stuff that is concrete and knowable as opposed to the artistic stuff I do, which is more abstract, and has no numbers attached to it. I think it's an incredible, dynamic mix between the two of us.*

But work on the new site was not yet complete. Signage was added to the front of the theater to give it some real identity, and a large grant from the Murdoch Charitable Trust brought in new, and much needed, lighting and sound equipment. Architect Doug Cooper came on board to develop donor recognition, the final phase of the project.

What is love? 'tis not hereafter; Present myrth hath present laughter. Twelfth Night, II, iii.

Kathleen Tague, Lady Macbeth.TM

Karen Wennstrom, Lady Macduff, *Macbeth*. TM

Carie Yonekawa, Witch, *Macbeth*. TM

Dianne Robertson (2002 program): *"As I welcome you to the 26th season of the Idaho Shakespeare Festival I realize anew how important the Festival is to our community and to the State of Idaho. The Festival employs ten full-time employees and each summer we are home to more than 100 actors, directors, designers and production personnel...During the Festival's third season, when my young daughters returned night after night hoping that Romeo would wait a little longer for Juliet to wake up, I knew that this young theater company had to survive and grow. I know that many of you have similar stories of our love for the Idaho Shakespeare Festival as it has become an important thread in the fabric of our lives."*

New Development Director Dawn Suleri started writing grants and helped bring the Festival a burst of additional contributions that came close to a million additional dollars. The money went toward a host of things that hadn't been finished, mostly furniture, fixtures and equipment. By the time the 26th season opened in June, the ISF park was beginning to look like a finished product. Board President Dianne Robertson's program letter offered up a personal look at just how far the Festival had come.

Charlie's season was chosen to reflect and distill the drama of life. The tragedy of Charlie's *Macbeth* was relieved by the comedy of *Much Ado About Nothing*, brought back from the previous season, and *Twelfth Night*, directed by Gordon Reinhart, whose lush *Amadeus* was a big hit the previous year. The fourth show in the repertory brought the debut of another great playwright on the ISF stage as Charlie also directed George Bernard Shaw's *Arms and the Man*. Drew Barr was back to tackle the season's musical, *You're A Good Man Charlie Brown*, which brought an exciting new talent to Boise in the person of Tom Ford. Ironically, Tom had heard about ISF long before he worked here. John Rice, who was an outstanding Iago in 1986 and returned to play the infamous Dr. Moriarity in '87, was a classmate in graduate school fifteen years earlier.

Steve Tague, *Macbeth*. TM

Mark Hofflund: *Just having the new theater gave us the foundation for what we could ultimately bring into it. For example, it was designed to allow for additional lighting equipment. It also gave us a fund raising potential, as well as a national profile when we hosted our colleagues, and it gave us the artistic frame to do more and better work.*

Tom Ford: *Charlie Brown was an incredibly idyllic situation because it was being directed by a friend of mine, it was a show I'd always wanted to do, and it was in this amazingly beautiful location. I remember there was this one moment where I would lay back on a bench and look up at the sky. I mean, that's what Charlie was doing and that's what I was doing, and there was this beautiful sky with these clouds and I was like, well, this is just glorious!*

L-R, Steve Tague, Major Petkoff; Davi
Smith, Major Saranoff, *Arms and th*

The expansion of John O'Hagan's educational programming, brought over with ITY, was paying dividends not even Charlie had seen coming. In addition to expanding ISF's reach into the community and across the state, he was able to use well-trained apprentices to fill out the stage in his productions, giving him ready-made crowd scenes. A few even landed small speaking roles. Before she had even graduated from high school, Karen Baughn was cast as Audrey in *As you Like It*, opposite Tom Ford.

Now, however, it was time for John to continue his own education, and that fall he left for graduate school at the University of Idaho, where he would study under former ISF actor and ITY Artistic Director David Lee Painter. But the daunting task of ensuring that the educational programs would continue to grow and remain an integral part of the Festival brought another member of the ISF family who had been absent for several years back into the fold.

Carole Whiteleather worked as an actress for ISF during the ParkCenter years, as well as doing several shows for ITY. She created the Holiday Interlude series with Mark Cuddy in the mid 1980's, and when Rod Ceballos dropped it in 1988, she continued it on her own. Charlie encouraged her to bring it back to ISF when he came on board, and it wasn't long before they were hiring two casts to handle the increased number of performances. When he mentioned he wanted to create a winter presence for ISF, Carole suggested play readings, and started the 3 x 3 reading series.

Carole Whiteleather: *I think things like that, along with the fact that I was teaching over at BSU, gave Charlie the idea that I might be the right candidate when John left. All of a sudden I had the Holiday Interludes, the Shakespearience tour, and then the ITY tour, which I create and direct. And on top of that there's the Drama School. Oh my gosh!*

By the end of its fifth season at the Barber Pool site, the capital campaign began to wind down, and the focus of fund raising efforts shifted more toward operations and maintenance. Without the impetus of a new theater to spur donors to action, and with federal as well as state funding for the arts in a decade-old decline, Charlie and Mark began to look for new ways to provide for the company. It was not a unique problem. Other arts organizations in Idaho and around the country were facing the same difficulty.

Following the example of Ballet Idaho, which had joined forces with a Eugene, Oregon company to co-opt productions, Charlie began exploring a similar strategic alliance with the faltering Great Lakes Theater Festival in Cleveland, Ohio.

...y Smith, Major Saranoff, *Arms.* TM

Kathleen Tague, Catherine Petkoff; David Anthony Smith, *Arms.* TM

L-R, Steve Tague, Major Petkoff; David Anthony Smith, Major Saranoff; Sara Bruner, Raina Petkoff; Kathleen Tague, Catherine Petkoff; *Arms.* TM

ISF director Charles Fee doubles his artistic vision

By Dana Oland
The Idaho Statesman

Idaho Shakespeare Festival artistic director Charles Fee will really start racking up the frequent-flyer miles in the coming year.

On Tuesday, Fee signed a one-year contract to become producing director at Great Lakes Theater Festival in Cleveland. But don't panic. He plans to remain at ISF, too, and commute between the two cities.

He can do this because the theater companies have opposite sea[...]

Charles Fee

theaters. That is something Fee and the ISF board have been interested in for a while.

"There are tremendous opportunities with this," Fee said. "It announces to the theater world that Idaho Shakespeare Festival is a player because its artistic director is now a national player."

Because Fee is continuing to develop [...] Idaho, that [...]

Saturday.

Arthur Lithgow founded the classical theater and it counts his son, actor John Lithgow ("3rd Rock from the Sun"), and Tom Hanks among its alumni.

It produces a five-play season in its 1,000-seat theater in Playhouse Square Center, one of the largest theater complexes in the country.

It's a great opportunity, Fee said, but he reiterated that he is not leaving Idaho. He and both theater boards will reevaluate the situation after a [...] meantime, he'll

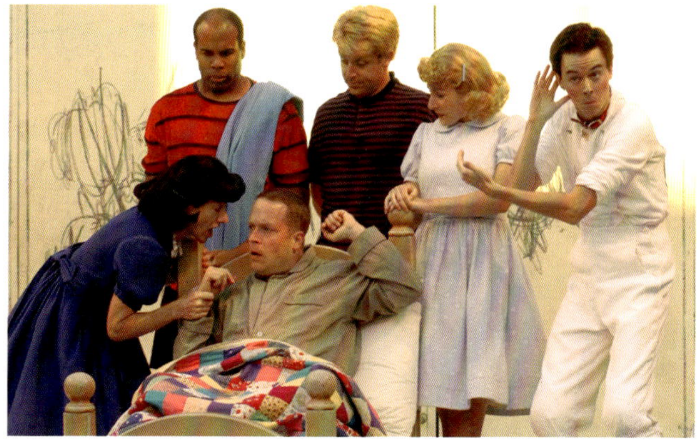

Clockwise top left: Kevin Free, Linus; Tony Capone, Schroeder; Jessica Walling, Sally; Daniel Kelley, Snoopy; Tom Ford, Charlie; Sandy Mulvihill, Lucy, *Charlie Brown.* TM

Charlie Fee: *When we looked at Cleveland it was clear that what the two companies were producing and how they were producing could be very similar. Their history had been in Shakespeare, but they had gotten away from that. I felt the company needed to return to those roots, and in doing that we could start to share more and more work between the two cities.*

L-R, Daniel Kelley, Snoopy; Kevin Free, Linus; Tony Capone, Shroeder; Sandy Mulvihill Lucy; Tom Ford, Charlie, *Charlie Brown.* TM

L-R, Kevin Free, Linus; Sandy Mulvihill, Lucy, *Charlie Brown.* TM

After much debate between boards and staffs, Charlie signed on as Producing Artistic Director at Great Lakes, while still retaining his position in Idaho. ISF's summer outdoor season contrasted nicely with Cleveland's winter indoor season, so the schedule allowed him to run both companies simultaneously. The cost savings were readily apparent, but for Charlie, the more important reason for the alliance was to extend the life of the work. One of his primary goals in coming to ISF was to build a company model in which he could realize long-term commitments from artists. Now he could begin to extend his actor contracts from a four month summer season to an additional four month winter commitment that included performing in two cities.

Charlie Fee: *It isn't because I think that's the way to get the best actors, it's because I think that's the way to make the best art. The longer commitment I can make to the actors the more I'm going to play a role in developing their work with them and the more they're going to play a role in developing our voice as a theater company. But one of the big problems is that the economic and artistic elements are inextricably linked. That's why we started doing remounts, because the sets and costumes are already there and the rehearsal period is shorter. With Cleveland in the loop I could extend the length of productions, get a second chance to direct them and bring them to a new audience, and give actors and all the other artists a great employment opportunity.*

That fall he took three productions from Idaho to Cleveland – *Much Ado* and *Arms and the Man* from the 2002 season, and the enormously popular *Midsummer* which had opened the new theater in 1998 and returned in '99. Not many of the Boise actors were available to go with the show, but he also needed to begin building a company

Clockwise from top left: Aled Davies, Toby Belch; Tracy Sunderland, Fabian; Joe Conely Golden, Andrew Agucheek, *Twelfth Night.* TM

in Cleveland, and he was able to integrate new actors into the remount in a way that he'd never done at ISF. The unknown factor was whether the Cleveland audience would embrace the idea of sharing work with a company in Boise, Idaho. National theater critic Tony Brown of The Plain Dealer answered that question with resounding clarity.

The Plain Dealer, October 28, 2002, Tony Brown, Theater Critic: *When I first heard that Great Lakes Theater Festival had hired a guy from the Idaho Shakespeare Festival to be its new CEO and would share productions with the Boise festival, a tiny company no one had ever heard of, I rolled my eyes and sighed a derisive, Oh, boy! Now that I have seen the first triumphant product of this unlikely-sounding arrangement, the thoroughly American and thoroughly hilarious Much Ado About Nothing that opened over the weekend at Playhouse Square, I hasten to amend that. Oh, Boise! Great Lakes' new Producing Artistic Director, Charles Fee, promised to return Cleveland's smart classical company to its central mission of Shakespeare. He also promised that the Shakespeare would be fun. He has delivered in a style Cleveland expects and deserves.*

Oliver Russell & Associates, cover design.

The following summer Boise's new Mayor, Carolyn Terteling-Payne, welcomed patrons to the 27th season of Shakespeare Under the Stars with a program letter that pointed out, "As Boiseans we are not only blessed to live in a city that continues to thrive, but to live and play in a city where the arts are valued and where resources like the Festival exist for us and our children."

Those values were reflected in growing attendance figures at the Festival, as well as expanded educational programs that take her message to young people

The Play: ***A Midsummer Night's Dream***
Director: Charles Fee
Scenic Design: Gage Williams
Costume Design: Star Moxley
Lighting Design: Rick Martin
Sound Design: Peter John Still

The Play: ***The Importance of Being Earnest***
Director: Charles Fee
Scenic Design: Gage Williams
Costume Design: Kim Krumm Sorensen
Lighting Design: Rick Martin
Sound Design: Peter John Still

The Play: ***The Comedy of Errors***
Director: Christopher Bayes
Scenic Design: Narelle Sissons
Costume Design: Caitlin Ward
Lighting Design: Mary Louise Geiger
Sound Design: Peter John Still

The Play: ***Henry V***
Director: Steve Tague
Scenic Design: Gage Williams
Costume Design: Star Moxley
Sound Design: Peter John Still

The Play: ***The Fantasticks***
Director: Drew Barr
Music Director: John Jay Espino
Scenic Design: Norelle Sissons
Costume Design: Jacqueline Firkins
Sound Design: Timothy Knox

The Fantasticks, the summer's musical offering.

JJF

2003

L-R, Christina Lang, Gwendolen Fairfax; Sara Bruner, Cecily Cardew, *The Importance of Being Earnest*. JJF

L-R, Douglas Frederick, John Worthing; David Anthony Smith, Algernon Moncrieff, *Earnest*. JJF

L-R, David Anthony Smith, Algernon; Sara Bruner, Cecily; Douglas Frederick, John; Christina Lang, Gwendolen; Kathleen Tague, Lady Bracknell, *Earnest*. JJF

L-R, Alad Davies, Rev. Chasuble; Tracy Sunderland, Miss Prism, *Earnest*. JJF

throughout the entire State, and to audiences on a national level as well, as board President Bob Wetherell proudly pointed out.

Bob Wetherell (2003 program): Since…ground was broken for this amphitheater, productions first seen on this stage have gone on to national acclaim. Much Ado about Nothing, Arms and the Man and A Midsummer Night's Dream were mounted this past year at Great Lakes Theater Festival in Cleveland. Cymbeline and Titus Andronicus have been staged in Seattle, Cymbeline appeared in New York and Stratford-Upon-Avon, where it was the first American produced Shakespeare play to be staged at the Royal Shakespeare Company, and Scapin played in Seattle and Chicago. Directors, composers, costume and scenic designers, and lighting designers have all received national awards based on work they originated for the Festival.

There were rewards closer to home as well.

Richard Klautsch: *The partnership between ISF and the Boise State Theatre Arts Department has been immeasurably valuable to both organizations. Very few undergraduate theater programs can offer their students and faculty the opportunities to compete for roles and technical positions on such a high level so close to home. For ISF, the department offers a diverse pool of talent of all ages!. It's one of our most important responsibilities in the professional regional theater – preparing the next generation of theater artists. And I have never, ever, seen someone after a summer working at ISF who wasn't better.*

Dana Oland: When they brought back the Beatles Midsummer for the third time I complained and complained and complained. And then I went and I laughed my ass off.

The Idaho Statesman • IdahoStatesman.com   Monday, June 9, 2003

Shakespeare Festival's 'Dream' still rings true

THEATER REVIEW

The Bard goes mod in rollicking, madcap opener

By Dana Oland
The Idaho Statesman

Director Charles Fee and his company could not have imagined a more triumphant return to the Idaho Shakespeare Festival of his "Dream."

But here it is.

A nearly sell-out crowd greeted the festival's "A Midsummer Night's Dream" with cheers and screams usually reserved for teen …k idols.

…pla is well de-

skirts, sleek Edwardian… and fur-trimmed coats… lovers. Her East Indian… flowing robes for Obe… tania hit the perfect s… Resident set desig… William's set is even… than the 1998 produ… ing, minimal doors… change of scene, and richly co… ored grasses create the mystical wilderness of enchanted woods.

Under resident lighting designer Rick Martin's lights, the whole production takes on an even more vivid dimension.

Thanks to new lighting equipment, even in the more daylike part of the evening, the intensity comes through.

As the four lovers, Carie … (Hermia), Jeffrey C. …

the Duke and appears the master of transcendental meditation as … Lynn's strong, grounded … welcome …

emote… mus. He also perfo… velous feat of being heard and understood through a donkey mask.

The rest of the mechanicals brings a delightful comic energy to a show that's filled with so much comedy.

Kudos to Mark Anthony Taylor, who directs as Peter Quince with ease, Douglas …rick as Snout the Tinker, A…rey as Sung the Joiner, … and Danny … the Tailor and … the Bellows

L-R, Mark Anthony Taylor, Pistol; Dan Peterson, Bardoph; Stitch Marker, Nym, *Henry V*. JJF

Mark Anthony Taylor, Pistol, *Henry V*. JJF

Aled Davies, Chorus with Cast, *Henry V*. JJF

The experiment with Cleveland came full circle for the first time in 2003 with the return of *A Midsummer Night's Dream*, which had just closed at Great Lakes Theater Festival. Its journey back and forth across the country had brought changes, some more visible than others, in the production itself, as well as in the way ISF was going about the business of professional theater.

Charlie Fee: *When we finished the two runs in Idaho the set was virtually destroyed, so we rebuilt the show entirely in Cleveland. We wanted to revisit costumes anyway, and we needed a full rehearsal period because it had been two years since the last performance. What we ended up with was a much fresher, brighter production when it came back here. I was able to remount it in six days instead of four weeks, and we saw enormous cost savings here in Idaho. For my money it was the best production of Dream that we had done.*

In addition to directing the "new and improved" *Midsummer*, Charlie continued his mission of bringing audiences the classics beyond Shakespeare by following the 2002 debut of George Bernard Shaw with that of Oscar Wilde, in the form of his rollicking comedy, *The Importance of Being Earnest*. Christopher Bayes, who directed the wild and crazy Scapin in 1999, was back to work his comic/clown magic on *A Comedy of Errors*, and Steve Tague, whom audiences had come to know as one of the company's leading actors for the past ten seasons, stepped outside the footlights to direct another first for ISF – *Henry V*.

Aled Davies: *One of the lovely things during Henry V was to have a four-month pregnant Kathleen Tague playing all those men in armor and swords and stuff. There's something moving about another generation of actors, being on stage in-utero.*

To close out the season, Drew Barr directed *The Fantasticks*, the third consecutive September musical, bringing back Tom Ford, who had wowed audiences the summer before as Charlie Brown, for another lesson in the unique community relationship that defines ISF.

Tom Ford: *People talk to you, out in the community, they feel completely comfortable talking to you. Which is sometimes strange. I was just at Albertsons the other day and this woman in the check out line says, "I'm sorry. You will always be Charlie Brown."*

And adding to our national exposure, the chairman of the National Endowment for the Arts, Dana Gioia, was on hand for the opening as part of a trip that included speaking at a statewide arts conference. It was a meeting that would reap further benefits for ISF down the road.

That summer, another small piece of the theater park was put in place. A small bronze embedded in sandstone now sits among the flowers in a raised planter near

brother's dead love, which she would keep fresh And lasting in her sad remembrance. O, she that hath a hea[rt of that fine] frame To pay this debt of love but to a brother, How will she love, when t[he rich golden shaft Hath k]ill'd the

the cottonwood dell. Dedicated by Bob and Dee Dee Copsey as part of the family's contribution to the capital campaign, it honors the group of artists and friends who brought their midsummer night's dream to reality on the lawn of One Capital Center in 1977.

Aled Davies: My fondest thing at the site is that little plaque about the first season. It's like a lifeline to the development of this theater and all the thousands of people who have had a hand in creating it. I'm moved always by the presence of Stitch Marker and Danny Peterson. To be around all these years later, and the history they've seen and the performances they've given. You leave things behind at every stage, but to be aware of where it started and just to honor that. In a way, that encapsulates all of the productions and people over the years that made it possible.

Allen Gilmore, Luce (also known as Nell), *The Comedy of Errors.* JJF

Christina Lang, Jailer, *Comedy.* JJF

L-R, Tom Willmorth, Dromio Twins; Joe Conely Golden, Antipholus twins, *Comedy.* JJF

The Comedy of Errors. JJF

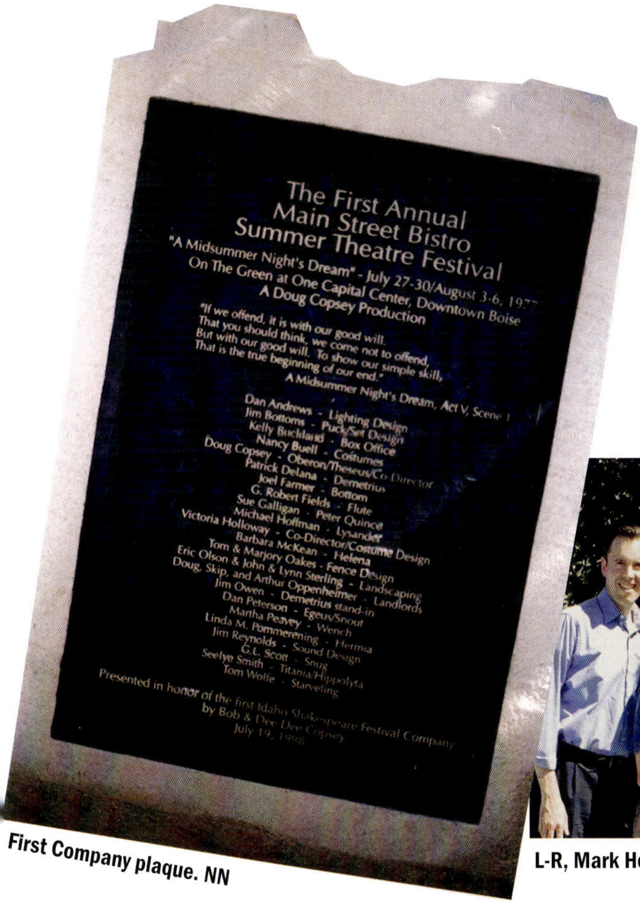

First Company plaque. NN

Dee Dee Copsey. UK

L-R, Mark Hofflund, Doug Copsey, Bob Copsey, Charlie Fee. NN

We are such stuff as dreams are made on, and our little life is rounded with a sleep. The Tempest, IV, i.

The beauty and the magic of theater is what we all continue to strive for as a

Oliver Russell & Associates, cover design.

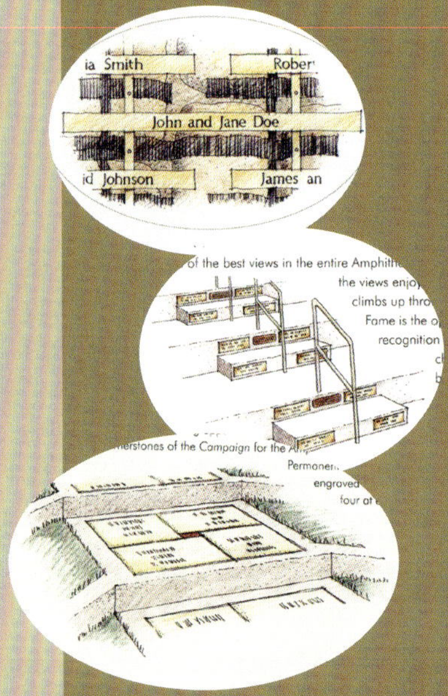

Donor recognition opportunities

That winter the British stonemasons who had done all the sandstone veneer work for the new theater were finally able to return to the U.S. after having to leave in the wake of 9/11. At last the final piece of exterior construction puzzle would be completed.

Mark Hofflund: *We knew that one day the board-and-batten was going to fall apart and we would have to repaint or whatever. Thanks to an anonymous donor and Gerhard Borbonus' ongoing contribution of sandstone rubble we were able to get the stonemasons to finish veneering that last building. Now it looks like the rest of the facility, it's really well insulated, and we'll never have to maintain it.*

In a fitting tribute to a former ISF apprentice who has been in a coma since the 1980's, Alan and Royanne Minskoff chose to use their naming opportunity to dedicate the green room in the theater's newest facility to their niece, Donna Lynn Sands. As further testament to the power of family, a group of nurses who care for Donna in New York, none of whom has ever been to Idaho, send a generous contribution each year to the Festival.

2004

Charlie shows off the new dressing rooms. TM

The Play: ***The Importance of Being Earnest***
Director: Charles Fee
Scenic Designer: Gage Williams
Costume Design: Kim Krumm Sorensen
Lighting Design: Rick Martin
Sound Designer: Peter John Still

The Play: ***As You Like It***
Director: Charles Fee
Scenic Designer: Gage Williams
Costume Design: Star Moxley
Lighting Design: Rick Martin
Sound Designer: Peter John Still

The Play: ***The Merry Wives of Windsor***
Director: Sari Ketter
Scenic Designer: Jarrett Bertoncin/Russell Metheny
Costume Design: B. Modern/Coleen Scott
Lighting Design: Less Dickert
Sound Designer: Tom Mardikes

The Play: ***Julius Caesar***
Director: Risa Brainin
Scenic Designer: Russell Metheny
Costume Design: Kim Krumm Sorenon
Lighting Design: Michael Klaers
Sound Designer: Tom Mardikes

The Play: ***I Love You, You're Perfect, Now Change***
Director: Victoria Bussert
Music Director: John Jay Espino
Scenic Designer: Jeff Herrmann
Costume Design: Nicole Frachiseur
Lighting Design: Less Dickert
Sound Designer: Peter John Still

... as we gamble with choices that we hope will put butts in the seats and bucks in the bank.

L-R, Sara Bruner, Rosalind; Neil Brookshire, Orlando, *As You Like It*. JJF

Donor recognition was still an ongoing project, and probably always will be, and while there were one or two items on the wish list that still had not been funded, for all intents and purposes the theater \was complete.

It was another year, and with it came another new mayor, "another star-filled sky, another delightful evening of Shakespeare along the river – not the Avon or the Thames, but the Boise, and a theater experience unlike any other in the world." Mayor David Beiter's program letter went on to say, "I invite you to pause and marvel at what you see, both on stage and all around you. The Festival Amphitheater & Reserve is a truly unique environment. A place where human creativity coexists with nature's artistry, set against the picture-postcard backdrop of the Boise Foothills and alongside the river that is the very lifeblood of our community. All the world's a stage, indeed, but you and I are fortunate to call this part of the world, and this incredible stage, our own."

What goes on that stage is a question offered up to audiences during the curtain speech toward the end of each season. It is a daunting task to try and figure out what will delight audiences and stretch their sense of theater in exciting and interesting ways. As Charlie put it in his annual message to patrons, "Shakespeare compares poets to lovers and madmen, the actors he calls players – gamblers one might say, betting the house every time they step on stage. Theater is a game of chance. ..all the repetition of rehearsal only prepares us to improvise. Every night, in every moment, we experience the play anew with our audience. And with every production we try and reinvent the wheel."

Sara Bruner: *I think Shakespeare is the king of them all. I think he's found the core and the heart of the human condition and the stories that we all need and want to hear and are willing to hear over and over again. And we never get sick of them. I loved doing Julia in Two Gents and Viola in Twelfth Night and Rosalind...I want to do them all again, as many times as I possibly can because they're so wonderful. There's nothing boring about exploring them and figuring out their similarities, and more importantly, their differences.*

L-R, Sara Bruner, Rosalind; Carie Yonekawa, Celia; Tom Ford, Touchstone, *As You Like It*. JJF

L-R, Tom Ford, Touchstone; Carie Yonekawa, Celia, *As You Like It*. JJF

Over the years, ISF has become known as a company that takes liberties with the Bard – a place where designers, directors and actors can experiment with ideas and concepts that larger, more traditional theater companies may not allow. But it has all been done with the audience in mind. Shakespeare did the same thing in his day, producing plays that shocked and amazed audiences with their boldness and audacity, that spoke about fantastical and beautiful things in real words that resonated with people on the most basic levels.

Sara Bruner: *One night I was out behind the audience waiting for my big entrance in Act II and this older woman came by and said, "I really like the play so far." And I'm like, great. She said, "You look a little tense," and I said, yeah, just a little nervous – trying to be nice but also trying to focus. And all of a sudden she starts rubbing my back! Then she said, "does that help?" And I'm like, oh yeah, thanks. And then she left."*

The beauty and the magic of theater is what we all continue to strive for as artists today, as we gamble with choices that we can only hope will put butts in the seats and bucks in the bank. One sure-fire way to accomplish those goals for the 28th season was to start off with the previous season's hit, *The Importance of Being*

Clockwise from top: Fabio Polanco, Emily Kraeger, Jeffries Thaiss, Trista Moldovan, *I Love You, You're Perfect, Now Change*. JJF

L-R, Fabio Polanco, Emily Kraeger, Trista Moldovan, Jeffries Thaiss, *I Love You*. JJF

L-R, Emily Kraeger, Jeffries Thaiss, *I Love You*. JJF

The New Court, *As You Like It.* JJF

Earnest. To follow that, Charlie chose to gamble with a show he had never staged before – *As You Like It*, setting it in late 18th century France and adding music by the Dave Matthews Band.

In another move that wasn't really a gamble at all, he hired Tom Ford, whose outstanding work in two previous musicals had earned him quite a following in the community, for the entire season.

> **Tom Ford:** *I was nervous about coming into the full company, and quite frankly, I was very cognizant of the fact that I was playing roles that other people could have played. And I was so welcomed. There was never a moment of competition or anything but really genuine support. That was really impressive to me because that doesn't happen very often.*

In the 1983 season at the Plantation, Mark Cuddy asked director Victoria Holloway to gamble on her production of *The Merry Wives of Windsor* by staging it as a

L-R, Lynn Allison, Mistress Page; Kathryn Cherasaro, Mistress Ford, *Merry Wives of Windsor.* JJF

Steve Tague, Falstaff, *Merry Wives.* JJF

L-R, Tom Ford, Master Ford; Steve Tague, Falstaff, *Merry Wives.* JJF

Tom Ford, Master Ford, *Merry Wives.* JJF

L-R, Neil Brookshire, Simple; Joe Conley Golden, Dr. Caius, *Merry Wives.* JJF

1950's sit-com. It worked beautifully. Sari Ketter took the same approach with her kitschy fifties version of the show in 2004, only this time it took place in a Howard Johnson's Motor Lodge.

> **Tom Ford:** *I think often times with these plays we think that we have to perform them in a certain way and be reverent to certain things, but we don't know how these plays were performed. We have some documents and some accounts, but I doubt there was any reverence for them when they were first performed.*

Julius Caesar is a gamble no matter how you produce it. The long, wordy production can be downright boring if the directing and acting aren't spot on. Director Risa Brainin stripped this troublesome script bare, letting the acting ensemble tell the story on an uncluttered set wearing non-descript black suits, incorporating just enough of today's political landscape to make this ancient plot chillingly immediate.

> **Tom Ford:** *Risa's process does sort of break down your idea of it and allows you to experience it. There were things that I may have had problems with, but at the same time I'm being challenged. If I'm having a problem with it it's because she's got an idea and I'm coming up against it. I think if you sort of embrace it, if you surrender to what she's doing, your safety net is removed a bit and your old habits are not helping. Not only are they not there, but if you rely on them you're not in the world of the play.*

> **Richard Klautsch:** *We had so many rainouts that summer. One night it started to rain during the bedroom scene and I was out there in slippers. I was slipping all over the place and I had to take them off in mid-scene and throw them off stage. I had to go barefoot. There's always something that teaches you how to stay in the moment and to stay focused up there.*

Perhaps feeling he had bet all of his chips on the repertory season, Charlie chose to take less of a gamble on the September musical, bringing in Victoria Bussert,

Carter Davis, Ensemble, *Julius Caesar.* JJF

L-R, Carter Davis, Ensemble; Aled Davies, Caesar; Tom Willmorth, Conspirator; Stitch Marker, Cicero; Richard Klautsch, Brutus, *Julius Caesar.* JJF

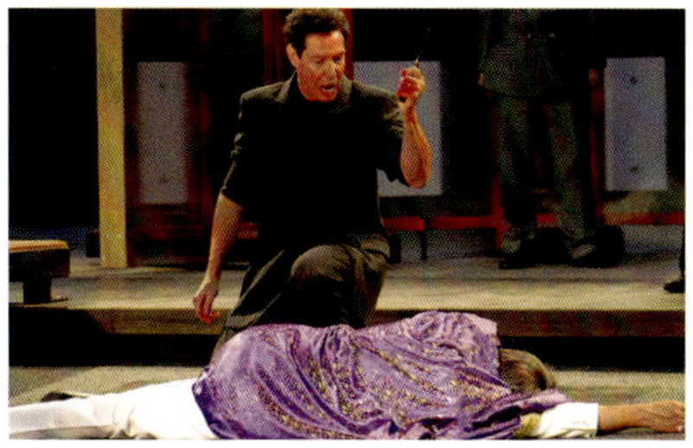

Richard Klautsch, Brutus; Aled Davies, Caesar, *Julius Caesar.* JJF

one of the hottest musical directors of the day, to direct one of the hottest musical revues of the year, *I Love You, You're Perfect, Now Change.*

In her first season as ISF's new Education Director, Carole Whiteleather did much more than just take over the long list of outreach programs she inherited from John O'Hagan. The Apprentice program once again auditioned high school students for fourteen spots on the summer roster. Each one receives over 200 hours of intensive training in voice, movement, acting and technical theater, as well as the opportunity to work on stage with the company.

Carole Whiteleather: *We started to realize the last couple of years that the chasm between the apprentices and the main company actors has gotten larger, primarily because of the high quality actors we're getting now. So to bring them closer together and make the summer a better experience for the apprentices, we created their own show, called the Apprentice Showcase. It's a complete two-act show that has become a really big deal to cap off their summer of hard work. All the company actors clamor to be in it, which just enhances the apprentice experience even more.*

As if that wasn't enough to handle during the already hectic summer season, yet another idea to educate the next generation of festival patrons surfaced from Development Director Ann Dehner.

Carole Whiteleather: *I was decrying the fact that we didn't have anything that tied the Drama School to the Shakespeare Festival. We were a separate function, running classes, and they didn't speak to who we were as a company. They didn't say anything about our mission as the ISF staff. So Ann said, "why don't you do a camp."*

Camp Shakespeare brought school children of all ages together twice that summer to study the words and wonders Shakespeare. Elementary students signed up for one week to study basic acting and work with Shakespeare's language and characters, while junior high and high school kids took a two-week session that focused on producing a one-hour version of a Shakespeare play. That first year over a hundred young artists signed up for the two sessions, making it another bona fide success story for the ITY arm of ISF.

Interpretive Center patio. TM

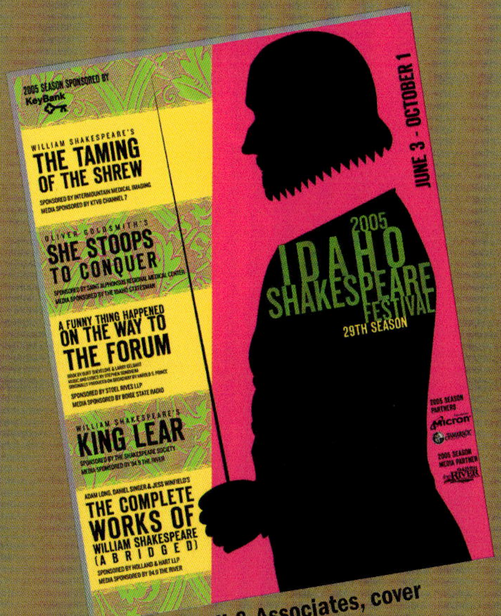

Oliver Russell & Associates, cover design.

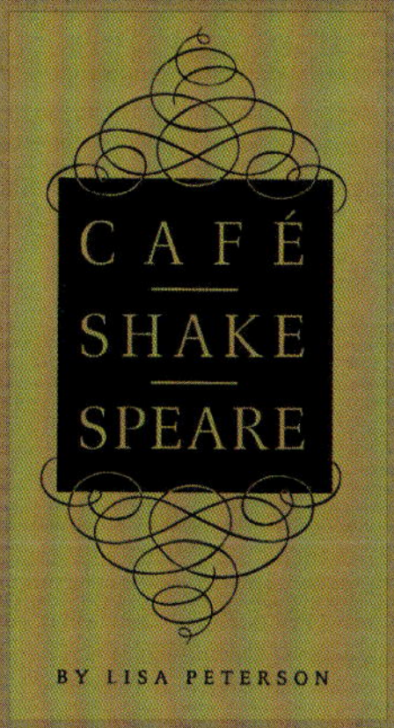

The 2004 season brought a change in catering services, and Charlie and Mark decided it was time to tackle one of the remaining wish list items.

They had always wanted the Interpretive Center to house a full kitchen, but as construction progressed and problems cropped up, the initial vision got reduced. Now they had the chance to go back to the drawing board and build what they really wanted.

Alan Minskoff: *Mark came to us and said, look, we're going to finish this kitchen. We've got this beautiful theater and here's sort of the cherry on top. So we said we'll reprise our leadership, but we'll do it completely the opposite of what we've done in the past. Instead of taking a long time to do it, we'll just invite people who care about the Festival to a one-time party and use that moment to raise the money.*

Lisa Peterson had just come on board as the new caterer, and a sumptuous layout of proposed dishes for the summer menu at that gathering helped accomplish that goal in record time, assuring that the new kitchen would be up and running for the opening of the 29th season. It was one of three capital projects touted in that season's program by second-term board president, Nick Miller, that were underway since completing the amphitheater and park. That fall the

The Play: ***The Taming of the Shrew***
Director: Drew Barr
Scenic Designer: Narelle Sissons
Costume Design: Kim Krumm Sorensen
Lighting Designer: Rick Martin
Sound Designer: Peter John Still

The Play: ***She Stoops to Conquer***
Director: Charles Fee
Scenic Designer: Gage Williams
Costume Design: Star Moxley
Lighting Designer Rick Martin
Sound Designer: Peter John Still

The Play: ***A Funny Thing Happened on the Way to the Forum***
Director: Victoria Bussert
Musical Director: John Jay Espino
Scenic Designer: Jeff Herrmann
Costume Design: Nicole Frachiseur
Lighting Designer: Michael Klaers
Sound Designer: Peter John Still

The Play: ***King Lear***
Director: Risa Brainin
Scenic Designer: Russell Metheny
Costume Design: Kim Krumm Sorenon
Lighting Designer: Michael Klaers
Composer: Brad Carroll
Sound Designer: Peter John Still

The Play: ***The Compleat Works of William Shakespeare (Abridged)***
Director: Charles Fee
Scenic Designer: Gage Williams
Costume Design: Charlotte Yetman
Lighting Designer: Rick Martin
Sound Designer: Peter John Still

2005

Grady cartoon, *The Idaho Statesman*

Cafe Shakepeare. TM

Festival purchased the old Dura-Top building just a stone's throw west of the theater and began renovating it into a scene and costume shop. No longer would set pieces have to be transported across town to the theater, they could be built almost in their back yard.

The third project was less visible than the others, at least at first. In an effort led by board member Bob Hay, the Festival's computers were converted to a state-of-the-art data system that enabled them to offer on-line ticketing and several other new features which greatly enhance the public's access to ISF and all its programs. One big reason the new projects were possible at all was because nearly a decade of Herculean efforts by the staff, board, and campaign committee, resulted in bringing the new festival site to the community debt free.

Meanwhile, one of the more visible areas of the Festival was attracting more and more attention each year. The meadows which formed the boundary between the Festival grounds and the river were prospering beautifully thanks to Carol Cole's gardening skills. A popular place for picnickers and strollers, they added yet another dimension to the beauty of the Festival and emphasized the unique partnership between ISF and the wildlife preserve in which it sat.

Another feather in the Festival's cap came that fall when the Shakespearience tour was selected to take part in a National Endowment for the Arts initiative to sponsor the largest tour ever of Shakespeare in America. In cooperation with Arts Midwest, "Shakespeare in American Communities" brought the Bard's works to small and mid-sized communities in all 50 states, not only in performance, but with workshops and educational programs as well. It was

Carol Cole: *The meadows are kind of experimental. Because we're located so close to the river, we get a lot of noxious weeds. Goldenrod has been our culprit the last couple of years because it just kind of takes over. The eco-system is pretty delicate. It's interesting to watch because the park has its own dynamic. If you get rid of one thing it makes room for something else, and then you get rid of that and it makes room for something else, and so on. I'm hoping one day I'm going to find the balance.*

U

Shakespearience Tour, *Romeo and Juliet*, TM

Hamlet costume designs, Star Moxley, DBB

basically what Shakespearience had been doing since it began in 1986, but the NEA grant gave ISF the ability to expand their reach into even more communities around the state with their spring tour of *Taming of the Shrew*.

2005 also brought international recognition for Star Moxley's costume design work, a staple of both ISF and ITY productions since 1978. She was asked to display her work at the U.S. Institute for Theatre Technology's World Stage Design exhibit, a bi-annual event honoring the technical theater arts. Star's designs for *Macbeth* and the Beatles version of *A Midsummer Night's Dream* toured with those of other honorees from around the world. The tribute stems from a similar honor she received for her 2001 *Hamlet* designs which, along with Gage Williams' set designs for that same show, toured for a year and hung in the main exhibit at the Prague Quadrennial in 2003.

That winter Charlie staged a new production of *The Compleat Works of Shakespeare, Abridged* in Cleveland with the idea of bringing it to Idaho in the September slot. Because of its small cast, this time consisting of Jeffrey Hawkins, Mark Anthony Taylor and Lynn Robert Berg, it became the first complete show to travel between the two companies since Charlie began his work there. Joe Golden and Tom Willmorth, two of the original 1996 cast, which also included Dan Peterson, were on hand for opening night and gave it an enthusiastic "two thumbs up."

Jeffrey Hawkins: *The absolute concrete foundation of the show is those three that started it. We just kind of built on top of that. So much of the spirit is them.*

At the same time, Charlie was selecting shows for the repertory season. He also produced *Taming of the Shrew* in Cleveland that winter, directed by Drew Barr, and though it did not come lock, stock and barrel, as did *Compleat Works*, it did bring Cleveland actress Laura Perotta to reprise her role as Kate. It also carried the distinction of being the first production originally staged by our sister company.

Looking once more at the classics beyond Shakespeare, Charlie chose to direct Oliver Goldsmith's restoration masterpiece, *She Stoops to Conquer*. According to dramaturg Diane Drielsma, the play is a perfect example of "laughing comedy," a new take on an old theatrical form developed in the middle of the 18th century that involves a skillful blending of quick comedic action, witty repartee and fashionable, modern dress.

Sara Bruner: *It seems insane, but last year when I came on stage for She Stoops I felt so free. Before I always felt like, what's my next line? Is it going to be funny? Is it going to be dramatic enough? And all of a sudden I was out there kind of in a really raw way, and it was a huge landmark for my career, like that was the first time after nine years I ever felt completely comfortable on stage.*

In another first for ISF, Charlie broke tradition with the

TM

Governor Dirk Kempthorne: *I always loved the Greenshows, and Tom was great once again this summer with his "I am smart pants" bit, where he says it and trys to get the audience to respond with, "No, I am smarty pants." Well, there wasn't much response, so he turns to me with a look that says help me out, and I yelled, "I am smarty pants!" And then everybody started to shout, "No, I am smarty pants."*

LIFE

Life editor Niki Forbing-Orr
Phone: 377-6444
E-mail: life@idahostatesman.com

The Idaho Statesman • Thursday, September 8, 2005 • IdahoStatesman.com

Neil Brookshire, Edgar; Lynn Robert Berg, Edmund, *Lear.* TM

previous four seasons and decided to incorporate a musical into the repertory, noting in the program that the decision was "partly in response to a request from our core acting company, who felt they were missing out on the fun!" Victoria Bussert followed her hilariously successful *I Love You, You're Perfect, Now Change* with Stephen Sondheim's *A Funny Thing Happened on the Way to the Forum.* The riotous romp had audiences rolling in the aisles all summer long, and it was more than apparent that the acting company was having a ball as well.

Tom Ford: *Vicki is a real task master. She's not a mean woman in any way, shape or form but she is very demanding and works really fast. So the first three days you just saw looks of terror on everyone's faces. And it was just so exciting to watch that transform into confidence and into an ownership of it. Aled Davies is now a musical performer. He'd never done it before and he's great.*

Steve Tague, Lear, *King Lear.* TM

The heavy of the season was *King Lear*, with Steve Tague taking on the title role in what he claimed would be his swan song on the ISF stage. And what a way to go out! As Charlie noted, "no play presents a more challenging face, even for the most experienced among us. The opportunity...only arises when you have the right team, extraordinary leaders, and a deep desire for the journey." Risa Brainin, who shed new light on *Julius Caesar*, once again brought the ensemble cast to the forefront, allowing them to weave the threads of one of the Bard's most daunting fabrics into a clear, concise story that had the audience on the edge of their seats from beginning to end.

Steve Tague: *When Charlie and I first talked, either he or Bart was going to direct it. Then when he told me Risa was going to do it I wasn't too happy. But she and I talked a couple of times over the winter and it went very well. Her process is super different from mine. She's always talking about why, and all I want to talk about is how. If I had to categorize it, she works from the inside out and my thing is outside in. I think the two approaches made a great combination.*

Bringing one of the Bard's most intriguing and introspective roles to life was indeed a fitting way to close out his career as an actor with ISF, but as another famous leading man once said, never say never.

Kristen De Angeli: *One night in King Lear when Steve was raging at the storm a huge Blue Heron flew right over the top of him and right through the sun. It was astonishing. Everyone stopped, you could hear that kind of collective gasp as it flew over him. That's one of the special things about Shakespeare and the outdoors, the environment gets incorporated into what we do. We have these beautiful evenings and we get to use them as settings.*

Richard Klautsch: *One night during the reconciliation scene, just when Lear recognizes Cordelia, we got this huge, kind of astonished, right-on-the-verge-of-laughing response from the audience. We couldn't believe it, but we just went on with the scene. We found out later that a skunk crossed the stage, and when he got just to center stage he stopped and looked out at the audience for a moment, then kept going off stage. We didn't know he was upstaging us!*

Tom Ford: *I was talking with a couple from Cleveland who were on the board at the Great Lakes Theater Festival. They had come out to see Shrew and Lear. They took a cab from the airport and the driver asked them why there were here. When they told him he said, "I've got to get out and see Lear." And they were just sort of dumbfounded that a cab driver was talking about going to see King Lear.*

Just when you think you can finally relax a little, that having a permanent

L-R, Richard Klautsch, Hardcastle; Sara Bruner, Kate Hardcastle, *She Stoops to Conquer.* TM

home, a world class, state-of-the-art theater complex and a board of trustees second-to-none, has given you a little breathing room, Mother Nature reminds you one more time that she's the real wild card in outdoor theater. For nearly thirty years she has thrown rain, wind, lightning and thunder, even hail at ISF productions, and through it all, loyal Treasure Valley audiences have stayed the course.

Tom Ford: *The one thing about this festival that sort of draws me to come back is that I've never worked at a theater where the community...it's their theater. When they don't like something or they're offended by something it's like, you shouldn't be doing that because this is my theater. And in a way that's fantastic that they feel so strongly. And vice versa, there are evenings where you perform and the response is unlike any response I've ever received. It's such a celebration at that theater, a theater which this community keeps running for four months every year. It's really astounding.*

L-R, Lynn Robert Berg, Hastings; Christina Lang, Mrs. Hardcastle, *She Stoops.* TM

On a hot afternoon in late July, a small grass fire broke out in the foothills just above Harris Ranch. In the parched cheat grass and sagebrush it quickly spread, and by the time volunteers and actors began showing up at the theater in the early evening a giant pall of smoke had darkened the sky not half-a-mile from the Festival site. Helicopters and tankers buzzed over the flames at regular intervals dropping water and retardant on the lower edge of the fire, trying desperately to keep it from reaching the homes just a few hundred yards below. At the same time, massive walls of flame could be seen climbing up the steep hillsides toward the treeline.

Undaunted, Festival patrons began to

L-R, Aled Davies, Senex; Tom Willmorth, Clown; David Anthony Smith, Gymnasium; Laura Perotta, Vibrata; Laura Miller, Geminae Twin, *Forum.* TM

Top: *A Funny Thing Happened on the Way to the Forum.* TM

Bottom: Dan Peterson, Erronius, *Forum.* TM

L-R, Sara Bruner, Bianca; Richard Klautsch, Baptista Minola; Tom Ford, Gremio; Lynn Robert Berg, Hortensio; Tom Willmorth, Lucentio, *Shrew*. TM

L-R, Laura Perotta, Kate; Lynn Robert Berg, Hortensio; Tom Ford, Gremio, *Shrew*. TM

L-R, M.A. Taylor, Grumio; David Anthony Smith, Petruchio, *Shrew*. TM

arrive for the next-to-last performance of *She Stoops To Conquer*. They trooped into the theater with their blankets and chairs as though nothing were out of the ordinary. After all, the fire was over on the foothills, and the smoke was, thankfully, drifting away from the theater. Shows had gone on in far worse conditions before. The question was what to do about the two helicopters dropping down from the hills every few minutes to dip their buckets in the Barber Pool, just behind the theater.

The Greenshow went off with barely a hitch, the actors either ignoring the *whump, whump, whump* of the giant rotary blades or offering exaggerated pauses, eyes turned skyward to follow the choppers as though they were willing them out of hearing before resuming their lines.

Managing Director Mark Hofflund's curtain speech recognized that the job of the firefighters was quite a bit more important than that of the actors on that particular evening, so if the audience was willing to put up with it, the actors would make the best of it, pausing intentionally to let the choppers make their rounds. Boise audiences had come for a show and were not about to be disappointed just because of a little noise and an occasional spray of water from the buckets passing almost directly overhead. Besides, watching the actors cope with such a major distraction just might add to the fun.

It would be interesting to know how many in that audience had sat through other natural disturbances at the Festival on previous occasions and felt somehow a part of something bigger than the performance they were there to enjoy. Suffice it to say that the actors did not disappoint, and some of the devices they employed to cover the entrances and exits of the helicopters added an extra measure of enjoyment for one and all. By intermission it had grown dark enough that the choppers were grounded. The second half of the show went on without distraction, unless you count the pungent odor of smoke and burnt grass that hung in the air. If the actors were relieved to have a quiet hour to complete their play, it didn't show. They went on as though nothing had changed.

Richard Klautsch: *That was one of those nights that accumulate over the years. I remember the days at ParkCenter when the wind would shift and those porta-potties hadn't been picked up for a few days. Suddenly you couldn't think about character, or what the hell you were saying on stage because of the odor. The helicopter night was one of those. That's a fun thing about outdoor theater. It teaches you to deal with stuff like that.*

When all was said and done, the audience went home knowing they had gotten a little more than their money's worth that night.

Just a few days later, August 2, the Festival received yet another national honor when Mark Hofflund was appointed to the National Council on the Arts by President George W. Bush. It was the first public step in a process that began in March, when NEA Chairman Dana Gioia casually asked him for a resume. Since that time he had gone through FBI background checks and a number of other vetting processes to assure the folks in Washington, D.C. that he was worthy.

Any audience on any given night at ISF could have saved them the trouble.

No doubt the best recommendation would have come on closing night of the Festival's 2005 season. The weather had been kind that summer. There were only two rainouts the entire season, but the second one was memorable because it was the final night of *Compleat Works*, and the last show of the season. The audience valiantly hung in there, using garbage bags, programs, cooler lids, whatever they could find to shield themselves from the downpour, refusing to leave because there were no more performances for which they could use a rain check. The actors, too, were giving it their all, and if ever there was a play where license could be taken due to unusual weather circumstances, *Compleat Works* is it.

But the rain would not stop, and when Mark stepped out to call the show, he was greeted with a chorus of boo's and calls for the show to go on. They were happy to sit through the storm. Mark explained that the rain was making the stage slippery, and therefore dangerous for the actors. Still the audience wanted them to continue. Mark relented, saying they would go until intermission, but that if the rain had not stopped by the time intermission was over, allowing them to dry the stage, they would have to call the show.

Intermission came and went, and still the rain fell. The stage remained wet. The audience still called for the play to continue – if they could take it, so should the cast. Making the ultimate sacrifice, a group of teenagers leaped on stage and began to roll around, mopping up the rainwater with their clothes. Finally Mark realized that the audience didn't understand that the rain was affecting more than just the three actors, there was an entire crew backstage as well. By way of explanation, he called each and every one of them on stage to take a bow. Greeted with this magnanimous opening of the mythical fourth wall, the groans changed magically to cheers and wild applause as the audience celebrated a valiant effort by the cast and crew that had served them faithfully all summer long. Though incomplete, it was a fitting end to the 29th season.

L-R, Jeffrey Hawkins; Lynn Robert Berg; M.A. Taylor, *Compleat Works*. TM

L-R, Lynn Robert Berg; M.A. Taylor, *Compleat Works*. TM

Attendance at Camp Shakespeare grew from 100 students in 2004 to almost 200 in 2005. Their success struck a chord with parents and students outside the Boise area as well, and Drama School teachers traveled to Shoshone to hold another of the two week sessions there.

The camp concept lent itself well to travel, and the idea of offering more satellite sessions in other communities has led to Caldwell, where *El Campo de Shake* will be held for Spanish-speaking students.

In the meantime, another new program called Camp Improv was formed to give students in grades 7-12 an opportunity to sharpen their acting and improv skills. And like Camp Shakespeare, each two week class culminated in a student show, with space donated by the Funny Bone Comedy Club in Boise. True to form, demand for that camp from elementary students and their parents has prompted Carole to expand the 2006 Camp Improv to include sessions for all ages, just as she did with Camp Shakespeare the year before.

The Play: ***A Funny Thing Happened to Me On The Way to the Forum***
Director: **Victoria Bussert**
Musical Director: **John Jay Espino**
Scenic Designer: **Jeff Herrmann**
Costume Design: **Nicole Frachiseur**
Lighting Design: **Michael Klaers**
Sound Designer: **Peter John Still**

The Play: ***Love's Labours Lost***
Director: **Drew Barr**
Scenic Designer: **Russell Metheney**
Costume Design: **Kim Krumm Sorenson**
Lighting Design **Rick Martin**

The Play: ***Major Barbara***
Director: **Steve Tague**
Scenic Designer: **Gage Williams**
Costume Design: **Charlotte Yetman**
Lighting Design: **Rick Martin**
Sound Designer: **Peter John Still**

The Play: ***Romeo and Juliet***
Director: **Charles Fee**
Scenic Designer: **Gage Williams**
Costume Design: **Star Moxley**
Lighting Design: **Rick Martin**
Sound Designer: **Peter John Still**

The Play: ***The Spitfire Grill***
Director: **Drew Barr**
Scenic Designer: **Jeff Herrmann**
Costume Design: **Kim Krumm Sorenson**
Lighting Design: **Rick Martin**
Sound Designer: **Peter John Still**

2006

Those that do teach young babes do it with gentle and easy tasks. Othello, IV, ii

Camp Shakespeare. UK

Buoyed by the huge response to the summer camps, Carole decided to return to ITY's roots and take some of these same concepts right to the students in the form of after school workshops. Shake It Up! finished it's first four week pilot program at Boise's Washington School in November, 2005, giving 20 elementary students an idea of how much fun it is to be involved in theater, and teaching them a little about Shakespeare at the same time.

Carole Whiteleather: *What we found was that at the end of the four weeks the kids were really beginning to get into the program and wanted more. And it's a great teaser program to give kids in the schools a taste of what it can be like at the summer camps.*

As if she weren't busy enough, the second round of the NEA Shakespeare tour selected ISF to lead the way in Idaho again that fall. That spring Shakespeare for a New Generation sponsored the Shakespearience production of The Tempest as it toured the state with what many believe to be the Bard's final play.

In the blink of an eye, summer was upon them again. The tech staff scrambled to complete the integration of the costume shop into the scene shop building, and the artistic staff contemplated the 30th anniversary season of Shakespeare Under the Stars. Indeed, there was much to contemplate. ISF has come a long way from that magical *Midsummer Night's Dream* at One Capital Center in 1977. Like some medieval troupe of wandering thespians we journeyed from downtown to the Plantation, only to move again, three years later, to Parkcenter where it finally found a long-term home for the next fourteen years.

During its first fifteen years, festival leadership changed hands a number of times as did the makeup of our board of directors, each time seeking to find the right mix to take the festival to greater heights. When Charlie Fee was hired in 1992, followed by Mark Hofflund in '93, the company finally achieved the stable, long-term management and leadership it had been seeking, and the second half of its 30 year existence has brought the community a new, state-of-the-art theater complex, a growing resident company of artists and technicians, and an alliance with Great lakes Theater Company that has further solidified the overall company financially and artistically as we begin to look toward the next 30 years and beyond.

Tom Willmorth: *I am so glad that from where we started to where we are now we have allowed ourselves to remain a picnic basket theater. It would have been so easy to install seats and turn this thing into every other outdoor theater. But people want to sit on the grass. People want to open a bottle of wine. I think it's important that we keep that informal relationship between the company and its community.*

The landmark 2005 season, with attendance topping 50,000 for the first time in the festival's history, coupled with the explosive growth of the Treasure Valley, produced visions of what the future could hold, and what needed to be done to prepare for that future.

Kristen De Angeli: *We always look for audience growth, and for ways to do what we do better. Technology is changing the way we communicate with our audience. On-line ticketing is a huge new part of performing arts, but it's expensive and the learning curve is very steep. At the same time it enables us to do things like e-mail responses for ticket requests, or send out a blast of e-mails saying we have tickets available for tonight, or here's a special for subscribers. That's a huge change in mindset for marketing. At the same time you still have to get out and talk to the service clubs, get into schools and meet new teachers and parents, and have information for neighborhood groups. So you've got to do the high-tech on the one hand, but you've still got to do the grass-roots stuff as well.*

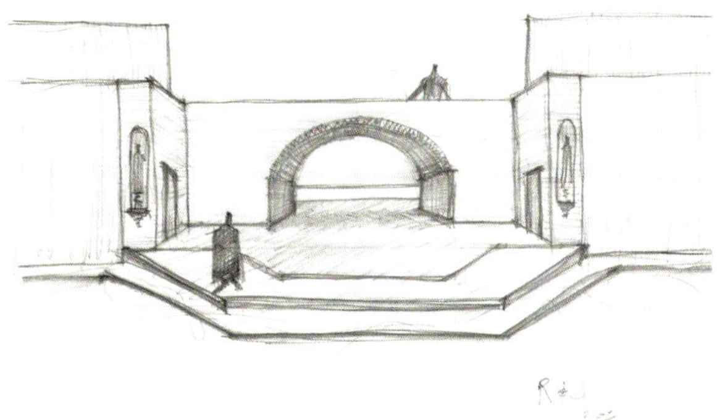

Preliminary set design, Romeo and Juliet, Gage Williams.

The 2006 season reflects our roots as a Shakespearean theater, our continuing effort to expand the reach of the classics beyond Shakespeare, and a nod toward the future with musical offerings that speak to the potential of a great outdoor theater company.

Aled Davies: *It was astonishing that the community of Boise would get together and fund and have the vision for something like that. To give themselves that. And to have watched now, eight years later, to see all those trees growing older, those bushes growing in...I don't know how many people know how beautiful that garden walk is. It's astounding, an utterly astonishing space.*

But audiences weren't the only ones benefiting from thirty years of Shakespeare in Idaho. For the first time since joining forces with the Great Lakes theatre Festival in Cleveland, an entire season of plays was shared by both companies. The savings in production costs brought about by the fulfillment of this revolutionary new alliance allowed Charlie to offer the acting company year-round, 52-week contracts, another first for ISF, and to include a package of health benefits, something few, if any , other theaters in the country provide for their actors.

Dana Oland: *To me, the growth of the company and the strength of the company is a reflection of the quality of the community. You can see it in the quality of the talent that comes here and wants to stay, as well as the audience that keeps coming back beyond what you would think could happen in a community this size. It's part of the magic that makes Boise what it is.*

The season kicked off with the return of *A Funny Thing Happened on the Way to the Forum*, the raucous musical hit from last season's repertory.

L-R, Sara Bruner, Geminae Twin; Steve Tague, Miles Gloriosis; Laura Miller, Geminae Twin, *Forum*. TM

L-R, Aled Davies, Senex; Tom Ford, Pseudolus; Jeffrey Hawkins, Hysterium, *Forum*. TM

L-R, Aled Davies, Senex; Kate Rockwell, Philia, *Forum*. TM

Drew Barr added his special touch to the often wordy and sometimes tedious Love's Labour's Lost to give audiences a delightfully charming exploration of Elizabethan love full of wit and good natured trickery.

Romeo and Juliet, first produced at One Capital Center in 1979, returned in it's fifth incarnation on the ISF stage. Charlie directed this classic tale of love and tragedy, working with costume Designer Star Moxley, who ironically helped build the costumes for that first production of *R&J*, to create the distinctly Japanese world of the Geisha. Charlie also directed *Major Barbara*, the second of George Bernard Shaw's classic comedies to hit the ISF stage. Set design for all the shows was once again in the capable and creative hands of Gage Williams.

In September the stage is transformed into an anonymous small town where a young woman tries to relinquish her broken past and start life anew in *The Spitfire Grill*.

And so the curtain falls on 30 years of Shakespeare in Idaho. But this is not the end. Far from it! The first three decades of the Idaho Shakespeare Festival are but prologue to the next 30 and beyond. I have often heard the comment from friends and colleagues from the early years of the festival that ISF just like a family any more, that it's lost a lot of that feeling because it's grown so big. But talk to any of the artists working with the festival today and there is still that overwhelming notion of the company as family. So perhaps it's not that the family has dissolved and moved on, it's just that the next generation has taken its rightful place in the spotlight.

Aled Davies: *Occasionally the local kids have gone away to train. I count Jeffrey Hawkins and M.A. Taylor as local because they've been here for so long what with the tours and everything else. Sara Bruner and Lynn Berg certainly are local. And I've really been moved to watch them now in their late twenties as trained, maturing artists, to see them take on the mantle of new adults. I know we're all limited actors here, but it's really kind of moving to see...okay, they're really stepping up into their own.*

Sara Bruner: *My first year here I was eighteen, and I was always feeling like I was the young one and they're the old ones. Then this past year it's like I'm sort of one of the middle-aged ones. It's fun to be the young one though, when you first get to know the festival and you start to realize what you're part of. It's so exciting to watch people like Stitch and Danny and Joe and Tom, and then all of a sudden to be working along side them. It's like being in a new relationship. It's like falling in love. And now it's like we've been married for a really long time, and it's still really wonderful, but I do miss the newness of it.*

The work of the Bard has survived more than half a millennium, bringing laughter and tears and all the emotions that great drama can provoke to countless audiences throughout the world. His words and characters are recognized in every society in every city and town that has experienced his timeless plays, and in the familiar faces that people our everyday lives. We have but to look, and they are there, even in the mirror.

TM

All's well that ends well; Still the fine's the crown. What'er the course, the end is the reknown. All's Well That Ends Well, IV, iv.

What the Future Holds

When Andy Erstad left the Board of Trustees at the end of the 2001 season, construction of the theater complex was essentially complete. The Building Committee that he had chaired was created to oversee the project on behalf of the board, but the theater would continue to evolve, and require careful tending over the years.

So before departing, he lobbied to give the Building Committee a permanent seat on the Executive Committee to ensure that the organization's single largest asset would serve them well into the future.

That one, small administrative action served notice that it was time to shift the focus of both board and staff from the single-minded purpose of creating a new theater to defining plans for the future of the company. It wasn't that no one had been thinking about the future, but after six long years of putting every ounce of energy into getting the Shakespeare park up and running, there was finally time to step back, take a breath, and begin to look at new directions.

Charlie Fee: *The work that I'm doing now in Cleveland is part of my desire to look at how we create the business model of the future for the tiny handful of large scale producers of classical work in this country, which is what we are. Because the cost of maintaining companies and casts of this size have continued to rise exponentially, you have to find ways to spread that cost. One of the ways to do that is create new markets.*

Great Lakes Theatre Festival photos courtesy of Playhouse Square Foundation.

At its core, ISF is a business, just like any other. And numbers are what drive any business. Not-for-profit wrinkles aside, it basically boils down to coming up with the money to produce a product and hoping you can sell enough of it to make a profit. Except for a few years in the 1980's when the Festival was forced to move the theater twice in a period of three years, ISF has always managed to do that, thanks in large part to the incredible support of a community that has learned to love its Shakespeare. For some, like Charlie Davis, who served on the Festival board from 1985-90 and again from 1993-99, only to come back on again in 2006, it has become much more than just a wonderful way to spend summer evenings.

Charlie Davis: *I love the Festival, I really do. And it's interesting to come back now that there's a new model and a new complexity, and try to help solve some of the new problems. I mean, how do you grow? That place holds X number of people and each season is has a very defined number of dates. Once you fill them all in you can't go above that. Charlie can play with extending the season, but you get into risky areas with weather. What do you do with a physical entity that is no longer being built but still needs to be maintained when raising money to build is a lot easier than raising money to maintain? It's a new set of challenges.*

One of the driving forces behind the Cleveland alliance was the downturn in federal spending on the arts in the early 1990's, and while that hasn't really changed on a national scale, something has been turning ISF into a very interesting national story.

Mark Hofflund: *The chairman of the NEA comes out and says, "Wow, this is fabulous!" Someone else comes and says, "Whoa, look at this!" And that word gets out. Our senior Snator, Larry Craig, has been out to see shows for two years in a row. People are coming now from 30 states every season. There's an article in an airline magazine, another one in Sunset Magazine, then one in the New York Times, and suddenly it becomes this ongoing, life-affirming process that says, "The more we do this the better we get at it, and because we're getting better, people who are important and can help us get even better are going to get involved."*

Ultimately, what Charlie and Mark want for Boise is a major, year-round theater center that produces everything from Shakespeare and other classics to musicals and contemporary theater that would share the work it produces with other companies. In the model he has created with Cleveland, a show doesn't play a dozen times and get thrown away, it plays twenty or thirty times between the two cities, and the incremental cost of remounting is much lower than the cost of a new production.

Charlie Fee: *The truth is, you're either growing, or you're shrinking, there's no in between. So what I'm aiming at here is in the next five years I think we need to be opening a second theater on the site – an indoor theater that would probably seat about 500 people. We've already mapped it out. We know where it sits and we know the size of the support facility that it will require. The models are obvious – Ashland, Cedar City, and on and on.*

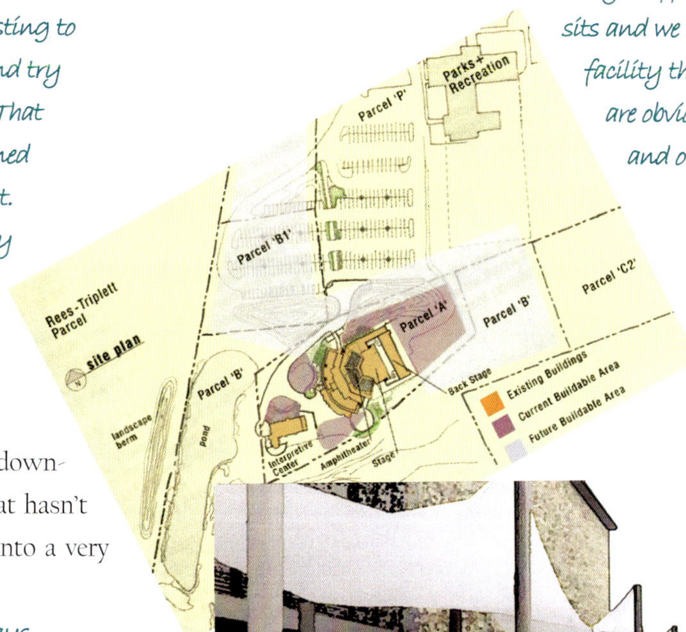

Site map and indoor theater rendering, Erstad-Thornton, Architects.

The mapping was done in the form of a twenty year site plan for the Festival, prepared by Andy Erstad and his team. The concept is based on bringing all the core facilities in to one location, which would require eventually bringing the costume and scene shop there, as well as rehearsal facilities and offices.

The outdoor amphitheater seats 700 and it's now become difficult to find a ticket for any weekend performance. Anticipating continued growth in attendance figures, it won't be that many more years before that same scenario becomes a regular occurrence on week nights as well. A second theater will give patrons another choice, and allow more people to come to the Festival more often. It also presents new options from an artistic point of view.

Charlie Fee: *You can start to craft which plays are right for which spaces. Arms and the Man, Importance of Being Earnest, and She Stoops to Conquer were really fun to do outside, but they are plays that were written for indoor theaters. Likewise, Shakespeare done inside would give audiences a whole different perspective on the work. Then you could start to mix and match as well.*

As the Festival moves into its fourth decade, it's also important to consider the larger picture – the growth of the city and the development of the valley around it. Charlie's vision sees ISF as a destination festival, complete with shopping, businesses, even a hotel. The Harris Ranch development will answer the first two parts of that equation with its proposed one million square foot office and retail park, just downriver. The hotel, however, has yet to make it to the drawing board.

Any plan for the growth of the Festival naturally takes into account its environmental setting. The fact that ISF is an integral part of a wildlife preserve is never far from anyone's mind, and maintaining the grounds in and around the theater is a key part of preserving that delicate balance.

Don Belts: *The sewage treatment ponds out along our western edge will eventually go away when those folks get hooked up to the sewer system. They might be a nice water amenity of some sort, or there could also be a housing development in there. Dave Triplett, the landowner, let us build a burm around the western side of the pond and put some plantings on it, and we cut a path through it with the thought that eventually we would have a continuous system with little overlooks and possibly a picnic site. It will be an important buffer to whatever happens over there.*

Charlie Fee: *We also need to continue to work with the environmental community to make this a location that really is a cultural center for theater and the environment, because those are the twin pieces of our site. So that you're coming as an audience member to environmental programming during the morning and afternoon, and to the theater at night.*

Events like Bald Eagle Days, held at the Interpretive Center each January when the eagles are roosting in Barber Pool, are addressing the environmental education part of the vision. The Idaho Bird Observatory, headed by Greg Kaltenecker, formed a partnership with the Idaho Foundation for Parks & Lands to help them implement their master plan for the preserve. That plan includes a series of nature trails, observation posts and, someday, a nature

Bald Eagle Days, 2005. Idaho Dept. of Fish & Game

Monte Tish and Slim. Idaho Dept. of Fish & Game

Liberty awes kids in the Interpretive Center. Idaho Dept. of Fish & Game.

center that will provide year-round education programs about the Pool and the 200 species that inhabit it, for kids and adults alike.

> **Mark Hofflund:** *This collaboration of having a private non-profit own and manage parkland is fantastic, because you get the best of both worlds. You get all this private support, all this private control when needed, and yet it's supervised by a public agency staffed with professionals in land management.*

This makes ISF's educational mission, as well as that of the Foundation for Parks and Lands, even more vital to the overall success of the company as it continues to grow toward that vision of becoming a destination festival. It also supports the idea of an on-site, indoor theater that could offer year-round student programming and student matinee performances. Add environmental education and tourism to that mix and you've got the perfect blend.

> **Mark Hofflund:** *So this facility continues the story that was established at the very beginning of the Festival, downtown at One Capital Center, the first great commercial development that got the downtown revitalization of the '70's started. The Oppenheimers helped get the Festival started and the Festival brought notoriety to the downtown business sector. It's all about good business practices.*

Ultimately ISF will have 2 theaters and a 6 million dollar annual budget, comparable to other large, regional theater companies. Charlie expects ISF's connection with the Actors' Equity Association to increase in the next three years. But that vision requires continued growth and actively pursuing consolidation of the proposed twenty-year site plan.

> **Charlie Fee:** *You've got to watch for opportunity. So when the shop building came on the market just down the road, instead of building that same shop space out at the site, we bought it for about half the price. We also need rehearsal space, drama school space, and administrative office space. Where we are right now is okay. We love the relationship with Matt Clark and Fulton Street Theater, but it's just not big enough. He's going to grow, and we already don't have enough space there. I ultimately want rehearsal space out at the theater because it's close to our costume shop. Maybe we'll move our offices out there, too. It's fun to come out there for meetings. It takes 15 minutes and you're out in a beautiful place.*

During my ten year tenure with the Festival, I used to have a little mantra I recited to myself as each summer season approached. There would always come a point in the spring when there was no turning back – the great machine had been put in gear, and each time I would remind myself that all we could do was hold on for the ride and try to keep it from running off the road.

As the Festival continued to grow, that machine seemed to slip into gear a little earlier every year until it was finally in permanent motion, lurching forward toward a future that always seemed to lie beyond some distant horizon. Some riders jumped off along the way, and others climbed on to take their turn at the wheel. Many of us who left for a time found we couldn't stay away. We were drawn back like bees to honey, longing for another taste of the wild ride.

I suppose no one really knows what the Idaho Shakespeare Festival will look like in twenty years, but given the pride and ownership that Boise and the rest of the Treasure Valley have taken in it, and the confidence and excellence built up in the organization by Charlie and Mark over the past fifteen years, no goal seems too high to reach. Over the course of three decades ISF has become so ingrained in the fabric of these communities that it's hard to imagine what it was like before that small, determined group of actors, looking for a way to make a living at their craft, dared to dream for eight midsummer nights in 1977. And maybe we don't want to anyway.

Photograph by Troy Maben

Acknowledgements

BENEATH IT ALL, THIS BOOK IS ABOUT FAMILY. Those of us who worked so hard together to create this festival during the early years became a family, and for the most part we remain so today. Along the way, many others have joined, and though some stayed around longer than others, each and every one of them had a role to play in the evolution of ISF and in the creation of this book, and they all deserve to be recognized for it. My deepest thanks to all the Shakespeare family members, past and present, who shared their stories and memories with me, and an extra nod to Sue Galligan, who helped me track down many of you. To those whose names did not make it to print, my apologies, but even a history book is limited by time, space and budget. To a person, you all remain a part of that family.

My own family became a part of ISF whether they wanted to or not. From my Mom and Dad, who instilled in me a strong belief in family and taught me that believing in yourself is the first step to achieving your dreams, to my brother and sister and their families, who more than once have been called upon to help keep their big brother's midsummer's night's madness alive with contributions—monetary and otherwise. They never hesitated, and they have my heartfelt thanks for that.

My beautiful wife Cheri has been incredibly supportive and patient with my journey down memory lane. She is the love of my life and I can't imagine having done this without her by my side. My daughters, Rachel and Cheri Catharine were both pressed into service for this project as photo-digitizers and interview transcribers. I hope they have gotten some small measure of enjoyment out of all the hard work. I have loved sharing my dreams with them.

This book would not have been possible without the leap of faith taken by Scott Gipson and the people at Caxton Printers. I shall be eternally grateful to them for allowing me to wallow in nostalgia for eighteen months at their expense.

When Chris Latter signed on to design this book, fresh from her excellent work on the Gene Harris biography, *Elegant Soul,* I don't think she had any idea what she was getting herself into. I hope she does now, and I hope she is as proud of her work as I am. Her spirit and enthusiasm show up on almost every page and bring a balance and integrity to this glorified family album.

To David Bogie, whose photography brings so many of those memories to life in ways no words could ever do, I owe a huge debt of gratitude for diving in head first, no questions asked, when this project became a reality. His tireless enthusiasm and sometimes off-the-wall ideas played a big part in making this book what it is.

Thanks, too, to Alan Minskoff and Vangie Osborn, who were kind enough to provide invaluable assistance in making sure people, places and events are depicted in a relatively correct fashion. Isn't it funny how we don't always remember things exactly the way they happened.

Finally, a nod to the Boise City Arts Commission, who saw fit to award a grant to the project that allowed me to spend some one-on-one time with a few key members of the ISF family and get their stories on tape for posterity. And to Alan Virta, Mary Carter-Hepworth, and the staff at the Boise State University Archives, where the bulk of the research that gave birth to this book now rests, waiting in boxes for curious eyes who want to know more about the unique, wonderful, and still growing family that is the Idaho Shakespeare Festival.

David Bogie

I remember taking every one of these photographs.

They are chromes. Composition, focus and exposure are preserved exactly as they came from my camera. Lusciously incomplete and vividly static on paper, they are frames from multi-projector films I created for the Idaho Shakespeare Company. Stretched shimmering upon the screen, these images elicited and shaped the memory of our ephemeral summers.

My thanks to all of you who unknowingly or patiently stood before of my lens, waiting for me to focus, allowing me to move you to better backlight or to find the catchlights in your eyes.

I hope you, too, will remember when I took every one of these photographs.

Chris Latter

Chris Latter has designed and illustrated several books, among them: *Elegant Soul, the Life and Music of Gene Harris*; *Harrison Boulevard: Preserving the Past in Boise's North End*; *Snake: The Plain and its People*; and *The Garage Band Method: How the Rest of Us Can Learn to Play*. She has also written and illustrated a children's book titled *The Elephant in My Stocking*. A native of the Bay Area, Latter attended Northwest Nazarene University in Nampa, Idaho. She and her husband have lived in Idaho for more than 20 years and have three grown children.

Appendix

1977

A Midsummer Night's Dream

Co-Directors ...... Doug Copsey & Victoria Holloway
Set Design ...... Jim Bottoms
Costume Design ...... Victoria Holloway
Lighting ...... Dan Andrews
Sound ...... Jim Reynolds

Acting Company / Role(s)

Doug Copsey	Theseus, Oberon
Dan Peterson	Egeus, Snout
Mike Hoffman	Lysander
Pat Delana	Demetrius
Seelye Smith	Hipployta, Titania
Linda M. Pommerening	Hermia
Barbara McKean	Helena
Sue Galligan	Peter Quince
Joel Farmer	Bottom
G.L. Scott	Snug
G. Robert Fields	Flute
Tom Wolfe	Starveling
Martha Peavey	Wench
Jim Bottoms	Puck

Production

Seamstress ...... Nancy Buell
Set Landscaping ...... Sterling Landscape Co.
Fence Design & Execution ...... Tom Oakes & Marjory Oakes

Administration

Producing Director ...... Doug Copsey
Artistic Director ...... Victoria Holloway
Box Office ...... Kelly Buckland

1978

The Two Gentlemen of Verona

Director ...... Doug Copsey
Set Design ...... Jon Ostrove
Costume Design ...... Victoria Holloway
Lighting ...... Dan Andrews
Sound ...... Jim Reynolds

Acting Company / Role(s)

Steve Marker	Valentine
Bruce Richardson	Proteus
John Elliott	Duke
Bruce Abas	Dogberry
David Painter	Walter
Erv Johnson	Antonio
Sue Galligan	Panthina
Victoria Holloway	Julia
Seelye Smith	Silvia
Barbara McKean	Lucetta
Janet Simmerman	Ursula
Ed Simmerman	Thurio
Patrick Delana	Eglamour
Michael Hoffman	Speed
Dan Peterson	Launce
Debra Groves	Valeria
Ginger Scott	Mae
Jim Campbell	Outlaw
Jon Ostrove	Outlaw
Patricia Cunningham	Outlaw
Peter Quince	Host
Cathy Charchalis	Dancer

Production

Costume Cutter ...... Victoria Holloway
Head Seamstress ...... Nancy Stover
Assistant ...... G. Robert Fields
Special Construction ...... Ginger Scott
Crew: Michelle Black; Laurie Anderton; Lance Brown; Patricia Bidwell; Star Moxley; Natalie Shanefelt; Edith Simmerman...and the Company

Set Construction: David Bogie; Jim Campbell...and the Company
Scene Painter ...... Jon Ostrove
Set Landscaping ...... Sterling Landscape Co.
Stage Manager ...... Nancy Stover
Properties: Diane Foster; Louann Blome; Laurie Anderton; Christina Gellert
Fencing Coach ...... John Charchalis

Administration

Producing Director ...... Doug Copsey
Artistic Director ...... Victoria Holloway
Box Office: David Painter; Jeannie Rice
Fence Design and Painting ...... Marjory Oakes
Program Sales ...... Victoria Holloway
...... Patrick Delana

1979

Romeo and Juliet

Director ...... Victoria Holloway
Set Design ...... Seelye Smith
Costume Design ...... Victoria Holloway
Lighting ...... Dan Andrews
Sound ...... Jim Reynolds

The Merry Wives of Windsor

Director ...... Pam Abas
Set Design ...... David Bogie
Costume Design ...... Bitsy Bidwell
Lighting ...... Dan Andrews
Sound ...... Jim Reynolds

Acting Company / Role(s)

Romeo and Juliet; Merry Wives

Sue Galligan	Chorus; Mistress Quickly
Doug Copsey	Escalus, Prince of Verona; Sir John Falstaff
Steve Marker	Paris; Simple
James E. Simmerman	Montague; Sir Hugh Evans
Patrick E. Nance	Capulet; Goatherd
Deb Groves	Lady Capulet; Laundress
Rebekah Oakes	Juliet
Spike Ericson	Tibalt; Fenton
Seelye Smith	Nurse
Ellen Mareneck	Percy; Mistress Ford
Jon B. Ostrove	Sampson; Shallow
Tom Pfenninger	Gregory
David Painter	Peter; John Rugby
Jenny V.A. Sternling	Lady Montegue
Stefan Wisniewski	Romeo; Pistol
Dan Peterson	Benvolio; Master Ford
Patrick Delana	Balthasar; Sackerson, a bear
Tracey Hollenbeck	Mercutio; Nym
Janet Simmerman	Jessie, a bawd; Dancer
Patrick Cunningham	Friar Lawrence; Dr. Caius
Dr. Allen Fletcher	Friar John; Bardolph
Jim Reynolds	A Monk; The Wizard
Louann Blome	Citizen of Verona
Bobbette Cunningham	Citizen; Dancer
Trish Elledge	Citizen; Dancer
Diane Foster	Citizen; Dancer
Erv Johnson	Citizen; John, a servant
Donna Sands	Citizen
G.L. Scott	Citizen; Host of the Garter
Natalie Shanefelt	Citizen; Dancer
Leslie Berger	Robin
Tom Willmorth	Slender
Nancy Suiter	–; Mistress Page
Joel Farmer	; Master Page
Kassie Reckamp	–; Anne Page
Alyssa Hurad	–; Elizabeth Page
Matthew Hurad	–; William Page
Stephanie Oqawa	–; Baby Page
Jason Patterson	–; Valentine
Sunshine	–; Sunshine, a dog
Miriam Hewes	–; Dancer

Production

Assistant Director for *Merry Wives* ...... Natalie Shanefelt
Set Construction: Jim Campbell; Jerry James; Lane Thomas; David Bogie: ... and the company
Scenic Painters: Jon Ostrove; Kathy Murphy
Set Landscaping ...... Sterling Landscape Co.
Costume Construction: Diane Foster; Martha Peavey; Katherine Taylor; Eleanor Foster; Ginger Scott; Bitsy Bidwell; Gueneth Omeron; Janet Simmerman; Edith Simmerman; Patrick Delana; Michelle Black; Bobbette Cunningham; Marian Scott; Trish Coonts; Catherine Rundquist; Martha Peavey; Chris Taderosa; Jodie Berger; Cindy Ferro; Vickie Baron; Kristina Berger; Chet Carpenter; ...and cast

Juliet's Costumes constructed by ...... Marjorie Oakes
Costume Painting for *Merry Wives* ...... Barbara Bancroft
Hair & Makeup ...... Shirley Hurley
Properties: Ginger Scott; Louann Blome
Stage Crew: Louann Blome; Donna Sands
Fencing Coach ...... Dr. Max Callao
Choreography: Natalie Shanefelt; Miriam Hewes
Red Tailed Hawk in R&J courtesy ...... Morley Nelson
Animals provided for *Merry Wives* by ...... Bill & Cindy Nance; Chet Carpenter; Gueneth Omeron

Administration

Producing Director ...... Doug Copsey
Artistic Director ...... Victoria Holloway
Ticket Committee: Patrick Cunningham, Chair; Victoria Holloway; Joyce Delana; Diane Foster; Louann Blome
Program Design ...... Dennis Chase
Program Sales ...... Patrick Nance
Patrick Cunningham; Patrick Delana; Tracey Hollenbeck; Rebekah Oakes; Ginger Scott
Fence Design and Painting: Scott Merrill; Dan Peterson; Jeannie Rice; Trace Hollenbeck
Patron Committee: Joyce Delena, Chair; Dianne Robertson; Louann Blome; Carmelyn Johnson; Peggy Stoddard; Alice Green; DeeDee Copsey

1980

The Taming of the Shrew

Director ...... Larry West
Set Design ...... Jerry Osborne
Costume Design ...... Victoria Holloway
Lighting Design ...... Lane Thomas
Sound Design ...... Jim Reynolds

The Merchant of Venice

Director ...... Larry West
Set Design ...... Jerry Osborne
Costume Design ...... Victoria Holloway
Lighting Design ...... Lane Thomas
Sound Design ...... Jim Reynolds

The Comedy of Errors

Director ...... Barry Press
Set Design ...... Jerry Osborne
Costume Design ...... Martha Shafer
Lighting Design ...... Lane Thomas
Sound Design ...... Jim Reynolds

Acting Company

Shrew; Merchant; Comedy

Curt Baker — Hortensio; Bassanio; Antipholous
Anthony Cesare — Grumio; Shylock; Dromio
William Coburn — Vincentio; Prince of Morocco/ Tubal; Duke/Balthasar
Doug Copsey — Petruchio; Lorenzo; Egeon
Tracey Hollenbeck — Lucentio; Gratiano; Angelo
Victoria Holloway — Widow; Portia; Adriana
Stitch Marker — Pedant; Salonio; –
Barbara McKean — Bianca; Jessica; Luciana
Patrick E. Nance — Gremio; Antonio; Town Crier/Nell
David Painter — Tranio; Prince of Aragon/ Launcelot; Dr. Pinch
Seelye Smith — Kate; Nerissa; Courtesan
Kevin Connell — –; Salerio; –
Spike Ericson — –; The Duke–
Nancy Lee — –; Singer/Servant; –
Martha Peavey — –; Singer/Servant:; –
Jenny Sternling — –; Seamstress; –
Stephen Williams — –; –; Antipholus/Jailer
Tom Willmorth — Biondello; –; –
Mary E. Markus — –; –; Emilia

Production

Asst. Director for *Shrew & Merchant* .... Stacy Lucas
Asst. for Sound .... Charley Schumaker
Set Construction Design Consultant ... Bill McCombs
Scenic Painting .... Jerry Osborne
Carpenter .... Carlos G. Salana
Trees .... Sterling Landscape Co.
Costume Construction: Michelle Black; Chris Cummings; Desiree McQueen; Nancy Lee
Hair & Makeup .... Shirley Hurley
Wigs: Robert Vasquez; Jeff Atkinson; Lynn Stacey
Technical Director .... Victoria Holloway
Assistant TD .... Seelye Smith
Stage Manager .... Louann Blome
Movement & Dance Coach .... Steve Mann
Fence Design & Painting .... Tom Oakes
Apprentice Program Manager .... Barbara McKean
Apprentice Instructor .... Martha Peavey
Apprentices: Bonnie Barker; Lisa Monaci; Valerie Mead; Jennie Ray; Julie Bayer; Ted Osborne; Katie Kilgrow; Donna Sands; Ann Marie Mills; Pam Pratt; Katie Whitman

Administration

Producing Artistic Director .... Doug Copsey
General Manager .... Jim Owen
Business Manager .... James T. Crowley
Box Office Manager .... Phil Hensley
Graphic Design .... Dennis Chase

Board of Directors

Doug Copsey, President
Victoria Holloway, Vice-President
Louann Blome, Vice-President
Ed Simmerman, Sectretary
Jim Owen

1981

Much Ado About Nothing

Director .... Eloise Bruce
Set Design .... Jerry Osborne
Costume Design .... Carrie Mather
Lighting .... M. Lane Thomas
Sound .... Homer Wise

The Tempest

Director .... Mark Cuddy
Set Design .... Jerry Osborne
Costume Design .... Michelle Thompson Black
Lighting .... M. Lane Thomas
Sound .... Homer Wise

As You Like It

Director .... Barry Press
Set Design .... Jerry Osborne
Costume Design .... Desiree McQueen
Lighting .... M. Lane Thomas
Sound .... Homer Wise

Acting Company

Much Ado; Tempest; As You Like It

Geoffrey Alm — Dogberry; Trinculo; Oliver
Jenny Brotherton — –; Spirit of the isle; –
John Cagan — Don John, A sexton; Caliban; Orlando
Doug Copsey — Don Pedro; Prospero; Duke Senior
Kevin Connell — Leonato; Alonso; Le Beau
Patrick Cunningham — –; Gonzalo; Adam, William
Mat DeCaro — Benedick; Stephano; Charles; Corin
Spike Ericson — Amiens
Janet Summers Eskew — –; Spirit of the isle; –
Sue Galligan — Ursula; –; –
Beverly Hainault — Beatrice; Ceres; Phebe
Hud Hudson — First Watchman, A gardener; Mariner; Dennis, A Person representing Hymen
Jim Hunt — –; Mariner; –
Christine Iaderosa — –; –; Lady of Frederick's Court
Brian King — Claudio; Ariel; Duke Frederick, Silvius
Nancy Lee — Juno; Celia
Geoffrey Leighton — Antonio; Boatswain
David Lewis — Messenger; –; –
Mark M. Mayo — Borachio; Sebastian; Touchstone
Ursula Meyer — Hero; Miranda; Rosalind
Charles Miller — Second Watchman; Mariner; –
David Painter — Friar FrancisVerges; Antonio; Jacques
Cammie Pavesic — –; Spirit of the isle;–
Mike Saben — –; Ferdinand; –
Carrie Sevy — –; Spirit of the isle; –
Doug Starnes — –; –; Lord of Frederick's Court
Billy Van Sickel — A serving man; Mariner; Lord of Frederick's Court
Katie Whitman — –; Spirit of the isle; –
Rod Wolfe — Conrade, Balthazar; Master of a ship; –
Melanie Yellen — Margaret; Iris; Audrey

Production

Apprentice Program, Director .... M. Lane Thomas
Apprentices: Aaron Allen, Sue Brewer; Jennifer Brotherton; Kevin Connell; Yvonne Gates; Christina Gellert; Hud Hudson; Christine Iaderosa; George Johnson; Cammie Pavesic; Pam Pratt; Douglas Starnes; Brian Sullivan; Bill Van Sickle; Katie Whitman; Johanna Winfield
Assistant Director for *As You Like It* .. Jenny Brotherton
Assistant Director for *Much Ado* ..... Johanna Winfield
Assistant Director for *The Tempest* ... Christine Iaderosa
Assistant, Costume Designer for *As You Like It* ... Jenny Brotherton
Stage Manager .... Louann Blome
Technical Director .... Jerry Osborne
House Manager .... James E. Simmerman
Assistant, Sets .... Andy Davidson
Master Carpenter .... Andy Davidson
Set Landscaping .... Sterling Landscape Co.
Sound & Lighting Crew: Johanna Winfield; Christina Gellert
Stage Crew: Christine Iaderosa; Jenny Brotherton; Yvonne Gates; Cammie Pavesic; Katie Whitman; Pam Pratt; Robin Kugler; Scott Campbell; Briane Pence; Kevin Connell
Costume Crew: Yvonne Gates; Christine Iaderosa; Pam Pratt; Sandy Thompson; Don Black
Costume Mistress .... Carrie Mather
Costumes, Special Acknowledgements.. Ariel & Spirit's Headdresses .... Star Moxley
Seamstresses: Carol Richardson; Gerry Sevy; Ginger Scott; Star Moxley; Jenny Brotherton; Johanna Winfield
Makeup Crew: .... M. Lane Thompson; Jenny Brotherton; Cammie Pavesic
Movement and Dance Coach .... Steve Mann
Musical Arrangements - *As You Like It* ...... Jim Savage
Props .... Louann Blome
Prop Crew: Hud Hudson; Bill Van Sickle; Gordon Pratt; Aaron Allen
Model T's courtesy of Southwestern Idaho Model T Club; Drivers Don Borchers, Kyle Lewis
Keystone Kops car courtesy of Preco Truck & Auto Electric Inc./Dennis Sheehy

Administration

Artistic Director .... Doug Copsey
Executive Producer .... Jim Owen
General Manager and Box Office Manager ... James T. Crowley
Assistant Business Manager .... Julie Bayer
Graphic Design .... Dennis A. Chase
Public Relations .... Pam Abas
Program Ad Sales .... Hugh Maffett
Billboards .... Bobbette Cunningham

Board of Directors

Doug Copsey, President
Lou Ann Blome, Vice President
Ed Simmerman, Secretary/Treasurer
Dianne Robertson, Patron Committee Chair
Jim Owen

1982

Hamlet

Director .... Doug Copsey
Set Design .... Jerry Osborne
Costume Design .... Martha Shafer
Lighting .... Phil Brotherton
Sound .... Sherilyn Paris

A Midsummer Night's Dream

Director .... Eloise Bruce
Set Design .... Jerry Osborne
Costume Design .... Star Moxley
Lighting .... Phil Brotherton
Sound .... Sherilyn Paris

Twelfth Night

Director .... Mike Hoffmann
Set Design .... Jerry Osborne
Costume Design and Set Decoration ... Odell England
Lighting .... Rozanne Robertson
Sound .... Phil Brotherton; Sherilyn Paris

Acting Company

Hamlet; A Midsummer Night's Dream; Twelfth Night

Mark Ancell –; –; Second Lord
Leslie Anderson –; Cobweb;–
Lynn Balesteri Gertrude; Titania; Viola
Julie Bayer Banner; Hippolyta; Revellers
Carol Brown Player; –; Revellers
Ray Chapman Bernardo, Gravedigger; Theseus; Fabian
Judith Dickerson Ophelia; Hermia; Olivia
John Elliott Player King; Francis Flute; Sir Toby Belch
Brady Frederick –; The Changeling Boy; –
Kate Gallun Gentlewoman to Gertrude;–; –
McCarthy Hanger Horatio; Puck; Sebastian
Nan Harms Player Queen; Helena; Maria
Mike Hoffman –; Demetrius;–
Trace Hollenbeck Hamlet; Philostrate; Antonio
T. J. Hopper Player, Osric; Snug ; –
Hud Hudson Francisco, Gravedigger; Robin Starveling; First Lord, Revellers
Brian King Claudius; Oberon; Orsino;
Andy Lawless Reynaldo; Second Fairy; Revellers
Stitch Marker Laertes; Lysander; Malvolio
Katherine Mason –; First Fairy; Revellers
Greg Pake Polonius; Nick Bottom; Feste
Cammie Pavesic Banner; Peaseblossom; –
Larry Reina Rosencrantz; Peter Quince; Sir Andrew Aguecheek
Kassie Reckamp –; Mustardseed; Revellers
James Sauve Marcellus; Egeus; A Sea Captain, Priest
Mike Sharp Player; –; Second Officer, Revellers
Juris Skujins Ghost of Hamlet's Father, Priest; Attendant; Curio, First Officer
Myrna Crooks Spencer Banner; Attendant; –
Tom Willmorth Guildenstern; Tom Snout; Valentine
Katy Whitman –; Third Fairy; –
Johanna Winfield Banner; Moth; –

Production

Assistant Director for *Hamlet* ....Carole Brown
Assistant Director for *A Midsummer Night's Dream* James Sauve ....
Assistant Director for *Twelfth Night* . .Johanna Winfield
Technical Director ....M. Lane Thomas
Stage Manager ....Jenifer Brotherton
Costume Crew: Julie Bayer; Carole Brown;Myrna Crooks Spencer; Leslie Anderson; Sherilyn Paris; Cammie Pavesic; Katie Whitman; Kate Gallun
Seamstresses: Jenifer Brotherton; Diane Dorman: Cindi Heavin; Alexa Howell; Maryjane Jorgensen; Cindy Spitz Ping
Makeup Design ....Nan Harms
Makeup Crew: Jenifer Brotherton; Johanna Winfield; Kassie Reckamp; Nan Harms; Katherine Mason; Kate Gallun; Frances Sase; Margaret Hopson
Prop Master ....Juris Skujins
Prop Crew: Kassie Reckamp; Cammie Pavesic; Pam Pratt: Mike Sharp
Piano ....Courtesy of Holsinger Music, Inc.
Movement and Dance Coach ....Johanna Winfield
Musical Director – Twelfth Night .....Myrna Crooks Spencer
Magic Instructor ....Greg Seely
Voice Coach ....Judith Dickerson
Stage Fighting Instructors: Greg Pake; Brian King
Apprentice Director ....Jenifer Brotherton
Apprentices/ Supporting Actors: Mark Ancell; Leslie Anderson; Julie Bayer; Jenifer Brotherton; Phil Brotherton; Carole Brown; Ray Chapman; Kate Gallun; T.J. Hopper; Hud Hudson; Andy Lawless Katherine Mason; Sherilyn Paris; Cammie Pavesic; Pam Pratt; Kassie Reckamp; Jim Sauve; Mike Sharp; Juris Skujins; Myrna Crooks Spencer; Katie Whitman; Tom Wilmorth; Johanna Winfield; Brady Franklin

Administration

Executive Producer ....Jim Owen
Artistic Director ....Doug Copsey
General Manager ....James T. Crowley
Box Office Manager ....Marlene Phillips
Graphic Design ....Dennis A. Chase
Banner Design – *Hamlet*: Ann Strawn; Marsha Barney
Public Relations ....Pam Abas
Program Sales: Patrick Nance; Marlene Phillips
Office Assistants: Katherine Mason: Mark Ancell; Mike Sharp; Juris Skujins
Program Advertising and Sales ManagerPatrick Nance
Box Office: Bea Moe Black; Jolene Dewald
House Manager ....Julie Bayer

Board of Directors

Doug Copsey, President
Lou Ann Blome, Vice President
Ed Simmerman, Secretary/Treasurer
Eloise Bruce
Alan Minskoff
Jim Owen
Beatrice Moe Black, Patron Committee Chair

Patron Committee

Jan Alden
Louanne Blome
Helen Copple
Mimi Copsey
Jolene Dewald
Evelyn Fowle
Marilyn Havelina
Chuck Hervey
Marsha Hoyt
Kay Naeve
Chuck Newhouse
Jaci Wilkins

1983

The First Part of King Henry the Fourth

Director ....Mark Cuddy
Set Design ....Jeffery Hunt
Costume Design ....Lowell Detweiller
Lighting ....M Lane Thomas
Sound ....Katherine Mason

The Merry Wives of Windsor

Director ....Victoria Holloway
Set Design ....Jeffrey Hunt
Costume Design ....Rozanne Robertsonx
Lighting ....M. Lane Thomas
Sound ....Jonathon Perry

Love's Labours Lost

Director ....David Ode
Set Design ....Jeffrey Hunt
Costume Design ....Martha Shafer
Lighting ....M. Lane Thomas
Sound ....Katherine Mason

Acting Company

Henry IV, Part One; Merry Wives of Windsor; Love's Labours Lost

Thom Allen Prince John/ Mortimer; Fenton; Nathaniel
Ken Bahn Vintner/Glendower; Doctor Caius; Boyet
Julie Bayer –; –; Maria
Mark Bennett Westmoreland/ Gadshill; –; Forester
Mara Berkley –; Robin; Understudy Jaquenetta
Delia Booth –; –; Trixie
Michael Connor Prince Hal; Nym; Dumaine
Wayne J. Cote Earl of Worcester; Ford; Don Armado
Patricia Denny –; –; Moth
Bill Fears King Henry IV; Pistol; Berowne
Sue Galligan Mistress Quickly; Mistress Quickly; –
Jon Irwin Northumberland/ Bardolph; Page; Holofernes
Wendy Lawless Lady Mortimer; Mistress Ford; Rosaline
Michael Leopard Sir John Falstaff; Sir John Falstaff; Dull
Geoffrey Lower Hotspur; Slender; King of Navarre
Troy Lunt Tapster; –; –
Michael J. McAlister, Jr. Sir Walter Blunt; Shallow; Mercade
Kathleen McNenny Bawd; Anne Page; Katherine
Ursula Meyer –; Mistress Page; Jaquenetta
Suzanne Perreault Lady Percy; Hostess; Princess of France
Jonathan Perry Francis; –; –
Alexis Strasheim Bawd; Roxie
Arne Swensen Tapster; Simple; Lord Arne
Michael Toot Peto; RugbyLongaville
Tom Willmorth Poins/Vernon; Hugh Evans; Costard

Production

Stage Manager – *King Henry* ....Mara Berkley
Stage Manager – *Merry Wives and Love's Labours* Stephen Jimenez ....
Assistant Stage Manager – *King Henry* ......Troy Lunt
Assistant Stage Manager – *Merry Wives* ....Delia Booth
Assistant Stage Manager – *Love's Labours* ....Alexis Strasheim ....
Technical Director ....M. Lane Thomas
Master Carpenter ....Micheal Baltzell
Costume Shop Director ....Jenny Brotherton
Wardrobe – *King Henry*: Delia Booth; Patricia Denny; Kathleen McNenny
Wardrobe – *Merry Wives*: Katherine Mason; Alexis Strasheim
Wardrobe – *Love's Labours*: Troy Lunt; Delia Booth
Makeup and Hair Design ....Nancy Harms
Assistant Make up Designer ....Shirley Hurley
Makeup Assistant: Jenny Horton; Tony Uberuaga; Michelle Arana ....
Property Mistress ....Louann Blome
Props Crew: Alexis Strasheim; Troy Lunt Jonathan Perry
Cannon courtesy of Civil War Skirmish Association
Fights Choreographer ....Stephen Jimenez
Combat Master/Assistant Fight ChoreographerMichael J. McAllister, Jr.
Combat Advisor ....Dr. Charles Lauterbach
Dance Choreographer ....Ursula Meyer
Voice and Movement Coach ....Ursula Meyer
Assistant Director – *Merry Wives* ....Louann Blome
Assistant Scenic Designer ....Jeffrey McDonald
House Manager ....Vickie Polnac
Production Assistant – *King Henry* ....Buffy Nailon
Production Assistant – *Merry Wives* ...Katie Whitman
Acting Interns: Thom Allen; Mara Berkley; Louann Blome; Delia Booth; Patricia Denny; Troy Lunt; Katherine Mason; Michael J. McAllister; Jonathan Perry; Vickie Louise Polnac; Alexis Strasheim Arne Swenson; Michael Scott Toot; Buffy Nailon, Apprentice

Administration

Artistic Director ....Mark Cuddy
General Manager ....James T. Crowley, Jr.
Box Office Manager ....Julie Bayer
Publicity: Cynthia Gaede; Glenn Oakley
Program Sales Manager ....Jeanne M. Dailey
Group Sales ....Marlene H. Phillips
Volunteer Coordinator ....Lori McAfee

Board of Directors

Jim Owen, President
Lou Ann Blome, Vice President
Chris Goode, Treasurer
Mark Ingram, Secretary
Beatrice Moe Black, Patron Committee
Doug Copsey, Artistic Director Emeritus

1984

The Taming of the Shrew

Director ....Tim McDonough
Set Design ....Jeffrey Hunt
Costume Design ....Sarah Campbell
Lighting ....Jonathan Langrell
Composer/Musical Director ....David Miller

Robin Hood

by Don Nigro

Director ....Mark Cuddy
Set Design ....Jeffrey Hunt
Costume Design ....Bitsy Bidwell
Lighting ....Jonathan Langrell
Composer/Musical Director ....David Miller

King Lear

Director ....Vincent Murphy
Set Design ....Jeffrey Hunt
Costume Design ....Sarah Campbell
Lighting ....Jonathan Langrell
Composer/Musical Director ....David Miller

Acting Company

King Lear; Taming of the Shrew; Robin Hood

Pam Abas — –; –; Old Queen Eleanor
Thom Allen — Duke of Burgundy/ Ensemble; Lucentio; Will Scarlet/ Lame Louie
W. Allan Batchelder — Doctor/ Ensemble/ Lear; Supporter; Biondello; Friar Tuck
Tony Carreiro — Edmund; Tailor/Comic; Sheriff of Nottingham/ Sam the Rag
Carissa Channing — –; Chorus; Bronwen/ Maid of Tuxford
Jonathan Chaus — Knight/ Peasant/ Ensemble; –; Davey o'Doncaster/ Arthur O'Bland
Doug Copsey — Duke of Cornwall; Pedant / Christopher Sly/ Comic; Robin Hood
Erin Corday — –; –; Grindl the Idiot Girl
Wayne Cote — Edgar; Gremio; Prince John
Mark Cuddy — –; Petruchio; –
Andrew Friedlander — Earl of Kent; –; –
Peter Giffin — Earl of Gloucester; Curtis/ Comic; Dark Monk/ King Richard/ Ghost/ Purvis the Peddler
Kim Gillingham — Captain/ Peasant/ Ensemble; Bianca; Jenny Brown/ Maid of Tuxford
Kirsten Giroux — Goneril; Katherina; Sally Serving Wench/ Gwenny
Dan Green — –; –; Alan a'Dale
James Henderson — –; –; Blind Benny
Laura Jones — Cordelia; Chorus; Maid Marian
Gavin Kirkpatrick — –; –; Deaf Danny
Patricia Knowlton — Ensemble; Peasant who kills Cornwall; Widow / Chorus; –
Ralph Lucas — The Fool; Grumio; Sir Stephan
Tedd McClellan — Ensemble; Gill Redcap/ Mitch the Miller
Tim McDonough — Lear, King of Britain; –; Little John
Ursula Meyer — Regan
Terri Morgan — –; Chorus; Prioress
David Lee-Painter — –; –; Yorick
Dan Peterson — Duke of Albany; Baptista Minola; Constable Watt / Eadom o' the Blue Boar
Brian Powell — –; –; Bell the Tinker
Toni Redman — –; Chorus; Sister Felicity / Maid of Tuxford
Don Schlossman — King of France / Herald / Ensemble; Hortensio; Dumb Duggan / Will Stutely
Gina Scorsone — Curan / Ensemble; –; Ellen Dear / Old Maid of Tuxford
Jay Sherlock — Old Man; Vincentio / Comic
Carole Whiteleather — –; –; Lady Quigley / Old Maid of Tuxford
Clay Wilcox — –; Bombshell / Comic; Diccon Cruikshank / Cootie the Drunk
Tim Willmorth — Oswald; Tranio Grok / Flint the Beggar

Production

Production Stage Manager ....Laurie Baker
Assistant Stage Managers: ......Paul Frellick; Patricia Knowlton; Jessica K. Peterson ....
Technical Director ....Jim Campbell
Production Manager ....David Lee-Painter
Production Assistant ....Gavin Kirkpatrick
Sound ....Katherine Mason
Scenic Artist ....Micheal Baltzell
Carpenter ....Phil Brotherton
Carpenter ....Steve Redmond
Lighting Crew: Jonathan Chaus; Lisa Klein; Laurie Utterback
Assistant Director – *Robin Hood* and *Lear* ..Paul Frellick
Assistant Director – *Shrew* ....Jessica Peterson
Costume Shop Supervisor ....Nancy Berger
Stitcher ....Cherrie Bragg
Steve Frank
Hair and Makeup Designer ....Nan Harms
Fight Choreographer ....David Boushey
Fight Captain ....Tony Carreiro
Properties: Carissa Channing; Tedd McClellan; .Terri Morgan; Jessica Peterson; Toni Redman; Gina Scorsone
Interns: Paul Frellick; Patricia Knowlton; Jessica K. Peterson; Jonathan Chaus; Lisa Klein; Laurie Utterback Carissa Channing; Tedd McClellan; Terri Morgan Jessica Peterson; Toni Redman; Gina Scorsone;
Katherine Mason, Artistic Associate: Director of Training ....Ursula Meyer
Apprentice Director ....Nancy Lee-Painter
Apprentice Company: Tina Browning; Lori Dickie James Henderson; Gavin Kirkpatrick; Toni Lawson Meesha Mangiaracina; Kassi Nelson; Alissalyn Paynter Brian Powell

Administration

Artistic Director ....Mark Cuddy
Managing Director ....Ron Wachholtz
"Shakescene" Editor ....Stu Evett
Administrative Assistant ....Lynda Irons
Box Office Manager ....Rita Morgan
Box Office Treasurer ....Nancy Lee-Painter
Box Office: Terri Morgan; Gavin Kirkpatrick
Volunteer Director ....Jay Sherlock
Publicity Director ....Sue Webster
Publicity Intern ....Laurie Utterback

Board of Directors

Dr. Charles Robertson, President
Brian Nye, Vice President
Chris Goode, Treasurer
Debbie Johnson, Secretary
Beatrice Black
Doug Copsey
Gene Fuller
Mark Ingram
Brian King
Richard McChrystal
Tina McChrystal
Alisa Pulver
Lee Pulver

1985

The Two Gentlemen of Verona

Director ....Roberta Levitow
Scenic Design ....Mike Baltzell
Costume Design ....Deborah Trout
Lighting ....Jim Henderson
Composer/Musical Director ....David Miller

Richard III

Director ....Robert Clare
Scenic Design ....Jeffrey Hunt
Costume Design ....Deb Brunneaux
Lighting ....Katherine Mason
Composer/Musical Director ....David Miller

The Winter's Tale

Director ....Mark Cuddy
Set Design ....Jim Campbell
Costume Design ....Star Moxley
Katherine Mason ....Barb Feige
Composer/Musical Director ....David Miller

Waiting for Godot

By Samuel Becket

Director ....Vincent Murphy
Set Design ....Jeffrey Hunt
Costume Design ....Star Moxley
Lighting ....Jeffrey Hunt
Composer/Musical Director ....David Miller

Acting Company

Two Gentlemen; Richard III; The Winter's Tale; Godot

Ken Bahn — Thurio; Norfolk; Camillo; –
W. Allen Batchelder — Outlaw/ Fighter; Blunt; 1st Lord / 2nd Gentleman / Shepherd Servant ; –
Mike Connor — Proteus; Dorset; Cleomenes / Shepherd; –
Janice Clawson — Ursula / Flower Seller;
Barry Edelstein — Outlaw / Fighter; 1st Citizen / Brandon; Jailer / Mariner / Shepherd; –
Paul Frellick — –; Richmond; –; –
Kate Gallun — –; –; Shepherdess; –
Rod Hansen — Outlaw / Butler / Fighter
Brakenbury — Officer / Archidamus / 1st Gentleman / Shepherd; –
Erv Johnson — –; Stanley; Antigonus; –
Joe Johnson — Musician #1; 2nd Citizen / Herbert; 2nd Lord / Bear; –
Bob Jones — –; Hastings; Polixenes; Pozzo
Stephanie Kallos — Sylvia; –; –; –
Kate Levy — –; Elizabeth; Hermione; Lucky
Gregg Loughridge — Valentine; Rivers Autolycus; –
Stitch Marker — –; Edward IV; –; –
Tedd McClellan — Speed; Grey; Dion / Shepherd; –
Lucas McClure — Outlaw / Gardener / Fighter Tyrrel; Leontes' Servant
Joseph McNally — Eglamour / Conductor Catesby Florizel; –
Kathleen McNenny — Julia; Lady-in-waiting; Perdita; –
David Miller — Panthino; Lord Mayor; –; –
Chris Odell — –; Margaret; Emilia; –
Al Oliver — Launce; Ratcliff; Leontes; –;
Dan Peterson — Antonio; Henry IV /

	Archbishop of Canterbury; –; Estragon
Maria Rocha	Lucetta; –; Dorcus; –
Rebecca Rosenbloom	–; Anne; Mopsa; –
Jay Sherlock	Gabby the Caretaker Archbishop of York; Old Shepherd; –
Russell Sommers	Host / Outlaw / Fighter
Richard III	3rd Lord / 3rd Gentleman; –
Michael Ward	–; Clarence; –; –
Jeff Ware	Duke; Buckingham; –; Vladimir
Carole Whiteleather	–; Duchess; Paulina; –
Clay Wilcox	Outlaw / Fighter
Scrivner / Oxford	Clown; –

Production

Production Stage Manager ....Timothy J. Ocel
Stage Manager – *Godot* ....Paul Frellick
Assistant Stage Manager ....David Moore
Assistant Stage Manager – *Godot* .....Casey Stousland
Assistant Stage Manager – *Richard* ....David Moore
Assistant Stage Managers – *Winter's Tale* .David Moore; James William Cox
Technical Director ....H. Kim Moon
Production Manager ....Barb Feige
Production Intern ....Jim Henderson
Carpenter: George Davis; Michael Hadley
Technician ....katherine Mason
Costume Shop Manager ....John Hill
Stitcher: Nancy Berger; Wendy Fountain; Elizabeth Kochneff; J. D. Thomas
Wardrobe ....Janet Elam
Wigs ....Paula Walton
Beard/Mustache Design ....Nancy Harms
Basketry – *Winter's Tale* ....Barbara Nelson
Director of Training ....Stephanie Kallos
Fight Captain ....Joe McNally
Fight Choreography – *Richard* ....Robert Clare
Fight Choreography – *Two Gents* ......Joseph McNally
Properties ....Sharon Church
Sound Archivist – *Winter's Tale* ....Jonathan Shever
Assistant Director – *Godot* ....Cynthia Gaede
Assistant Director – *Richard* ....James William Cox
Assistant Director – *Winter's Tale* .....Casey Stousland

Administration

Producing Director ....Mark Cuddy
Development Director ....Vangie Osborn
Office Manager ....Pamela Hawley
Photographer ....David Bogie
Box Office Assistants: Jeff Holley; Teresa McLaughlin
Photographer ....Thomas Murphy
Publicity Assistant ....Paula Pamperian
Box Office Manager ....Carole Quartz
Associate Producer ....Christine S. Selian

Board of Directors

Doug Copsey, President
Brian Nye, Vice President
Martin Hurbi, Treasurer
Debbie Johnson, Secretary
Susan Berry
Michael Brush
Larry Chase
Linda Darrow
Dr. Charles Davis
Ann Erstad
Janie Gjording
Barbara Gruendemann
Neal Hundt
Brian King
Don Lojek
Michael McCarthy
James McGee
Michael Murie
Bonnie Quinn
Thomas Saldin
Glenn Selander
Artie Stone
Wayne Waldorph

1986

A Midsummer Night's Dream

Director ....Mark Cuddy
Scenic Design ....Jeffrey Hunt
Costume Design ....Bitsy Bidwell
Lighting ....Tom Coatey
Music Director ....Joseph Weisnewski

Pendragon
By Don Nigro

Director ....Andrew Traister
Scenic Design ....Micheal Baltzell
Costume Design ....Frances Kenny
Lighting ....Tom Coatey
Music Director ....Joseph Weisnewski

Othello

Director ....Vincent Murphy
Scenic Design ....Philip W. Atlakson
Costume Design ....Matty Shafer
Lighting ....Tom Coatey
Music Director ....Joseph Weisnewski

All's Well That Ends Well

Director ....Paul Frellick
Scenic Design ....Scott Beseman
Costume Design ....Ted Bernard
Lighting ....Shaun Sites
Music D\irector ....Joseph Weisnewski

Acting Company

A Midsummer Night's Dream; Pendragon; Othello; All's Well That Ends Well

Claudia K. Benbow	Peaseblossom; –; Girl;–
Linda Bloom	Cobweb; Benny Wong; – ;–
Shelley K. Booker	–; –; –; Widow
Douglas Copsey	Oberon; Pendragon; Brabantio King
Judi Dickerson	Hermia; –; Emilia; Helena
John W. Elliott	–; Roosevelt/ Hemingway; –; –
Tom Elliott	Lysander; Banjo Picker; Gratiano/ Senator; Lord
Paul Frediani	Snug; Jeffries; Soldier #3; –
Peter Greenberg	Philostrate; Charley Wong; –; Soldier/ Interpretor
V. L. Holloway	Helena; Alison; Desdemona; –;
Jennifer Langsam	Mustardseed; Isabel/ Daughter; –; –
Steven Matt	Theseus; Othello; Rinaldo
Paul Mayer	–; Joe Navarro; –; Lord
Tedd McClellan	Flute; Revelations Red; Soldier #1; Younger Dumain
Lucas McClure	Starveling; –;Montano; –
David Mears	Egeus; Mr. McPherson /Mr. Bengoa; Duke; Lafew
Jana Norris	Hippolyta; Anne Pendragon; –; Diana
Dan Peterson	Bottom; Mark Twain; Roderigo Lavatch
John Plummer	Flick; –; Soldier #2; Lord
John Rice	Demetrius; –; Iago; Lord
Richard Robertson	Snout; Boone; Lodovicio / Senator; Elder Dumain
Jay Sherlock	Quince; Stationmaster; –; Duke
Joel Summerlin	Thorn; –; –; Prince
Barbara Svoboda	Moth; Ama; Navarro; Mariana
Carole E. Whiteleather	Titania; –; Bianca; Countess
Tom Willmorth	Puck; –; Cassio; Bertram
Jenny Reid	
Laura Johnson	Attendants
Benjamin David Whiteleather	Changling Boy
Micheal Baltzell	
Hillary Atkinson	
Jim Sprouls	
Joseph Weisnewski	Musicians
Pilar Witherspoon	Basque Girl
Ted McClellan	First Soldier
John Plummer	Second Soldier
Paul Frediani	Third Soldier
Claudia K. Benbow	Girl
Paul Mayer	
Kelly A. Bickford	
David Duncan	Torchbearers

Production

Stage Manager – *King Henry* ....Mara Berkley
Production Stage Manager ....Timothy J. Ocel
Stage Manager ....David Moore
First Assistant Stage Manager – *All's Well* ....Mary Catherine Gilson
First Assistant Stage Manager – *Midsummer/Othello* ....David Moore
First Assistant Stage Manager – *Pendragon* ....Joel Summerlin
Second Assistant Stage Manager – *All's Well* ....Jennifer Langsam
Second Assistant Stage Manager – *Midsummer* ....Aaron Hudson
Second Assistant Stage Manager – *Othello* ....Cynthia Gaede
Second Assistant Stage Manager – *Pendragon* ....Pilar Witherspoon
Technical Director ....Tom Coatey
Site Manager ....Shaun Sites
Master Carpenter ....George Davis
Sound Technician ....Katherine Mason
Costume Shop Director ....Guy Beutller
Sitcher / Wardrobe Claudia Benbow; Mary Catherine Gilson ....
Stitcher ....Lisa Leftowich
Stitcher / Crafts ....Ted Bernard
Hair ....Graeber & Company
Properties Director ....Lowell Grant
Fight Captain – *Othello* ....Richard Robertson
Assistant Fight Captain – *Othello* .....Tedd McClellan
Assistant Director – *All's Well* ....Lila Mirochin
Assistant Director – *Midsummer* ....Cynthia Gaede
Assistant Director – *Othello* ....Christine S. Selian
Assistant Director – *Pendragon* ....Lila Mirochin
Interns: Claudia Benbow; Shelley K. Booker; Paul Frediani; Cynthia Gaede; Peter Greenberg; Jennifer Langsam; Lila Mirochin; Paul Mayer; Jana Norris; John Plummer; Joel Summerlin; Barbara Svoboda

Administration

Producing Director	Mark Cuddy
Development Director	Vangie Osborn
Associate Producer	Christine S. Selian
Office Manager	Carole E. Whiteleather
Publicity Director	Trish Elledge
Administrative Asst.	Jay Sherlock
Box Office Assistant	Theresa McLaughlin
Associate Director	Paul Frellick
Photographers	Dave Bogie; Thomas G. Murphy
Concessions	Jeff Holley

Board of Directors

Michael McCarthy, President
Karen Justus, Treasurer
Brian King, Secretary
James Brandstetter
Michael Brush
Dr. Charles Davis
Janie Gjording
Don Lojek
Raquel Pascoe
Bonnie Quinn
Thomas Saldin
Glenn Selander
Barbara Skinner

1987

Romeo and Juliet

Director.....Mark Cuddy
Scenic Design.....Jenny Guthrie
Costume Design.....Michael Chapman
Lighting.....Tom Coatey
Sound.....Mark Cuddy
Music Composed by.....Joseph Weisnewski

The Comedy of Errors

Director.....Dennis Bigelow
Scenic Design.....Jenny Guthrie
Costume Design.....Guy A. Beuttler
Lighting.....Tom Coatey
Music Composed by.....Joseph Weisnewski

Pericles

Director.....Paul Frellick
Scenic Design.....Micheal Baltzell
Costume Design.....Ted Bernard
Lighting.....Tom Coatey
Music Composed by.....Joseph Weisnewski

The Adventures of Sherlock Holmes by Mark Rosenwinkel from the stories of Arthur Conan Doyle

Director.....Timothy J. Ocel
Scenic Design.....Tom Coatey
Costume Design.....Nancy Phillips Berger
Lighting.....Shaun Sites
Sound.....Joseph Weisnewski

Acting Company

Romeo and Juliet; The Comedy of Errors; Pericles; The Adventures of Sherlock Holmes

Norman Armour	Abram/ Apothecary; Dr. Pinch/ Merchant; –; Eustace Brakenstall
Betsy Byng	Helena; Courtesan; Antiochus' Daughter Escanes; –
Tony Carreiro	Mercutio; –; Pericles; –
Thea Clark	Lavinia; –; Thaisa Prostitute; Madame Saskras
William C. Cochran	The Watch; –; –; –
Kevin Connell, S. J.	Prince Escalus; Angelo; Cleon / Crewman; Inspector Lestrade
Trish Elledge	–; –; Lychorida/ Diana; Prostitute
Bradley T. Fontanesi	Peter; Jailer; Leonine / Knight Crewman / Antioch Guard Johnny Randall
Stan Garner	Friar Laurence; Antipholus of Syracuse; Cerimon; Sherlock Holmes
Peter Greenberg	Balthasar; Riff-Raff; Philemon Fisherman; Man
Nelson Handel	Sampson; Balthazar; Thaliard / Knight Businessman; –
Arthur Glen Hughes	Tybalt; Dromio of Syracuse; Simonides Businessman; Mr. Nazim
Jennifer Langsam	Juliet; Luce Philoten / Tharsian; Lord Native of Terminus; Woman
James Newcomb	Romeo; –; –; –
Victoria Otto	Lady Capulet; Adriana; Dionyza Lady Brakenstall
Skip Parry	Gregory; Duke; Knight / Pirate Native of Terminus; Bobby Randall
Dan Peterson	–; Drominio of Ephesus; Antiochus; Fisherman; Dr. Watson
John Plummer	Paris / Friar John; Riff-Raff; Boult / The Marshal Native of Terminus; Mick Randall
Karen Pollard	Rosaline; Luciana; Marina
John Rice	Benvolio; Antipholus of Ephesus; Lysimachus / Knight / Scavenger; Professor Moriarty
Daniel Richards	Capulet; Egeon; Helicanus Pirate; xCaptain Jack Croker
Jay Sherlock	Old Capulet; Officer; Pander / Scavenger; –
Greg Snyder	Montague; Merchant Engineer / Knight Prostitute; Man
Suzanne Sturn	Nurse; Emilia; Bawd/ Native of Terminus; Mrs. Watson
Robin Wennberg	Lady Montague; Riff-Raff; The Helm Pirate; Woman
Carole Whiteleather	–; –; The Knower; Theresa Wright
Nate Taylor	Anthony; –; –; –
John Costello	
C. John Siebel	Guards
Shaun Varner	Young Boy
Heather I. Denton	Maria
Tammy S. Ferrell	Anna
Tami D. Ferguson	The Fruit Seller
Colleen McCleary	Young Girl
C. Joseph Siebel	Junior Officer
Jennifer Wees	Guard / Tharson Citizen
Heather Ayers	Tharson Citizen
Lei Blasingame	Tharson Citizen

Production

Associate Director.....Paul Frellick
Assistant Director – Sherlock Holmes.....Christina S. Selian
Assistant Director – Comedy of Errors.....Christina S. Selian
Assistant Director - Pericles.....Norman Armour
Assistant Director – Romeo and Juliet..Cynthia Gaede
Production Stage Manager.....Timothy J. Ocel
Stage Manager.....David Moore
First Assistant Stage Manager – Comedy of Errors.....Becky Brizee
First Assistant Stage Manager – Pericles..Becky Brizee
First Assistant Stage Manager – Romeo and Juliet.....Violet M. Lynch
First Assistant Stage Manager – Sherlock Holmes.....Violet M. Lynch
Second Assistant Stage Manager - Comedy of Errors.....Heather I. Denton
Second Assistant Stage Manager – Pericles..Abi Maala
Second Assistant Stage Manager - Romeo and Juliet.....John Costello
Second Assistant Stage Manager – Sherlock Holmes.....Karen Pollard
Technical Director.....Martin Gwinup
Technical Director – Pericles.....George Davis
Electrician.....Shaun Sites
Scenic Painters: Micheal Baltzell; Karl Brake
Carpenters: Michael Hartwell; Marshall Lutz; Chad Sheen
Advisor.....Dave Bogie
Shop Foreman.....George Davis
Special Effects Consultant.....Tim McNeil
Sound Recording.....Sanctuary Sound Recording
Assistant Sound Production.....P. Kathy Robran
Costume Shop Director.....Guy A. Beuttler
Crafts Master.....Ted Bernard
Cutter.....Gail Gwinup
Stitchers: Christine A. Bentley: Gail Gwinup; Karen W. Ross; Susan R. Trenery
Wardrobe.....Jane Lark Mckie
Wig and Wardrobe Mistress.....Kimberly A. Thurston
Properties Director.....Karl Brake
Production Assistant.....Abi Maala
Fight Choreographers.....Tony Carreiro
James Newcomb.....
Fight Captain – *Sherlock Homes*.....Peter Greenberg
Dance Choreographer.....Marius Zirra
Voice and Movement Coaches: Tony Carreiro; James Newcomb; John Rice; Suzanne Sturn.....
Grounds Maintenance: Aaron Hudson; Shaun Sites
Interns: Norman Armour; Betsy Byng; Thea Clark; Bradley T. Fontanesi; Nelson Handel; Skip Parry; Karen Pollard; Greg Snyder; Robin Wennberg

Administration

Producing Director.....Mark Cuddy
General Manager.....Vangie Osborn
Associate Producer.....Christina S. Selian
Publicity Director.....Trish Elledge
Correspondence.....Carole Whiteleather
Administrative Assistant.....Jay Sherlock
Box Office Staff.....Jeana McClure
Camile Thom.....
Photographers: Dave Bogie; Thomas G. Murphy
Concessions.....Trease Koutnik
Marketing Intern.....Leah Butler
Administrative Intern.....Sarah M. Payne
Publicity Intern.....Robin Smith
Poster and Brochure Design.....Dennis Chase
Development Brochure Production.....Ken Poulsen

Board of Directors

Glenn Selander, President
James Brandstetter, Vice President
William Keller, Treasurer
Brian King, Secretary
Colin Cannon
Dr. Charles Davis
Janie Gjording
Roxanne Jensen
Karen Justus
Dr. Richard Steele
Don Lojek
Brent Lloyd
James McGee
Brian Nye
Raquel Pascoe
Mary Puccio
Bonnie Quinn
Thomas Saldin
Odette Sutton
Mello Dee Thornton

1988

As You Like It

Director.....William Glover and Rod Ceballos
Scenic Design.....Micheal Baltzell
Costume Design.....Ted Bernard
Lighting.....Robert Parsley
Composer/Sound Design.....Benjamin Masterson

Quilters By Molly Newman and Barbara Damashek

Director.....Theresa Larkin
Scenic Design.....Micheal Baltzell
Costume Design.....Guy Beuttler
Lighting.....Robert Parsley
Music Director.....Joseph Weisnewski

Measure for Measure

Director.....Peggy Shannon
Scenic Design.....Micheal Baltzell
Costume Design.....Thom Heyer
Lighting.....Robert Parsley
Composer/Sound Designer.....Benjamin Masterton

Titus Andronicus

Director.....Rod Ceballos
Scenic Design.....Micheal Baltzell
Costume Design.....Ted Bernard
Lighting.....Robert Parsley
Composer/Sound Designer.....Benjamin Masterton

Acting Company

As You Like It; Quilters; Measure for Measure; Titus Andronicus

Robert G. Anderson	Touchstone; –; Lucio; Saturninus
Betsy Byng	–; Daughter; Francisca; Rabble/ Goth
Jim Campbell	–; –; Roman/ Goth
Will Casey	Jaques; –; Friar/Abhorson; Titus Andronicus
David Clements	Silvius; –; Barnadine; Quintus/ Goth; –
Bridget Connors	Lady Amiens; Daughter; Mariana
A. Bernard Cummings	Le Beau; –; Escalus; Aaron
Dennis Mark Delaney	Duke Frederick; Angelo; Martius/ Goth
David Eichman	Charles/ Amiens; –; Gentleman; Bassianus/ Goth
Laurie Flanigan	Page; Daughter; –; Roman Woman
Karen Fuller	–; Daughter; Juliet; Nurse
Elizabeth Kelly	Phebe; –; Isabella; –
Tom Kelly	Orlando; –; Musician; Captain/ Messenger/ Caius
Sandra Lindberg	Rosalind; Daughter; –; Tamora
Mikel MacDonald	Duke Senior; –; Vincentio; Marcus
Stitch Marker	Lord/ Martext Prairie Man
Pompey	Alarbus/ Rabble/ Clown/ Goth
Jennifer McCarthy	Page; Daughter; Musician; Rabble/ Goth
Kenneth R. Merckx, Jr.	William/ Lord Claudio; –; Lucius
Susan Mundell	Celia; –; Lavinia
Scott Olson	Oliver; –; Elbow; Chiron
Dan Peterson	Corin; –; Provost; Aemilius
David Poynter	Lord; –; Gentleman; Demetrius
Jay Sherlock	Adam; –; Justice/ Varrius; Senator
C. E. Whiteleather	Audrey; Sarah McKendree Bonham; Mistress Overdone; –
Casey Wood	–; –; –; Young Lucius
Buffy Davis	–; Daughter; –; –
Beth Johnson	–; –; –; Roman Woman
Jason Knight	–; –; Mutius/ Rabble/ Sempronius
John J. O'Hagan	–; –; –; Rabble/ Publius

Production

Stage Manager – *As You* ....Violet Lynch
Assistant Stage Manager – *As You* ......Ingrid Kottke
Stage Manager – *Quilters* ....Richard Feldman
Assistant Stage Manager – *Quilters* ....John Hadley
Production Consultant – *Quilters* ......Karen McBride
Stage Manager – *Measure* ....Violet Lynch
Assistant Stage Manager – *Measure* ......Ingrid Kottke
Stage Manager – *Titus* ....Richard Feldman
Assistant Stage Manager – *Titus* ....John Hadley
Technical Director ....Kevin S. Walker
Technical Director – Site Electrician ......Shaun Sites
Shop Foreman ....George Davis
Carpenters: ....Mark Aitchison; Michael Hartwell
Costume Shop Supervisors ....Ted Bernard
Guy Auguste Beuttler ....
Wigmaster/Crafts ....Kevin Brainerd
Props Mistress/Crafts ....Joanna Medioli
Stitchers: Nancy Berger; Linda Campbell; Aaron Elmore; Karen Ross
Fight Choreographer ....Robin H. McFarquhar
Artistic Associate/Vocal Coach ....Theresa Larkin
Feldenkrais Instructor ....Robert Spencer
Apprentice Director ....Jenifer Brotherton
Apprentices: Chris Chambers; Jamie T. Dugger; Bevin Etheridge; Nicole Afton Fox; Sheri Gress; Shawn Kyle; Lisa Lechner; Chelsie Richter; Erin Shackelford; Alan Steed; Sally Thomas; Scott E. Vandusen; Technical Interns: Buffy Davis; Beth Johnson; Jason Knight; John J. O'Hagan

Administration

Artistic Director ....Rod Ceballos
General Manager ....Vangie Osborn
Office Manager ....Jeana McClure
Publicity Director ....Trish Elledge
Publicity Associate ....Robin Austin Smith
Administrative Assistant ....Jay Sherlock
Box Office Staff: ....Kirstin Allen; Renae Knapp
Marketing Intern ....Shannon Solaas
Poster and Brochure DesignSperling Guy & Associates
Toni Rome; Lynn Bernasconi
Program Design: Jeana McClure; Robin Austin Smith
Program Consultant ....Jay Flaherty
Printing ....Joslyn Morris, Inc.
Cover Design: Toni Rome, Sperling Guy & Associates
Cover Art ....Lynn Bernasconi

Board of Directors

James Brandstetter, President
Glenn Selander, Vice President
William Keller, Treasurer
Brian King, Secretary

Colin Cannon	Doug Oppenheimer
Dr. Charles Davis	Raquel Pascoe
Janie Gjording	Mary Puccio
Roxanne Jensen	Bonnie Quinn
Karen Justus	Dick Steele
Brent Lloyd	Odette Sutton
Don Lojek	Mello Dee Thornton
Richard McChrystal	Scott Tunnell
James McGee	

1989

Much Ado About Nothing

Director ....Douglas Jacobs
Scenic Design ....Micheal Baltzell
Costume Design ....Ted Bernard
Lighting ....Robert Parsley
Musical Director ....Susan Nelson Phillips
Sound ....Benjamin Masterton

Waiting for the Parade By John Murrell

Director ....Penny Metropulos
Scenic Design ....Micheal Baltzell
Costume Design ....Guy Auguste Beuttler
Lighting ....Robert Parsley
Sound ....Benjamin Masterton

King Richard the Second

Director ....Kenneth Kelleher
Scenic Design ....Micheal Baltzell
Costume Design ....Pamela Davis
Lighting ....Robert Parsley
Sound ....Joseph Weisnewski

Troilus and Cressida

Director ....Rod Ceballos
Scenic Design ....Micheal Baltzell
Costume Design ....Lisa Vollrath
Lighting ....Robert Parsley
Sound ....Joseph Weisnewski

Acting Company

Much Ado About Nothing; Waiting for the Parade; Richard II; Troilus and Cressida

Rick Anderson	; –; –; –Nestor
Robert G. Anderson	Leonato; York; Pandarus
Kevin Connell, S.J.	Don Pedro; Richard II; Aeneas
Susan Coromel	Marta; Lady; Cassandra
John J. Freeman	Claudio; –; Henry Percy; Paris
Karen Fuller	Hero; Eve; –; Andromache
Joseph Hulser	Balthazar; –; Mowbray/ Salisbury; Diomedes
David Ivers	–; –; Gardener/ Attendant; Soldier
Tracey Komoski	–; –; Janet; Duchess of Gloucester; –
Sandra Lindberg	Beatrice; Margaret; Duchess of York; –
Mikel MacDonald	Benedick; –; Bolingbroke; Achilles
Stitch Marker	Borachio; –; Northumberland; Thersites
Robert McDonough	–; –; Willoughby; Helenus
Susan Mundell	Margaret; Catherine; –; Helen
Hugh O'Gorman	Watch; –; Busy; Patroclus
Sean O'Shea	Watch/Messenger; –; Green/ Keeper; Ajax
Dan Peterson	Dogberry; –; Bishop of Carlisle; Agamemnon
Susan Phillips	Lute Player; –; –; –
Kimberly Rhodes	–; –; Queen; Servant
William L. Salyers	Conrade; –; Aumerle; Menelaus
Jay Sherlock	Verges; –; Gardener; Priam
Ty Smith	Antonio/ Friar; –; Francis; John of Gaunt/ Groom; Ulysses
Michael Strickland	Watch; –; Bagot; Troilus
Christopher Thometz	Sexton; –; Ross; Antenor
Anne Marie Tremko	Ursula; –; Lady; Cressida
Tim True	–; –; Attendant/ SoldierCalchas/ Soldier
David Weber	Watch; –; Welsh; Captain; Deiphobus
Eric Briant Wells	Don John; Exton; Hector
Lisa Sorenson	Musician

Tac Anderson Adam Toothaker Lisa Lechner	Attendants/ Servants
Tac Anderson John J. Freeman Jospeh Hulser David Ivers Mark Learned Shannon Lynch Hugh O'Gorman Scan O'Shea Dan Peterson Jay Sherlock Michael Strickland Adam Toothaker Tim True David Weber	Lords, Heralds, Officers, Soldiers, Messenger, and other Attendants
Susan Coromel Anne Marie Tremko	Ladies Attending on the Queen
Tac Anderson Mark Learned Jonathan Nechas Chelsie Richter Adam Toothaker	Myrmidons
Lisa Lechner Shannon Lynch	Servants to Helen

Production

Production Stage Manager ....Becky Brizee
Technical Director ....Robert Katkowsky
Shop Foreman ....Michael Hartwell
Costume Shop Supervisor ....Ted Bernard
Head Stitcher ....Nancy Berger
Stitchers: Arlette Bankston; Jinny DeFoggi; Sally Thomas; Lee Woods
Wardrobe: Sydney R. S. Anderson; Chelsie Richter;
Master Carpenter; Robert E. Riddle, Sr.
Carpenters: Peter K. Dully; John Hadley; Kent Saleska
Electricians: Pamela Eden Parker; Deborah Penrod
Crafts ....Christina Rosendaul
Props ....Denise J. Grillo
Stage Manager – *Much Ado* ....Kati Sipp
Assistant Stage Manager – *Much Ado* Elizabeth D'Wolf
Light Board Operator – *Much Ado* .....Deborah Penrod
Sound Board Operator – *Much Ado* ....Minda Perry
Dressers – *Much Ado*: Laurel DeFoggi; Halle Longeteig; Sarah Shackelford
Stage Manager – *Waiting* ....Behn Rudo

Assistant Stage Manager – *Waiting* . . Susan Kattwinkel
Light Board Operator – *Waiting* . . . Pamela Eden Parker
Sound Board Operator – *Waiting* . . . . Jonathan Nechas
Assistant Director – *Richard* . . . . Terri April Dillion
Fight Choreographer – *Richard* . Robin H. McFarquhar
Assistant Stage Manager – *Richard* . . Susan Kattwinkel
Light Board Operator – *Richard* . . . . Deborah Penrod
Sound Board Operator – *Richard* . . . . Jonathan Nechas
Dressers – *Richard*: Laurel DeFoggi; Megan Hutchinson
Stage Managers – *Troilus*: Becky Brizee; Kati Sipp
Assistant Stage Manager – *Troilus* . . . Elizabeth D'Wolf
Light Board Operator – *Troilus* . . . . Pamela Eden Parker
Sound Board Operator – *Troilus* . . . . Minda Perry
Dressers: Megan Hutchinson; Halley Longeteig
Movement Instructors: Robert Spencer; LeeAnn Garton
Photographer . . . . Dave Bogie
Director of Training . . . . Robin McFarquhar
Directing Intern . . . . Terri April Dillion
Dramaturg . . . . Deborah Palmes
Vocal Instructor . . . . Susan Coromel
Technical Interns: Robert Drewes; Lisa Lechner
Apprentices: Tac Anderson; Shannon Lynch; Minda Perry; Adam Toothaker; Mark Learned; Jonathan Nechas; Lisa Sorenson; Kym Williams

Administration

General Manager . . . . Vangie Osborn
Artistic Director . . . . Rod Ceballos
Office Manager . . . . Jeana McClure
Publicity Director . . . . Robin Smith
Box Office . . . . Renae Knapp
Cencessions . . . . Maria Lewis
Marketing Intern . . . . Deanna McWhirter

Board of Directors

Glenn Selander, President
Mello Dee Thornton, Vice President
Brent Lloyd, Secretary
William Keller, Treasurer
Candice Allphin
James Brandstetter
Colin Cannon
Dr. Charles Davis
Roxanne Jensen
Brian King
Don Lojek
Richard McChrystal
Doug Oppenheimer
Mary Puccio
Bonnie Quinn
Dick Steele
Scott Tunnell
Carolyn Bancroft, Recording Secretary

1990

Merry Wives of Windsor

Director . . . . Cynthia White
Scenic Design . . . . Micheal Baltzell
Costume Design . . . . Ted Barnard
Lighting . . . . Robert Parsley
Sound Designer/Composer . . . . Pete Weaver

A Woman of Means
By R.N. Sandberg

Director . . . . Penny Metropulos
Scenic Design . . . . Micheal Baltzell
Costume Design . . . . Christina Rosendaul
Lighting . . . . Robert Parsley
Composer/Music Director . . . . Joseph Weisnewski
Lyricist . . . . R. N. Sandberg

Merchant of Venice

Director . . . . David Hay
Scenic Design . . . . Micheal Baltzell
Costume Design . . . . Paula Davis
Lighting . . . . Robert Parsley
Sound Designer/Composer . . . . Pete Weaver

Henry VIII

Director . . . . Rod Ceballos
Scenic Design . . . . Micheal Baltzell
Costume Design . . . . Lisa A. Vollrath
Lighting . . . . Robert Parsley
Composer/Music Director . . . . Joseph Weisnewski

Acting Company

Merry Wives of Windsor; A Woman of Means; Merchant of Venice; Henry VIII

Anna Affleck	–; Fiddle Player; –; –
Rick Anderson	Shallow; –; Gobbo; Lord; Chancellor
Bill Arbogast	Dr. Caius; –; –; Lovell, Dancer
Kim Ataide	Quickly; –; –; Patience
Ronald Bashford	Simple; Joe; –; Campeius
Jordan Berlant	Fenton; –; Lorenzo; Gent 1, Vision
J. Paul Boehmer	Slender; –; Bassanio; Gardiner
Rod Ceballos	–; –; Shylock; –
Warren Cegleck	–; Guitar, Banjo; –; –
Sean Coleman	Nym; –; –; Surrey
Susan Coromel	Mrs. Ford; –; Lil Katherine
Raylene Dodson	Anne's Friend; –; Attendant; –; Dancer, Lady
John Farrange	–; Smith; Morocco; Griffith
Michael Goldberg	Robert; –; Soanio; Surveyor/ Butts Dr.
Julie Greenberg	–; Starr; Nerissa; Lady, Dancer, Vis.
Scott Hayes	–; Harry; Salerio; Sands, Dancer, Vis.
Christina Lang	–; –; Portia; Old Lady, Dancer
Mikel MacDonald	Falstaff; Scotch; –; Henry
Stitch Marker	Pistol; –; Antonio; Norfolk
Michael M. Marlin	John; –; Tubal; Capuchius; Gent 2
Susan Murdoch	Mrs. Page; –; Jessica; Lady; Dancer, Vis.
Sean O'Shea	Host; –; Gratiano; Suffolk
Dan Peterson	Ford; –; Stephano; Cranmer
Susan Phillips	Musician, Lute; – Musician; Musician, Lady
Michael Pocaro	Page; –; Arrogon; Buckingham/ Linc.
Berta Jo Smith	–; Bass Player; –; –
Christ Thometz	–; –; –; Abergav/ Gent 3
Anne Marie Tremko	Anne Page; Kate; –; Ann Bullen/ Vis.
William Westenberg	Rugby; –; Duke; Lord Chamberlain
William Wood	Bardolph; –; Launcelot; Cromwell
Tracy Young	Evans; Steele; –; Wolsey

Rick Anderson
Mindee Clem
Esther de Veuve
Raylene Dodson
Mark Learned
Heather Munday
Jonathan Neches
Michael Pocaro
Ryan Richards
Adam Toothaker
Andrew Wyke

Magnificoes, Officers, Jailers, Servants, and other Attendants Ladies, Pages, Attendants, Spirits in Queen Katherine's vision

Production

Assistant Director – *Merchant* . . . . Stacey Spain
Production Stage Manager . . . . Becky Brizee
Stage Mangers . . . . Lisa Marie Flegel
Jeffrey Jones
Jason Lowry (assistant) . . . .
Technical Director . . . . Micheal Baltzell
Michael Hartwell (assistant) . . . .
Master Carpenter . . . . Robert E. Riddle, Sr.
Carpenters: Michael Fegley; BJ Weber
Electricians . . . . Pamela Parker
Shaun Sites . . . .
Costume Shop Supervisor . . . . Robert Haven
Crafts . . . . Christina Rosendaul
Props . . . . Lisa Abbe
Crafts/Props Assistant . . . . Sydney Anderson
Cutter . . . . Laney D'Aquino
Stitchers: Elizabeth Bloukos; Jinny DeFoggi; Chelsie Richter; Judith A. Senk; Sally Thomas; Lee Woods
Wigs – Make-up . . . . Nancy Doi
Wardrobe . . . . Debbie Brigante
Nikki Shell . . . .
Technical Intern . . . . Tamara Cameron
Dressers: Laurel DeFoggi; Josh Howard; Megan Hutchinson; Halle Longeteig

Administration

General Manager . . . . Vangie Osborn
Artistic Director . . . . Rod Ceballos
Administrative Assistant . . . . Jay Sherlock
Publicity Director . . . . Jennifer Russell
Box Office . . . . Renae Knapp
Concessions . . . . Peter Lablanc
Administrative Intern . . . . Stacey Spain
Souvenir Program Design and Execution . . . . . Jennifer Russell
Souvenir Program Cover . . . . Bethann Anderson
Souvenir Program Cover Graphics . . . . . Jeffrey Conger
Sperling Guy & Associates . . . .
Souvenir Program Photographer . . . . David Bogie
Souvenir Program Advertising Sales . . . Jeana McClure
Jennifer Russell . . . .

Board of Directors

Glenn Selander, President
Mello Dee Thornton, Vice President
Brent Lloyd, Secretary
William Keller, Treasurer
Candice Allphin
Mike Bessent
Dr. E. Manley Briggs
Colin Cannon
Dr. Charles Davis
Everett Halfhide
Jim Hansen
Brian King
Doug Oppenheimer
Mary Puccio
Sandra Shook
Dick Steele
Carolyn Bancroft, Recording Secretary

1991

The Tempest

Director . . . . Doug Copsey
Scenic Design . . . . Micheal Baltzell
Costume Design . . . . Christina Rosendaul
Lighting . . . . Robert Parsley
Sound . . . . Joseph Weisnewski

Twelfth Night

Director . . . . Paul Frellick
Scenic Design . . . . Michael Hartwell
Costume Design . . . . Ted Barnard
Lighting . . . . Robert Parsley
Sound . . . . Joseph Weisnewski

Spring Awakening
by Frank Wedekind, translated and adapted for the American stage by Rick Foster

Director .... Dennis Bigelow
Scenic Design .... Micheal Baltzell
Costume Design .... Debra Bruneaux
Lighting .... Deborah Penrod
Sound .... Joseph Weisnewski

Macbeth

Director .... Kenneth Kelleher
Scenic Design .... Micheal Baltzell
Costume Design .... Ron Erickson
Lighting .... Deborah Penrod
Sound .... Joseph Weisnewski

Acting Company

The Tempest; Twelfth Night; Spring Awakening; Macbeth

Tony Carreiro*	–; –; –; Macbeth
Sean Coleman	Ferdinand; Orsino; –; Young Siward; Apparitian/ Attendant
Kevin Connell	–; Preacher/ Sailor; Herr Gabor/ Sunprick/ Locksmith/ Masked ManRoss
Susan Coromel	Juno; –; Frau Gabor/Pudgycudgel; Lady Macbeth
Jamie Dugger	–; –; Robert / Toungebeat/Ruprecht; –
Kelley Dunn	–; ViolaMartha; 3rd Witch
Kevin Fabian	–; Aguecheek; Hans Rilow/ Reinhold; Malcolm
John Farrage	Alonso; Fabian; –; Banquo/Soldier
Debbie Funkhouser	Miranda; –; Wendla Bergmann; Gentlewoman
Lorenzo Gonzalez	–; Sebastian; Moritz Stiefel/ Pastor; Baldgut; Donalbain/ Soldier/Apparitian
Seth Jacobs	Master; Sea Captain/ Officer; –; Macduff
Rob H. Kimmel	Sebastian; –; Georg/ Flypaper/ Gaston; Angus
Stitch Marker	Stephano; Malvolio; Herr Stiefel/ Slitherquick/ Dr. Fizzwater; –
Susan Murdoch	–; Olivia; Frau Bergmann/ Hungergut; 1st Witch
Dan Peterson	Prospero; –; –; –
Ron Richardson	Antonio; Sailor/ Officer; ; Bloody Captain/ Dr/ Attendant/ Apparitian
Erika Rolfsrud	Ariel; –; Ina Mueller/ Bonebreak; Lady Macduff
James Matthew Ryan	–; Antonio; Otto/ Helmuth/ Mother Schmidt; Lennox
Martie Sanders	–; Maria; Ilse/ Dr. Cutitoff; 2nd Witch
Jay Sherlock	Gonzalo; –; –; Old Man
Ty Smith	Mariner; Toby Belch; –; Duncan/ Siward
Travis Swartz	Mariner; –; Melchior Gabor; –
Kevin Warren	Caliban; Feste; –; Menteith
Rod Wolfe	Trinculo; Valentine; –; Caithnes/ Apparitian/ Soldier/ Attendant
Tracy Young	Boatswain; –; Ernst/ Diethelm; Seyton/ Porter/ Messenger
Kelly Miller	Ceres; –; –; –
Kate Shea	Iris; –; –; –
Erin Clem	
Mindee Clem	
Megan Marchetti	
Heather Munday	
Ryan Richards	Spirits
Scott Learned	
Jeremy Miltenberger	Mariners; Curio
Warren Ceglecki	
Amy Nelson	Musicians
Estella Fairbanks	
Scott Learned	
Ryan Richards	Gentlemen, Officers, Soldiers,

Murderers, Attendants, Messengers, the Ghost of Banquo, and other Apparitions

Production

Assistant Director – *The Tempest* .... Jamie Dugger
Assistant Director – *Twelfth Night* .... Travis Swartz
Assistant Director – *Macbeth* .... Stacey Spain
Stage Managers: .... Carol Charles; Becky Brizee
Assistant Stage Managers: ..... Eve Hilgenberg; Jamie Dugger; Jennifer Russell
Technical Director .... Micheal Baltzell
Assistant Technical Director .... Michael Hartwell
Production Manager .... Jeffrey Jones
Production Assistant .... Jennifer Russell
Master Carpenter/Shop Foreman.. Robert E. Riddle, Sr.
Master Electrician/Carpenter .... Shaun Sites
Carpenter .... Peggy Atkingson
Carpenter .... Tamera Cameron
Costume Shop Manager .... Ted Barnard
Cutter/Draper .... Nancy Berger
Stitchers: Cheryl Adox; Jinny DeFoggi; Laurelel Horton; Crystal Powers
Stitcher/Assistant Crafts .... Pauline Smith
Stitcher .... Sally Thomas
Wardrobe: Nickie Shell; Lynn Sims
Wigs/Make-up .... Nancy Doi
Make-up .... Manuel Flores
Dresser .... Laurel DeFoggi
Dresser .... Halle Longteig
Props .... Andrew D'zmura
Crafts .... Christina Rosendaul
Assistant Crafts .... Pauline Smith
Translator/Adaptor – *Spring Awakening* ..... Rick Foster
Movement Coach/Choreographer ..... Rebecca Stone
Apprentices: Erin Clem; Mindee Clem; Scott Learned; Megan Marchetti; Kelly Ann Miller; Jeremy Ann Miller; Jeremy Miltenberger; Heather Munday; Ryan Richards; Kate Shea; Karen Silvester; Amy Zuroeveste
Other Players .... Warren Ceglecki, Musician
Amy Nelson, Musician
Rian Riddle, Actor

Administration

General Manager .... Vangie Osborn
Photographer .... David Bogie
Box Office .... Susan Boyd
Concessions .... Connie Hopkins
Box Office .... Renae Knapp
Marketing Publicity Director .... Peter Lablanc

Board of Directors

Mello Dee Thornton, President
Dr. Charles Davis, Vice President
Bill Keller, Treasurer
Candice Allphin, Secretary
Carolyn Bancroft, Recording Secretary
Mike Bessent
Dr. Manley Briggs
Colin Cannon
Michael Fery
Everett Halfhide
Jim Hansen
Arthur B. Lane
Richard McChrystal
Doug Oppenheimer
Sandra Shook
Ray E. Smith
Dick Steele

1992

Romeo and Juliet

Director .... Charles Fee
Scenic Design .... Micheal Baltzell
Costume Design .... Ron Erickson
Lighting .... Shaun Sites
Composer/Sound .... Peter Still

The Taming of the Shrew

Director .... Barry Edelstein
Scenic Design .... Micheal Baltzell
Costume Design .... Ted Barnard
Lighting .... Shaun Sites
Sound .... Peter Still

Richard III

Director .... Bartlett Sher
Scenic Design .... Deborah L. Jensen
Costume Design .... Kim Krumm Sorenson
Lighting .... Shaun Sites
Composer/Sound .... Peter Still

Scapino!
By Frank Dunlop and Jim Dale

Director .... Dale "AJ" Rose
Scenic Design .... Deborah L. Jensen
Costume Design .... Clare Henkel
Lighting .... Shaun Sites
Composer/Sound .... Peter Still

Acting Company:

Romeo & Juliet; The Taming of the Shrew; Richard III; Scapino!

Tina Marie Abas	Ensemble; Bridesmaid; Ensemble; –
Peter Burford	–; Fireman/ Petruchio's Servant; Ensemble; –
Anthony Casper	Balthasar; Fireman/ Petruchio's Servant; Murderer/ Blunt
Franz Elizondo	Ensemble; –; Ensemble; –
Daniel Foley	Friar Laurence/ Chorus; Gremio/Tailor;Edward IV; –
Joseph Golden	Gregory; Lucentio; Stanley; Leondro
Andrew Harkins	Paris; –; Ratcliffe; Ottavio
Brad Heberlee	Ensemble; Fireman/
Petruchio's	Servant; Lord Grey; Carolo
Don Hiatt	–; –; –; Scapino
Terry Hoff	–; Ensemble; Bridesmaid; Ensemble; –
Dave Knapp	Apothecary; Biondello; –; –
Stitch Marker	Peter; Tenor (Pedant); Lovell; Sylvestro
Brian T. McCarthy	Friar John; Fireman/ Petruchio's; Servant; Dorset; Waiter
Sheri Novak	Lady Montague; Bridesmaid; Ensemble; –
Colin O'Connor	Sampson; Curtis/ Fireman; Richmond/ Archbishop of York; Waiter
Katherine Patmont	Ensemble; –; Mistress Shore; –
Martha Perantoni	–; –; Elizabeth; Zerbinetta
Alex Robertson	Abram; Grumio; Ensemble; –
Ted Rooney	Prince; Hortensio; Buckingham; Geronte
Mhari Sandoval	Juliet; Bianca; Lady Anne; Giacinta
Triney Sandoval	Romeo; Tranio; Rivers/Tyrell; Nurse
Jay Sherlock	Montague; Vincentio; Ely/ Brackenbury/ Lord Mayor; –
Marcel Shipman	Nurse; Widow; Duchess of York; Waitress
Thaddeus Smith	Benvolio; Christopher Sly; Hastings; Head Waiter
Ty Smith	Capulet; Baptista; Clarence/ Catesby; Argante

Janis Stevens — Lady Capulet; Kate; Queen Margaret;
Steve Tague — Mercutio; –; Richard III; Robert Titlow; Cardinal; –
Austin Hunt
Rian Riddle
David Cardoza. — Other Actors

<u>Production</u>

Dramaturg .... Rick Foster
Equity Stage Manager .... Margaret J. Soch
Stage Manager .... Laura Sims
Assistant Stage Managers: ... Carolyn Koch; Kathleen Sigelman
Assistant Technical Director .... Michael Hartwell
Production Manager .... Robert Titlow
Technical Assistant .... Jeremy Miltenberger
Carpenters: Jarett Bertoncin; Bob Parsley
Cutter .... Nancy Berger
Stitchers: Cheryl Adox; Kristen Castillo; Jinny DeFoggi; Kira Gray; Laurelei Horton
Fight Choreographer .... Dexter Fidler
Crafts .... Laurelei Horton
Hair .... Nancy Doi
Wardrobe: Halle Longeteig; Nickie Shell; Lynn Sims
Props Master .... Angela Conte
Apprentices: Will Hoppins; Lisa Kerrick; Timothy C. Knox; Tony Lowe; Kim Mosier; Shawna Sherburn; Tony Vega; Joshua Webb; Karen Wennstrom; Amy Zuroeveste

<u>Administration</u>

Artistic Director .... Charles Fee
General Manager .... Vangie Osborn
Marketing Director .... Peter Leblanc
Box Office .... Shanon Sale
Administrative Assistant .... Kevin Peterson
Box Office .... Renae Knapp
Concessions .... Connie Hopkins
Administrative Intern .... Katherine Patmont
Program Design and Layout .... Robin Bergin and Peter LeBlanc
Cover Design .... Tereasa Guy, Sperling Guy & Associates
Cover Photo and Illustration .... Mark Lisk
Advertising Sales .... Renee Morse
Photographer .... David Bogie
Printing .... Joslyn & Morris, Inc. Lithoprinters
Program Entry ... Carolyn Wolfe, Kevin Peterson, and many others

<u>Board of Directors</u>

Dr. Charles Davis, President
Candice Allphin, Vice President
Ray E. Smith, Secretary
Bill Keller, Treasurer
Mike Bessent
Colin Cannon
Michael Fery
Sandy L.S. Fery
John Glaza
Everett Halfhide
Jim Hansen
Jill Kuraitis
Arthur B. Lane
A. K. Leinhart
Richard McChrystal
Doug Oppenheimer
Dick Steele
Mello Dee Thornton
Carolyn Bancroft, Recording Secretary

1993

Quilters
By Molly Newman and Barbara Damashek

Director .... Theresa Larkin
Scenic Design .... Micheal Baltzell
Costume Design .... Star Moxley
Lighting .... Shaun Sites
Musical Director .... Michael Koerner

A Midsummer Night's Dream

Director .... Kirk Boyd
Scenic Design .... Deborah L. Jensen
Costume Design .... Kim Krumm Sorenson
Lighting .... Rick Martin
Composer and Sound Designer .... Peter Still

Tartuffe
by Moliere

Director .... Charles Fee
Scenic Design .... Deborah L. Jensen
Costume Design .... Kim Krumm Sorenson
Lighting .... Rick Martin
Composer and Sound Designer .... Peter Still

The Comedy of Errors

Director .... Barry Edelstein
Scenic Design .... Narelle Sissons
Costume Design .... Rafi Mercado
Lighting .... Rick Martin
Composer and Sound Designer .... Peter Still

<u>Acting Company</u>

Quilters; Midsummer; Tartuffe; Comedy of Errors

Lynn Allison — Daughter; –; –; Emilia
Philip Atlakson — –; Starveling;–; –
Anthony Casper — –; Snout; – ; Merchant
Kathleen Clancy — Helena; Dorine; Adriana
Susan Coromel — Daughter: –; –; –
Kathryn Estep — Daughter; –; –; –
Carol Flanders — Daughter; –; –; –
Knekoh Fruge — Daughter; –; Flipote; –
Joseph Golden — –; Lysander; –; Dromio of Syracuse
Michael Hacker — –; Philostrate; –; Jailer
Richard Klautsch* — –; Oberon;/Theseus; Orgon; –
Nancy Lee-Painter — Daughter; –; –; –
Brian Linden — –; Flute; –; –\
Stitch Marker — Prairie Man; –; Madame Pernelle; Dr. Pinch/Solinus
Sheri Novak — –; Moth; –; Courtesan
Dan Peterson — –; –; –; Egeon
Heather Lea Pool — –; Peaseblossom; –; Nun
Diane Ragsdale — –; –; –; Angelo
Toni Rayborn — –; Cobweb; –; Nun
Mhari Sandoval — –; Hermia; Mariane; Luciana
Triney Sandoval — –; Puck; Damis; Dromio of Ephesus
Jennifer Schapiro — Daughter; –; –; –
Ty Smith — –; Peter Quince; Cleante; Antipholus of Syracuse
Janice Stevens* — –; Titania/Hippolyta; Elmire; Luciana
Michael Surabian — –; Snug; –; Merchant
Steve Tague* — –; Bottom; Tartuffe; Antipholus of Ephesus
Karen Wennstrom — –; Mustardseed; –; Nun
Carole Whiteleather* — Sarah McKendree Bonham; –; –; –
Tom Willmorth — –; Demetrius; Valere; –
Warren Ceglecki
John Cochrane
Berta Jo Smith — Musicians

<u>Production</u>

Equity Stage Manager .... Margaret J. Soch
Stage Manager .... Karen Fernandez
Assistant Stage Managers: Jenny Lynn Elmore; Lynn . Sims
Technical Director .... Micheal Baltzell
Asst. Technical Director .... Scott Cavin
Master Carpenter .... Monica R. Coburn
Carpenters: .... James Chesick; John Hadley
Props Artisan .... Stacey Spain
Assistant Props Artisan .... Megan Marchetti
Technical Intern: .... Andrew Ellis; Kristy Martin
Costume Shop Manager .... Nancy Berger
Assistant Costume Shop Manager .... Dagny Haug
Crafts Artisan, Cutter .... Christina Rosendaul
Stitchers: Cheryl Adcox; Jinny DeFoggi; Dianna Kay Slade; Maxine Waite
Hair and Wig Coordinator .... Odell England
Hair and Make-up Coordinator .... Shirley Hurley
Wardrobe: Kristen Castillo; Nickie Shell
Dance/Movement Choreographers: Marla Brittain; Hansen; Alfred Hansen; Carl Rowe
Fight Choreographer .... Dexter Fidler
Dramaturg .... Rick Roster
Rehearsal Pianist .... Betsy Brunner
Assistant Director – *Quilters* .... April Scott-Goss
Assistant Director – *The Comedy of Errors* .... Kim Todd
Apprentices: Tamara Bauman; Vanessa Ferrell; Chad Matheson; Nicole Michel; Erin Miller; Kimo Muraki; Chris "Dutch" Olson; Terese Reynolds

<u>Administration</u>

Artistic Director .... Charles Fee
Managing Director .... Mark Hofflund
Director of Marketing and Publicity .... Peter Leblanc
Box Office Manager .... Hillary L. D. Gorrell
House Manager .... Kim Todd
Concessionaire .... Marie Helene Peterson
Marketing Assistant .... Rob Bergin
Box Office Assistant .... Marc Malone
Receptionists: .... Kristen Castillo; Heather Farber

<u>Board of Directors</u>

Candice Allphin, President
Ray E. Smith, Vice President
James D. Hansen, Secretary
Bill Keller, Treasurer
Brad Andrews
Mike Bessent
Jamie Dater
Dr. Charles Davis
Sandra Fery
John A. Glaza
Everett Halfhide
Michael Hoffman
Grove Hummert
Jill Kuraitis
Arthur B. Lane
A. K. Leinhart
Richard McChrystal
Tom Nunamaker
Doug Oppenheimer
Dr. Bruce Robbins
Dick Steele
Odette Sutton
Carolyn Bancroft, Recording Secretary

1994

Dancing at Lughnasa
By Brian Friel

Director .... Joan Robbins
Scenic Design .... Micheal Baltzell
Costume Design .... Ann Hoste
Lighting .... Rick Martin
Sound Design and Musical Coordinator .... Peter John Still

Much Ado About Nothing

Director .... Charles Fee
Scenic Design .... Gage Williams
Costume Design .... Star Moxley
Lighting .... Rick Martin
Music and Sound Design .... Peter John Still

Julius Caesar

Director .... Anne Justine D'Zmura
Scenic Design and Costume Design .... Nephelie Andonyadis
Lighting .... Rick Martin
Composer and Sound Designer .... Peter John Still

As You Like It

Director .... Bartlett Sher
Scenic Design .... Jack Balance
Costume Design .... Kim Krumm Sorenson
Lighting .... Marcus Dilliard
Additional Music and Sound Design .. Peter John Still

Acting Company

Dancing at Lughnasa; Much Ado; Julius Caesar; As You Like It

* Casting information incomplete for this season.

Lynn Allison	Chris; –; –; –
Danny Camiel	–; Claudio; –; –
Susan Coromel	Agnes; –; Calphurnia; –
Ted Deasy	Gerry; –; Casca; Amien
Debra England	Kate; –; –; –
Kristin Flanders*	–; –; –; Rosalind
Jim Fisk	–; Balthasar; –; Charles
Deb Funkhouser	–; Hero; –; Phebe
Joseph Golden	–; Verges; –; Silvius
Michael Hacker	–; Borachio; Caesar; Duke Frederick/Duke Senior
Amber Hartley	–; –; –; –
Matthew Hoverman	–; –; –; –
Arthur Glenn Hughes	Michael; –; –; –
JoAnn Johnson*	Maggie; –; –; –
Richard Klautsch*	–; Don Pedro; Marcus Brutus; Touchstone
Matthew Letscher	–; –; Mark Anthony; Orlando
Stitch Marker	–; Don John; Cicero; Sir Oliver Martext
Louise Moore	Rose; –; –; –
Ray Newton	–; –; –; –
Dan Peterson	Jack; Antonio; Lepidus; –
Matthew Richards	–; Friar Francis; –; LeBeau
Michael Roberts	–; Lord; –; Dennis
Dana Slamp	–; Margaret; Cinna; Audrey
Michael Surabian	–; –; Cimber; –
Kathleen Tague*	–; Beatrice; Portia; Celia
Steve Tague*	–; Benedick; Cassius; Jaques
Mark Anthony Taylor	–; –; Popilus; –
Greg Watanabe	–; –; –; –
Karen Wennstrom	–; Ursula; –; –
Tom Willmorth	–; Dogberry; Publius; –

Production

Assistant Director – *Dancing at Lughnasa* ... Mike Steele
Assistant Director – *Julius Caesar* .... Mike Steele
Equity Stage Manager .... Margaret J. Soch
Stage Managers: Tamara Cameron; Karen Fernandez
Assistant Stage Managers: Toni Guffey; Jill Snyder
Technical Director .... Michael Hartwell
Technical Interns: .... Kristy Martin; Kimo Muraki
Master Carpenter .... James Chesick
Master Electrician .... Shaun Sites
Electrician .... Tim Knox
Carpenter .... John Hadley
Costume Shop Manager .... Nancy Berger
Stitchers: Jinny DeFoggi; Lito-John Demitita; Sharla McAndrew; Bonnie Preacher
Assistant Crafts .... Michelle Tolub
Assistant Cutter .... Rebecca A. Williams
Wardrobe: Debra Bogie; Kritin Castillo; Megan Marchetti; Nickie Shell
Craftsperson .... Anne Hoste
Hair and Make-up Design .... Shirley Hurley
Props Artisan .... Gavin Thompson
Props Assistant .... Jodi Nelson
Running Crew .... Dano Madden
Fight Choreographer .... Dexter Fidler
Movement and Dance Choreographer ..... Carl Rowe
Dialect Coach .... Ann Klautsch
Dramaturg .... Rick Foster
Circus Techniques .... Lane Thomas
Apprentices: Ira Amyx; Nathan Bainbridge; Urusula A. Bartels; Scott Duff; Joe Fairbanks; Nicholas Fouch; Maria Headley; Rich Heist; Rachel Hunt; Kate Milette; Kimo Muraki; Pamela Wiensz

Administration

Artistic Director .... Charles Fee
Managing Director .... Mark Hofflund
Box Office Assistant .... Betsy Lloyd
Box Office Managers:.. Kristen Castillo; Diane Ragsdale
Concessionaire .... Shannon Smith
Development Intern .... Stephanie Hunt
Director of Marketing and Publicity .... Peter Leblanc
Educational Outreach Coordinator ... Helene Peterson
House Managers: ...... Brad Hunt; Linda Byron; Kelly Duklet
Publicity Intern .... Stephanie Leavitt

Board of Directors

Ray E. Smith, President
A.K. Lienhart-Minnick, Vice President
James D. Hansen, Secretary
Mike Bessent & William Keller, Treasurers
Candice Allphin
Brad Andrews
Tina Bess
Jamie Dater
Dr. Charles Davis
Dana Divin
Sandra Fery
John A. Glaza
Michael Hoffman
Grove Hummert
Arthur B. Lane
Richard McChrystal
Tom Nunamaker
Dr. Bruce Robbins
Odette Sutton
Henry W. Taylor, Jr.
Carolyn Bancroft, Recording Secretary

1995

Two Gentlemen of Verona

Director .... Anne Justine D'Zmura
Scenic Design .... Jack Ballance
Costume Design .... Elizabeth Hope Clancy
Lighting .... Rick Martin
Composer and Sound Designer .... Peter John Still

Love's Labours Lost

Director .... Bartlett Sher
Scenic Design .... Jack Ballance
Costume Design .... Alec Hammond
Lighting .... Rick Martin
Composer and Sound Designer .... Peter John Still

The First Part of King Henry the Fourth

Director .... Charles Fee with Rick Foster
Scenic Design .... Gage Williams
Costume Design .... Ann Hoste
Lighting .... Rick Martin
Composer and Sound Designer .... Peter John Still

The Second Part of King Henry the Fourth

Director .... Rick Foster with Charles Fee
Scenic Design .... Gage Williams
Costume Design .... Ann Hoste
Lighting .... Rick Martin
Composer and Sound Designer .... Peter John Still

Acting Company

Casting information incomplete for this season

The Two Gentlemen of Verona; Love's Labours Lost; The First Part of Henry IV; The Second Part of Henry IV

James Anderson	–; Sir Nathaniel; Walter Blunt; –
James Asher	–; Moth; –; –
Matthew Clark	Outlaw; –; Colville; Colville
Sean Coleman	Panthino/Outlaw; –; Poins; Poins
Paul de Cordova	Outlaw; –; Thomas of Clarence; Thomas of Clarence
David Dollase*	–; Don Armado; Lord Percy/Hotspur; earl of Northumberland
Jaque Drew	Lucetta; –; –; Doll Tearsheet
Sally Eames	Ursula; –; –; –
James Fisk	–; –; –; Bullcalf
John H. H. Ford	–; Ferdinand; Archibald, Earl of Douglas; Lord Hastings
Mark Fossen	Thurio; –; Scroop, Archbishop of York; Scroop, Archbishop of York/Pistol
Joe Golden	Valentine; –; Westmorland; Silence
Michael Hacker	–; Holofernes; Mortimer; Rumor
Peter Hadres*	–;Longaville; –; Lord Chief Justice
Tina Jones	Sylvia; Maria; Lady Percy; Lady Percy
Richard Klautsch*	–; Boyet; King Henry IV; King Henry IV
Eric Liddell	–; Dumaine; Prince John of Landcaster; Lord Mowbray
Stitch Marker	Antonio; –; Henry Percy; Shallow
Karla Mason	–; Princess of France; –; –
Doug Miller	–; Berowne; Prince of Wales; Henry V
Doyne Mraz	Duke of Milan; –;–; Earl of Warwick
Ollie Nash*	–; –; Falstaff; Falstaff
Erin Neill	–; Katherine; –; –
Dan Peterson	–; Dull; Bardolph; Bardolph
Rebecca Prescott	–; Jaquenetta; Lady Mortimer; –
Matthew Ramsey	Outlaw; –; Vernon; Shadow
Samuel Read	Eglamour; Marcade; –; Mouldy
Mike Ryan	Proteus; –; Humphrey of Gloucester; Francis
Ty Smith	–; –; Glendower; Gower
Dana Slamp	Julia; –; –; Falstaff's Page
Mark Anthony Taylor	Speed; –; Peto; Peto/Wart
Tom Willmorth	Launce; Costard; –; –
Shana Wride	–; Rosaline; Mistress Quickly; Mistress Quickly

Production

Equity Stage Manager .... Jennifer Kimball
Stage Managers: .. Mary Cummins; Brenna St. George Jones; Gretchen Lynn Wingerter
Assistant Stage Manager .... Jill Snyder
Technical Director .... Shaun Sites
Technical Assistant .... Tim Knox
Scenic Artist .... Carol Carson
Carpenter: Nicholas Fouch; Kurt Hammes; Elliott Hansen; Stuart Schatz
Electricians: Scott Duff; Ryan Richards
Technical Interns: Erich Hamm; Amber Herdich; Rachel Hunt
Costume Shop Manager .... Nancy Berger
Costume Crafts .... Rebecca Hoffman
Stitchers: Jinny DeFoggi; Lito-John Demetita; Sharla McAndrew; Sally Thomas
Assistant Cutter .... Rebecca A. Williams
Costume Shop Interns: ... Julia Berger; Maria Headley
Wardrobe Mistress: Debra Bogie; Lisa Lassis-Skosberg; Susan Lawrence;
Dresser .... Hannah Read
Hair Design .... Shirley Hurley
Wig Design .... Marsha Knipple
Props Master .... David Hoth
Props Assistant .... Deb Bogie
Fight Choreographer .... Dexter Fidler
Movement and Dance Choreographer .... Carl Rowe
Dialect and Vocal Coach .... Ann Klautsch

Dramaturgy ....Rick Foster; Christina Sibul
Assistant Director, *Henry IV 1st Part and 2nd Part* ....Dexter Fidler
Directing Assistant ....Flint Weisser
Apprentice Advisors: Lynn Hofflund; Stitch Marker
Apprentices: Sarah Anderson; Belynda Starr Hubler; Jarrett Hult; Jennifer Knighton; Kate Millet; Lisa Peacock; Tamera Portrey; Jill Seetin; Allen Traylor; Jennifer Todd; Chad Winks

Administration

Artistic Director ....Charles Fee
Managing Director ....Mark Hofflund
Box Office Managers: Dwayne Blackaller; Renae Knapp
Director of Marketing ....Kristen Robertson
Education Outreach Coordinator ....Helene Peterson
House Manager ....Stephanie Hunt
Box Office Assistant ....Dano Madden

Board of Directors

William Keller, President
Brad Andrews, Vice President
Jamie H. Dater, Secretary
Mike Bessent, Treasurer
Tiane Bess
Dr. Charles Davis
Sandra L.S. Fery
John A. Glaza
Michael Hoffman
Grove Hummert
Arthur B. Lane
A. K. Leinhart-Minnick
Richard McChrystal
Pamela F. Meals
Royanne Minskoff
Tom Nunamaker
Dr. Bruce Robbins
Judith Kish Ruud
Ray E. Smith
Odette Sutton
Henry W. Taylor, Jr.
Carolyn Bancroft, Recording Secretary

1996

The Complete Works of William Shakespeare (Abridged) By Jess Borgeson, Adam Long and Daniel Singer

Director ....Charles Fee
Scenic Design ....Gage Williams
Costume Design ....Rebecca Hoffman
Lighting ....Rick Martin
Sound Designer ....Peter John Still

The Merry Wives of Windsor

Director ....Sari Ketter
Scenic Design ....Jack Ballance
Costume Design ....Kim Krumm Sorenson
Lighting ....Rick Martin
Sound Designer ....Peter John Still

The Tempest

Director ....Bartlett Sher
Scenic Design ....Alec Hammond
Costume Design ....Kim Krumm Sorenson
Lighting ....Rick Martin
Composer ....Peter John Still

Twelfth Night

Director ....Charles Fee
Scenic Design ....Gage Williams
Costume Design ....Star Moxley
Lighting ....Rick Martin
Sound Designer ....Peter John Stil

Acting Company

Complete Works; Merry Wives; The Tempest; Twelfth Night

Blake Abramovitz	–; Nym; Master of the Ship/Mariner/ Spirit; Officer/ Sailors/ Attendants
Karl Allen	–; John; –; –
Drew F. Brhel*	–; Sir Falstaff; –; –
Sara Bruner	–; Robin; Miranda; –
Danny Camiel	–; Abraham Slender; Sebatian; Valentine
Randy Davison	–; John Rugby; Francisco;
Officer/	Sailors/ Attendants
Craig Franson	–; Pistol; Boatswain/ Mariner/ Spirit; Officer/ Sailors/ Attendants
Daniel Garton	–; Peter Simple; Ferdinand; –
Mark Gladue	–; Host of the Garter Inn
Mariner/ Spirit	Officer/ Sailors/ Attendants
Joe Conley Golden*	Cast; –; Trinculo; Sebastian
Kelli Kerslake	–; Mistress Quickly; –; Olivia
Naomi Kingsbury	Dancer
Richard Klautsch*	–; Francis Ford; Antonio; Sir Toby; Belch
Christina Lang	–; Mistress Page; –; Maria
Michelle Lockhart	–; Kate; Mariner/ Spirit; –
Dano Madden	–; Robert; –; –
Stitch Marker	–; Justice Shallow; Alonso; Antonio
Danan Pere*	–; George Page; Caliban; Orsino
Dan Peterson	Cast; Bardolph; –; Sea Captain/ Priest
Rebecca Prescott	–; Anne Page; Ariel; –
Matthew Ramsey	–; Fenton; Adrian; Curio
Nick Sceirine	–; William Page; –; –
Ty Smith	–; Sir Evans; Gonzalo; Feste
Kathleen Tague*	–; Mistress Ford; –; Viola
Steve Tague*	–; –; Prospero; Malvolio
Mark Anthony Taylor	–; Doctor Caius
Mariner/ Spirit;	Fabian
Tom Willmorth	Cast; –; Stephano; Sir Andrew; Aguecheek
Erin Cunningham	
Blythe Staley	
Chad Winks	Townspeople

Production

Equity Stage Manager ....Brenna St. George Jones
Stage Managers ....Megan Kelly
Stage Manager Interns: Scott Blades; Lisa Kerrick; Emilie Woodbridge
Directing Intern ....Dano Madden
Technical Director ....Shaun Sites
Technical Assistant ....Elliott Hansen
Sound Engineer ....Tim Knox
Scenic Artist: Scott Gerwitz; Jessica Wade
Master Electrician ....Penny Lippert
Carpenter: Kimo Muraki; Daina Sites
Scenic Intern: Jarrett Hult; Eric Wiesemann
Electrics Intern ....Sheila Kole
Hair Design ....Shirley Hurley
Wig Design ....Marsha Knipple
Costume Shop Manager ....Nancy Berger
Costume Crafts ....Rebecca Hoffman
Stitchers: Jinny DeFoggi; Lito-John Demetita; Fairy Hitchcock; Sharla McAndrew;
Costume Shop Interns: Michelle Allred; Carrie Jones Kietra King;
Wardrobe Mistress: Susan Lawrence; Hannah Read
Dresser: Julia Berger; Bill Bowes
Props Master ....Nicholas Fouch
Props Intern ....Belynda Hubler
Fight Choreographer ....Dexter Fidler
Movement and Dance Choreographer .....Carl Rowe
Dialect and Vocal Coach ....Ann Klautsch

Administration

Artistic Director ....Charles Fee
Managing Director ....Mark Hofflund
Director of Marketing ....Kristen Robertson
Education Outreach Coordinator ....Helene Peterson
Box Office Managers: Shelly Krois; Carrie Shanafelt
House Manager ....Leah Stephens
Concessions Manager ....Andrea Gibbons
Box Office Assistant ....Danielle Prescott

Board of Directors

William Keller, President
Brad Andrews, Vice President
Jamie H. Dater, Secretary
Mike Bessent, Treasurer
Barbara Bauer
Tiane Bess
Dr. Charles Davis
Brent Fery
Sandra L.S. Fery
John A. Glaza
Michael Hoffman
Grove Hummert
Cheryl Larabee
A. K. Leinhart-Minnick
Richard McChrystal
Pamela F. Meals
Royanne Minskoff
Tom Nunamaker
Dr. Bruce Robbins
Ray E. Smith
Odette Sutton
Henry W. Taylor, Jr.
Carolyn Bancroft, Recording Secretary

1997

Private Lives By Noel Coward

Director ....Charles Fee
Resident Scenic Designer ....Gage Williams
Costume Design ....Ann Hoste
Lighting ....Tracy Odishaw
Composer ....Peter John Still

The Merchant of Venice

Director ....Bartlett Sher
Resident Scenic Designer ....Gage Williams
Costume Design ....Kim Krumm Sorenson
Lighting ....Tracy Odishaw
Composer ....Peter John Still

The Taming of the Shrew

Director ....Sari Ketter
Resident Scenic Designer ....Gage Williams
Costume Design ....Kim Krumm Sorenson
Lighting ....Tracy Odishaw
Composer ....Peter John Still

The Tragedy of Macbeth

Director ....Charles Fee
Resident Scenic Designer ....Gage Williams
Costume Design ....Star Moxley
Lighting ....Tracy Odishaw
Composer ....Peter John Still

Acting Company

Private Lives; The Merchant of Venice ;The Taming of the Shrew The Tragedy of Macbeth

Ira Amyx	–; Ensemble; Servant; Nobleman
Danny Camiel	–; Bassanio; Biondello; Malcolm
Jared Dalley	–; Leonardo/ Ensemble; Vincentio/Servant; Nobleman/ Murderer
Paul Eggington	Victor Prynne; –; –; –
Craig Franson	–; Balthazar/ Ensemble; A Tailor/

	Servant; Nobleman/ Captain;
Mark E. Gladue	–; Tubal; A Pedant/ Servant; Nobleman/ Murderer
Joe Conley Golden*	–; Launcelot Gobbo; –; Rosee
Brad Heberlee	–; Lorenzo; Lucentio; Seyton
Grant W. Hetherington	–; Ensemble; An Officer; Nobleman
Kelli Kerslake	Sybil Chase; Nerissa; –; Lady Macduff/ Witch
Richard Klautsch*	Elyot Chase; Duke of Venice; Petruchio; Macduff
Sitch Marker	–; Solanio; Baptista Minola; Duncan/ Hecate;
Kimo Muraki	–; –; –; –
Rebecca Olson	Stephano/ Ensemble; A Widow/ Servant
Dan Peterson	–; Old Gobbo; Christopher Sly; Porter
Rebecca Prescott	–; Jessica; Bianca Minola; Witch
Janis Stevens*	Amanda Prynne; –; –; Lady Macbeth
Tracy Sunderland	Louise; –; –; –
Kathleen Pirkl Tague*	–; Portia; Katharina –; Minola
Steve Tague*	–; Shylock; Macbeth; –
Mark Anthony Taylor	–; Salerio; Hortensio; Witch
Eden Teagle	–; Ensemble; Hostess; Gentlewoman
Joel Weaver	–; Prince of Arragon; –; Donalbain/ Young Siward
Tom Willmorth	–; Gratiano; Tranio; –
Andrew Wyke	Prince of Morocco Haberdasher/ Servant; Lenox
Ty Smith	–; Antonio; Gremio; Banquo/ Siward
T. J. Little	–; Ensemble; –; –
Lisa Reynolds	–; Ensemble; –; –
Clay Blaha	–; –; –; Fleance

Production

Assistant Director ....Jeremy Miltenberger
Assistant to the Director – *Merchant* ..Catherine Bettis
Equity Stage Manger ....Cheryl Carabelli
Stage Managers: Bonnie Hildebrand; Amy Miranda Warner
Stage Manager Interns: Joshua Pilote; Roger L. Quinte III
Technical Director ....Shaun Sites
Technical Intern ....Karl Allen
Sound Engineer ....Tim Knox
Scenic Artist ....Jessica Wade
Master Electrician ....Penny LIppert
Carpenter: ....John J. O'Hagan; Eric Ragan
Scenic Intern: ....Leslie Hammon; Amber Herdich
Electrician ....Brian Hallada
Props Master ....Mark Cruise
Props Intern ....Colleen Jones
Props Running Crew ....Julia Berger
Costume Shop Manager ....Rebecca A. Hoffman
First Hand ....Sally Thomas
Sitichers: Jinny DeFoggi; Lito-John Demetita; Amber Hartley; Ginger Robertson;
Assistant Crafts ....Lito-John Demetita
Cutter/Draper ....Randall Exton
Wardrobe: ......Susan Lawrence; Hannah K. E. Read
Fight Choreographer ....Dexter Fidler
Movement and Dance Choreographer Helene Peterson
Dialect and Vocal Coach ....Ann Klautsch
Greenshows – *Merchant and Shrew* . .Joe Conley Golden
Tom Willmorth
Greenshows – *Private Lives and Macbeth* Rebecca Prescott
Matt Ramsey
Apprentices: Carey Acker, Sound; Clay Blaha, Acting; Adam Hale, Sound; T. J. Little, Acting; Lisa Reynolds, Acting

Administration

Artistic Director ....Charles Fee
Managing Director ....Mark Hofflund
Director of Marketing ....Kristen Robertson
Director of Development ....Beth B. Markley
Education Outreach Coordinator ....Helene Peterson
Box Office Manager ....Kit Knox
House Manager ....Errica Long
Concessions Manager ....Richard Comstock
Night Box Office Manager ....Paul Roberts

Board of Directors

Bradley G. Andrews, President
Sandra L.S. Fery, Vice President
Barbara Bauer, Secretary
Mike Bessent, Treasurer
Candice Allphin
Jamie H. Dater
Dr. Charles Davis
Brent Fery
Michael Hoffman
Grove Hummert
William H. Keller
Cheryl Larabee
Kevin Kline, Honorary Campaign Chair
A. K. Leinhart-Minnick
Royanne & Alan Minskoff,Campaign Co-Chairs
Richard McChrystal
Royanne Minskoff
Michael M. Mooney
Tom Nunamaker
Dr. Bruce Robbins
Dianne H. Robertson
Ray E. Smith
Henry W. Taylor, Jr.
Carolyn Bancroft, Recording Secretary

1998

A Midsummer Night's Dream

Director ....Charles Fee
Resident Scenic Designer ....Gage Williams
Costume Design ....Star Moxley
Lighting ....Rick Martin
Composer ....Peter John Still

Cymbeline

Director ....Bartlett Sher
Resident Scenic Designer ....Gage Williams
Costume Design ....Caitlin Ward
Lighting ....Chris Akerlind
Composer ....Peter John Still

Romeo and Juliet

Director ....Paul Barnes
Resident Scenic Designer ....Gage Williams
Costume Design ....Janet L. Swenson
Lighting ....Rick Martin
Composer ....Peter John Still

Acting Company

A Midsummer Night's Dream; Romeo and Juliet; Cymbeline

Lynn Berg III	Guest; Attendant to Escalus/ Friar John/ Officer; Guiderius
Neil Brookshire	Guest; Balthasar; Ensemble
Leslie Brott*	Nurse; Queen
Sara Bruner	Snug; Ensemble; Apparition/ Ensemble; Leonda Clendenen Guest ; Helen/ Ensemble
Aled Davies*	Theseus/ Oberon; Friar Lawrence; Story teller
Joe Conley Golden*	Bottom; Sampson; Cloten
Nathan Guisinger	Snout; Romeo; Apparition/ Ensemble
Jeffrey C. Hawkins	Lysander; Abram; Posthumous Leonatus
Cheri Lynn Johnson	Hippolyta/ Titania; Lady Montague; Caius Lucius
Richard Klautsch*	–; Capulet; Pisanio
Stitch Marker	Egeus; Escalus; Cymbeline
Kenneith R. Merckx, Jr.*	–; Mercutio; Iachimo
Isaac N. Perelson	Guest; Anthony; Ensemble
Maren Perry	–; Lady Capulet; –
Dan Peterson	Flute; Montague/ Apothecary; Belarius
Tim Redmond	Starveling; Tybalt; A Frenchman/ Ensemble
Jessica Ripple	Guest; Ensemble; Ensemble
Michael Shipley	Demetrius; Paris; A Dutchman/ Apparition/ Ensemble
Rachel Sledd	Hermia; Juliet; Apparition/ Ensemble
Gregory Ivan Smith*	–; Benvolio; Arviragus
Belynda Starr	Guest; Ensemble; Ensemble
Tracy Sunderland	Helena; Potpan/ Ensemble; Ensemble
Mark Anthony Taylor	Quince; Gregory; Storyteller
Tom Willmorth	Philostrate/ Puck; Peter
Martha Bradford	
John Peterson	Dancers; –; –
T.J. Little	–; Page/ Ensemble; Ensemble
Clay Blaha	
Brett Larabee	
Paul Munson	Ensemble

Production

Assistant to the Director – *Cymbeline* ..Matthew Clark
Equity Stage Manager ....Sue Karutz
Stage Managers: Emily Compton; Joshua R. Pilote
Assistant Stage Managers ....Jennifer C. Gadda; Nickie Shell
Technical Director ....Jeremy Miltenberger
Technical Consultant ....Shaun Sites
Scenic Artist: Monica Coburn; Amber Herdrich
Master Electrician ....Penny M. Lippert
Sound Engineer ....Adam Hale
Carpenter: Devid Ledger; Jesus Soto
Carpenter Intern: Joshua Patrick Brown; Eric B. Higer Thomas E. Wells
Technical Intern ....Christina Velasquez
Electrician ....Christine A. Engle
Props Master ....Thomas Verdos
Costume Shop Manager ....Rebecca S. Hoffman
First Hand ....Katherine Rundquist
Costume Shop Intern ....Jill Bowen
Stitchers: Jinny DeFoggi; Lito-John Demetitia; Amber Hartley
Stitcher Intern ....Lito-John Demetita
Cutter ....Ginger Robertson
Wardrobe Mistress: Deb Bogie; Elizabeth Giesel
Dresser ....Lisa Collins
Fight Choreographer ....Kenneth R. Merckx, Jr.
Movement and Dance Choreographer ......M. Helene Peterson
Tango Choreographers: Martha Bradford; John Peterson
Greenshows: Joe Conley Golden; Tom Willmorth
Apprentices: Clay Blaha, Acting; Brett E. Larabee, Acting; T. J. Little, Acting; Paul V. Munson, Acting; Lisa Reynolds, Technical; Claire Yunker, Technical

Administration

Artistic Director ....Charles Fee
Managing Director ....Mark Hofflund
Director of Marketing ....Kristen L. R. De Angeli
Director of Finance ....Sherrill Livingston
Director of Development ....Beth Markley
Director of Educational Outreach .M. Helene Peterson
Box Office Manager ....Anne M. Allen
Night Box Office Manager ....Sandy Capozzi
Night Box Office ....Alissa Fizer
Box Office ....James R. M. Hopper
House Manager ....John O'Hagan
Souvenir Manager ....Gerry Rodriguez
Box Office ....Jennifer Jo Rogien
Concessions Manager ....Burk Tarrant

1999

A Midsummer Night's Dream

Director .... Charles Fee
Resident Scenic Designer .... Gage Williams
Costume Design .... Star Moxley
Lighting .... Rick Martin
Sound .... Peter John Still

Scapin
By Moliere

Director .... Christopher Bayes
Resident Scenic Designer .... Gage Williams
Costume Design .... Caitlin Ward
Lighting .... Tracy Odishaw
Music Director .... Peter John Still

The Winter's Tale

Director .... Charles Fee
Resident Scenic Designer .... Gage Williams
Costume Design .... Star Moxley
Lighting .... Trace Odishaw
Sound .... Peter John Still

Titus Andronicus

Director .... Bartlett Sher
Scenic Design .... Deborah Jensen
Costume Design .... Caitlin Ward
Lighting .... Christopher Akerlind
Sound .... Peter John Still

The Compleat Works of Wllm. Shkspr. (Abridged) by Jess Borgeson, Adam Long and Daniel Singer

Director .... Charles Fee
Resident Scenic Designer .... Gage Williams
Costume Design .... Rebecca Hoffman
Lighting .... Christopher Akerlind
Sound .... Peter John Still

Acting Company

A Midsummer Night's Dream; Scapin; The Winter's Tale; Titus Andronicus; Compleat Works

Robert Gerard Anderson*	Geronte; Antigonus/ Ensemble; Bassianus/ Clown/ 1st Goth Soldier
Lynn Berg III	Demetrius; Carle; Ensemble; Martius/ Caius/ 3rd Goth Soldier
Courtney Bohl	Masques; Dorcas/ Ensemble; Ensemble
Sara M. Bruner	Snug/ Lion; Zerbinette; Perdita; Ensemble
Betsy Brunner	Pianist
Adam Cotterell	Masques; Nerine/ Policeman and Porter; Ensemble; Ensemble
Sean Robert Cox	Starveling/ Moonshine; Policeman and Porter; Cleomenes/ Ensemble; Quintus/ Valentine/ 2nd Goth Soldier
Aled Davies*	Theseus/ Oberon; Camillo;
Marcus	Andronicus
Nick Garcia	Snout/ Wall; Octave; Dion/ Ensemble; Chiron
Allen Gilmore*	Argante; Aaron
Joe Conley Golden*	Bottom/ Pyramus; Autolycus; Cast
Jeffrey C. Hawkins	Lysander; Leandre; Florizel; Lucius; Cast
Cheri Lynn Johnson	Hippolyta/ Titania
Devin Kearns	Masques; Emilia/ Ensemble; Ensemble
Richard Klautsch*	Leontes; Saturninus
Patrick Knudsen	Young Lucius
Brett Larabee	Mamillius/ Ensemble
T. J. Little	Masques; Ensemble; Ensemble
Stitch Marker	Egeus; Archidamus/ Mariner/ Ensemble/ Time; Aemilius
Kimo Muraki	Policeman and Porter/ Musician
Dan Peterson	Thisby/ Flute; Old Shepherd; Cast
Joshua R. Pilote	Ensemble; Mutius/ Publius
Samantha Quan	Hermia; Hyacinte; Lavinia
Tracy Sunderland	Helena; Paulina; Ensemble
Kathleen Pirkl Tague*	Hermione; Tamora
Steve Tague*	Polixenes; Titus Andronicus
Mark Anthony Taylor	Quince/ Prologue; Silvestre; Clown/ Jailer; Sepronius/ Alarbus
Jennifer Walker	Masques; Mopsa/ Ensemble; Nurse
Tom Willmorth	Philostrate/ Puck or Robin Goodfellow; Scapin; Demetrius

Production

Equity Stage Manager: Emily Compton ; Christopher Sadler
Stage Managers .... Joshua R. Pilote
Assistant Stage Managers/Interns: Jodi Briscoe; Lisa M. Kerrick; Elizabeth Littman; Erin C. Nelson; Jorja Ackers
Technical Director .... Jeremy Miltenberger
Scenic Artist .... Monica Fabbi
Master Electrician .... Christopher Wood
Sound Engineer .... Seth Asa Sengel
Carpenters: Mike Czerepinski; Ray Firkins; Eric Higer; Ken Pierson; Carpenter Intern; Mehul Asher; Andrea Bryn Bush
Sound Intern .... Zach Stinnet
Electrician .... Jason A. Rollins
Electrician Intern .... Sam C. Samuelson
Properties Master .... Thomas Verdos
Costume Shop Manager .... Katherine Rundquist
First Hand .... Birgit Bishop
Costume Crafts .... Rebecca S. Hoffman
Cutters .... Carole Bloomsburg-Urquhart
Nancy Berger King ....
Stitchers: Marya L. Cline; Danyale K. Cook; Jinny DeFoggi; Fairy Hitchcock; Karen Milena Lyons
Crafts Assistant .... Danyale K. Cook
Wardrobe Mistress .... Lisa M. Collins
Assistant Wardrobe Mistresses: Deb Bogie; Nickie Shell
Dresser: Jorja Ackers; Jessamine Jones; Claire Yunker
Fight Choreographer: Dexter Fidler; J. Steven White
Movement and Dance Choreographer: M. Helene Peterson; Amy O'Brian
Voice and Speech Coach .... Steve Tague
Greenshows .... Joe Conley Golden
Tom Willmorth ....
Apprentices: Jorja Ackers, Stage Management; Patrick Knudsen, Acting; Brett Larabee, Acting; T. J. Little, Acting; Christy Waybright, Technical; Claire Yunker, Wardrobe

Administration

Artistic Director .... Charles Fee
Managing Director .... Mark Hofflund
Director of Marketing .... Kristen L. R. De Angeli
Director of Finance .... Sherrill Livingston
Director of Development .... Anne M. Allen
Director of Educational Outreach . M. Helene Peterson
Box Office Manager .... James R. M. Hopper
Administrative Assistant .... Nickie Shell
Assistant Box Office Manager .... Burk Tarrant
House Manager .... Leonda Clendenen
Box Office Assistant .... Rebecca Olson
House Manager .... Cathleen Reese
Box Office Assistant .... Shaun R. Thomas

Campaign for the Idaho Shakespeare Festival

Kevin Kline, Honorary Chair
Alan & Royanne Minskoff, Campaign Co-Chairs
Jamie H. & Tom Dater, Co-Chairs of Major Gifts
Cheryl A. Larabee & Dianne H. Robertson, Co-Chairs of Partnership Gifts
Sandra L.S. Fery, Chair of Public Campaign
Andrew Erstad, Chair of Building Committee
Barbara Bauer, Campaign Treasurer

Advisory Board

Bradley G. Andrews
Michael Hoffman
Richard McChrystal
Alan & Royanne Minskoff
Michael M. Mooney
Tom Nunamaker
Ray E. Smith

2000

The Compleat Works of Wllm. Shkspr. (Abridged)
by Jess Borgeson, Adam Long and Daniel Singer

Director .... Charles Fee
Resident Scenic Designer .... Gage Williams
Costume Design .... Rebecca Hoffman
Lighting .... Rick Martin
Sound .... Peter John Still

The Three Musketeers
by Alexander Dumas, adaptation by Linda Alper, Douglas Langworthy and Penny Metropulos

Director .... Charles Fee
Resident Scenic Designer .... Gage Williams
Costume Design .... Star Moxley
Lighting .... Rick Martin
Sound .... Peter John Still

The Two Gentlemen of Verona

Director .... Charles Fee
Resident Scenic Designer .... Gage Williams
Costume Design .... Kim Krumm Sorenson
Lighting .... Rick Martin
Music Director .... Peter John Still

Othello

Director .... Victor Papas
Scenic Design .... Gage Williams
Costume Design .... Rose Pederson
Lighting .... Tracy Odishaw
Sound and Composer .... Peter John Still

Pump Boys and Dinettes
Conceived and Written by John Foley, Mark Hardwick, Debra Monk, Cass Morgan, John Schimmel and Jim Wann, original stage production by Dodger Productions.

Director .... Dennis Jones
Scenic Design .... Dennis Jones
Costume Design .... Kristin Cooper
.... (based on a design by Gail Russell)
Lighting .... Mary Louise Geiger
Musical Director .... Travis Jones

Acting Company:

Compleat Works; Three Musketeers; Two Gents; Othello; Pump Boys

Lynn Berg –; Count de Wardes/ Ensemble; Ensemble; –
Sara Bruner –; Kitty; Julia; Bianca; –
Dan Crane –; Patrick/ Ensemble; Outlaw; Ensemble; –
John Jay Espino* –; –; –; L. M.
Nick Garcia –; Grimaud/ Ensemble; Eglamour; Ensemble; –
Allen Gilmore* –; Aramis; –; Othello; –
Joe Conley Golden* Cast; –; –; –
Jeffrey C. Hawkins –; D'Artagnan; Proteus; Ensemble; –
Sheila Hennessey –; Abbess/ Mlle. d'Astree; Ensemble; –
Dan Hiatt* –; Porthos; Launce; Roderigo; –
Julie James* –; –; –; –; Prudie
Travis Jones –; –; –; –; Jim
Felton Page Kennedy –; Jussac/ Ensemble; –; Montano; –
Richard Klautsch* –; –; Athos; –; Brabantio; –
Donald Sage Mackay* –; The Count de Rochefort; –; Cassio; –
Stitch Marker –; De Treville/ Reilly Outlaw/ Panthino; Ensemble; –
Doug Miller* –; Duke of Buckingham; Duke of Milan; Duke of Venice; –
Sandy Mulvihill* –; –; –; –; Rhetta
Justin Ness –; Bazin/ Ensemble; Host; Ensemble; –
Dan Peterson Cast; M. Bonancieux; Antonio; Gratiano; –
Rebecca Prescott –; Queen Anne; –; Desdemona; –
Matt Ramsey –; John Felton/ Ensemble; Valentine; Lodovico; –
David Sahadi* –; –; –; –; Eddie
Jack R. Sinclair –; –; –; –; Bubba
Shane T. Stokes –; Biscarrat/ Ensemble/ Lubin Thurio; Ensemble; –
Tracy Sunderland –; Mme. De Coquenard; Speed; Ensemble; –
Kathleen Pirkl Tague* –; Countess de Winter; –; Emilia; –
Steve Tague* –; Cardinal Richelieu; –; Iago; –
Mark Anthony Taylor –; Planchet/ Ensemble; Outlaw; Ensemble; –
Karen Wennstrom –; Mme. De Chevreuse; Lucetta; Ensemble; –
Tom Willmorth Cast; King Louis XIII; –; Ensemble; –
Carie Yonekawa –; Mme. Constance Bonancieux Silvia Ensemble

Production

Associate Director – *Two Gents* .... Sari Ketter
Equity Stage Manager .... Emily B. Compton
Equity Stage Manager .... Christopher Sadler
Technical Director .... Stephen G. Smith
Assistant Technical Director .... Jennifer Schmidt
Costume Shop Manager .... Katherine Rundquist
Scenic Artists: Monica Fabbi; Jennifer Price
Master Electrician .... Adam Travis
Sound Engineer .... Seth Asa Sengel
Carpenter: Ricky Harrison; Josh Mason; Caroline Mulcahey; Jeremiah Smith
Carpenter Intern .... Scott Iseri
Electrics Intern: Dante Smith; Willis Sullivan
Props Artisan .... Woody Hearn
First Hand .... James Haycock
Costume Crafts .... Rebecca Hoffman
Cutter/Draper .... Carole Bloomsburg-Urquhart
Cutter .... Sharla McAndrew
Stitchers: Marya Cline; Lisa Collins; Jinny DeFoggi; Fairy Hitchcock; Sabrina Thorson
Wardrobe Mistress .... Deb Bogie
Dresser .... Jessamine Jones
Choreographers: Matthew Hope
Equity Member and Fight Choreographer .Kenneth R. Merckx, Jr. ....
Choreographer .... Leah Stephens Clark

Administration

Artistic Director .... Charles Fee
Managing Director .... Mark Hofflund
Director of Marketing .... Kristen L. R. De Angeli
Director of Finance .... Sherrill Livingston
Director of Development .... James R. M. Hopper
Director of Education .... M. Helene Peterson
Director of Idaho Theater for Youth .... John O'Hagan
Box Office Manager .... Ted Hurliman
Site Coordinator & Marketing Associate ... Dawn Lea
Administrative Assistants: Monica Hopkins; Nickie Shell
Box Office Assistants: Kayla Avery; Jenny Brown; John O'Hagan; Laura Soldati; Burk Tarrant; Eden Teagle; Ron Torres
House Managers; Jenny Brown; Eden Teagle
Site Facilities Coordinator .... Dawn L. W. Lea

Board of Directors

Brent Fery, President
Michael D. McIntyre, Vice President
Lorie Nies-Pettiette, Secretary
Barbara Bauer, Treasurer
Steve Arnold
Margaret Buchanan
Richard P. Clark
Linda Dixon
Andrew Erstad
Leann Gilberg
Norena Gutierrez
Sus Helpenstell
Cheryl A. Larabee
Debbie McDonald
Theresa McLeod
Nicholas G. Miller
Thomas V. Munson
Anthony W. Olbrich
Dianne H. Robertson
Caren W. Sage
Henry W. Taylor, Jr.
Shirley Tierney
Robert T. Wetherell
Kathryn Zimmerman
Carolyn Bancroft, Recording Secretary

Consulting Members

Rory Farrow
Cathy Frasure
Kathy Harris
Sandy Patano

Campaign for the Idaho Shakespeare Festival

Kevin Kline, Honorary Chair
Royanne & Alan Minskoff, Campaign Co-Chairs
Jamie H. & Tom Dater, Co-Chairs of Major Gifts
Cheryl A. Larabee & Dianne H. Robertson, Partnership Co-Chairs
Sandra L.S. Fery, Public Campaign Chair
Andrew Erstad Building Committee Chair
Barbara Bauer, Campaign Treasurer

Advisory Board

Candice Allphin
Bradley G. Andrews
Mike Bessent
Doug Copsey
Charles Davis
Sandra L.S. Fery
Michael Hoffman
William H. Keller
Richard McChrystal
Alan Minskoff
Royanne Minskoff
Michael M. Mooney
Tom Nunamaker
Charles L. Robertson
Ray E. Smith

2001

The Two Gentlemen of Verona

Director .... Charles Fee
Resident Scenic Designer .... Gage Williams
Costume Design .... Kim Krumm Sorenson
Lighting .... Rick Martin
Sound .... Peter John Still

Amadeus
By Peter Shaffer

Director .... Gordon Reinhart
Resident Scenic Designer .... Gage Williams
Costume Design .... Ann Hoste
Lighting .... M. L. Geiger
Sound .... Peter John Still

Much Ado About Nothing

Director .... Drew Barr
Resident Scenic Designer .... Gage Williams
Costume Design .... Kim Krumm Sorenson
Lighting .... Rick Martin
Sound .... Peter John Still

Hamlet

Director ....Charles Fee
Resident Scenic Designer ....Gage Williams
Costume Design ....Star Moxley
Lighting ....Rick Martin
Sound ....Peter John Still

Forever Plaid

Written and originally and choreographed by Stuart Ross. Musical continuity supervision and arrangement by James Raitt.

Director ....Jim Giancarlo
Scenic Design ....Gage Williams
Costume Design ....Kerri Lee Robbins
Lighting ....Elizabeth Gaines
Musical Director ....John Jay Espino
Sound ....Peter John Still

Acting Company

Two Gents; Amadeus; Much Ado; Hamlet; Forever Plaid

Ira Amyx –; Citizen of Vienna/ Valet; The Watch; Reynaldo; –
Lynn Berg Thurio; Venticelli; Borachio; Guildenstern; –
Neil Brookshire –; Salieri's Valet; The Watch; Other; Player; –
Sara Bruner Julia; –; Margaret; Ophelia; –
Frederick Charles Canada* –; Johann Kilian; Von Strack; –; Friar Francis; Marcellus; –
Kathryn Cherasaro –; Constanze Weber; –; –; –
Daniel Crane Outlaw; Conrade; Barnardo; –
Luke Daigle –; –; A boy; –; –
Aled Davies* Antonio; –; Leonato; Claudius; –
Katie Dubman –; Citizen of Vienna/ Valet; –; Attendant
John Jay Espino* –; –; –; –; Piano Player
Douglas Frederick* Duke of Milan; Joseph II; Don Pedro; Horatio; –
Joe Conley Golden* Launce; –; –; –; –
Reggie Gowland Citizen of Vienna/ Valet
Jeffrey C. Hawkins* Proteus; Claudio; Player Queen
Dan Hiatt* Polonius
Francis Kelly* Franky
Richard Klautsch* Antonio Salieri; The Ghost/ Player King/ The grave-digger's companion
Michael Jenkinson* Sparky
Kristen Looper Other
Stitch Marker Panthino/ Outlaw
Giuseppe Bonno Antonio; Osric
Blain McFeely –; Citizen of Vienna/ Valet; –; –; –
Justin Ness* Host; Salieri's Cook; Balthasar/ The Watch; Other Player/ Priest; –
Alice Royer –; –; –; Other; –
Jack Rucker Eglamour; Citizen of Vienna/ Valet; A Sexton; –; –
David Sahadi* –; –; –; –; Bass Player
Chad Scheppner Valentine; Major Domo; Don John; Francisco; –
David Anthony Smith* –; Gottfried Von Sweiten; Benedick; Laertes; –
Jim Sorenson* –; –; –; –; Smudge
Chad Summervill –; –; –; –; Jinx
Tracy Sunderland Speed; –; –; –; –
Kathleen Pirkl Tague* –; –; Beatrice; Gertrude; –
Steve Tague* –; –; Dogberry; Hamlet; –
Mark Anthony Taylor Rosenberg Outlaw; Franz Orsini-Rosenberg; Verges; Rosencrantz; –
Nicole Vernon –; –; Nicole Vernon; –; –
Karen Wennstrom Lucetta; Teresa Salieri; Ursula; Attendant; –
Tom Willmorth –; Wolfgang Amadeus Mozart; –; A grave-digger; –
Carie Yonekawa Silvia; Katherina Cavalieri; Hero; Attendant
Jamie Young –; Citizen of Vienna/ Valet; –; Attendant

Production

Equity Production Stage Managers: Christopher Sadler; Jeffrey S. Williams
Assistant Stage Managers: Jodi Briscoe; Jennifer Gadda; Hannah Read
Intern Stage Manager ....Jorja Ackers
Production Assistant ....Ian Mundorff
Production Manager ....Michael Hartwell
Technical Director ....Stephen G. Smith
Assistant Technical Director ....Jennifer Schmidt
Master Carpenter ....Ted O'Neil
Carpenters: ....Holly Grabowski; Williams Wood
Carpenter Interns: .....Dov Markowitz; Bill Williams
Props Master ....Craig Doer
Props Stitcher ....Fairy Hitchcock
Props Assistants: Joe Leporati; Caroline Mulcahy
Scenic Artists: Jennifer Bean; Joe Donovan
Master Electrician ....Kenneth Elliott
Electrican ....Katrina Elliott
Electrics Apprentices: Dante Smith; Dylan Smith
Spot Operator: Lyn Hezeltine; Rosela Moseng
Costume Crafts ....Rebecca Hoffman
Crafts Assistant Costume Production ...Hannah Read
Costume Shop ....Kathy Rundquist
First hand ....Rebecca Foster
Cutter ....Karen Ross
Assistant Cutter ....Carole Urquhart
Stitchers: Tracy Arrington; Rosey Bock; Marya Cline; Sarah Fonnesbeck; Dorothy Hopkins; Reenie Sudduth
Wardrobe Supervisor ....Jessamine Jones
Head Dresser ....Nikka Freeman
Dresser: Whitney Barnhill; Megan Huston; Sarah Spencer; Emily Vetsch; Kelsey Westerland; Emma Weston

Administration

Artistic Director ....Charles Fee
Managing Director ....Mark Hofflund
Co-Directors of Marketing: Susan Platt; Lisa Wilson
Director of Finance ....Sherrill Livingston
Director of Education ....James R. M. Hopper
Director of Patron Relations ....Kelly Moore
Director of Development ....Dawn Suleri
Company Manager ....Nickie Shell
Administrative Assistants ......Christine Zimowsky
Box Office Manager ....Michael Aaron Milette

Board of Directors

Michael D. McIntyre, President
Dianne H. Robertson, Vice President
Lorie Nies-Pettiette, Secretary
Leann R. Gilbert, Treasurer
Steven P. Arnold
Barbara Bauer
Margaret Buchanan
Richard P. Clark
Linda Dixon
Andrew Erstad
Brent Fery
Norena Gutierrez
Sus Helpenstell
Cheryl Larabee
Jane Loge
Debbie McDonald
Theresa McLeod
James McNorton
Nicholas G. Miller
Thomas V. Munson
Anthony W. Olbrich
John Parrish
Shirley Tierney
Robert T. Wetherell
Shawn Del Ysursa
Carolyn Bancroft, Recording Secretary

Consulting Members

Cathie Frasure ....Shirley O'Neil
Kathy Harris ....Sandy Patano
Suzanne Lierz ....Diane Rigby

Advisory Board

Candice Allphin ....Richard McChrystal
Bradley G. Andrews ....Alan Minskoff
Mike Bessent ....Royanne Minskoff
Doug Copsey ....Michael M. Mooney
Charles Davis ....Tom Nunamaker
Sandra Fery ....Charles Robertson
Mike Hoffman ....Ray E. Smith
William H. Keller ....Henry W. Taylor, Jr.

2002

Much Ado About Nothing

Director ....Drew Barr
Set Design ....Gage Williams
Costume Design ....Kim Krumm Sorenson
Lighting ....Rick Martin
Sound ....Peter John Still

Arms and the Man
By George Bernard Shaw

Director ....Charles Fee
Set Design ....Gage Williams
Costume Design ....Star Moxley
Lighting ....Tracy Odishaw
Sound ....Peter John Still

Twelfth Night

Director ....Gordon Reinhart
Set Design ....Gage Williams
Costume Design ....Clare Henkel
Lighting ....Rick Martin
Sound ....Peter John Still

Macbeth

Director ....Charles Fee
Set Design ....Gage Williams
Costume Design ....Star Moxley
Lighting ....Rick Martin
Sound ....Peter John Still

You're a Good Man, Charlie Brown

Based on the comic strip "Peanuts" by Charles Schulz. Book, music and lyrics by Clark Gesnerr. Additional music and lyrics by Andrew Lippa. Original direction for this version of You're a Good Man, Charlie Brown by Michael Mayer. Originally produced in New York by Arthur Whitelaw and Gene Persson.

Director ....Drew Barr
Set Design ....Narelle Sissons
Costume Design ....Jacqueline Firkins
Lighting ....Rick Martin
Sound ....Peter John Still

Acting Company

Much Ado; Arms and the Man; Twelfth Night; Macbeth; Charlie Brown

Ira Amyx Watch; –; Sailors and Officers; Nobleman; Murderer; –
Karen Baughn –; Villager; –; –; –
Lynn Robert Berg –; –; –; –; –
Dwayne Blackaller Balthasar; –; Curio; Nobleman; –
Neil Brookshire Watch; –; Sebastian; Drummer; –
Sara Bruner* –; Raina Petkoff; Viola; Witch; –

Tony Capone	–; –; –; –; Schroeder
Andy Carey	Watch; –; Sailors and Officers; Donalbain; Nobleman; –
Kathryn Cherasaro	–; Louka; Maria; Gentlewoman; –
Daniel Crane	Conrade; Russian Officer Villager; –; Nobleman; Young Siward; Captain; –
Luke Daigle	A boy, other; –; –; –; –
Aled Davies*	Leonato; Nicola; Sir Toby Belch; –; –
Carter Davis	–; –; –; Drummer; –
Bianca Dillard	–; Villager; –; –; –
Katie Dubman	Other ; –; –; –; –
Tom Ford*	–; –; –; –; Charlie Brown
Douglas Frederick*	Don Pedro; –; Malvolio; Duncan; –
Kevin Free	–; –; –; –; Linus Van Pelt
Nick Garcia	Don John; –; Valentine; Nobleman; Murderer; –
Joe Conley Golden*	Verges; –; Sir Andrew Aguecheek; Rosse; –
Reggie Gowland	–; –; Fleance; –
Richard Klautsch*	–; –; Orsino; Macduff; –
Daniel Frank Kelley	–; –; –; –; Snoopy
Stitch Marker	Antonio; –; Feste; Seyton; –; –
Blaine McFeeley	–; Villager; –; Nobleman
Sandy Mulvihill*	–; –; –; –; Lucy Van Pelt
Dan Peterson	Friar Francis; –; Antonio; Porter; –
Aaron Preusse	Borachio; –; Sea Captain; Lenox; –
Jessica Ramsey	–; Villager; –; –; –
Alice Royer	Other; –; –; –; –
Jack Rucker	A Sexton; –; Priest; Nobleman; –
Evan Sesek	–; –; –; Boy; –
Ashley Smith*	Claudio; Captain Bluntschli; –; Malcolm; –
David Anthony Smith*	Benedick; Major Sergius Saranoff; –; Banquo; Siward; –
Tracy Sunderland	Margaret; –; Fabian; Witch; –
Kathleen Pirkl Tague*	Beatrice; Catherine Petkoff; –; Lady Macbeth; –
Steve Tague*	Dogberry; Major Paul Petkoff; –; Macbeth; –
Stephanie TeBeau	Villager
Jessica Walling	–; –; –; –; Sally Brown
Karen Wennstrom	Ursula; –; –; Lady Macduff; –
Carie Yonekawa	Hero; –; Olivia; Witch; –

Production

Equity Stage Manager ....Jennifer Gadda
Equity Production Stage Manager Christopher Sadler
Production Manager ....Michael Hartwell
Assistant Stage Manager ....Jorja Ackers
Assistant Stage Manager ....Hannah Read
Production Assistants: Ian Mundorff; Olivia Lebens; Kyle Barrow
Technical Director ....Philip R. Hendren
Assistant Technical Director ......Joshua Frachiseur
Master Carpenter ....Robert Riddle
Scenic Carpenter ....Richard May
Scenic Intern: Dov Markowitz; Scott Price
Charge Scenic Artist ....Robert Vaughn
Scenic Painters: Marsha McFarland; Clint L. Sperl
Electrician ....Matthew Robert Curtis
Electrics Intern ....Andy Iverson
Electrics/Running Crew ....Dante Smith
Properties Master ....Craig Dorer
Properties Assistants: Andrew Fitts; Fran Maxwell
Sound Engineer ....Seth Asa Sengel
Sound Operator ....Zach Stinnett
Sound Intern ....Cody Hyslop
Costume Shop Manager ....Katherine Rundquist
First hand ....Nicole Frachiseur
Cutter ....Karen Ross
Cutter/Draper ....Jackie Arrington
Costume Crafts: Rebecca Hoffman; Lito-John Demetita
Stitchers: Eileen Louise Albert; Tracy Forbes; Nancy Mosby; Sarah Reever
Scenic Stitcher ....Fairy Hitchcock
Wardrobe Mistress ....Mika Freeman
Fight Choreographer ....Kenneth R. Merckx, Jr.
Dance Choreographer ....Helene Peterson
Apprentice Company: Karen Baughn; Luke Daigle; Bianca Dillard; Katie Dubman; Reggie Gowland; Kristen Looper; Blaine McFeeley; Jessica Ramsey; Alice Royer; Stephanie TeBeau

Administration

Producing Artistic Director ....Charles Fee
Managing Director ....Mark Hofflund
Director of Marketing & PR ...Kristen L.R. De Angeli
Director of Finance ....Sherrill Livingston
Director of Education ....John O'Hagan
Director of Patron Relations ....Kelly Moore
Grants Manager ....Ann Dehner
Production Manager ....Mike Hartwell
Campaign Associate ....Liz Littman
Box Office Manager ....Aaron Milette
Company Manager ....Nickie Shell
Administrative Assistant ....Christine Zimowsky
Box Office Assistant: Kayla Avery; Jodi Briscoe; Jennifer Crane; Libby Fox; Renee Racan; Jess Stanley; Eden Teagle; Marika Warilla; Chandra Woodward
Master Gardener ....Carol Cole
Assistant Gardener ....Shelli Mittmann
House Managers: Amanda Costello; Hartley Miller
Souvenir Managers: Carrie Schweitzer; Dante Smith

Board of Directors

Dianne H. Robertson, President
Robert T. Wetherell, Vice President
Margaret Buchanan, Secretary
Leann R. Gilbert, Treasurer
Richard P. Clark
Linda Dixon
Brent Fery
Cathie Frasure
Norena Gutierrez
Robert & Ann Hay
Sus Helpenstell
Cheryl A. Larabee
Jane Loge
Michael D. McIntyre
Theresa McLeod
James McNorton
Nicholas G. Miller
William T. Mooney
Anthony W. Olbrich
John Parrish
Lorie Nies-Pettiette
Carolyn Ticknor
Shirley Tierney
Shawndel Ysursa
Carolyn Bancroft, Recording Secretary

Consulting Members

Jerry Brady	Suzanne Lierz
Susan Carlise	Shirley O'Neil
Lynn Darling	Sandy Patano
Kathy Harris	Diane Rigby

Advisory Board

Candice Allphin	Richard McChrystal
Bradley G. Andrews	Alan Minskoff
Barbara Bauer	Royanne Minskoff
Mike Bessent	Michael M. Mooney
Doug Copsey	Thomas V. Munson
Charles Davis	Tom Nunamaker
Sandra L.S. Fery	Charles L. Robertson
Michael Hoffman	Ray E. Smith
William H. Keller	Henry W. Taylor, Jr.

Campaign for the Idaho Shakespeare Festival

Kevin Kline, Honorary Chair
Royanne & Alan Minskoff, Campaign Co-Chairs
Jamie H. & Tom Dater, Co-Chairs of Major Gifts
Cheryl A. Larabee & Dianne H. Robertson, Partnership Co-Chairs
Sandra L.S. Fery, Public Campaign Chair
Andrew Erstad, Building Committee Chair
Barbara Bauer, Campaign Treasurer

2003

A Midsummer Night's Dream

Director ....Charles Fee
Set Design ....Gage Williams
Costume Design ....Star Moxley
Lighting ....Rick Martin
Sound ....Peter John Still

The Importance of Being Earnest
By Oscar Wilde

Director ....Charles Fee
Set Design ....Gage Williams
Costume Design ....Kim Krumm Sorenson
Lighting ....Rick Martin
Sound ....Peter John Still

The Comedy of Errors

Director ....Christopher Bayes
Set Design ....Narelle Sissons
Costume Design ....Caitlin Ward
Lighting ....Mary Louise Geiger
Sound ....Peter John Still

Henry V

Director ....Steve Tague
Set Design ....Gage Williams
Costume Design ....Star Moxley
Lighting ....UK
Sound ....Peter John Still

The Fantasticks
Book and lyrics by Tom Jones. Music by Harvey Schmidt

Director ....Drew Barr
Set Design ....Narelle Sissonr
Costume Design ....Jacqueline Firkins
Lighting ....Mary Louise Geiger
Sound ....Timothy Knox

Acting Company

Midsummer; Earnest; Comedy of Errors; Henry V; The Fantasticks

Karen Baughn	Ensemble; –; –; –; –
Lynn Robert Berg*	Demetrius; Lane\Balthazar; Archbishop of Canterbury/ Sir Thomas Grey/ Captain MacMorris/ The Dauphin; –
Aaron Bloom	–; –; –; –; –
Jimmy Bowman	Ensemble; –; –; –; –
Sara Bruner*	–; Cecily Cardew; Courtesan;
John	A Boy; Isabel; –
Andy Carey	Starveling/Ensemble; –; –; –; –
Aled Davies*	Theseus/Oberon; Rev. Canon Chasuble; –; Chorus/Duke of Burgundy
Carter Davis	Snug/Ensemble; –; Ensemble; –; –
Kate Dubman	Ensemble; –; –; –; –
Douglas Frederick*	Snout; John Worthing, J.P; Solinus; Charles Delabreth Earl of Westmoreland; –
Chloe Fritz	–; Servant; –; –; –
Allen Gilmore*	–; –; Angelo; Luce; Henry Captain Fluellen; Charles the Sixth; –

Joe Conley Golden*	Bottom; Antipholus of Ephesus and of Syracuse; Captain Gower; Earl of Grandpre; French Soldier;–
Jeffrey C. Hawkins*	Lysander; –; Second Merchant of Ephesus; Tour Guide; Richard John Bates; Montjoy Ambassador to King of England; Alice; –
Christina Lang	–; Hon. Gwendolen Fairfax; Jailer; –; –
Cheri Lynne*	Hippolyta; –; Titania Adriana; Duke of Orleans; Governor of Harfleur; Messenger; –
Stitch Marker	Egeus; Merriman; Aegeon; Bishop of Ely; Sir Thomas Erpingham; Nym; Lord Rambures; –
Meghan McCurdy	Ensemble; –; –; –; –
Dan Peterson	Flute, –, First Merchant of Ephesus; Humphrey; Bardolph; –
Lisa Reppell	Ensemble; –; –; –; –
Colin Sesek	–; Servant; –; –; –
Mike Sharp	Ensemble; –; –; –; –
David Anthony Smith*	–; Algernon Moncrieff; –; King Henry V;
Tracy Sunderland;	–Helena; Miss Prism; Emilia; –; –
Kathleen Pirkl Tague*	–; Lady Bracknell; –; Duke of Exeter; Captain Jamy; Hostess of the Tavern; –
Mark Anthony Taylor*	Peter Quince; –; Doctor Pinch; Pistol; Earl of Salisbury; –
Sophie Thomas	–; Servant; –; –; –
Mark Vashro	Ensemble; Servant; –; –; –
Tom Willmorth	Philostrate; Puck; –; Dromio of Ephesus/Dromio of Syracuse; –; –
Carie Yonekawa*	Hermia; –; Luciana; Michael Williams Messenger; Katherine; –

Production

Equity Stage Manager .... Jeffrey Williams
Equity Production Stage Manager .Christopher Sadler
Production Manager .... Michael Hartwell
Assistant Stage Manager .... Jennifer Gadda
Assistant Stage Manager .... Kyle Barrow
Production Assistant .... Tim Saunders
Production Assistant .... Megan Schwarz
Technical Director .... Philip R. Hendren
Assistant Technical Director .... Joshua Frachiseur
Master Carpenter .... Richard Destasio
Scenic Carpenter: Logan Doughty; Richard May
Scenic Intern .... Jessica Hill
Charge Scenic Artists: .Micheal Baltzell; Gary Benson
Lead Paint Artist .... Karl Hermanson
Scenic Artist Intern .... Angie Grow
Master Electrician .... Matthew Robert Curtis
Electricians: Josh Nelson; Dante Smith
Electrics Intern .... Angie Grow
Properties Masters: Craig Dorer; Joseph Day
Properties Assistants: Andrew Fitts; Fran Maxwell
Sound Engineer .... Seth Asa Sengel
Sound Interns: Leisha Fastabend; Tim Long
Costume Shop Manager .... Katherine Rundquist
First Hands:
Christine Bentley Johnston; Vicky Nebecker-Destasio
Cutter/Draper: .... Sylvia Rognstad; Karen Ross
Costume Crafts .... Nicole Frachiseur
Costume Crafts Artisan .... Lito-John Demetita
Stitchers: Eileen Louise Albert; Jodi Briscoe; Eve Heidenreich; Kelly Pantzlaff; Carla Troughber
Properties Stitcher .... Fairy Hitchcock
Wardrobe Mistress .... Mika Freeman
Dance Choreographer .... Helene Peterson
Fight Choreographer .... Ken Merckx
Apprentice Company: Karen Baughn; Jimmy Bowman; Angela Derisio; Chloe Fritz; Meghan McCurdy; Lisa Reppell; Colin Sesek; Mike Sharp; Sophie Thomas; Mark Vashro; Meaghan Vernon; Ali Wight

Administration

Producing Artistic Director .... Charles Fee
Managing Director .... Mark Hofflund
Director of Marketing & PR ...Kristen L.R. De Angeli
Director of Finance .... Sherrill Livingston
Director of Education .... John O'Hagan
Director of Patron Relations .... Kelly Moore
Grants Manager .... Ann Dehner
Production Manager .... Mike Hartwell
Campaign Associate .... Liz Littman
Box Office Manager .... Aaron Milette
Assistant Box Office Manager .... Kaelen O'Shea
Company Manager .... Nickie Shell
Administrative Assistant .... Christine Zimowsky
Box Office Assistants: Carter Davis; Libby Fox; Cody Hyslop; Janie Reynolds; Lisa Reynolds; Alice Royer; Kari Schweitzer; Jess Stanley; Tracy Streebel; Jimmy Strohmaier; Chandra Woodward; Christine Zimowsky
Master Gardener .... Carol Cole
Assistant Gardener .... Casey O'Leary
House Manager: .... Amanda Costello; Martha Miller
Souvenir Managers: Lauren Blaesing; Julie Durham

Board of Directors

Robert T. Wetherell, President
Nicholas G. Miller, Vice President
Margaret Buchanan, Secretary
Leann R. Gilberg, Treasurer
Paul M. Boyd
Linda Dixon
Paul J. Dubman
Brent Fery
Norena Gutierrez
Robert & Ann Hay
Sus Helpenstell
Joy Kealey
Cheryl A. Larabee
Jane Loge
Gwen Lytle
Michael D. McIntyre
Theresa McLeod
James McNorton
William T. Mooney
Anthony W. Olbrich
John Parrish
Carolyn Pereira
Lorie Nies-Petteitte
Rosie Reilly
Dianne H. Robertson
Carolyn Ticknor
Shirley Tierney
Shawndel Ysursa
Carolyn Bancroft, Recording Secretary

Consulting Members

Jerry Brady
Susan Carlise
Lynn Darling
Diane Kiehn
Shirley O'Neil
Sandy Patano
Martha Ripple

Advisory Board

Candice Allphin
Bradley G. Andrews
Barbara Bauer
Mike Bessent
Richard P. Clark
Doug Copsey
Charles Davis
Andrew Erstad
Sandra L.S. Fery
Michael Hoffman
William H. Keller
Richard McChrystal
Alan Minskoff
Royanne Minskoff
Michael M. Mooney
Thomas V. Munson
Tom Nunamaker
Doug Oppenheimer
Charles L. Robertson
Henry W, Taylor, Jr.

Foundation for the Idaho Shakespeare Festival

Leann R. Gilberg, President
Charles L. Robertson, Vice President
Melville W. Fisher, II, Secretary
William H. Keller, Treasurer
Theresa McLeod
Carey H. McNeal
Nicholas G. Miller

Campaign for the Idaho Shakespeare Festival

Kevin Kline, Honorary Chair
Royanne & Alan Minskoff, Campaign Co-Chairs
Jamie H.** & Tom Dater, Co-Chairs of Major Gifts
Cheryl A. Larabee & Dianne H. Robertson, Partnership Co-Chairs
Sandra L.S. Fery, Public Campaign Chair
Andrew Erstad, Building Committee Chair
Barbara Bauer, Campaign Treasurer

2004

The Importance of Being Earnest By Oscar Wilde

Director .... Charles Fee
Set Design .... Gage Williams
Costume Design .... Kim Krumm Sorenson
Lighting .... Rick Martin
Sound .... Peter John Still

As You Like It

Director .... Charles Fee
Set Design .... Gage Williams
Costume Design .... Star Moxley
Lighting .... Rick Martin
Sound .... Peter John Still

The Merry Wives of Windsor

Director .... Sari Ketter
Set Design .... Jarrett Bertoncin
Costume Design .... B. Modern
Lighting .... Les Dickert
Sound .... Tom Mardikes

Julius Caesar

Director .... Risa Brainin
Set Design .... Russell Metheny
Costume Design .... Kim Krumm Sorenson
Lighting .... Michael Klaers
Sound .... Tom Mardikes

I Love You, You're Perfect, Now Change

Director .... Victoria Bussert
Set Design .... Jeff Herrmann
Costume Design .... Nicole Frachiseur
Lighting .... Les Dickert
Sound .... Peter John Still

Acting Company

The Importance of Being Earnest; As You Like It; The Merry Wives of Windsor; Julius Caesar; I Love You, You're Perfect, Now Change
Book and lyrics by Joe DiPietro. Music by Jimmy Roberts.

Lynn Allison –; –; Mistress Margaret Pae; –; –
Kyle Barrow –; –; Nym; –; –
Karen Baughn –; Audrey; –; –; –
Aaron Bloom –; Ensemble; –; –; –
Jimmy Bowman –; Ensemble; Ensemble; –; –
Neil Brookshire –; Orlando; Peter Simple; Ensemble; –
Sara M. Bruner* Cecily Cardew; Rosalind; –; –; –
Kathryn Cherasaro –; Phoebe; Mistress Alice Ford; Calphurnia; –
Casey Crowley –; –; Ensemble; –; –
Aled Davies* Rev. Canon Chasuble; Jaques; –; Julius Caesar; –
Carter J. Davis –; –; Pistol; Ensemble; –
Katie Dubman –; –; Robin; –; –
Tom Ford* –; Touchstone; Master Frank Ford; Casca; –
Douglas Frederick* John Worthing Charles; Sir Hugh Evans Cassius; –
Chloe Fritz Servant; –; –; –; –
Joe Conley Golden* –; Silvius; Doctor Caius; –; –
Reggie Gowland –; Ensemble; John Rugby; Ensemble; –
Lauren Guicheteau –; –; Ensemble; –; –
Tori Horn –; –; Ensemble–; –
Shawn Kelly Servant; –; Ensemble; Ensemble
Val King –; –; Ensemble; –; –
Richard Klautsch* –; –; Duke Frederic/Duke Senior; Master George Page; Marcus Brutus; –
Emily Krieger* –; –; –; –; Woman Two
Christina Lang Hon. Gwendolen Fairfax; –; Mistress Quickly; Soothsayer; –
Olivia MacFadden –; –; Ensemble; –; –
Stitch Marker Lane Merriman; Le Beau, Second Lord; Robert Shallow; Cicero; –
Trista Moldovan* –; –; –; –; Woman One
Noah Moody –; –; Ensemble; Ensemble; –
Nicole Orabona –; –; Ensemble; –; –
Dan Peterson –; Adam/ Ensemble; Bardolph; Ensemble; –
Fabio Polanco* –; –; –; –; Man One
Gordon Reinhart* –; Corin; The Host; Decius Brutus; –
Lisa Reppell Servant; Ensemble; –; –; –
Christopher Scheeren* –; –; Master Fenton; Octavius Caesar; –
Seth Asa Sengel –; Ensemble; –; –; –
Colin Sesek Servant; –;–; Ensemble; –
Evan Sesek –; –; William Page; –; –
David Anthony Smith* Algernon Moncrieff; –; Oliver; Mark Antony; –
Tracy Sunderland Miss Prism; –; –; –; –
Kathleen Pirkl Tague* Lady Bracknell; –; –;
Steve Tague* –; –; Sir John Falstaff; –; –
Jeffries Thaiss* –; –; –; –; Man Two
Nick White –; –; –; Ensemble; –
Ali Wight –; –; Ensemble; –; –
Tom Willmorth* Sir Oliver Martext; Master Abraham ; Slender; Trebonius; –
Carrie Yonekawa* –; Celia; Anne Page; Portia; –

Production

Equity Stage Managers: Christopher Sadler; Jeffrey Williams
Assistant Stage Managers: Jorja Ackers; Jenaiah Shoop; ....Kyle Barrow
Production Assistants: Kyle Barrow; Tim Saunders
Production Manager ....Philip R. Hendren
Technical Director ....Michael Hartwell
Assistant Technical Director ....Joshua Frachiseur
Assistant to the Director ....Richard Sparks
Scenic Carpenters: Joseph Leporati; Geoffrey Bennett .
Welder/Scenic Carpenter ....Richard Destasio
Scenic Intern ....Nate Pohl
Charge Scenic Artist ....Karl Hermanson
Scenic Artist ....Micheal Baltzell
Scenic Artist Intern ....Angie Grow
Master Electrician ....Matthew Robert Curtis
Assistant Master ....Peter J. Vomocil
Electrician ....Dante Smith
Electrics Intern ....Kelli Groskopf
Properties Masters: Nathan Michael; Emily Steger
Properties Assistant ....Beth Goldfischer
Sound Engineer ....Seth Asa Sengel
Sound Intern ....Tim Long
Costume Shop Manager ....Vicky Nebecker-Destasio
First Hands: Louise Everett; Kelly Pantzlaff
Cutter/Drapers: Jackie Arrington; Matthew Lewis
Design Assistant ....Mika Freeman
Costume Crafts Artisan ....Nicole Frachiseur
Nicola Gardiner ....
Stitchers: Eileen Louise Albert; Elizabeth Burk; Nicole Laeger; Reenie Sudduth; Shawn Walton-Hill
Hair and Wigs ....Cecil Kester
Wardrobe Mistress ....Katherine Rundquist
Resident Dance Choreographer ......Helene Peterson
Resident Fight Choreographer ....Ken Marckx
Apprentice Company: Karen Baughn; Jimmy Bowan; Casey Crowley; Chloe Fritz; Reggie Gowland; Laren Guicheteau; Tory Horn; Shawn Kelly; Valerie King; Olivia MacFadden; Noah Moody; Nichole Orabona; Lisa Reppell; Colin Sesek; Nick White; Ali Wight
2004 Understudies: James Auw; Joshua Belville; Geoffrey Bennett; Dwayne Blackaller; Liberty Leeds; Jenny Newbry; Noah Hostetler; Luke Messengill; Tim Pakutka; Jeffrey Petersen

Administration

Producing Artistic Director ....Charles Fee
Managing Director ....Mark Hofflund
Director of Marketing & PR ...Kristen L.R. De Angeli
Director of Development ....Ann Dehner
Director of Finance ....Sherrill Livingston
Director of Education ....Carole Whiteleather
Director of Patron and Corporate Relations ....Kelly Moore
Campaign Associate ....Liz Littman
Box Office Manager ....Aaron Milette
Company Manager ....Hannah Read
Development Assistant ....Christine Zimowsky
Assistant Box Office Manager ...Chandra Woodward
Box Office Assistants: Lauren Blaesing; Kymm Corneilson; Sean Costello; Ian Mundorff; Kaelen O'Shea; Tim Pakutka; Janie Reynolds; Kari Schweitzer; Jess Stanley; Tracy Streebel; Echo Waldron; Cheryl Williams
Master Gardener ....Carol C. Cole
Assistant Gardener ....Casey O'Leary
House Managers: Amanda Costello; Lauren Tyler
Souvenir Manager ....Julie Durham

Board of Directors

Nicholas G. Miller, President
Leann R. Gilberg, Vice President
Robert Hay, Secretary
Joy Kealey, Treasurer

Barbara Bender	James McNorton
Paul M. Boyd	William T. Mooney
Linda Dixon	Lorie Nies Pettiette
Paul J. Dubman	Anthony W. Olbrich
Brent Fery	John Parrish
Norena Gutierrez	Caroline Pereira
Anne Hay	Leacadia Powell
Sus Helpenstell	Carolyn Ticknor
Val Heusinkveld	Shirley Tierney
Cheryl A. Larabee	Robert T. Wetherell
Gwen Lytle	Shawn Del Ysursa
Michael D. McIntyre	Carolyn Bancroft, Recording Secretary
Theresa McLeod	

Consulting Members

Jerry Brady	Shirley O'Neil
Lynn Darling	Sandy Patano
Diane Kiehn	Martha Ripple
Anju Lucas	

Advisory Board

Candice Allphin	Jane Loge
Bradley G. Andrews	Richard McChrystal
Barbara Abuer	Alan Minskoff
Mike Bessent	Royanne Minskoff
Richard P. Clark	Michael M. Mooney
Doug Copsey	Thomas V. Munson
Charles Davis	Tom Nunamaker
Andrew Erstad	Doug Oppenheimer
Sandra L.S. Fery	Charles L. Robertson
Michael Hoffman	Dianne H. Robertson
William H. Keller	Henry W. Taylor, Jr.

Foundation for the Idaho Shakespeare Festival

Leann R. Gilberg, President
Melville W. Fisher, II, Secretary
William H. Keller, Treasurer
Thomas G. Dater
Sandra L.S. Fery
Joy Kealey
Carey H. McNeal
Royanne Minskoff

Campaign for the Idaho Shakespeare Festival

Kevin Kline, Honorary Chair
Royanne & Alan Minskoff, Campaign Co-Chairs
Jamie H.** & Tom Dater, Co-Chairs of Major Gifts
Cheryl A. Larabee & Dianne H. Robertson, Partnership Co-Chairs
Sandra L.S. Fery, Public Campaign Chair
Andrew C. Erstad, Building Committee Chair
Barbara Bauer, Brent Fery & John Parrish, Campaign Treasurers

2005

The Taming of the Shrew

Director ....Drew Barr
Set Design ....Narelle Sissons
Costume Design ....Kim Krumm Sorenson
Lighting ....Rick Martin
Sound ....Peter John Still

She Stoops to Conquer
By Oliver Goldsmith

Director ....Charles Fee
Set Design ....Gage Williams
Costume Design ....Star Moxley
Lighting ....Rick Martin
Sound ....Peter John Still

A Funny Thing Happened on the Way to the Forum
Book by Burt Shevelove & Larry Gelbart. Music and lyrics by Steven Sondheim. Originally produced on Broadway by Harold S. Prince.

Director ....Victoria Bussert
Set Design ....Jeff Herrmann
Costume Design ....Nicole Frachiseur
Lighting ....Michael Klaers
Sound ....Peter John Stil

King Lear

Director ....Risa Brainin
Set Design ....Russell Metheny
Costume Design ....Kim Krumm Sorenson
Lighting ....Michael Klaers
Sound ....Peter John Still
Composer ....Brad Carroll

The Compleat Works of William Shakespeare (Abridged)
By Jess Borgeson, Adam Long and Daniel Singer

Director .... Charles Fee
Set Design .... Gage Williams
Costume Design .... Charlotte Yetman
Lighting .... Rick Martin
Sound .... Peter John Still

Acting Company

Taming of the Shrew; She Stoops to Conquer; A Funny Thing Happened...; King Lear; Complete Works

James Auw –; –; –; Servant; –
Lynn Robert Berg* Hortensio; Hastings; Marcus Lycus; Edmund; Guy One
Sara M. Bruner* Bianca; Miss Kate Hardcastle, A Geminae Twin; Cordelia; –
Jonathon Buffington Other Servant; –; Servant; –
Luke Daigle Other Servant; Servant
Aled Davies* –; Sir Charles Marlow; Senex; Earl of Gloucester; –
Carter Davis Biondello; Tom Twist; –; –; Servant; Oswald
John Jay Espino* –; –; –; Curan; –
Tom Ford* Gremio; –; Pseudolus; Fool; –
Joe Conley Golden* –; Tony Lumpkin; –; Duke of Albany; –
Jeffrey C. Hawkins* Tranio' Young Marlow, *his son* Hysterium Edgar; Guy Two
Richard Klautsch* Baptista Minola; Hardcastle; –; Earl of Kent; –
Christina Lang –; Mrs. Hardcastle; Domina; Goneril; –
Liberty Leeds A Widow; –; –; –; –
Matt Lillo* –; –; Hero; King of France; –
Stitch Marker Vincentio; Jack Slang; –; –; Crony ; –
Hartley Miller A Hostess; –; –; –; –
Laura Miller –; Maid; A Geminae Twin; –; –
Noah Moody Other Servant; –; –; –; –
Laura Perrotta* Katherina; –; Vibrata; Regan; –
Dan Peterson A Pedant/A Priest; Landlord Jeremy; Erronius; Crony; –
Kate Rockwell* –; –; Philia; –; –
Maria Katrina Sermonia –; –; Tintinabula; –; –
Evan Sesek Other Servant; –; –; –; –
David Anthony Smith* Petruchio; –; Gymnasium; Duke of Cornwall; –
Steve Tague* –; –; Miles Gloriosis; King Lear
M.A. Taylor* Grumio; Aminidab Diggory; –; Duke of Burgundy Crony; Guy Three
Karen Wennstrom –; Miss Neville; Panacea; –; –
Tom Willmorth* Lucentio; –; –; –; –
Rod Wolfe Curtis A Tailor; Dick Muggins Servant; –; Crony; –

Production

Assistant Director – *Lear* .... Emily Weisberg
Equity Production Stage Managers: Corrie E. Purdum; Christopher Sadler
Equity Stage Manager .... Kyle Barrow
Production Manager .... Philip R. Hendren
Production Assistants: Robert Shoquist; Brecca Chabot-Olson; Hartley Miller; Jorja Ackers; Tim Saunders
Technical Director .... Michael Hartwell
Assistant Technical Director .... Joshua Frachiseur
Master Carpenter .... Leslie Hammond
Welder/Scenic Carpenter .... Richard Destasio
Scenic Carpenters: Vincent A. Sylvester; Christopher J. Weddle
Scenic Intern .... James Matthew Godwin
Charge Scenic Artist .... Karl Hermanson
Assistant Charge .... Micheal Baltzell
Scenic Artist .... Angie Grow
Master Electrician .... Matthew Robert Curtis
Assistant Master Electrician .... Peter J. Vomocil
Electrician .... Kelli Groskopf
Electrician Intern .... Erica A. Deshner
Spot Operator .... Kurtis Workman
Properties Master .... Joe Day
Properties Assistant .... James Koehnle
Properties Intern .... Heidi Draay
Sound Engineer .... Tim Long
Sound Intern .... Kaylie Hoffman
Changeover Supervisor .... Jason McGrath
Changeover Crew Members: Mark Aadlard; Crystala Haylett; Jerome Nelson; Bobbo Pattersen; Victorita Raaen; Kurtis Workman
Costume Shop Manager .... Vicky Nebecker-Destasio
First Hands: Christina Caverly; Kristine Davies
First Hand/Costume Crafts .... Rebecca Hoffman
Cutter/Drapers: Kelly Pantzlaff; Karen Ross
Design Assistant .... Nicole Laeger
Costume Crafts Artisan .... Jerry Johnson
Stitchers: Deb Bogie; Jodie Briscoe; Brittany Loar; Rachel Reisenauer; Brian Turpin
Intern Stitcher .... Katia Jade Monasterio
Hair and Wigs .... Cecil Kester
Wardrobe Mistress .... Katherine Rundquist
Resident Fight Choreographer .... Dexter Fidler
Choreographers: Dexter Fidler; Janet Louer; Ken Merckx; Helene Peterson
Dance Captain .... Laura Miller
Speech & Dialect Coach .... Aled Davies
Greenshow Producers: Joe Conley Golden; Tom Willmorth
Musicians: Jerry Jensen; Todd Chavez; Sean Rogers
Apprentice Company: Emma Ayers; Becca Ballenger; Julie Bean; Lina Chambers; Lauren Guicheteau; Tori Horn; Ryan King; Valerie King; Noah Moody; Justine Olnes; Nicole Orabona; Anneliese Rice; Evan Sesek; Catherine Sherwood; Andrew Storms
Interns/Understudies: James Auw; Karen Baughn; Jonathon Buffington; Luke Daigle; Marc Ewins; Liberty Leeds; Hartley Miller; Maria Katrina Sermonia

Administration

Producing Artistic Director .... Charles Fee
Managing Director .... Mark Hofflund
Director of Marketing & PR .... Kristen L.R. De Angeli
Director of Development .... Ann Dehner
Director of Finance .... Sherrill Livingston
Director of Education .... Carole Whiteleather
Campaign Associate .... Liz Littman
Box Office Manager .... M. Aaron Milette
Company Manager .... Hannah Read
Development Assistant .... Christine Zimowsky
Box Office Assistant Managers: Chandra Woodward; Lauren Blaesing
Box Office Assistants: Kymm Corneilson; Lisa Reppell; Mary Jane Reynolds; Alice Royer; Seth Asa Sengel; Jess Stanley
Master Gardener .... Carol Cole
Assistant Gardener: .... Rachel Airmet; Dallas Gilbert
House Managers: .... Kari Schweitzer; Lauren Tyler

Board of Directors

Nicholas G. Miller, President
Leann R. Gilberg, Vice President
Robert Hay, Secretary
Joy Kealey, Treasurer
Steven B. Andersen
Cindy L. Bateman
Barbara Bender
Paul M. Boyd
Chip Browndyke
Viki Dater
Paul J. Dubman
Brent Fery
Anne Hay
Sus Helpenstell
Val Keusinkveld
Leslie Hurst
Sondra Juetten
John Kennevick
W. Patrick Knibbe
Gwen Lytle
Jeff Malmen
Michael D. McIntyre
Theresa McLeod
James NcNorton
William T. Mooney
Anthony W. Olbrich
John Parrish
Carolyn Pereira
Georgiann Raimondi
Janelle Reilly
Martie Rowen-Bronson
Ike Tanabe
Carolyn Ticknor
Shawn Del Ysursa
Carolyn Bancroft, Recording Secretary

Consulting Members

Jerry Brady	Anju Lucas
Lynn Darling	Shirley O'Neil
Diane Kiehn	Sandy Patano
Ken Lamson	Martha Ripple

Advisory Board

Candice Allphin	Alan Minskoff
Bradley G. Andrews	Royanne Minskoff
Barbara Bauer	Michael M. Mooney
Mike Bessent	Jane Motes
Richard P. Clark	Thomas V. Munson
Doug Copsey	Tom Nunamaker
Charles Davis	Doug Oppenheimer
Andrew Erstad	Lorie Nies Pettiette
Linda Dixon	Charles L. Robertson
Sandra L.S. Fery	Dianne H. Robertson
Norena Gutierezz	Henry W. Taylor, Jr.
Michael Hoffman	Shirley Tierney
William H. Keller	Robert T. Wetherell
Richard McChyrstal	

Foundation for the Idaho Shakespeare Festival

William H. Keller, President
Royanne Minskoff, Vice President
Melville W. Fisher, II, Secretary
Joy Kealey, Treasurer
Thomas G. Dater
Sandra L.S. Fery
Leann R. Gilberg
Gwen Lytle
Carey H. McNeal

Campaign for the Idaho Shakespeare Festival

Kevin Kline, Honorary Chair
Royanne & Alan Minskoff, Campaign Co-Chairs
Jamie H.** & Tom Dater, Co-Chairs of Major Gifts
Cheryl A. Larabee & Dianne H. Robertson, Partnership Co-Chairs
Sandra L.S. Fery, Public Campaign Chair
Andrew C Erstad, Building Committee Chair
Barbara Bauer, Brent Fery & John Parrish, Campaign Treasurers

2006

A Funny Thing Happened on the Way to the Forum
Book by Burt Shevelove & Larry Gelbart. Music and lyrics by Steven Sondheim. Originally produced on Broadway by Harold S. Prince

Director .... Victoria Bussert
Set Design .... Jeff Herrmann

Costume Design ....Nicole Frachiseur
Lighting ....Michael Klaers
Sound ....Peter John Still

Love's Labours Lost

Director ....Drew Barr
Set Design ....Russell Metheney
Costume Design ....Kim Krumm Sorenson
Lighting ....Rick Martin

Major Barbara
By George Bernard Shaw

Director ....Steve Tague
Set Design ....Gage Williams
Costume Design ....Charlotte Yetman
Lighting ....Rick Martin
Sound ....Peter John Still

Romeo and Juliet

Director ....Charles Fee
Set Design ....Gage Williams
Costume Design ....Star Moxley
Lighting ....Rick Martin
Sound ....Peter John Still

The Spitfire Grill
Based on the 1996 film by Lee David Zlotoff, James Valcq and Fred Alley

Director ....Drew Barr
Set Design ....Jeff Herman
Costume Design ....Kim Krumm Sorenson
Lighting ....Rick Martin
Sound ....Peter John Still

Acting Company

A Funny Thing Happened...; Love's Labours Lost; Major Barbara; Romeo and Juliet; The Spitfire Grill

Lynn Allison –; –; Lady Britomart; Lady Montague; –
Lynn Robert Berg* Marcus Lycus; Sir Nathaniel; Bill Walker; Tybalt; –
Courtney Bohl Gemini; Maria; Jenny; –; –
Neil Brookshire –; Moth; Stephen; Balthazar; –
Sara M. Bruner* Vibrata; Jaquenetta; –; Juliet; –
Cathryn Cherasaro* Tintinabula; Rosaline; Sarah; –; –
Luke Daigle Protean; Forester; –; Gregory; –
Aled Davies* Senex; Boyet; Undershaft; –; –
Carter J. Davis –; Forester; –; Paris; –
Katie Dubman –; –; –; –; –
Tom Ford* Pseudolous; Navarre; –; Friar Laurence; –
Joe Conley Golden* –; –; Snobby Price; –; –
Jeffrey C. Hawkins* Hysterium; Costard; –; Romeo; –
Richard Klautsch* –; Don Armado; –; Prince of Verona/Chorus; –
Stitch Marker –; Marcade; Peter Shirley; –; –
Douglas Miller Protean; Holofernes; Cusins; –; –
Michael Mueller Protean; Dumaine; –; Sampson; –
Ben Nordstrom Hero; –; –; –; –
Laura Perrotta* Domina; Princess; Mrs. Baines; Lady Capulet; –
Dan Peterson Erronius; –; Morrison/Bilton; –; –
Scott Plate* Miles Gloriosis; Longaville; –; Benvolio; –
Kate Rockwell* Philia; –; –; –; –
David Anthony Smith* Gymnasium; Berowne; –; Mercutio; –
E.B. Smith Protean; Forester; –; –
Kathleen Pirkl Tague* –; –; Major Barbera; Nurse; –
Steve Tague* –;–;–; Capulet; –
M.A. Taylor* Protean; Dull; –; Peter
Laura Welsh Gemini; Kathryn; –; –; –
Karen Wennstrom Panacea; –; –; –; –
Tom Willmorth* –; –; Lomax; –; –
Jamie Young –; –; –; –; –

Production

Production Manager ....Philip R. Hendren
Technical Director ....Michael Hartwell
Assistant Technical Director ......Joshua Frachiseur
Master Electrician ....Matthew Robert Curtis
Properties Master ....Joe Day
Costume Shop Manager ....Nicole Frachiseur
Fight Choreographer ....Ken Merckx
Dance Captains: ....Helene Peterson; Janet Louer
Greenshow Producers: ......Joe Conley Golden; Tom Willmorth

Administration

Producing Artistic Director ....Charles Fee
Managing Director ....Mark Hofflund
Director of Marketing & PR ...Kristen L.R. De Angeli
Director of Development ....Ann Dehner
Director of Finance ....Sherrill Livingston
Director of Education ....Carole Whiteleather
Development Assistant ....Liz Littman
Box Office Manager ....M. Aaron Milette
Company Manager ....Hannah Read
Information Specialist ....Christine Zimowsky
Box Office Assistant Manager ...Chandra Woodward
Master Gardener ....Carol Cole

Board of Trustees

Robert Hay, President
Joy Kealey, Vice President
Cindy L. Bateman, Secretary
Gwen Lytle, Treasurer
Steven B. Andersen
Barbara Bender
Jeanette Bennion
Paul M. Boyd
Vicki Brinkmeyer
Chip Browndyke
Viki Dater
Charles Davis
Linda Dixon
Paul J. Dubman
Anne Hay
Val Heusinkveld
Andrew Huang
Sondra Juetten
John Kennevick
W. Patrick Knibbe
Kathleen Kustra
Kenn Lamson
Michael D. McIntyre
James McNorton
Nicholas G. Miller
William T. Mooney
John Parrish
Carolyn Pereira
Georgiann Raimondi
Janelle Reilly
Martie Rowen-Bronson
Lari Jane Rumpp
John Sims
Brnady Stemmler
Ike Tanabe
Martin Tanner
Carolyn Ticknor
Shirley Tierney
Susan Delana Walker
Shawn Del Ysurza
Carolyn Bancroft, Recording Secretary

Consulting Members

Jerry Brady
Richard E. Hall
Diane Kiehn
Ken Lamson
Shirley O'Neil
Sandy Patano
Martha Ripple

Advisory Board

Candice Allphin
Bradley G. Andrews
Barbara Bauer
Mike Bessent
Richard P. Clark
Doug Copsey
Charles Davis
Andrew Erstad
Brent Fery
Richard McChrystal
Theresa McLeod
Alan Minskoff
Royanne Minskoff
Michael T. Mooney
Jane Motes
Thomas V. Munson
Tom Nunamaker
Anthony W. Olbrich
Sandra L.S. Fery
Leann R. Gilberg
Norena Gutierezz
Sus Helpenstell
Michael Hoffman
William H. Keller
Cheryl A. Larabee
Doug Oppenheimer
Lorie Nies Pettiette
Charles L. Robertson
Dianne H. Robertson
Henry W. Taylor, Jr.
Robert T. Wetherell

Foundation for the Idaho Shakespeare Festival

William H. Keller, President
Royanne Minskoff, Vice President
Melville W. Fisher, II, Secretary
Joy Kealey, Treasurer
Cindy L. Bateman
Thomas G. Dater
Sandra L.S. Fery
Leann R. Gilberg
Gwen Lytle
Carey H. McNeal

**Members of Actors' Equity Association, the Union of Professional Actors and Stage Managers in the United States*

***deceased*

****Information as known at press time.*

Index

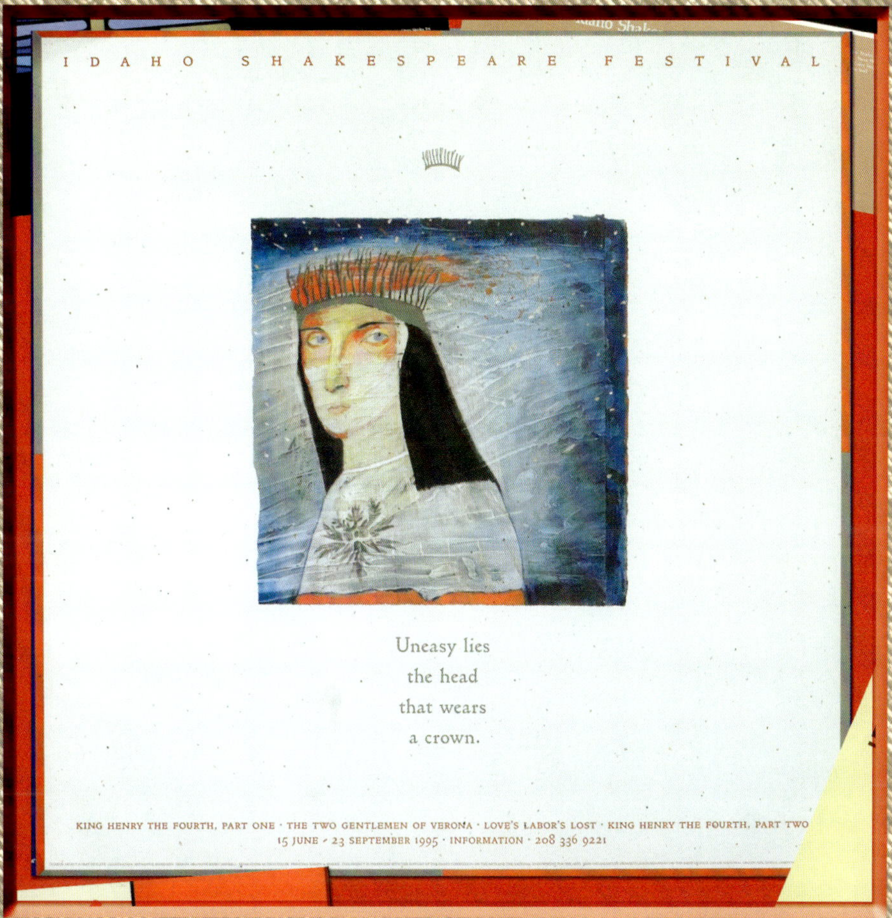

30 Years of Posters

Join us July 8th. through August 9th. For the 1980 Idaho Shakespeare Festival
Shakespeare
July 8th-August 9th Monday-Saturday 8:15 Curtain
Admission $5.00
Seniors and Children $3.50
Ray's Seafood Restaurant
999 Main St. Boise, Idaho
Tickets: 342-0720
345-0060
Idaho Shakespeare Festival
Beginning July 6th through August 8th.
The Tempest
As You Like It
Much Ado About Nothing
For Tickets and Reservations Call 345-0060
THE FIRST ANNUAL
ONE CAPITAL CENTER
BOISE
Main Street Bistro
SUMMER THEATRE FESTIVAL
PRESENTS
WILLIAM SHAKESPEARE'S
A Midsummer Night's Dream
July 27-30 & August 3-6
8:30 p.m.
Tickets $3.50 Kids Under 12 $1.00
Seating on the Lawn.
Refreshments on Sale
Except During Performance.
For Reservations Call 345-4757
or the Main Street Bistro at 345-2261.
A DOUG COPSEY PRODUCTION
THIRD ANNUAL SUMMER
Shakespeare
THEATRE
"Romeo and Juliet"
July 10 - 20
"The Merry Wives of Windsor"
July 23 - August 4
TICKETS: 342-0720
One Capital Center
999 MAIN STREET, BOISE
The Two Gentlemen Of Verona
July 11-29, 1978 — 8:30 p.m.
Tickets $3.75
$2.50 For Kids Under 12
And Seniors
by William Shakespeare
For Reservations
Phone 345-4757
or Ray's at 342-0700
A Doug Copsey Production
CELEBRATING 25 YEARS

The Eighth Annual
Idaho Shakespeare Festival
The Taming of the Shrew
Robin Hood
The Tragedy of King Lear
In Repertory
At ParkCenter
July 6 – August 12, 1984
Reservations: 336-9221
Shakespeare
IDAHO SHAKESPEARE FESTIVAL
Uneasy lies the head that wears a crown.
KING HENRY THE FOURTH, PART ONE · THE TWO GENTLEMEN OF VERONA · LOVE'S LABOR'S LOST · KING HENRY THE FOURTH, PART TWO
15 JUNE – 23 SEPTEMBER 1995 · INFORMATION · 208 336 9221
IDAHO SHAKESPEARE FESTIVAL
THE 1985 IDAHO SHAKESPEARE FESTIVAL
Presents
Shakespeare Under The Stars
Our Biggest Season Ever!!
Return Engagement!
ROBIN HOOD by Don Nigro June 14-20 Only!
In Repertory, June 28 - August 25
The Two Gentlemen of Verona by Wm. Shakespeare
Richard III by Wm. Shakespeare
Waiting for Godot by Samuel Beckett
The Winter's Tale by Wm. Shakespeare
Gate opens at 6:30 p.m. for picnic dinners on the lawn.
All performances begin at 8:15 p.m.
$9.00 Sunday - Thursday, $11.00 Friday and Saturday
$5.00 Previews. Tickets available at all Citizens National Bank branches and at the Festival Box Office at Park Center or
Call 336-9221 For Reservations and Discount Subscription Prices.
Shakespeare
AHO
Shakespeare
FESTIVAL '82
July 6 - August 13
Hamlet
Midsummer Night's Dream
Twelfth Night
SPECIAL SUBSCRIPTION OFFER
For Reservations Call 345-0060

SHAKESPEARE
In Repertory At ParkCente
1991
JUNE 20-AUGUST 24
Twelfth Night • Spring Awakening • Macbeth
IMAGES
IDAHO SHAKESPEARE FESTIVAL
In Repertory At Parkcenter June 27-August 24, 1986
- A Midsummer Night's Dream
- Pendragon (World Premier)
- All's Well That Ends Well
- Othello
ANNIVERSARY
IN REPERTORY AT PARK CENTER
JUNE 26 – AUGUST 23 1987
ROMEO & JULIET
THE COMEDY OF ERRORS
PERICLES
THE ADVENTURES OF SHERLOCK HOLMES
MARK TWAIN, HISOWNSELF
The GOOD The BAD & The UGLY
Coming To An Amphitheater Near You!
Some people are bad and some people are good.
It's too bad the bad can't be like the good.
But everything changes a little and it should.
Good ain't forever and bad ain't for good.
But ugly goes clear to the bone.
IN REPERTORY AT PARKCENTER
New Split Season
JUNE 19TH-JULY 25TH
JULY 31ST-SEPTEMBER 5TH
IDAHO SHAKESPEARE FESTIVAL

1 9 9 8
What visions have I seen
A Midsummer Night's Dream
Cymbeline
Romeo and Juliet
Enchanted Evening Gala | July 17
Starlit Gala | July 18
A Midsummer Night's Dream • The Comedy of Errors • Tartuffe by Molière • July 1 – September 18
In Repertory at Park Center
June 3 – June 26
Molly Newman and Barbara Damashek's Quilters
Et tu, Brute?
June 9 - September 23
1994
Dancing at Lughnasa
Much Ado About Nothing
Julius Caesar
As You Like It
Idaho Shakespeare Festival
"FRAME YOUR MIND TO MIRTH AND MERRIMENT"
Idaho Shakespeare Festival
Macbeth
20th Anniversary • June 12-September 13 • Information 208.336.9221
IDAHO SHAKESPEARE FESTIVAL
WHAT'S PAST IS
prologue
The Merry Wives of Windsor
The Tempest
Twelfth Night
1996

Idaho Shakespeare Festival
ye GLOBE
Queen Admits to Affair with Donkey Man
Half donkey, half man, "all hunk!" declares love-crazed queen.
Candidate's Cannibalism Rocks Capital
KeyBank
Shakespeare Festival
June 14 - August 19, 1990
24th Season
Shakespeare
Under the Stars
June 8–September 23, 2000
Tickets 336-9221
www.idahoshakespeare.org
Celebrating 25 Years
Silver Anniversary 2001
The Two Gentlemen of Verona
shakespeare
festival
Summer in the city...
In Repertory At Park Center June 22 - August 21, 1988
As You Like It
Measure For Measure
Titus Andronicus
Quilters

TICKETS 336-9221 OR WWW.IDAHOSHAKESPEARE.ORG
idaho shakespeare festival 2002
much ado about nothing
by William Shakespeare
arms and the man
by George Bernard Shaw
twelfth night
by William Shakespeare
macbeth
by William Shakespeare
JUNE 7 - SEPTEMBER
2002 season sponsored by
KeyBank
2002 season partners
Micron
2006
EXPERIENCE
IDAHO WILDLIFE
KeyBank
2003 season sponsored by
idaho shakespeare festival 2003
JUNE 6 - SEPTEMBER 27, 2003
a midsummer night's dream
by William Shakespeare
the importance of being earnest
by Oscar Wilde
the comedy of errors
by William Shakespeare
henry v
by William Shakespeare
the fantasticks
2003 season partners
Micron
TAMARACK
2003 media partner
336-9221 OR WWW.IDAHOSHAKESPEARE.ORG
2004 SEASON SPONSORED BY
KeyBank
WILLIAM SHAKESPEARE'S
AS YOU LIKE IT
THE IMPORTANCE OF BEING EARNEST
BY OSCAR WILDE
WILLIAM SHAKESPEARE'S
THE MERRY WIVES OF WINDSOR
WILLIAM SHAKESPEARE'S
JULIUS CAESAR
I LOVE YOU, YOU'RE PERFECT, NOW CHANGE
JUNE 4 - SEPTEMBER 25
2004
IDAHO SHAKESPEARE FESTIVAL
28TH SEASON
2004 SEASON PARTNERS
Micron
TAMARACK
2004 SEASON MEDIA PARTNER
RIVER
TICKETS 336-9221
WWW.IDAHOSHAKESPEARE.ORG
2005 SEASON SPONSORED BY
KeyBank
WILLIAM SHAKESPEARE'S
THE TAMING OF THE SHREW
OLIVER GOLDSMITH'S
SHE STOOPS TO CONQUER
STEPHEN SONDHEIM'S
FUNNY THING HAPPENED
THE WAY TO
E FORUM
JUNE 3 - OCTOBER 1
2005
IDAHO SHAKESPEARE FESTIVAL
29TH SEASON
2005 SEASON PARTNERS
Micron
TAMARACK
2005 SEASON MEDIA PARTNER
RIVER
TICKETS 336-9221
WWW.IDAHOSHAKESPEARE.ORG